CHINESE THEOLOGY

CHINESE THEOLOGY

THEOLOGY

Text and Context

Chloë Starr

Yale
UNIVERSITY
PRESS
New Haven & London

Published with assistance from the foundation established in memory
of James Wesley Cooper of the Class of 1865, Yale College.

Yale University Press books may be purchased in quantity for educational, business,
or promotional use. For information, please e-mail sales.press@yale.edu (U.S. office)
or sales@yaleup.co.uk (U.K. office).

Set in PostScript Electra with Weiss display types by Newgen North America.
Printed in the United States of America.

Library of Congress Control Number: 2016936590
ISBN 978-0-300-20421-6 (hardcover : alk. paper)

A catalogue record for this book is available from the British Library.

This paper meets the requirements of ANSI/NISO Z39.48–1992 (Permanence of Paper).

10 9 8 7 6 5 4 3 2 1

In memory of

Zhang Boda
(Béda Chang, 1905–1951)

Zhao Zichen
(T. C. Chao, 1888–1979)

the martyred and the bereft

CONTENTS

Contents

ACKNOWLEDGMENTS

It is a pleasure to thank the many friends and colleagues who have helped me in numerous ways over the years, from offering advice, to procuring materials or texts, to providing enlightening comments and conversation. Among these I am especially thankful for Glen Dudbridge, Ryan Dunch, He Guanghu, Jason Lam, Leo Leeb, Don Starr, Philip Wickeri, Gerda Wielander, Jean-Paul Wiest, Zhang Jing, and colleagues at Yale Divinity School, East Asian Languages and Literatures, and the Council on East Asian Studies at Yale. For helpful comments on chapters, I am most grateful to Peter Ditmanson, Sharon Kim, Rana Mitter, Linn Tonstad, John Yueh-Han Yieh, the two anonymous readers at Yale University Press, and the six inadvertently onymous readers whose critiques of draft chapters for promotion review helped me hone the volume. I would like to thank the Visiting Fellows and students who patiently read early chapters in class, particularly Liu Jiafeng and Anna Wu Qing; Chen Lang, Xu Xiaohong, and Liu Boyun for translation work, especially help with Buddhist terminology; Christian Meyer and the Globalization team; Henrietta Harrison for hospitality during Harvard-Yenching visits; and colleagues and friends at Yale Divinity School who have read portions, made life more pleasant, or improved my grasp of theology, including mentors Denys Turner and Harry Attridge.

I am very glad of the opportunity publicly to thank Yang Huilin for supporting my initial research at Renmin University in 2008–2009 via a Hanban fellowship, and to Liu Xiuyan and Geng Youzhuang at Renmin; to Daniel Yeung for a visiting fellowship at the Institute of Sino-Christian Studies in Hong Kong in 2009; to the Henry Luce Foundation for a Theology Fellowship in 2011–2012, with particular thanks to Michael Gilligan at the Luce Foundation and to

Stephen Graham at the Association for Theological Schools. St. Anne's College, Oxford, proved a congenial place to write up the final sections of the volume with its Plumer Fellowship in 2014–2015, for which especial thanks to Tim Gardam and Robert Chard. Thanks also to Rana Mitter (and Dirk Meyer) for a home in the China Centre during my Oxford sabbatical, and to Greg Sterling and the Yale Divinity School, and the Council on East Asian Studies at Yale (and the indomitable Helen Siu), for their generous financial support and sabbatical leave.

The book would have been much depleted without tremendous help from librarians at Yale, Harvard, Beijing, and Oxford. Particular thanks to librarians Michael Meng, Tang Li, Martha Smalley, and Cindy Lu for their help over the years in the East Asian and Divinity School libraries at Yale, and to David Helliwell and Joshua Seufert at the Bodleian.

Sincere thanks and gratitude to Jennifer Banks, Heather Gold, and Mary Pasti at Yale University Press, whose cheerful professionalism and rapid responses to emails have made the stressful process of reviews and revisions so much more pleasant, and to Jessie Dolch for her meticulous and thoughtful copy-editing (and painstaking excision of British English).

And finally, thanks to Peter Ditmanson, Joshua Seufert, beer, Margaret Hillenbrand, and Henrietta Harrison for the title, and to my mother for pretty much everything else in life.

A shorter version of Chapter 3 was published as "Surveying Galilee from a Chinese Observation Tower: Zhao Zichen's *Life of Jesus* (1935)," *English Language Notes: Scriptural Margins* 50.2 (Fall/Winter 2012): 63–76, www.english.colorado .edu/eln. Material from Chapters 3 and 4 appears in Chinese in "读经"——民国时期神学的当代意义" [Reading *Jing*: The Relevance of Republican Era Theology], *Jidujiao Wenhua Xuekan Journal for the Study of Christian Culture* No. 31 (2014): 207–36. Chapter 6 draws in part on material forthcoming in "Religion, Politics and Sino-Christian Theology," in Markus Höfner, ed., *Theo-Politics? Conversing with Barth in Western and Asian Contexts* (Minneapolis, MN: Fortress, 2016). Chapters 6 and 8 contain some material from "The Chinese Church: A Post-Denominational Reality?" in Stanley D. Brunn, ed., *The Changing World Religion Map: Sacred Places, Identities, Practices and Politics* (Dordrecht: Springer, 2015), Chapter 108, pp. 2045–58, reproduced with kind permission from Springer Science+Business Media; and Chapter 8 draws in part on an earlier essay, "Sino-Christian Theology: Treading a Fine Line between Globalisation and Self-Determination," in Thomas Jansen, Thoralf Klein, and Christian Meyer, eds., *Chinese Religions and Globalization* (Leiden and Boston: Brill, 2014). Permission to reproduce copyright materials is gratefully acknowledged.

ABBREVIATIONS

CASS	Chinese Academy of Social Sciences
CCP	Chinese Communist Party
CCPA	Chinese Catholic Patriotic Association
CCYB	China Christian Year Book
CMB	China Missionary Bulletin
CR	Chinese Recorder
NCC	National Christian Council of China
PRC	People's Republic of China
SARA	State Administration for Religious Affairs
TSPM	Three-Self Patriotic Movement (of the Protestant Churches of China)
YMCA	Young Men's Christian Association
YWCA	Young Women's Christian Association

Chinese Theology

INTRODUCTION

A mirror called theology has been given to us to reflect
the image of God implanted in those of us Christians
who are also heirs to Chinese civilization.
—C. S. Song[1]

In an ideal world, this volume might have two separate introductions, like those children's books with multiple narrative threads where you can choose your own beginning and ending: one for theologians, and one for readers interested in Chinese literature. Word counts and press deadlines join with the argument of the book to insist on the less amusing but perhaps more radical task of integrating the two. If this causes any dissonance, the tension only reflects something of that which Chinese theologians have faced as they tried to write of and conceive of a Christian God in a language in which the concepts did not readily exist and in literary forms that bore little relation to those in which they themselves had inherited the gospel.

This volume aims to do two things: first, to present a general history or overview of Chinese theology through background chapters and studies of individual texts, and second, to offer the argument that Chinese theology cannot truly be understood without a sense of Chinese literary form and of the social meaning of the text. Dynastic politics, anti-imperialism, social reform movements, and Communism have left deep striations in Chinese theology, but Chinese theological texts and thinking have also been molded and influenced by Chinese literary traditions.[2] Benoit Vermander, musing on Michel de Certeau, has written that "an authentic Christian discourse is elaborated within a common experience of the Word of God, an experience which it precisely endeavours to translate into a language. In this regard, the crafting of a Christian community is akin to the crafting of a theological style."[3] The argument in this volume is that this common experience of the Word and the crafting of a community and theology have, for a great number of Chinese Christians, been based in a shared reading of texts.

Chinese Theology traces currents of thought and major figures of Chinese theology from the writings of literati Christians in imperial China to the sermons and micro-blogs of theological educators and pastors in the twentieth and twenty-first centuries. Chinese theology has been written in a great array of forms and styles, from the diary to the imaginary, via the essay, the hymn, and the sermon, and the volume attempts to do some justice to its richness. The volume traverses a range of eras and beliefs, incorporating Roman Catholic and Protestant voices and a variety of church affiliations.[4] While there are evident losses to such a breadth—any number of scholars could have written stronger individual chapters—a single volume allows a keener sense of overall development and new comparisons and insights. The setting up of the state patriotic movements ("official churches") in the 1940s and 1950s, for example, looks very different when viewed in the light of Republican Christian aspirations rather than from a contemporary perspective. A longer trajectory allows the anti-Christian literature of the 1930s to be set alongside the anti-Christian treaties of the 1630s, or parallels to be made between the ways Christianity was regarded as a corrective to corrupt Neo-Confucian metaphysics in the Ming and as a corrective to Marxist methodologies in contemporary academia.

Chinese Theology is first a study of Chinese theological texts. It takes texts that are representative of the most important periods of Chinese Christianity—as seen in the flourishing of theological writing, rather than in the divides of dynastic or mission history—and studies them as theological and literary works. The volume argues that Chinese theology has been necessarily tied to the (Chinese) literary forms in which it has been written and that the theological content cannot be separated from its literary expression. The thought is molded by the genre in which it is expressed: we cannot read Chinese theology as if it were written in English, and we cannot study it as if the form of writing had no bearing on the thought constructed. Chinese theological texts have to be understood in their *textual* context as well as their contextual context. The sociopolitical background is critical to this highly engaged theology, but we also have to be able to read the texts within their own history of meaning construction. To limit "Chinese theology" to those works that look like or read like Western systematics may fundamentally misconstrue how Chinese Christians have written of, and understood, God. In the same way, as Western scholars used to debate whether or not Chinese philosophy was philosophy, since it did not adhere to certain logical and structural norms of the (Western) genre of philosophy, a new debate is needed on what Chinese theology is, not just from the perspective of the inverse of the expected and the systematic, but starting out from the texts that comprise this theology.

Literary form and theological content are indivisible, an integrated whole. If the true "form" of theology, the mode in which it reflects, is divine ideas or divine thought, these still need capturing in human words.[5] For us to understand Chinese theology, we need a sense of its craft, of how the Chinese literary forms operate through which the theology has been created. One conclusion we might reach, for example, is how much Chinese theology, like Chinese text reading, is essentially relational: this is not the virtuoso performance of a scholastic, where the reader, or student, follows along the steps to their logical conclusion, but a more open process, where the reader, conceived as a peer, is invited to make connections from within a shared intranet of allusion. A common heritage in the Chinese classics and a reading pattern that proceeds via a series of implicit associations in the mind of the reader create a more participative and open-ended way of reading and of engaging with theology. It is a theology that does not just draw from the church and reflect back church thinking, but asks readers to comment on and add to the debates as the texts are written and circulated. This might be more evident in classical Chinese writings than in the modern essay, but the canonical learning that so thoroughly shaped the worldview of the late-imperial elite has remained stubbornly vital even into the People's Republic. An understanding of precepts such as human nature, for example, remains in good part a result of dialogue between the classics and the classics as reinterpreted through a Christian lens.

The volume is structured around periods of theological activity, rather than church activity or national politics. The late Qing, for example, may have been a time of great mission work and translation activity, paving the way for many of the writings here, but it was not in itself a time of exciting new theological thinking by Chinese Christians and is not covered in any detail.[6] The periodization here delineates *Chinese* theology, not the church in China, not mission history, not even the attacks on the church or the path of church, but the response by thinking, writing Christians to those events, the formation of sustained Christian discourse and reflection. While some excellent studies of quotidian Christian life exist,[7] historical studies of Chinese Christianity have tended to be event-dominated, particularly those events that affected missionaries, such as the Taiping Rebellion or Boxer Movement. Theological history has different milestones and junctures and has thrived during times of relative peace, or at least during periods when Christians were not being singled

out for special treatment. Moments of intense development in the history of
the expression of God in Chinese thought include the 1630s to 1660s, 1920s to
1930s, and 1990s to 2000s. (While theological history does not track neatly onto
standard historical narratives, it evidently interacts with this history—so we see
the Kangxi emperor reading Matteo Ricci's catechism almost a century after its
publication and basing his 1692 Edict of Toleration on his reading of that text; or
the notorious case of the effect of Protestant preacher and tract-writer Issachar
Jacox Roberts in the 1840s on Hong Xiuquan, the "younger brother" of Jesus
and founder of the Taiping Movement.)

Chinese Theology concentrates on those thinkers who have taken seriously
the "Chinese" element to their theology. In a survey necessarily horizontal as
well as vertical, it inquires into individual theologians' relations with God, with
their faith, with philosophical and scriptural texts—and with their compatriots
and the state. It might be possible to read the writings of twentieth-century
evangelists like Song Shangjie (John Sung) or Ni Tuosheng (Watchman Nee),
whose theology presupposes a universal truth and universally applicable Christianity, while knowing little of the situation in China. It would be much more
difficult to read the writers discussed here without knowing something of the
history and political preoccupations of each era: the background chapters
(Chapters 2, 6, and 8) are included for that purpose. These chapters join the
dots, outlining the social and historical circumstances that form the backdrop
to the Christian theology. They could be read as a continuous history, or may be
skipped by those with knowledge of Chinese Christian history: the text studies
are the main point.

The theology explored here is one of engagement: with historical theology,
with Chinese textual traditions, with the World Council of Churches and international bodies, and most of all, with Chinese society and its governors. Ni
Tuosheng provides, in fact, an excellent case in point to explain the focus of this
volume. Ni was a widely read (in Chinese and English) and influential preacher
and writer who suffered long imprisonment for his faith. His writings—whether
on atonement, kingdom theology, or ecclesiology—are peppered with Chinese
examples and cases, but he uses these primarily to illustrate Christian truths,
rather than to determine them. The writers and thinkers selected here use a
Chinese viewpoint in a more radical sense: to develop and inform their understanding of God and the world. If we were to strip Ni Tuosheng's Chinese
examples away, his point would almost always still stand, whereas the theology
of those "Chinese theologians" studied here is more dependent on the particular lens or narrative frame in operation for its force and validity, whether those

theologians are engaging with literary or philosophical traditions or the social environment.

In an era of interest in popular Christianity and its sectarian and nonorthodox expressions, and when we understand theology to be so much more than the texts of academic or church theologians, a narrative that showcases elite male voices and mainstream Han theologians might seem a throwback to prewar or pre–Vatican II sensibilities—an anachronism before it is even published. There are grounds for persisting, however: Chinese theology is so little known and understudied that even major figures and writers have yet to make it into systematic theology courses outside of the Chinese-speaking world. While women's church leadership as *beata*, as Bible women, as evangelists and revival leaders, and more recently as priests and seminary deans, has been a prime force in the development and perpetuation of the Chinese church, as discussed in the explanatory chapters below, the writings of such women have until recently represented a minor stream in the record. The current flourishing of church and academic theology in China will soon alleviate the contemporary, if not historical, gender imbalance and allow for a different approach in future studies of Chinese theology, as church theologians such as Gao Ying or Cao Shengjie and great numbers of female academic scholars are contributing to new directions in theology and a new body of work.

Recent scholarship on "popular" Christianity in China has highlighted the tremendous growth in evangelical and independent churches throughout the twentieth century, and there has been prolific publishing in English of Chinese evangelical writings; but there has been no recent equivalent monograph study of the issues that intellectuals and liberals faced, such as the fraught issue of Chinese Christian identity in a postmissionary world or how to relate Christianity to wider society. There is no suggestion that this academic, intellectual stream of literary Christianity is the sum total of Chinese Christianity, or even its most important strand, any more than scholars who have worked on popular Christianity or Christian sects, or even a rarefied cultural Christianity, would make such a claim for their subject matter.[8] It is one strand of Chinese Christianity. But because of the correlation of leadership—in both academia and the church—and writing, and the continued valorization of the textual heritage in China, it is a particularly important one.

Like many academics, Chinese theologians frequently come to doctrinal theology at a slight tangent, with a sense of questioning rather than givenness. All that does not make rational sense or sense within a Chinese worldview or Chinese language context is tested and thought through—a stance that has put some of those theologians at odds with the stance of their teachers, who regarded theology more as a transmitted given. In a study of the Holy Spirit in the "found" of Christianity as opposed to the "given," Ben Quash noted two challenges of the English Reformation: "the Catholic-leaning concerns of those who would translate the Bible only on the assumption that English could add nothing new whatsoever to Latin, and the Calvinist concerns of those who thought that historical experience could add nothing new whatsoever to one's confidence of election."[9] Whatever their personal or denominational inclinations, the Chinese theologians explored in this volume were to discover that a Chinese Christ brought new things of God, which could not be theorized from within an attachment to Latin (or English) and the universal meaning it stood for, and that defending their own historical experience of faith would be an integral part of their task. If "radical generativity" is the mark of the divine, and the story of Jesus Christ is at home in all contexts and meaning systems, the narrative of how this infinitely "re-presentable" story took form in China is necessarily both an exciting tale of creativity and a challenge to those who derive their authority from previously fixed forms.[10]

THEOLOGY AND THE STUDY OF CHINESE CHRISTIANITY

The argument over what constitutes Chinese theology bears similarities to debates in other fields. In a recent study of the work of Xu Bing 徐冰 (the artist whose installation 天书 *A Book from the Sky* created thousands of fabricated characters in a text that cannot be "read"), editors Hsingyuan Tsao and Roger Ames discuss the question of how "Chinese" contemporary Chinese art is. As they suggest: "it is not exactly 'Chinese' even though it does address the Chinese experience and issues. And on the other hand, it cannot abandon this 'Chinese' identity because it is only by labeling itself 'Chinese' that it can gain a place in the international art arena."[11] While commercial cynicism might be lacking in the religious case, the same cultural dilemma and external direction of the field (as Tsao and Ames note, contemporary art discourse is pretty much synonymous with "Western contemporary art discourse") mean that Christianity is often caught in the cleft of being seen as a "foreign" religion by insiders and as "Chinese" by outsiders and having to defend itself against similar charges of "cultural self-colonization." The problem of identity, whether imposed or adopted, has strongly influenced both the questions that Chinese theology has asked, particularly in the past century, and the institutional location of "Chinese theology" as a discourse (a field all too frequently relegated to "Asian religion" courses and not regarded as part of a standard systematic curriculum by right).

In his essay in the same volume, Roger Ames sets out to show how Xu Bing's work can be read not just in terms of its Western associations, but as squarely located within Chinese tradition, and that an understanding of Chinese cosmologies gives a richer meaning to the artwork by an order of magnitude, as well as opening up new religious questions of the text. Ames also notes, significantly for our discussion, that Xu Bing's "meaningless" book has a logic and coherence at the textual level, the level of the binding, the pagination, the interlinear commentary and calligraphy, all of which "arouses an anticipation of meaning" in a Chinese observer.[12] This volume has the same aims as Ames: to read the texts from within Chinese traditions to gain a deeper understanding of their meaning and to explore that "third place" where Chinese theologians appropriate ideas from both traditions to address "Chinese cultural issues within a Chinese cultural discourse."[13]

The relationship between the study of Chinese theology and other fields of research into Chinese Christianity, especially history, is a developing entity and has remained undertheorized in part because of the paucity of theological studies. Historical events and their later record have significantly affected the reception of Christianity in China and so the development of theology, just as theological texts have inflected the course of church history. If intellectual historians are more interested in outcomes, of prime importance to theologians are the texts themselves, their wisdom and insight. This volume shares with other recent historical work, much of it drawing on newly opened archives, an interest in reevaluating the narrative of Chinese Christianity, a narrative suppressed in Communist historiographical and literary records and subject to frequent revisions in interpretation. If Christianity has been seen as inimical to the Chinese state for much of PRC history, this narrow viewpoint and narrow tranche of history are currently being contested by Chinese and foreign scholars researching areas such as the Christian contribution to infrastructure, education, and nation-building during the late Qing and Republican China.[14]

In her recent book on the Taiping Rebellion, *What Remains*, Tobie Meyer-Fong relates how reading account after account of deaths of the "loyal and righteous" Qing subjects in Yangzhou gazetteers changed her perception of the Taiping Movement (ca. 1850–1864). Like others, Meyer-Fong had taught courses on the Taiping that focused less on the horrific deaths of twenty million Chinese and more on the strange visions of "Jesus Christ's Younger Brother," Hong Xiuquan. As Meyer-Fong narrates, as soon as the dynasty fell, the martyrs of the Qing resistance were sidelined in the historical narrative, displaced by newer, more politically correct martyrs to the Republic.[15] Just as the meaning of the Taiping Rebellion has continuously evolved, so too the narrative of Chinese Christianity has been through multiple editions, transposed over time and space. Early encounters between (foreign) missionaries and Chinese interested in Christianity were inevitably documented and transmitted most readily by the foreigners, who had a greater incentive to produce records of their work for a home audience, whether that audience was the Pope or a mission board. The dominant initial narrative of nineteenth-century Chinese Protestantism, for example, was a tale of travel, of translation studies and printing presses, and of the persecution of "native" converts, threaded through with amateur anthropological musings about the "Chinese personality" and descriptions of the cultural and religious rites of a people who had grown up "as isolated as if they had been the inhabitants of another planet," in the words of one missionary historian.[16]

The interpretations of Christianity and of the church have differed wildly over time and across different groups in Chinese society: from object of curiosity and scientific allure during the Ming dynasty, to hated harbinger of imperial might among late Qing gentry, to oppressor of women among Republican feminists, and to opiate of the masses for liberated Communists. These changing perceptions of Christianity more broadly in society have conditioned the theology emerging from Christians living in that society. A hospital eye clinic in rural Fuzhou in the late nineteenth century was a symbol of salvation to some, of imperialist incursion to others. Accounts of Christian intellectuals from the 1920s may tell of how they struggled with questions of faith during the Anti-Christian Movement (1925–1927), but, as in Meyer-Fong's case, it takes reading journal article after journal article, in an Anti-Christian Federation magazine such as *Juewu* (覺悟 Awakening), to appreciate why so many educated Christians during the 1920s were so badly affected by the emotive force of essays attacking their religion. In a period of trenchant secular philosophies and pro-science rhetoric like the early Republic, it is easy to see how Christian thought was shaped by wider social beliefs, as week after week, editorial writers and essayists amassed an array of material and argument to expose Christianity as a tool of imperialism, antithetical to modern life and scientific inquiry, and, more wrenchingly for young idealists, an obstacle to the realization of Chinese identity and nationhood.

Much has been written on the "paradigm shift" over the past few decades from mission-centered studies of Chinese Christianity to sinological ones focused on the Chinese recipients and developers of the message and on Chinese-language materials.[17] This has been a profound corrective, and the exploration of Chinese materials and of Chinese subjectivities has challenged entrenched narratives and brought new perspectives, opening up whole new fields of research, such as studies of Chinese independent churches (where the majority of Protestant believers worshipped!). The pendulum shift has been so marked, in fact, that some scholars have more recently criticized the tendency to downplay or efface the mission contribution to Chinese Christianity and have called for recognition of the interdependence and reciprocity in the work of missionaries and local churches.[18] There are good grounds for eschewing clear distinctions between "mission church" and "Chinese church," between "Western theology" and "Chinese theology." Many of the individuals studied in this volume had trained abroad; almost all received theological training from non-Chinese teachers; several write in multiple languages; all have dedicated their lives to the study of something both transcendent and localized.

In a recent editorial in the *Journal for the Study of Christianity in China*, Geng Youzhuang delineates the differences between *hanxue* (汉学 "Chinese studies," sinology), *guoxue* (国学 "national studies," study of Confucian classics), and *Zhongxue* (中学 "China studies"). The first, *hanxue*, is understood as sinology as practiced by Western scholars—a Western academic discipline with a pedigree reaching back to the days of the new chairs in Chinese in Germany and at Oxford in the late nineteenth century.[19] *Guoxue* denotes the recent rise in China of traditional Chinese studies, which was out of favor during much of the twentieth century but now is reestablishing itself as a field of classics, in much the same way that Latin and Greek are taught in European universities. *Zhongxue* is a newly delineated category, that is, Chinese studies as done by Chinese scholars rather than by foreign scholars. The distinction is hard to maintain in Chinese Christian studies. Jesuit-era missionaries such as Matteo Ricci (Italian/Papal States), Nicolas Trigault (Flemish), or Diego de Pantoja (Spanish) wrote in Chinese and attempted to use Chinese literary forms and tropes; their work is usually counted as part of Chinese (Christian) literature. In the modern era, the Jesuit Zhang Boda wrote natural, exquisite French; Bishop Jin Luxian wrote his personal diary in Latin as late as the 1950s; and figures like Zhao Zichen or Xu Zongze, who trained for their doctorates in the United States or Europe, thought and wrote in modes influenced by their "Western" training as well as their national heritage. Contemporary academics like Yang Huilin draw on Giorgio Agamben and Alain Badiou as readily as Chinese philosophical thinkers, and yet another generation of academic scholars of Christianity (including Liu Xiaofeng and Li Qiuling) trained in Germany, Switzerland, and beyond during the 1980s and 1990s.

While "Chinese Christianity" has indeed been studied, as critics hold, as part of mission history tracing a meta-narrative of global evangelism—a tale that focuses on such facts as which denominations were "given" which provinces of China as their mission field and which texts missionaries translated and when as focal to the development of the church, as if the sum total of Chinese Christianity could be told in English through European and American eyes—there is no alternative, pristine "China-only" version of history (or theology) waiting to be constructed. The artificial distinction proposed between Western and Chinese academic studies of Chinese classics is paralleled by an artificial distinction between the "mission" and "Chinese" churches and between "Western" and "Chinese" theology. Scholars have rightly moved away from seeing inculturation as a unidirectional application of Christianity to a culture to an understanding of the much more interactive, reciprocal processes at work; but an easy sino-centrism is no solution either.

Barnett Newman, who wrote of the Greek invention of beauty as "the bugbear of European art" in his call to dissociate art from the question of beauty, claimed in 1948: "We are freeing ourselves of the impediment of memory, association, nostalgia, legend, myth, or what have you, that have been the devices of Western European painting. Instead of making cathedrals out of Christ, man, or 'life,' we are making it out of ourselves, out of our own feelings. . . . The image we produce is the self-evident one of revelation, real and concrete, that can be understood by anyone who will look at it without the nostalgic glasses of history."[20] The same impossible attempt to transcend to the sublime without being mired in the "props of an outmoded and antiquated legend," as Newman puts it, is visible in some Republican-era and later Sino-Christian theology attempts to break away from European modes and the historical accumulation of theology and contemplate Christ directly. They are visible also in the attempts of critics to create a "Chinese" theology that is entirely centered in Chinese critical writings, or in the notion that *Hanxue* and *Zhongxue* are two separate fields of discourse.

An alternative paradigm that has been developing in Chinese Christian studies situates Chinese Christianity within world Christianity, focusing not just on national histories, but on transnational flows and comparisons. Again, the project has merit: the missions of Jesuits and Franciscans and others to the Chinese courts were clearly part of a wider story of mission history and development, just as the influence of the Social Gospel Movement in China during the 1920s aligned with trends elsewhere around the globe and cannot be read as an isolated event. The international character of the Roman Catholic Church and mainline Protestant denominations means that member churches are inherently tied to decisions and thought patterns from elsewhere (a source of dispute and danger for church members and governments alike who believe in the attainability of absolute independence). What is not wholly clear is whether we yet have the data to support such meta-studies, or perhaps rather, whether it is wise to pull back from local or detailed studies to move on to the broad-scale histories at this point. Historical studies of the Chinese Roman Catholic Church, its spread, methods, theologies, liturgies, and interaction with wider society, are indeed numerous and well-researched in both Chinese and non-Chinese languages. Academic studies of the Protestant churches are fewer, predominantly historical in scope, and barely scratch the surface of the vast data in libraries, archives, and private collections. Studies of Chinese theology are fewer still, and exceedingly limited in English.

This study has modest aims. It sets out to read, and draw together, a series of theological texts (broadly defined, as discussed in the chapters that follow) and locate them within their own textual and reading histories, giving enough background for readers to grasp the political and social aspects to those reading histories. The studies are intended to highlight particular moments and readings, to stand as in-depth essays producing an encounter where the reader can engage with the text and author, without the pretense of producing a comprehensive history of Chinese theology. The interest is how Chinese Christians write, and conceive of the tenets of their faith, and what aspects of Christianity come to the fore when Christian thought is conceptualized in Chinese textual modes. In its close text readings, the study builds up a narrative of Chinese theology that naturally intersects with other narratives and histories but does not foreground these links. Given the stifling of Christianity in Chinese historiographical and literary records, recent studies reevaluating Christianity (including Christian theology) also contribute to a wider understanding of each period. Christian periodical literature adds an important dimension to Republican-era political debates and social movements; the nationalistic sentiment of itinerant hymn writers in the 1990s contributes to studies of folk religious movements and migration. Readers who know something of the history of other religions in China will note many correspondences in the history of governmental influence, interpretation, and stipulation of religion and of religious response; the parallels are not dwelled on here explicitly, but the Christian case provides examples common to other narratives. There are parallels, for example, in the political selection of leadership; in disputes over the rightful Catholic bishop of a diocese and the whereabouts of top Roman Catholic leaders with those of the child reincarnations of the Panchen lama (with dual bishops and dual child lamas in place); and parallel histories of support for the New China, seen, for example, in the Dalai Lama's 1955 "Ode to Mao" and in Christian magazine articles effusively welcoming the New China and supporting the Korean War. State-church relations form a separate field of inquiry, but many of the questions asked by sociologists of religion are also theological questions, addressed in the theological texts presented here.

If the volume as a whole produces an overview of Chinese Christian theology, it is selective in its sources: for every theologian here, another could have been discussed. There are some serious omissions: any comprehensive study of early twentieth-century theology could hardly fail to include detailed study of Jia Yuming (賈玉銘) or Xie Fuya (謝扶雅 N. Z. Zia), for example. Given that the primary audience for this volume is an English-speaking one, English-language references among secondary materials have been given where possible, especially for the historical or background chapters, so readers can access more information (the primary texts for each chapter are in most cases not available in English). This is not (just) wholesale capitulation to Western academic norms, or lazy scholarship, but acknowledges the constant dialogue in the history of reading China; it is naïve to think that we can dismiss non-Chinese-language scholarship, especially in periods when outside scholars have had access to archives and materials unavailable within China.

On a technical note, names are given in Chinese format (surname first) and in pinyin. Where individuals have used other styles of name (e.g., K. H. Ting, T. C. Chao), these are given on first mention, with the standardized pinyin form used thereafter for consistency with other scholarship. The only exception to this is made for Cantonese names and/or historical figures known in wider English-language scholarship by an earlier Romanization (e.g., Chiang Kai-shek). Characters are given in the form appropriate to the text: long form for classical-language and early twentieth-century texts, and short form for modern PRC texts that postdate character simplification.

CHAPTER OUTLINE

Chapter 1 presents three texts from the late sixteenth and early to mid-seventeenth centuries (catechisms by Michele Ruggieri and Matteo Ricci, and a record of conversations with missionaries by Li Jiubiao 李九標 and others) to show the evolution from a Chinese-language to a Chinese-authored theology, setting the scene for the discussion of the remainder of the volume. The theology of the early encounters of Chinese with Christianity—whether Church of the East monks in the seventh century, Jesuits in the sixteenth century, or the first Protestant missionaries in the nineteenth century—was naturally strongly influenced by the missionaries' own backgrounds and theological training, tempered over time by their improved grasp of the Chinese language and understanding of what was most helpful for, or acceptable to, their audience. As missionaries' appreciation of Chinese literary form developed, and as Chinese Christians began writing their own philosophical essays or evangelistic tracts, the form and scope of the dialogue evolved. The three texts discussed in Chapter 1 trace this evolution from missionary to Chinese theology.

The 1920s and 1930s produced some of the most exciting and voluminous theology in Chinese history as Chinese leaders gained more prominence in churches, revival movements drew in new converts, mission education began to provide a stream of theology graduates, and the Chinese Christian press expanded. Chapters 2 through 5 explore the theology of an era when church growth was buoyant and Christians were prominent in national politics, education, and social movements, yet when a strong backlash against Western imperialism seemed to threaten the foundations of the church. The nature of "Chinese Christianity" was a prime source of reflection, but so too was the Chinese state itself and the nature of Christian duty to the nation. Chinese Christian intellectuals overwhelmingly conceived of Chinese theology as a theology for China: for the nation, and for its people. Engaging with this strand of nationalism (and how the nation was conceived as a positive factor) is critical to understanding the emerging theologies of the twentieth century, seen in different ways in each of the three texts studied from this era.

Chapter 2 surveys the state of Chinese Christianity at the beginning of the twentieth century and explores the notion of theology as a collective publishing exercise via a reading of Republican Christian journals. Chapter 3 discusses the *Life of Jesus* (Yesu zhuan 耶穌傳) by Zhao Zichen (趙紫宸 T. C. Chao) (1935), a semifictional biography written to respond to the call for a new "Chinese Christian literature" and replete with literary references. The study focuses on the structure of the narrative, on Jesus's self-understanding as the Messiah, and on the role of landscape in the novella. Chapter 4 considers another literary form, the *biji* 筆記, or "jottings," to show how the Jesuit theologian and archivist Xu Zongze (徐宗澤 P. Joseph Zi) was able to express himself and his theology differently in different forms within the same journal. The unofficial, lowbrow "jottings" comprise a personal view to complement the "official" theological essays in the *Shengjiao zazhi* (聖教雜誌, Revue Catholique) magazine. Chapter 5 analyzes the desire of Wu Leichuan (吳雷川 L. C. Wu) to build the Kingdom of God on earth in his *Christianity and Chinese Culture* (Jidujiao yu

Zhongguo wenhua 基督教與中國文化), also from the mid-1930s. Wu has often
been labeled a "Confucian-Christian," but this chapter considers the dialogue
in his work with U.S. and European proponents of the Social Gospel.

Chapters 6 and 7 tackle the difficult transition to unity and a "postdenominational" church in China, as well as the closed period of the church during the
1960s and early 1970s. Chapter 6 discusses the very different response of Roman
Catholic and certain Protestant church leaders to the leadership of New China
and to the creation of state patriotic bodies in the 1950s. Anti-imperialism and
self-determination dominate the discourse, played out in increasingly shrill, patriotic language. As the chapter points out, very little "theology" is published
during this period. Chapter 7, discussing the work of preeminent Protestant
bishop and statesman Ding Guangxun (丁光訓 K. H. Ting), concentrates on
his writings from the late 1930s through the mid-1950s, including his difficult
debates with the staunchly separatist church leader Wang Mingdao (王明道).

The contemporary or post-Reform-era church (1978–) is the subject of Chapters 8, 9, and 10. The great growth in the Chinese church, and what this might
mean for a future China, has been the source of much recent media debate,
from the *New Yorker* to the *Financial Times*, as the world has begun to catch up
with the astounding development of Chinese Christianities over the past three
decades. Chapter 8 assesses how state regulation has attempted to channel and
control that growth and discusses the three broad categories of writing that have
emerged from the attempt, in the form of official church, unofficial church,
and academic writings. While "theology" proper designates the output of the
state seminaries in an official Chinese construct of categories, the chapter also
addresses theological writings in academia and outside the state church. Chapters 9 explores the work of Renmin University professor Yang Huilin (楊慧林)
as an example of Sino-Christian, nonchurch theology; and Chapter 10 analyzes
some of the recent writings of Chengdu house-church pastor and former academic Wang Yi (王怡), the biographies collated by dissident Yu Jie (余杰), and
The Canaan Hymns (迦南诗选) by Lü Xiaomin (吕小敏).

FROM MISSIONARY WRITINGS TO CHINESE CHRISTIAN TEXTS: AN INTRODUCTION

If you do not serve the teaching of the Lord
you cannot do truly good works.
—Wang Zheng, *Renhui yue*, 1634[1]

In the eighth month of the seventh year of the Chongzhen reign, in 1634, Shaanxi scholar Wang Zheng 王徵 put the finishing touches on the introduction to his "Benevolent Society Regulations" (*Renhui yue* 仁會約). Local charitable organizations were a common feature of gentry involvement in the community during the late Ming, and recent scholarship had paved the way for statecraft and its preoccupation with regulations to be seen as a more acceptable part of the life and work of a scholar-official.[2] As a member of the local elite Wang was well-placed to contribute time, finances, and expertise to his Benevolent Society project. The regulations of the proposed society are extensive and define the duties of members and leaders; detail daily, monthly, and annual contributions payable by supporters; and offer practical instruction on such matters as feeding the indigent and providing coffins for the dead. What makes Wang's text extraordinary is the radically Christian nature of the organization proposed. Wang's rationale is theological (the new virtue of "love" is the ideological cornerstone of the project, on occasion combined with the cardinal Confucian virtue in the phrase "the benevolence of loving others");[3] the basis is scriptural (the new teachings are achievable by all; quotes the author, "My commandment is not too high or too far away but is in your heart; it is most easy");[4] the virtues of almsgiving are laid out in the Catholic terms of the seven corporal and seven spiritual acts of mercy; and the wisdom of the Christian canon (in citations from St. Thomas, St. Augustine, St. Paul, and St. James, among others) undergirds the principles of mutual love, practical charity, and egalitarian membership on which the society was based.[5]

Wang Zheng is best known for his writings on Western machinery and phonetics,[6] yet this practical text of little renown achieves something remarkable: in it Wang sets the aims and duties of a Confucian scholar within a Christian worldview, creating a generically recognizable text with a backdrop in Ming statecraft and philanthropy that is also thoroughly imbued with Christian precepts and evangelical in its emphasis on the true love of neighbor and God. The "Benevolent Society Regulations" starts out from Jesus's summary of the law, combines Christian injunctions and language with the principles and vocabulary of Confucian (or Mencian) moral action, and at the same time offers subtle theological insights, such as the notion that looking for a reward for one's good works is to indebt God.[7] If Matteo Ricci assumed a Chinese worldview to write his great explanation of the Christian faith in 1603, Wang Zheng's writing, steeped in Christian rhetoric and example, strains toward the opposite extreme.[8] Another work of Wang's, a translation of stories of the desert fathers produced in collaboration with the Jesuit Johann Adam Schall von Bell, extols the virtues of fasting and privation as means to cultivate the soul in a series of fabulous-sounding tales of virgins rescued, desires chastened, and girls disguised as boys.[9] Yet even in these accounts of monastic life in the Egyptian desert, the stories echo Chinese hero tales, the lessons of virtue express a distinctly Chinese morality, and the preface discusses the merit of sponsoring texts in terms that draw on Buddhist religiosity as much as Catholic.

To understand Chinese theology, we have to understand Chinese texts. This bald statement might seem self-evident when considering a written, historical theology, but the ramifications in the Chinese case are particularly extensive. As this chapter explores, there are two integrated aspects to the development of Chinese theology: content and text. The Jesuits, creators of a great wealth of theological texts in late Ming and early Qing China, understood this and were ideally suited to the task of learning to read, appreciate, and philosophize with Chinese texts by dint of their own text-reading and philosophical training.[10] Over the course of the seventeenth century, Roman Catholic texts were printed and distributed; improved by their Jesuit authors in terms of language, intelligibility of the concepts to Chinese readers, and literary form; and then composed and circulated by Chinese Christians, completing the shift of the center of perception. The creation of Christian texts, Chinese in form and embedded in a Chinese understanding of the meaning of the written word, was integral to the creation of a Chinese theology.[11] In a neat, if dispiriting, parallel, an almost identical three-stage pattern of text production occurred in the nineteenth century, as the first Protestant missionaries labored to improve their Chinese; then develop, sinicize, and disseminate their writings; and subsequently watch as Chinese Christians took the ideas forward in surprising and exciting new ways. (Because the Jesuits aimed their evangelism at the literate elite, what happened over the course of thirty or forty years in the early seventeenth century, as literati converts incorporated new Christian ideas into their daily habits of writing and scholarship, took the best part of a century in the Protestant church, as missionaries first built the institutions to educate converts.)

To trace this great process of theological and textual development, which takes us to the starting point of this volume and its study of Chinese-authored theological texts, this introductory chapter looks at three works that might represent the three early stages of development. The differences and transitions between these presentations of the gospel provide a case study, or an analogy, of the process of the re-creation in Chinese language and text of Christian thought and its selective appropriation and transformation by Chinese scholars. The three texts are all well-known, they all predate the worst of the Rites controversy,[12] and two are available in English translation; collectively they show the steep, and mutual, learning curves of Jesuit writers and Chinese converts. Michele Ruggieri's catechism *Tianzhu shilu* (天主實錄 True Record of the Lord of Heaven) was published in 1584; Matteo Ricci's revised catechism *Tianzhu shiyi* (天主實意 True Meaning of the Lord of Heaven) was published in 1603; and Li Jiubiao's *Kouduo richao* (口鐸日抄 Daily Excerpts of Oral Admonishments) was compiled between 1630 and 1640. Following this exposition in miniature of the pattern of theological growth, which culminated in the flourishing of Chinese theology by Chinese Christian scholars in texts of all manner and type in the mid and late seventeenth century, the chapter concludes with a note on subsequent publications that challenged the theological proclamations of these texts, the so-called anti-Christian writings.

The process of Christianity emerging in Chinese thought and form in Ming and Qing China has traditionally been termed "accommodation," with reference to Matteo Ricci's methods of recasting Christianity in philosophical terms amenable to his Chinese audience and with a sympathetic interpretation of Chinese ritual. The term is used pejoratively by those who opposed his methods, but "accommodation" is not a bad term if it describes a two-way making room for, or adaptation of, religious thought, liturgy, and method within a new philosophical house or religious casing. It implies a generosity, and hospitality, on the part of both the one making room for the metaphysical newcomer and the one accommodating Christianity to a new sphere of religious experience. Later terms, such as "inculturation," "enculturation," and "contextualization," have been much debated in the models they propose for this overall process of religions being adapted to, emerging from within, and acting as transformative agents in another culture. The concern in this volume is not to critique such models or produce a grand new schema but to describe one strand of the process—that pertaining to theology, and particularly, the inscription of Chinese Christian thought in, and through, Chinese writing.[13] Accommodation was not just a matter of language and of cultural norms, as it has often been presented, but of texts too. The creation of a written theology is clearly related to broader processes of inculturation but has its specific background in an understanding of the social setting of Chinese texts and of how given literary forms create new readings and insights. Textual form is not neutral. If biblical studies has taught us to see, for example, how the "bare bones" narrative of Genesis 1 incorporates a distinct theological perspective or how ancient Near Eastern literary motifs function, then we need to be equally astute in our reading of how Chinese texts inform theology in particular, God-revealing, ways.

FROM SCHOLASTIC AND JESUIT TO CHINESE, SCHOLASTIC, AND JESUIT

Michele Ruggieri and Matteo Ricci, two of the first Jesuits to reside in mainland China, shared much in common beyond their coauthored texts, which began with a tract on the Ten Commandments in 1583—quite probably the first piece of Chinese Christian literature from within the Western, Latin church.[14] Their cultural backgrounds and training were to affect and shape Chinese theology for decades to come, but the differences between their writings also show the effect of Ricci's longer time in China and more profound understanding of the Chinese canon and its interpretation.[15] Ruggieri and Ricci both grew up in an environment of Christian humanism and of church reform following the Council of Trent. Both missionaries had excelled within a rigorous Jesuit curriculum that entailed systematic study of Greek and Latin classical authors and a course of study that progressed from philosophy through physics, geometry, and astronomy to metaphysics and, finally, theology.[16] The ideas transmitted by the Jesuits in China might not always have been the cutting-edge science of Copernicus or Kepler and were sometimes more culture-bound than the universalism Jesuits proclaimed,[17] but the breadth of their education conferred important advantages in a society where literacy and status were so tightly related.

As Haun Saussy has reminded us, the knowledge we have of Matteo Ricci's texts and of Counter-Reformation Catholicism makes Ricci seem less remote than he really was—and the Ricci of Chinese sources is not the Ricci of Western-language writings.[18] But if Counter-Reformation theology cannot tell us the full story of what Chinese readers took from Jesuit writings, the Jesuit curriculum is a starting point for the ideas that the first Jesuits developed in China. Classical scholarship furnished the language and textual analysis skills for learning difficult, untranslated texts in the Chinese canon. More importantly, the positive value attached to Greek and Roman moral thought enabled Jesuit scholars to approach the Confucian ethical system with an expectation of gain. Jesuit probabilism gave wide latitude of interpretation, and the positive theology of the society sat well with Confucian sensibilities in areas such as the individual's role in attaining salvation.[19] The role of Jesuit science, and in particular astronomical and calendrical knowledge, in paving the way to the Chinese court is well-known, but a pedagogy that placed scientific knowledge before theology in the curriculum was also to play a critical role in the methodology and writings of Ricci. Certain other global features of sixteenth-century Roman Catholicism aided the incipient Chinese mission: the expansion of evangelism in the Americas, for example, had provoked a flurry of new thinking on salvation and on whether a good life lived in "natural" knowledge of God outside of Christ or the church could justify a person. The range of opinions in the early sixteenth century on dealing with "virtuous pagans" was wider than it would be again for several hundred years, and Ricci and other Jesuits in China wrote of the hope that some of "the ancients" might be saved by natural law.[20]

Michele Ruggieri's catechism of 1584, the *Tianzhu shilu*, was one of the first introductions to Christian doctrine in Chinese and was distributed across Chinese-reading areas as far as the Philippines and Korea. It was deliberately discontinued once Ricci's revised text was published in 1603,[21] making the text of interest as a baseline for later translations and explanations, a point of departure for comparison, and an example of a rejected formula—the textual equivalent of Ricci's policy reversal in ditching Buddhist clothing for the robes of the literati once the top-down policy of evangelism to the elite was put into effect. Ruggieri's text engages with Chinese thinking, but his substantial introduction to the faith remains firmly rooted in its author's own background.

The opening to *Tianzhu shilu* is dotted with Chinese concepts such as the Five Virtues or Five Relationships, as it sets out its aim of teaching how to achieve "the salvation of the soul and ascent to heaven, and avoid falling to hell."[22] This is not a hard teaching to keep, advises Ruggieri—just worship the Lord with your whole heart and do not doubt, and God will bring blessings. Keen to distinguish at the outset this "teaching" from Buddhist practice, the introduction points out that there is no need to leave one's profession or follow a teacher far away.[23] In situating himself, the author adds that he is not a (lowly) merchant, come to China for profit, but is here to serve the Lord. As regards Confucian (or Ruist) teachings, the text immediately engages its world of thought by identifying a transnational quest to understand *li* (理), the underlying principles of a thing—principles at the heart of literati debate for the previous several centuries. The text itself is offered as an agent of change: before *Tianzhu shilu* existed, writes Ruggieri, readers did not know the origins of life and death and lived as if in a dark night, but now the record has appeared, and the foundations of knowledge of the Lord of Heaven are clear.[24]

The starting point for Ruggieri's explanation of Christianity, as for all good Bible-based catechism, is creation, with God as Creator of the world. Ruggieri offers a selection of standard contemporary proofs for the existence of God—including the analogies of watching a boat on a stream navigating currents and knowing there must be an oarsman inside or seeing smoke from a chimney and knowing there is a fire in a room—to suggest intelligent design; or "only stupid people think that if they cannot see it, it doesn't exist."[25] Ruggieri lists the attributes of the Lord of Heaven, explains how the Lord of Heaven did not need matter to create, and offers answers to potential objections from a Chinese perspective on creation. In common with the later catechisms, Ruggieri writes at length of the nature of the soul and its faculties, of the four Aristotelian elements as the basis of matter, and of the three epochs of God's law (the "natural" era of innate knowledge of God, the period of the Mosaic law, and the period after Christ's revelation). This latter concept was to prove pivotal in Chinese literati discussions of salvation outside of Christianity and is discussed further below.

Ruggieri's text is a fine explanation of contemporary European thinking on creation and its chronology of 5,550 years and of the tripartite nature of the soul and such late medieval topics, but the structure is confused, with long, detailed questions and answers and little apparent progression. As others have noted, the work is somewhere between a catechism (i.e., a work directed at a non-Christian audience) and a doctrina, or a text for the faithful: it includes explanations of Jesus's miraculous birth and of "Maliya's" postpartum purity, detail on the nine heavens, and an explanation of the distinction between laypeople and monastics, alongside heavy-going philosophizing and scientific explanations of European astronomy.[26] Episodes from Old Testament narratives are interspersed with ethical categories, but the human history as retold appears as a monophonic record of human evil and punishment, with rare exceptions in the characters of Luoduo (Lot) and Nuoye (Noah). The mode of explanation in this first catechism is iterative, sometimes exhaustively so. Ruggieri makes ample use of Buddhist terminology in his explanation of Christian doctrines yet vigorously derides Buddhist thought: the mind of the text is firmly centered in the rightness of Christianity. Ideas found in Śākyamuni's writings are dismissed as "unbelievable," such as the notions that when heaven is full, some get to be reborn on earth, or that the rich who can purchase scripture recitation go to heaven while the poor go to hell.[27]

All three texts discussed in this chapter take the form of a dialogue, echoing both Jesuit school methods and canonical texts like the *Analects* (論語) or *Great Learning* (大學).[28] In Ruggieri's *Tianzhu shilu*, the dialogue is a constructed, internal one, which produces a self-affirming progression of thought. When an answer or explanation is given, the unnamed questioner accepts it and moves on to a related question in a step-by-step progression familiar to readers of, say, Aquinas. Questions such as "how is loving money, possessions, or parents more than God a sin?"[29] evidently derive from translated catechetical texts rather than from live repartee. In comparison with later texts, the language of Ruggieri's catechism inevitably seems rough, in phrases such as "God transformed himself into a male"; in Jesus being born in "Western India"; in transliterations like "Resuo" for Jesus (later "Yesu"); and in a depiction of Mary that makes her sound like an immortal in the Chinese pantheon.[30] (Awkward transliterations and terms were a feature of the first generation of Protestant missionary-authored Bible and Prayer Book translations too.) Ruggieri's text, moreover, assumes a level of prior knowledge that readers could scarcely have had of non-Chinese concepts.

A degree of contextualizing of interpretation is evident, particularly over ethical precepts. The Decalogue is analyzed at length in the main text and re-presented at its conclusion along with some basic prayers from the daily office.[31] The command to honor one's parents, for example, is explained in terms of filial piety and repayment; the distinction between murder and judicial killing is made inherent in the translation of the fifth commandment; and the prohibition on adultery explicitly condemns the taking of a concubine, an interpretation less evident in the Mosaic law. In answer to the question of how to avoid violating the command to respect the Lord, a detailed, legalistic explanation is overlain with a layer of local cultural interpretation in spelling out such specific violations as worshipping the sun, moon, or gods; believing in dreams and auspicious auguries; selecting particular days for events; or trusting in geomancy and other divinatory arts. For detail of why these offenses are folly, we must turn to Ricci.

SINICIZED MISSIONARY TEXTS: RICCI'S *TIANZHU SHIYI*

If Ruggieri's catechism threatens to pull apart at the seams with the wealth of novel material and concepts introduced to its readers, Matteo Ricci's revisions produced a refined, more directed composition. Ricci's 1603 *Tianzhu shiyi* marked the confluence of late Ming philosophical thought and method and the scholastic and Jesuit theology of his own training and was inscribed with the textual and sociocultural knowledge garnered over twenty years in China. Some have regarded *Tianzhu shiyi* as *the* great work of early Catholicism in China, a magisterial synthesis of Chinese and Christian thought, molding subsequent mission and evangelism.[32] To a greater degree than Ruggieri's text, Ricci's is not (just) a Christian treatise, but a Christian response to, and explanation of, life shaped by Chinese philosophical and religious concerns. It is certainly a text that aims to start out from a Chinese perspective. In the introduction Ricci adopts the modest tones of a Chinese scholar, noting that his friends had cautioned against perfection and urged him to publish, even as he "implored Heaven with tears" for the day when true orthodoxy would come to be known in China.[33] *Tianzhu shiyi* was not the first Chinese text Ricci published and came on the heels of the success of his map of the world and his short text "On Friendship." This latter, a work that collated maxims and aphorisms on friendship from Greek, Roman, and Christian writings, demonstrated Ricci's keen knowledge of Ming literati trends and was well-received in literati circles, producing the acclaim that smoothed the way for Christian publications.[34]

If Ruggieri's introduction to the faith was generically confusing, with its combination of philosophical argument, doctrine, and science, Ricci's work offers a text that is more Chinese in thought and in form. The mediated nature of the text is deliberate. As preface writer Feng Yingjing suggests, Ricci's text "proves the west with the west, and uses what is Chinese to transform China," that is, he uses the thinking of the (far) west to argue against that of the (Buddhist) west and quotations from the Chinese classics to bring a new interpretation to China's ancient texts.[35] Ricci takes care to place the text in a Chinese reading frame, just as he does to express its thought in terms meaningful to his audience. One way of doing this was paring down the text to a more recognizable genre, or in European terms, by following the scholastic distinction between doctrines that belong to natural revelation and can be understood through reason, and those of positive revelation, which are grasped through faith.[36] While Ruggieri's catechism wove explanations believed amenable to reason, such as the existence of a Creator, with articles of faith, such as miracles or soteriological pronouncements, Ricci's approach is to structure his catechism so that rational people, with no prior understanding of Christian doctrine, could read, comprehend, and assent to the essence of what was being proposed.

This was, as Ricci explained to his Italian readers, an attempt to "open the way" to deeper mysteries by establishing the existence of a Creator and by "bringing Confucius . . . to our doctrine" through showing what Confucius himself reveals of God and Christ.[37] While later critics of Ricci's methods made much of this as an attempt to "hide" core Christian teachings and accused him of promoting a "Confucian monotheism" and eviscerating Jesus,[38] the grounds for this generic and theological move are clear, since the *Tianzhu shiyi* was never intended to present the entirety of the Christian faith. Separate texts, such as *Tianzhu jiao yao* (天主教要 Essentials of Catholic Teaching) of 1605, were produced by missionaries to teach believers or catechumens the Lord's Prayer, the Beatitudes, the Decalogue, and other such doctrinal basics. *Tianzhu shiyi* was, as one translator has written, a "pre-evangelical dialogue" bringing out points of contact with Chinese thought and inviting further consideration.[39]

To show how Ricci set his teachings within a Chinese frame and integrated the intellectual content of the message with a new textual form to make both as acceptable and intelligible as possible to his readers, we might turn to the authorial preface and first chapter of Ricci's text. Chinese prefaces are important, integrated components of texts. They convey status, and the quality of the (handwritten, block-printed) calligraphy of prefaces is an aesthetic marker. Ricci's *Tianzhu shiyi* was embraced into a network of scholarly association by the authority of its prefaces penned by high government officials: censor Feng Yingjing for the first imprint of 1603 and future "pillar of the faith" Li Zhizao for a 1607 edition. Ricci's own preface starts out with the cardinal Chinese concept of good governance. His bold opening, echoing so many early "Confucian" texts, affirms the canonical Chinese theory of relationships, pointing to the pivotal role of the ruler in the Five Relationships and Three Bonds, but it segues adroitly into the suggestion that from the early ages of disunity onward it has been clear that every state needs a ruler—why should the universe be any different?[40] Linking governance to the existence of a cosmic ruler in this way, Ricci continues by suggesting that all scholars ought to know, and look up to, the source of the universe (the term used for scholars is *junzi*, often translated as "superior man" or "gentleman," the epitome of morality, scholarship, and rule in classical thought and the personification of that to which his readers aspire).

Ricci employs gentle flattery a number of times in his opening: here to suggest that a focus of scholarship must be the Creator; a few lines later to question whether the people of the great Yao and Shun, the inheritors of the Duke of Zhou and of Confucius, can really have allowed knowledge of the true doctrines of heaven to be corrupted. While modestly implying that his own language is not up to the job of correcting the errors introduced over the centuries, Ricci also points to the mystery and ineffability of the truth of the Most-Wise and All-Knowing and issues a challenge to his readers: the benefit of a paltry knowledge of the Lord of Heaven is "greater than knowing much about other things."[41] By piquing curiosity and presenting a philosophical proposition to appeal to scholars by dint of its difficulty, Ricci's preface encourages a rethinking of the source of all being, the governance of the world, and the nature of judgment.

As Thierry Meynard has shown, the structure of *Tianzhu shiyi* as a whole is composed of sets of mini-dialectics: Chapters 1 and 2 on the question of God, with Chapter 1 showing the necessity of God and Chapter 2 refuting alternative theories; Chapters 3 and 4 on theological anthropology, with Chapter 3 a presentation on the soul and Chapter 4 refuting pantheism; and Chapters 5, 6, and 7 refuting transmigration and exploring the nature of the human.[42] Chapter 8 stands alone, answering implied questions on the strangeness of Western customs and the Christian religion.[43] This first chapter begins with "the Chinese scholar" musing on how self-cultivation—the achievement of which allows one to be called a *junzi*—is a universal phenomenon. This Chinese voice then conveniently questions where this Way (or Dao) might lead after death. The Way of Heaven, the "Western Scholar" counters, is followed in all great nations; it has textual pedigree and is transmitted through canons and commentaries. Ricci/the Western Scholar explains that in the catechism he will start out from the principles on which the teaching is based, rather than talk about its adherents or scriptures. Creating neologisms as needed (such as *lingcai* 靈才, spiritual intelligence, for "intellectus"),[44] Ricci outlines what differentiates humans from other animals, in Christian terms that resonate with this central Confucian topic. (As Sun Shangyang has noted, Ricci was selective in his choice of Confucian texts, drawing most heavily on early texts and those amenable to a theist or Christianized reading.)[45] There is common cause across cultures, Ricci holds, in the pursuit of truth, as he establishes the basis for his dialogue in an unforced, mutual acceptance of reason. "What the intellect makes manifest cannot be forced to comply with what is not true," he points out, but "everything which principles affirm as true I cannot but take as true."[46] The primacy of reason is tempered by the humility of accepting that we cannot know everything—but what we do know cannot go against the truth. Following the conventions of Chinese texts, Ricci refers to readers as his listeners and invites debate with his audience.

When the Chinese interlocutor has affirmed Ricci's method and the project, Ricci begins his set-piece argument for the existence of God, transposing the usual scholastic catechistical order and beginning with arguments for a supreme ruler first, since the argument for creation ex nihilo was a hard sell to

Confucian minds. Taking three examples of design from nature (and borrowing heavily from Ruggieri), Ricci shows how the order inherent in the universe points to an authority in control of the world. To the further point of whether this authority must necessarily also have created the world, Ricci explains how these are one and the same question. Ricci tailors his examples to his scholarly audience: things that cannot bring themselves into being need an external cause, he writes—the need for someone to bring order can be seen in the example of writers who cast characters in bronze, where a compositor is needed to line up the sentences and build sentences into a whole article.[47] This Creator of order, who has endowed humans with the Five Virtues, has in Ricci's text also given them a notably Chinese physiology: eyes to see the Five Colors, ears to hear the Five Notes, a tongue to taste the Five Flavors. The old rejoinder from the Chinese scholar "if God created everything, who created God?" soon draws Ricci into a lengthy explanation of the Aristotelian Four Causes and of the Lord of Heaven as the active, final cause.[48]

Once the Chinese scholar has accepted the argument for a supreme Lord and asks for a fuller explanation of the Christian teaching, it is time to end the first day's discussion. Ricci concludes this first chapter with a teasing anecdote attributed to Augustine to show how we can never fully grasp the truths of God, let alone record them in a single book, and tells how the Lord of Heaven can be spoken of only negatively, being beyond all categories of language and being.[49] If the dialogue format allows Ricci to start from a Chinese perspective, the chapter ends with his interlocutor announcing, in the simulated oral narration style common to novels, "in listening, I have for the first time seen the Great Way, and thereby returned to the Great Source," following with more conventional phrases also implying the pretense of a narrator. (The beginning of Chapter 2 likewise recalls the opening conventions of a novel chapter, "I've washed my ears and am ready to listen," with its "your mysterious doctrines satisfy the ear and intoxicate the mind; I've been thinking about them all night without sleep.")

Ricci's catechism was honed over more than a decade of reading and debate. If the background to Ruggieri's text lay primarily in the Jesuit curriculum of his own training, Ricci's revised version was more attuned to the ideological currents of the late Ming and its debates over textual orthodoxy and political culture. As various scholars have noted, Ricci's understanding of Buddhist thought and of the different schools of Neo-Confucianism as shown throughout *Tianzhu shiyi* was far from comprehensive and frequently informed by his own philosophical background, at times marring a comparative explanation of Christianity.[50] The thinking Ricci drew on in his interpretations of classical texts did, however, reflect contemporary Chinese debates.[51] His own interpretations, influenced by his tutors like Zhang Huang (from whom he derived Confucian anti-Buddhist arguments) and the experience of public debate with Buddhists, developed considerably over the period while the text was circulating in manuscript form in the late 1590s. This is an important point in terms of the "Chineseness" of the text and its acceptability: as Ricci's manuscript circulated among friends and colleagues in the manner of any Chinese text, it was edited and improved, with corrections incorporated into later editions.[52]

There were at least three sources of textual input into Ricci's work: earlier catechisms, Ming intellectual writings, and inspiration (directly or indirectly) from Chinese Jewish and Islamic writings.[53] Ricci's text drew heavily on earlier catechisms, borrowing some thirty passages from Ruggieri and sharing approximately forty passages in common with a Japanese catechism of 1591 produced by the Jesuit head of the Asia mission, Alfonso Valignano.[54] Passages reproduced verbatim from Ruggieri include proofs for the existence of God and discourse on the faculties of the soul, while Valignano's arguments against Buddhism were adapted to refute the Chinese concept of *taiji* (太極, The Great Ultimate).[55] In his sparring with Ming intellectual thought, Ricci benefited from a receptiveness to new streams of thought that was itself a function of multiple competing schools teasing apart late Ming orthodoxy, in what has been described as a "general climate of spiritual effervescence."[56] Reactions against narrow orthodoxy and the materialism of the age came from various syncretistic movements and new schools.[57] The absorption of elements from Daoist and Buddhist streams within orthodox Song-Ming *lixue* (理學 School of Principles) provoked much internal debate, at the same time as Wang Yangming's *xinxue* (心學 School of the Mind) was challenging standard Neo-Confucian interpretation on matters such as innate good or the unity of knowledge and action—questions on which Ricci and fellow Jesuits had much to say.[58] Ricci's arguments on individual Neo-Confucian concepts may have been unconventional, and in places unsupportable, but the text passed the first hurdle: it was readable. In this much, it surpassed Ruggieri.

Some of Ricci's own sections were, in fact, the least successful as arguments. But what Ricci did, apart from reducing the number of phonetic equivalents and improving the translation terms, was to restructure the catechism and make it a more fluid text. Ricci had been asked by Valignano to contextualize the work for a Chinese audience, and to do so he reordered certain arguments, removed details on Buddhism, and developed a more profound dialogue on Confucian morality.[59] Of great importance to the final product, however, was Ricci's ability to craft a decent piece of writing, which can be seen in his initial references to statecraft and the series of quotations from the Chinese classics in Chapters 2, 4, and 6 and in the detail of narrative conventions. *Tianzhu shiyi* read, mostly, as a Chinese text, and so its arguments were at least circulated and considered. The reach of the text affirms this: official recognition of Christianity in 1692 was directly related to the Kangxi emperor's reading of Ricci's text; *Tianzhu shiyi* was one of the few Christian works catalogued in the Qing imperial repository, the *Siku quanshu* (Complete Works of the Four Treasuries); and Ricci's text was translated into Korean, Mongol, and Manchu. Its citation figures and circulation throughout the seventeenth century would be the envy of many a modern scholar.

Tianzhu shiyi can be seen as a genuinely intermediate text. In terms of its thought, as Sun Shangyang argues, Ricci harmonized elements compatible with Confucianism and rejected or disputed those that were incompatible,[60] and a bilateral process can be seen at work as Christianity was itself transformed as it responded and adapted to Chinese thought and textual form. Ricci's text bequeathed a series of precedents and questions to later theologians that shaped both Chinese Christian writings and debates among the mission community. Some decisions on principle or method went against Ricci, such as the decision among missionaries in 1629 to cease the use of *"Shangdi"* as a term for God or the Rites ruling (on the Roman side). But in terms of the text, there is a clear development from previous missionary writings in literary form, in the range of citation, and in the paratextual materials that were so critical to the reception of Chinese texts. As Meynard argues tellingly, however, *Tianzhu shiyi* is not a true dialogue but a teaching, since the Chinese scholar's questions always bring a response and resolution from Ricci himself.[61] For a more ingenuous narrative, we have to wait for the appearance of Chinese-authored texts.

TEXTS WITHIN TEXTS AND THE WRITING OF A CHINESE THEOLOGY: *KOUDUO RICHAO*

By the end of the seventeenth century more than three hundred Christian texts were circulating in China. The majority of these were still authored by Europeans, but an increasing number by Chinese converts, and represented a great array of genres and subject matter, from apologetics, to explanations of the Mass, to lives of the saints, to texts on almsgiving. One title which demonstrates richly the intellectual questions that Christianity raised for new believers is the *Kouduo richao*. It is also a work that shows the clear effect of Chinese concepts of the text on contemporary theology. This hefty compilation of eight volumes presents extracts of conversations recorded over the course of a decade between

Chinese Christians in Fujian and local Jesuit missionaries. Among the most frequent conversation partners are editor Li Jiubiao (d. ca. 1647) and his brother Li Jiugong (李九功 d. 1681), and Jesuits Giulio Aleni (d. 1649) and Andrzej Rudomina (d. 1632).[62]

The five hundred entries in *Kouduo richao* cover topics ranging from the nature of the soul, punishment, and theodicy to Christian relics, piracy, and the calculation of longitude. The questions raised, the circumstances of publication, and the assumptions implicit in the text about reading and living faithfully tell us much about how Chinese scholars and editors expected theology to function. The extracts, chronologically organized and presented, reflect a Chinese scholar's lifetime habit of writing and the daily recording of observations and self-reflection. The majority of entries are dialogic in form, while a few record particularly noteworthy points from sermons preached by resident Jesuits.[63] Unlike Ruggieri's or Ricci's texts (or even Aleni's own text recording conversations in 1627 with the official Ye Xianggao),[64] the encounters in *Kouduo richao* are characterized by a natural, spontaneous feel: the text is a record of life, a miscellany, not a systematized didactic presentation of Christian faith. Conversations arise out of quotidian life: provoked by an event, such as a typhoon, or prompted by an object, such as a map on the wall, or, as in many entries, questions on a book just read. This was to be a defining feature of later Chinese theological texts, where questions are woven into life and explain life, deriving from the experience of Christianity rather than starting from abstract theological concepts. A great variety of topics is addressed, but certain thematic areas recur in the conversations, and in these we can see how Chinese sensibilities frame the questions asked and shape the Christian message as recorded by the Chinese editors and compositors. Two concepts that run throughout *Kouduo richao* are considered further below: the text and the nature of merit.

Aleni's dialogue partners in Fujian of lower-gentry elite mirror in certain ways Ricci's literati circles. The respondents are highly educated and intelligent but have little knowledge of Christian concepts and few texts to guide them. A question such as "are not omniscience and predestination incompatible?" from Yan Zanhua shows how sharp the discussants might be on difficult topics, while Aleni's retelling of biblical pericopes in paraphrase reminds us that even local Christian leaders had no knowledge of the greater part of the Bible and needed missionaries to link experiences to biblical models.[65] Conversations might be initiated by one of the Jesuits, often with a pointed question, but more usually the starting point is a query from a visitor or Christian passing through town. Because of the peripatetic nature of mission and the occasional trips to the city of the converts, the conversations are often a catch-up, touching base after an absence. Conversation threads in the text are dropped and taken up again days later, depending on the interests of the particular interlocutor; there is a strong sense of happenstance in this chronological or diary style of writing.[66] As with Ricci, Aleni draws on Chinese concepts wherever possible to make his point. In one discussion, for example, visitor Xie Zhongsheng comments how difficult it is to feel remorseful over minor transgressions. Aleni responds that not repenting of minor sins equates to not recognizing the supreme nature of the Lord and explains with an analogy that utilizes a Chinese sense of hierarchy: for a disrespectful comment to a peer, he notes, one might not feel any particular remorse, while such a comment to a superior would leave one ashamed; if the same comment were made to someone in a position of great authority, one would feel extremely embarrassed and mollified only after begging forgiveness. What sin could be greater, Aleni parries, than to belittle the Lord?[67]

The scholars who come to converse with Aleni often have scientific questions to put to him, which the Jesuit frequently uses to disprove erroneous religious beliefs or to turn to more spiritual points. An explanation of longitude turns into a discussion of why the astrological selection of auspicious dates can have no logical foundation;[68] a discussion on the clavichord leads to the observation that all should learn to tune their own minds; and mention of the telescope results in the insight that we should use one end to look at other people and the opposite to look at the self.[69] The new technical and scientific knowledge being introduced can be quite disorientating: for Li Jiubiao, an explanation of longer days and nights nearer the poles left him "forgetful and sick at heart."[70] Conversations on maps and armillary spheres may change the scholars' way of viewing the universe—so may serve well as an evangelistic tool—and might, as Li reflects, challenge "narrow-minded literati" who think that whatever they cannot see with their own eyes does not exist (a phrase present in the earlier catechisms).

It is clear from a number of entries that more mature Christians occasionally get others to ask questions that might be unseemly for them, such as when Li Jiubiao sends Lin Zizhen back to Aleni to ask him why geomancy is untrue, if areas like Fuzhou produce more graduates than other regions.[71] (Aleni's answer, as is often the case, marries common sense with logic: since other areas produced more graduates in the late Song dynasty, and the landscape hasn't changed since, how can the success be attributed to *fengshui*? he asks.) Aleni takes every opportunity presented to plug Western inductive reasoning. He teaches through conversations, sermons (which often have a dialogic element to them and are conducted after the church service), illustrated volumes, and church paintings and through his own and others' texts.[72] Just as Li Jiubiao and

his friends will often bring queries about books they have read to Aleni, he also
frequently refers them back to published works. In a discussion on Jesus's nature
with Lin Yijun, for example, Aleni asks whether Jesus's human nature was his
body and his divine nature his soul. Lin's incorrect response of "yes" prompts
an explanation by Aleni of body, soul, and divine nature and how the three
substances combine in the one person of Jesus, followed by the comment, "On
the one person of Jesus, if you read what it says in my *Yiji* on the wonders of the
Trinity, it talks precisely about this."[73]

Discussions on texts form a leitmotif throughout *Kouduo richao*.[74] If Ricci's
catechism can be seen as an intermediate stage in both thought and textuality,
a close replica of Chinese form and debate but with foreign elements and assumptions, Li Jiubiao's volume inhabits by right the Chinese textual sphere.
This inheritance involved a wealth of ingrained beliefs about texts and text-
reading practices: from early perspectives on texts reflecting the patterning
of the universe, to the textual authority invested in the emperor and the state, to
the classics as the repository of morality and source for inculcating the virtues
that enable growth into full humanity. Because the Confucian canon remained
so central to learning and statecraft throughout late imperial China, certain
early assumptions continued to inform reading practices, and Chinese Christian texts entered a library where the meanings attached to them as ritual objects, the functions attached to their teaching, and their authority as a reflection
of divine truth were preinformed by this Confucian heritage, overlain by Buddhist and Daoist textual histories. Where Ricci had attempted to grapple with
Neo-Confucian philosophies and concepts in his presentation of the Christian
message, the concerns of the dialogue partners in *Kouduo richao* who approach
their Jesuit teachers with issues raised by the new Christian religion are played
out more gently against this assumed backdrop of moral, religious, and state-
authoritative functions of texts.

The Chinese state was itself a textual foundation, and the canon was the
source of imperial authority.[75] To begin to reflect the authority of the Lord of
Heaven—not even as befits God, but just to reach par with the emperor—a
textual canon was needed, and an illustrious history of interpretation. Ricci had
attempted to create this by appropriating the authority of the early canon, via
its references to *Shangdi* (上帝 Supreme god) and *Tian* (天 Heaven), as Jewish
scholars had earlier done.[76] In *Kouduo richao*, the preface writers buttress the
impression of orthodoxy and authoritative transmission of the text. Zhang Geng
quotes a snippet of the *Zhongyong* (Doctrine of the Mean) to the effect that one
should not leave the Way even for a single moment, and Li Jiubiao also picks
up the question of transmission, claiming (pace Ricci) that the masters from the

pacific West had come precisely because the "true transmission" of the Lord of Heaven had long been obscured, especially after the crooked sayings of the Daoists and Buddhists permeated China.[77]

The social production of *Kouduo Richao* by a network of disciples implicitly invested authority in the figure of "the Master," Aleni. This happened in two ways. In the relation between Aleni and the recordings that his disciples make of conversations, a distant echo sounds of the model of Confucius.[78] Hangzhou convert and local gentry Li Jiubiao compiled and edited the first two volumes of the book, soliciting entries from others for later volumes, which were published serially over several years: two dozen people had some form of input in writing, editing, or producing notations. The collective voice of the editors speaks to the authority of the "Master" (as the Jesuits are named in the text) in a system where the disciple was necessary to text production and therefore to the Master's authority, just as descendants were necessary to the existence of an ancestor.[79] More practically and immediately, text production in China was a social process. Having patrons of the highest possible social standing write prefaces and lend their cachet to projects was as important as having patrons pay for the carving of wood blocks and printing of texts. The collaborative nature of the text has theological ramifications: Chinese textual practice, as a communal forum, militated against the notion of theology as produced by a single, systematizing mind or, by extension, as individual revelation.

Morally, Chinese texts functioned as the means of self-cultivation and the source for rule—a link that Ricci had made in the opening section to his own catechism. This moral purpose had to be ingested and embodied by each aspiring official: every scholar of the lowest standing in the Ming had learned by heart the Confucian canon and possessed an ability to cite and interrelate at will, and every local official shared in the premise of the canon's efficacy as a vehicle of guidance for the individual and the state. The role of the text in believers' lives is underscored in the paratextual material at the very beginning of *Kouduo richao*. The diary extracts are, as Lin Yijun's preface suggests, a model for conduct and the training of the mind; the perfect copy of the text is transcribed in the believer's life "like a rubbing made of an inscription on precious stone."[80] Whereas writing is, for other Chinese literati, a means to examination success and glory, the production of this book will bring glory only in "the hometown of the soul," Lin notes, in an apt Christianizing of a standard trope. As the title of the work explains, the text is composed of daily entries that serve as a "warning bell" to a dissolute world, part of a broader Ming genre of texts and novels to "awaken the world." Editor Li Jiubiao explains in his own authorial preface how the sounds of this warning bell are to "awaken the obtuse and discipline the obstinate." *Kouduo richao* is, as Lin Yijun suggests, a "mirror for one's mind, penetrating one's heart and marrow,"[81] a series of pithy texts that need, as Aleni advises his interlocutors, to be digested slowly.[82]

In one early entry in the volume, Aleni questions Lu Liangbi over whether he has read a certain book that he had requested. The answer fails to impress: I treasure that book and cannot bear to read it, responds Lu, "fearing to dirty it." "The book will be dirty but the person will be clean," Aleni retorts.[83] The anecdote underlines the fact that for the literate elite among whom Jesuits like Aleni worked, much discipleship was text-based. In his master-disciple role, Aleni took an interest in the spiritual progress of his conversation partners, testing and questioning them on what they had read. It is clear from various entries that the new disciples in the 1630s were themselves writing and circulating their own tracts and texts to explain their faith. In one seemingly harsh lesson, Aleni responds to the news of Lin Yijun grieving over the death of his son by pointing out that the author of the essay "Clarifying Misconceptions" ought to be able to clarify his own understanding and comfort himself through a reading of Job.[84]

When a group of disciples suggest that texts on *Tianxue* 天學, or "Heavenly Studies" (i.e., Christianity, including astronomy), be translated and distributed more widely, Aleni advises that books can indeed cure souls, but a medicine store can cure diseases only when the various products "are all present and prepared."[85] In other words, the more books the better and the broader the spectrum to cure diseases more broadly: the production of Christian texts is linked to social well-being. Since morality and state stability are essentially coterminous and the state is closely linked to the textual canon, it is unsurprising that the disciples anticipate that the printing and distribution of Christian texts will serve to "expose the heterodox and exalt the orthodox."[86] The orthodox (正) or true teachings are a goal in themselves and a pursuit for loyal Christians. This notion of orthodoxy, in its association with harmonious society and its proclamation of truth and a properly ordered universe, comes as close as any canonical idea to a sense of social salvation.

It did not take long for an indigenous hagiographical literature to develop in China. When Li Jiubiao comes across a text titled "The Testimony of Michael" (*Mike'er yiban*), he is surprised by its contents and goes straight to Aleni for elucidation. As Li had surmised, Aleni was indeed connected to the author Zhang Jianbo and recounts the tale of the teenager's death, his out-of-body experience in heaven being scolded by Jesus, and subsequent narration of events to family members before his second, final death.[87] Liu Jiubiao's response is given as a comment on the text, in the manner of a historian adding applicable comment to an event: if young Zhang had so much merit and yet made it to heaven only via the intercession of the Archangel Michael and Matteo Ricci as recounted, what a terrifying warning this should be for those of lesser merit!

The text as a motif in *Kouduo richao* thus figures as an aid to self-cultivation or purification, a teaching tool, and a means of accumulating merit. The volume as a whole can be read as an ongoing class on, and exegesis of, Chinese Christian texts. Visitors come, ask questions on texts they have read, and seek answers from the Master, whose responses produce a further text. The entries function as an annotation, in person, of the explanation of texts. An example illustrates this: in October 1631, we are told that a certain Dai came to visit, asking for instruction on the Incarnation, a topic he has failed to grasp despite his reading of the Ten Commandments, Diego de Pantoja's *Qi Ke* (七克 Seven Overcomings), and Aleni's *Sanshan lunxue ji* (三山論學記 Sanshan Discussions on Learning). In response to his questioner, Aleni makes skillful use of both Christian and early Chinese texts to illustrate how God can be simultaneously in heaven and on earth and why suffering was permitted, using an analogy for Jesus in the self-offering of the Shang king, Cheng Tang, as a sacrificial victim.[88] The web of textual learning is seen even more clearly in another example, when official Wang Zheng (he of the Benevolent Society discussed above) is praised for not taking a concubine.[89] Aleni commends Wang's piety, as seen in a letter written to his family explaining his refusal. Later, under pressure, Wang did take a concubine, but on subsequently reading in *Kouduo richao* of his own earlier virtue (!), he was overcome with shame and repented in a public confession.[90]

While texts may bring merit to an individual (Aleni suggests to Li Jiubiao at one point that much labor over a text on the Lord of Heaven will bring much merit to its author, akin to the merit achieved by martyrdom or maintaining chastity),[91] literati views on the matter were occasionally taken to the extreme. Two days after the discussion on printing Christian books, Aleni asks Li Jiubiao what was the prime means of merit for repaying the favor of the Lord. Li naturally answers, reading books and being tireless in our relations with others.[92] Aleni is forced to contradict him: the prime way is not by reading Christian books but "by bearing one's cross for the Lord," he suggests. Jesus, notes the Jesuit, told his disciples to carry their cross and follow him each day but mentioned nothing about interactions with people. Aleni comments further that the cross becomes all the heavier for those who are unwilling to bear it and end up dragging it along; virtue lies in overcoming patiently and curbing one's desires. While Aleni discusses physical and metaphysical crosses, Li brings the topic back to the morality ledger, once again interpreting his teacher's words in terms of merit.

The relationship between Chinese and Catholic notions of merit, good works, and individual or social salvation is complex. Merit (*gong* 功) is akin to effort, a struggle against the current of life;[93] it can be gained through adversity[94] and is frequently prayed for.[95] In the latter case, where an examination candidate tells Rudomina he has prayed for merit and fame—that is, examination success—Rudomina suggests limiting oneself to striving for merit, since fame follows naturally. A long discussion related to sea pirates on whether evil is innate and corrigible leads Aleni to suggest that despite differences in human strengths and natural dispositions, what divides most between good and evil is practice, or habit.[96] When a good person strenuously turns from evil, notes Aleni, his merit is even greater than that of a good person. Here "merit" becomes something like standing with God. Rudomina has elsewhere expressed a similar view when he says that for those diligently practicing Confucian ways, it is easy to proceed to Heavenly Studies, with the implication that the practice, or discipline, is the important factor.[97]

Aleni expounds a classic Christian position in discussing the merit of someone being praised for establishing a new religious association. All good human work comes from God, notes Aleni: the Lord bestows his grace on people, and if people use it well, then "the Supreme Lord records it as merit."[98] The language of "recording merit" used in the text recalls strongly the widespread sixteenth- and seventeenth-century "ledgers of merit and demerit" (功過格), a genre of ethical handbooks and a practice of noting merit and wrongs in daily moral life derived from Daoist tradition but widespread in both popular and elite Neo-Confucian and Buddhist life. Moral merit was held to parallel material gain and to presage good or ill in future life, with elements in the system that human effort could influence.[99] Aleni himself is clear about the Thomist relation of grace to salvation. When regular discussant Lin Yongyue asks Aleni whether good works performed during a human lifetime might constitute a voucher or ticket for admittance to heaven, Aleni confirms that merit alone is not sufficient but that individual rewards differ, depending on the amount of *gratia* given and responded to.[100]

Lin's follow-up question—what of those who have accumulated merit from good works but lack grace?—points back to a question underlying much of the discussion of merit in *Kouduo richao*: what of good Chinese people within the Christian schema? Aleni's response acknowledges the implicit question in arguing that the motive behind doing good is what is important: no *gratia* accrues if there is an ulterior motive to the good. God does not reward what a person does, but why a person does good.[101] This allows for the possibility of God rewarding those who do good without knowing God (in keeping with the teaching of the three stages of revelation: natural revelation; revelation through the book, that is, Mosaic law; and revelation through Jesus, where God can be known and pleased through actions that accord with naturally revealed good before the teachings of the law or Christ) but requires a certain blurring of time lines and doctrinal clarity to achieve.[102] Elsewhere, in a lengthy discussion with Li Jiugong on the Incarnation and atonement, Aleni clarifies the discussion on merit by explaining that the Lord has paid the price for the sins of all by donating his own self, but only when people accept this price are they steeped in the grace of redemption.[103] The discussion continues into difficult territory: the virtuous before the Incarnation can ascend to heaven from limbo, suggests Aleni, as can (potentially) infants, but no one can ever rely on his or her own merit, only on the grace of the Incarnation. As Erik Zürcher notes in his discussion of this passage, the "fate of pagan but virtuous Chinese in the hereafter" remained a thorny issue without clear-cut answers.[104] That the discussion is complex, and this is a particularly difficult topic, is seen in the fact that Aleni has to refer his audience to three other Jesuit-authored works for further explanation. His listeners will have to trust the authority of the text on this central question for Chinese believers.

REPERCUSSIONS AND DEVELOPMENTS

In the sequence of works discussed above, the text functions as a metaphor for the processes of translating, rethinking, and inscribing Christianity in China. The chronology is not, of course, as straightforward as the three examples might suggest: different strands of debate run throughout seventeenth-century texts, and missionary writings and reevaluations of earlier texts overlap, just as Chinese Christian writings of various kinds interact with missionary writings and each other, and Chinese apologetics create their own discussion threads. The emergence in the early seventeenth century of Chinese writers whose works weave these strands together—including the defense of Christianity against emerging attacks—and who could take up the philosophical and theological work between Chinese canonical and scriptural texts that Ricci would have wanted to do himself and recalibrate Christian ideas in a Chinese frame marks the culmination of Jesuit work and the true beginnings of Chinese theology.[105]

Beyond the networks of believers, the text functions as a vehicle for dialogue with the rest of China. During the decade in which the positive account of *Kouduo richao* was being compiled by Christians in Fujian (even though Christianity was prohibited and churches were confiscated in Fujian in 1637, there is little in the compilation that discusses persecution directly), trouble was brewing on two fronts: first from the newly arrived Dominican and Franciscan missionaries in the province, whose growing opposition to Jesuit "accommodation" to Chinese ritual practice and beliefs led to some sharp correspondence with Rome, and second from an expanding body of literature collectively categorized as "anti-Christian writings." A war of texts that began around 1620 saw a series of skirmishes throughout the century, including the 1639 compilation *Shengchao poxieji* (聖朝破邪集 The Sacred Dynasty's Anthology of Writings to Expose Heresy), and notable altercations around 1660 with the publication of two collections defending Confucian orthodoxy, *Pixie lun* (闢邪論 Discourse on Exposing Heresy) and *Budeyi* (不得已 variously translated as "I have no alternative," or "I can't contain myself"). As in the late nineteenth century (when some of the anti-Christian texts really were lurid and libelous), the volume of Christian texts coming into circulation prompted a defensive reaction from other scholars.

The broad category of "anti-Christian writings" in the seventeenth century includes essays denouncing the political threat of Christians (whose arrival was seen as a prelude to foreign invasion), works that show the intellectual misadventure of believing in a foreign religion, and writings that tackle in a more detailed manner perceived contradictions in Christian doctrine and philosophy. While there are examples of vitriol and rancor, there are also essays that evince a genuine intellectual bafflement at tenets of the new doctrine as seen in the circulating texts, and that might more fairly be regarded as theological debate. Some of the points contested by the detractors as illogical or absurd are no longer articles of faith for many Christian believers: the consignment of the unbaptized to hell, the precise relationship between soul and body (how can the soul be distinct from the body? asks Xu Dashou),[106] or scientific challenges to a span of creation only seven thousand years long. Questions of theodicy asked by Chinese literati get to the heart of much Christian debate on the same topic (and are not dissimilar to questions from contemporary New Atheists): if all good comes from the Lord of Heaven and bad from humanity, where did the Lord of Heaven find the early seeds of evil? Is it not unjust of God to forgive a lifetime of evil for one act of repentance but damn those who do not know God after a lifetime of good? If it was a "miracle" that saved Christian homes from fire, did God not love the others who lost their houses?[107] In some ways, it is to the non-Christian writings that we have to look to understand the struggles that Chinese Christians must have been going through.

Alongside a philosophical perplexity at the Christian message, there were other rational expressions of consternation. Some hostile writings were penned by monks: the wide circulation of the missionaries' catechisms with their contemptuous derision of concepts like transmigration naturally evinced a range of reactions from religious thinkers, from denunciation of misunderstandings to outright attack. There was also common ground between the Christian detractors of Jesuit (especially Ricci's) theology and methods and that of the anti-Christian factions.[108] The *Pixie lun*, for example, deconstructed Ricci's identification of the Lord of Heaven with Shangdi, a point already debated within the order. Some criticism in the circulating texts related to the presentation of Christianity. Ricci's decision to produce works appealing to reason brought repercussions from some quarters, where there were (understandable) criticisms of a perceived "duplicity" in the appearance of two sets of writings—one for interested literati and another for neophyte Christians—with different emphases.[109] As noted above, the category of Christian writings, or *Tianxue* included both religious or theological texts and works on science and astronomy. The inclusion of astronomy and science as part of the Christian oeuvre encouraged a coalescing of genuine philosophical unease at Christian doctrine with antagonism against the position of the Jesuits at the Ming and Qing courts (and much personal political maneuvering over appointments, which turned deadly at flash points).[110]

Systemic differences in worldviews were real and were also exploited by those who felt threatened by the new religion. While missionary doctrines and texts were criticized, Chinese converts bore the brunt of attack.[111] Disparities over the function of religion and of the authority structure of Chinese society left Christians isolated: since worship of heaven was the prerogative of the emperor alone and the Ming law code forbade commoners to address Heaven, critics could legitimately accuse Christians who "sacrificed" to Shangdi of treason; Aleni and Ricci both skirted around such questions. The fact that Chinese cosmology provided a totalizing worldview that structured society and social order meant that metaphysical challenges were in effect criticisms of the state and Chinese life and naturally brought Confucian scholars leaping to a defense of tradition. Certain Christian claims exacerbated this chauvinism, including any appropriation of Chinese history narratives, such as the suggestion that Chinese were descendants of Judeans.[112] During an early wave of anti-Christian aggression in 1616/17, Vice Minister of Rites Shen Que played the orthodoxy card in his memorials to the emperor, accusing the Christian barbarians of spreading teachings that conflicted with the emperor's role as Son of Heaven and of malevolent intent against the state.[113] Shen's memorials did not produce the intended result of the complete banishment of foreigners, but they did lead to expulsions, death warrants for Chinese collaborators, and a temporary cessation of mission activity.

The work of Jacques Gernet and others has done a great service to scholarship in documenting so meticulously the texts, sources, and arguments of the "anti-" factions. But where these writings excoriating Christian beliefs and practices are read in isolation from the entirety of the debates and the Christian perspective, the conclusions that may be reached showing the irreconcilability of worldviews are inevitably partial. Chinese Christians clearly have been able to reconcile intellectual and cultural disparities to their own satisfaction in their thinking and writing. Even if missionaries did not fully appreciate the scale of difference in perception, as Gernet assumes, Chinese Christians often did, and their work reconciling Christian and Chinese frames of belief over the past four centuries is the important story. (The problem in accounts of cultural clash is often not so much sinological as theological, with doctrinal assumptions among contemporary critics coloring the discourse.)[114] The anti-Christian writings in China had a broader historical impact than their effects on subsequent theologies, but they sharpened the questions for Chinese Christians and directed their apologetic responses. While the label "anti-Christian" may in certain cases be a misnomer, the writings underscore the importance of the textual networks in which Christian and counter-Christian messages were disseminated and received, as well as the high social valorization of the texts. So much time and ink would scarcely have been expended in denouncing Christianity but for the perceived power of the written word.[115]

CONCLUSIONS

This chapter has traced the development of early Roman Catholic theological texts in the sixteenth and seventeenth centuries across a shift in background from Counter-Reformation Europe to late Ming society and across a change in language quality and textual format. These changes were, as the chapter has suggested, interdependent: a Chinese theology had to be created in Chinese textual form. The text was, moreover, not just a material object, a literary form or style of commentary, but came bound with a whole set of assumptions about its role in pedagogy, in society, in worship, and in friendship that were to shape the creation and meaning of the theology as printed.

The translator and great scholar of the *Kouduo richao*, sinologist Erik Zürcher, called the work "an invaluable mirror of early Chinese Christianity," but one "shattered into a thousand pieces," where "to find information on a specific topic, the researcher has to plod through . . . from cover to cover."[116] While we might understand immediately what Zürcher means, the metaphor of the shattered mirror is the textual complement to the notion of "accommodation": it assumes a "complete" whole that is systematically organized and ordered and needs re-creating in that unified form by a scholar. Just as "accommodation" might suggest that Christian orthodoxy resides in Western teachers and not Chinese scholars, the shattered mirror assumes the normativity of systematic theological thought. As this chapter has shown, the evolution of Christian writings in China into Chinese Christian writings involved not just content and patterns of thought, but textual forms too, symbiotically linked to the theology. Its transformation meant the discarding of prior ("Western") norms and requires still the acceptance that theology does not need to follow—and indeed, cannot follow—the forms of other textual cultures.

Much seventeenth-century theology was textual debate: argument about whether Shangdi of the early classics was God, or what knowledge of God existed in ancient China. In a society where state, religion, and education were bound up in a well-defined canon, Chinese theology was always going to be a process of entering into that textual world and transforming it from within. Theology in the Ming and Qing dynasties can be seen as a process of textual integration, the continued reconciliation of Christian thinking with Confucian texts and distinction from other religious texts. The role of interpreting the classics was a substantial part of missionary work and not confined just to Jesuit scholars.[117] Chinese Christianity developed within and against a reading of the classics: drawing on their language, affirming or challenging their concepts, and being inscribed in a textual world where the meaning of reading scripture came from the dominant tradition. The grounds on which Christianity was transmitted and contested were those of hermeneutics, of textual reasoning, commentary, and reinterpretation. The Rites question, which simmered throughout the seventeenth century and drew to such a decisive climax at its end, is often taken to be about ritual praxis and ancestor worship—but it is more properly a textual issue, concerning the whole question of how the texts of one culture are received in another and their locus of authority. The ban on further discussion of the Rites issue effected by Pope Benedict XIV in 1742 asphyxiated not just ancestor worship, but theology itself in the Chinese Catholic Church until its reversal in the 1930s.

To be literate in China was, at some level, to accept Confucian doctrine.[118] Much has been written on the "blending" or "synthesis" of Christianity and Confucianism, although some scholars have also downplayed this component of Chinese Christianity as "a minor movement of the time."[119] While elite Jesuit Christianity was certainly only one strand of the growth of the church in seventeenth-century China, and the field has benefited from recent studies of local Christian communities led by Chinese Christians, dismissive claims of blending do not take seriously the textual element of the transmission of Christianity that of necessity involved sinicization: the sinicization was textual. Two related misperceptions about contextualization persist. The first is that it happened in the early twentieth century—an error made most frequently among Protestants. The second is that contextualization was a question of authority transfer and ecclesial structures. This perception relates to a European narrative, or a historical view, rather than a theological one. Theology itself was, as this chapter has explored, sinicized much earlier, and much more comprehensively, than church structures.

In his fascinating study of eighteenth-century local Catholic communities based around Fuan in Fujian, the same province where converts recorded their conversations with Aleni a century earlier, Eugenio Menegon suggests that in contradistinction to the "elite vision" of the Jesuits and the view of Christianity in China that privileged "doctrinal debates among the higher echelons of literati converts"—a discourse which held that missionaries had to accommodate to Confucian intellectual and social norms for Christianity to survive, propagated by later scholars of these texts—the real setting where Christianity was transformed into a local religion was in local environs, away from texts, in a world where personal devotions and daily rituals took precedence.[120] Chinese Christianity is not, however, a zero-sum game. Working on elite theological texts does not detract from studies of local religious life and its diurnal forms and liturgies. Elite scholars took part in local life when in their hometowns, as well as participating in transregional networks. Just as Christianity was being transformed into Chinese forms by local adaptation and innovation in communities and patterns of prayer built around a church or mission house, so Chinese Christian theology underwent its own process of transformation into a local textual religion. The localization of Christianity did take place among the *beata* groups of empowered Christian women, and in communities where Dominicans and Franciscans worked among nonliterate congregations, and accelerated in the prohibition period after 1724 as local religious spaces were transformed through ritual acts and interaction with other religious groups—but there was also a deep, and enduring, textual sinicization that began with missionaries but was developed most rapidly and abidingly by Chinese Christian writers and believers.

2

THE CHRISTIAN IMPRINT: THE SHAPING
OF REPUBLICAN-ERA THEOLOGY

As for the theoretical theology of religion, it is entirely in
disagreement with the racial characteristics of the Chinese
people, and therefore, has very little chance of spreading.
—Hu Shi, 1922[1]

In the early twentieth century, Chinese intellectuals were confronted with a
new twist on the old philosophical conundrum: if you replace, plank by plank,
the educational system, the government, and the written language, is what remains still "China"? And if the philosophical and cultural premises sustaining
those institutions are rethought, who has the authority to determine the answer?
As each board was stripped and relaid—from the outdated bureaucratic system
to China's defeated naval forces, and even imperial rule itself—the ship of state
listed and careened. In just a little more than a decade from around 1905, most
major institutions in China and the means of creating those institutions had
gone. The 1911 Revolution confirmed China's new course, even as foreign con-
tractors continued to vie for the right to supply replacements for the dynastic
compass and binnacle.

The church came of age under Chinese leadership just as the nature of social
and intellectual leadership was being rethought. As revolutionaries ousted the
reformists who curtailed the old "feudal" rule, systemic changes opened up unimagined new possibilities for urbanites to determine the ideologies by which
they lived and the structures governing their common life. New political groups
(constitutional monarchists, restorationists, revolutionaries) competed for members with new literary groups, and new broadcast media appeared daily. Women
worked as journalists, models, and preachers. The growth and development of

Chinese Christianity is inseparable from these surrounding political and historical events. Foreign aggression and the treaty system, language reform and literary renaissance, worldwide expansion of higher education, attacks on Confucianism, the rise of the Social Gospel Movement, changing Vatican policies, Darwinism and scientism, higher criticism and Pentecostalism—all were instrumental in fashioning the incipient church. Meanwhile, Chinese-led revival movements flourished; new denominations were created; the first Chinese bishops were appointed by Rome; Chinese Christian intellectuals founded colleges, developed university theology departments, and began the task of creating an indigenous theology in the new modern Chinese language.

The Republican period produced a disproportionate number of exciting and lasting Chinese theological texts and insights. Important thinking and inspiring writing on doctrine, Christian education, social and virtue ethics, the relation of the local church to the church universal, and a great range of other topics filled the pages of new journals and book series. This chapter first considers the reasons for this productivity, exploring the environmental factors and social forces shaping debate, and second where theological texts were being produced and by whom.

Among the many interacting factors on which the growth of the church and the theology of its proponents were contingent, two stand out. The first is the question of identity. As church communities debated practical matters, from new Bible translations to interdenominational unity, and as preachers and leaders grappled with theologies of biblical criticism and budgets for church hospitals, one question preempted all other debate and action: who are we, as Chinese Christians? To whom is loyalty due? How can an individual identity as a Christian be reconciled with a social identity as Chinese? The dual nature of Chinese and Christian proved a weighty proposition at a time when national identity was rocked by political, cultural, and literary revolution, and simultaneously threatened by foreign invasion and the influx of foreign products, yet was also nourished by international currents, new gender understandings, and solidarity movements. The question of identity cuts across the five background factors to the growth of Republican theology discussed in the first half of the chapter (internal church developments, anti-imperialism, Christian education, elite social responsibility, and the effects of the Anti-Christian movements).

Christian intellectuals shared with other educated reformers a desire to see China recover and prosper as a nation and a tension over how to achieve that aim—to liberate from the worst aspects of patriarchal authority in Confucian family life and social rule without losing a sense of "China" that for conservatives was predicated on those values. Where secular iconoclasts were seen as "anti-Chinese" for seeking in their own past the reasons for China's weakness and not attributing them to foreign aggression, Christians were inherently suspect.[2] The association of "Christian" with "Western" retarded Christianity for most of the twentieth century, but during the Republican era, as Roman Catholics were debating what "indigenous" might mean and as Protestant churches were making the slow transition from foreign-run and foreign-financed bodies to self-supporting, self-governing churches, Chinese Christians were still held responsible for the actions of foreigners. Many had benefited from the foreign presence and were schooled or trained by foreign organizations. Most felt a sense of spiritual indebtedness and held a genuine, considered support for aspects of the foreign cause; yet they were convinced of the damage of the foreign link to the credibility of Christianity, of the pressing need for autonomy and secession of the church and the imperative to reclaim the positive within Chinese culture.

As China looked abroad for technological expertise and democratic inspiration to remedy the military and economic weaknesses demonstrated in recent wars against the French, Russians, and Japanese, the West represented both model for emulation and imperial enemy. Christians were caught up in the same debates as other citizens, divining to what degree westernization was the way to "modernize" China, but their identification with the foreign complicated responses. Pressure mounted as a more aggressive nationalism took hold into the 1920s. Those who left to join new, "Chinese" churches found one solution. Chinese leaders within the historic churches had to defend Christianity to the Chinese public at the same time as fight their own battles for authority and intellectual autonomy within the church. Their pivotal role, and the means by which they presented their case to a wider public, is explored over the next three chapters.

The question of identity was central also to the second aspect shaping theological growth: the rise of the modern press. Rapid, cheap circulation of print media enabled Christian thought to be widely distributed and debated, but the expanding print culture was also closely tied to the role anticipated for literature by the leaders of the (secular) New Culture and May Fourth Movements in saving China.[3] The Christian press, in parallel with the secular press, shouldered the mantle of determining what China was and what the Chinese church should become. An era of social and ecclesial flux demanded rapid theological reflection and strong action. Christian elites who took on the intellectual leadership in the mainstream churches responded robustly to the scientific and nationalist critiques of Christianity of their peers, developing their own visions of what a Chinese Christian church and thought might look like. They did so, by and large, in the periodical press, a medium chosen because of its contemporaneity, mass distribution, and shared space with other reformist groups. The background factors to Republican Christianity considered in the first half of this chapter are relatively well-known from historical and literary studies of the period, but the role of print culture in enabling the new Chinese theology of the twentieth century has yet to be fully appreciated.[4] Print determined the form of the theological literature that appeared and frames discussion of its literary aspects. The revolution may have ousted the Confucian canon from the center of elite life and the emperor from his role as guardian of the textual heritage, but the status of the printed word was not so easily eroded. As the power of print became the power of the press, it was naturally to this medium that educated young Christians turned to express their ideas. The second half of the chapter takes up the story of the new print media and Chinese-authored Christian literature.

THE CHURCH CHINESE: THE ENVIRONMENTAL AND SOCIAL BACKGROUND

THE ECCLESIAL LANDSCAPE

A decade on from the 1911 Revolution, the Chinese church was in the throes of its own revolution, a less bloody affair but no less long-lasting. "The die has been cast. The Foreign Mission has abdicated its throne," wrote one Protestant missionary commentator, with a flourish of hyperbole but little apparent sense of irony.[5] There was a widespread belief among foreign communities that a turning point had been reached, that as of 1922 or 1923, "the centre of gravity of the movement was shifted from the missions and foreign Christian workers to the churches and the Chinese Christians."[6] Among Roman Catholics, preparations were under way for the 1924 plenary council in Shanghai, during which Chinese clergy and missionaries were accorded equal rights with foreign ones, and Chinese was designated the primary language of the church.[7] The National Christian Council (NCC), appointed in 1922, stood as a symbol of a new Protestant unity, with equal representation of Chinese among its leadership. Report after report from mission stations and churches around the country contributed to the consensus that moves toward self-government and financial devolution were coupled with a new self-assertion, of which "the most conspicuous and most important development is a consciousness THAT THE CHURCH IS CHINESE!"[8] The growing number of Chinese leaders of new independent churches needed no such headline reminders from the mission press:

they had spent the previous decade building up their own thriving, autarchic congregations.[9]

Beneath the capitalized emotions of missionary reports, a more complex picture emerges. Growth in the historic churches was buoyant:[10] the number of Catholics, which had shot up in the years following the Boxer Rebellion, reaching 1.3 million by 1910, stood at just under 2 million in 1920.[11] Communicants in Protestant churches had increased by 50 percent in the same decade, to 366,000, and the ratio of Chinese salaried workers to foreign ones in historic Protestant churches was growing steadily.[12] The Russian Orthodox Church, which had suffered heavy losses among its Chinese members during the Boxer Rebellion, saw a similar period of growth in baptisms and school enrollments in the early twentieth century.[13] New, independent congregations were reshaping the ecclesial landscape. There was a striking energy to envision the future during the early 1920s, a determination across church and para-church organizations to think creatively and programmatically about institutional life. The creation of the NCC was hailed as a landmark event for Protestants, "the first real step towards putting the responsibility of Christianizing China into the hands of Chinese Christians," as one Chinese commentator wrote;[14] and its subcommittees set to work on a variety of tasks, from deepening spiritual growth and improving religious education to tackling an array of social problems. The YWCA held its first national convention in 1923 under acting general secretary (Ms.) Ding Shujing 丁淑靜, while the YMCA began campaigning against low wages and unsanitary conditions in the industrial field.[15]

At the same time, structural challenges to the church were evident. Within the historic churches, discrimination against Chinese priests and leaders was widespread. Progressive critics of the European domination in the Catholic Church in China, such as Vincent Lebbe or Antoine Cotta, were transferred or recalled. Institutional inertia prevented long-held goals of amalgamations among Protestant denominations from being realized. The optimism that heralded Christianity as part of the Chinese religious landscape came from mission reports, not Chinese ones, and was frequently tinged with a paternalistic sense that the Chinese church had not yet grown into "full maturity."[16] New ways of thinking among Chinese believers caused consternation among the more conservative-minded. The NCC saw groups disaffiliate almost immediately over theological differences,[17] while independent congregations faced their own challenges of leadership produced by growth. Churches across the spectrum faced serious critiques from the pro-science and Anti-Christian movements and from the force of nationalist rhetoric that charged all Christians, not just those under foreign leadership, with imperialism. From the late 1920s, churches also faced the disruption common to institutions encountering the civil war and the Japanese occupation.

Changing church structures were motivated by new worldwide understandings of the relationship between church and local culture. Among the historic churches, the Roman Catholic Church saw particular tensions in a period when not all were convinced that "only under Chinese leadership would the church become Chinese and prosper."[18] World War I had disrupted Roman Catholic mission, but growth accompanied revival in Europe, and Propaganda Fide was kept busy apportioning provinces in China as new groups — Salvatorians, Tyrolese Franciscans, Salesians, Ursulines, and many more — arrived to take up their missions. Between 1918 and 1927, almost as many Catholic organizations began work "as in all the previous history of the Middle Kingdom."[19] On the ground, this meant the establishment of new sisterhoods, new orphanages, and a new daily newspaper, the *Yi shi bao* (益世報 Social Welfare) — and also new tensions, as non-Chinese-speaking priests and religious arrived without the capacity to institute the changes Rome was calling for. The encyclical Maximum Illud in 1919 had stressed the formation of a native clergy, and a papal brief to Chinese bishops in 1926 urged the implementation of a national church structure.[20] There were some changes: the percentage of Chinese clergy increased, and more inculturated church architecture and liturgical chanting were developed.[21] New prefectures apostolic were created in Zhili and Hubei in 1924, entrusted to the care of Chinese clergy, signifying the move from missionary regions to regular church dioceses; and in 1926 six Chinese bishops were consecrated in Rome, to great fanfare.[22] The creation of a Chinese episcopate was a huge step forward, and yet, as Kenneth Latourette notes, "the most important positions continued to be held by the foreigner and nine-tenths of the bishops were still of alien birth and allegiance."[23]

Protestants had a small head start on the question of leadership, although many of the historic Protestant churches were also struggling to create structures to transfer final authority to Chinese priests and pastors. Although Protestant churches had prioritized the handing over of financial responsibility to Chinese, disparities persisted in definitions of what "self-supporting" meant, and many local congregations struggled with an expensive inherited model of church.[24] The problem of proliferating denominations represented a major stumbling block for Chinese Christians. A disjuncture between ecclesial structures and ideals was felt acutely. As Zhao Zichen argued in an address of 1922, it was not "that the genius of the Christian religion is alien to the Chinese mind and heart," but "the church which expresses Christianity is so variously and rigidly organized that it does not fit with the Chinese genius."[25] For Zhao and many others, denominationalism was the worst expression of this Western rigidity, coupled with a lack of vision for a nationwide, unified Christian consciousness.[26]

The Protestant church as a whole grew through a combination of separatist and coalition movements, the former to create independent congregations and the latter through the mergers and the slow movement toward a single Protestant congregation.[27] Nineteenth-century church practices had encouraged local difference, but by the end of the century strong centripetal forces were at work, evident in joint liturgical texts and pan-mission projects, such as the *Chinese Recorder*, a journal for the entire mission field. Uniting societies of the same denomination was often a first step toward the aim of a united Protestant church. The various Presbyterian assemblies consulted on creating a unified, autonomous church body between 1901 and 1907, and Anglicans from different nations agreed to form the Zhonghua sheng gong hui (Holy Catholic Church of China) in 1909. Denominational mergers overcame the problems of overlapping jurisdictions and inefficiencies and chimed with global moves toward ecumenical partnership. The largest such partnership came into being in 1927 when the Church of Christ in China, a body comprising at least ten Reformed groups, held its first general assembly.[28]

The greatest change to the Chinese church landscape came with the mushrooming of dozens of new, Chinese-led churches: evangelical, Pentecostal, charismatic.[29] Most were nonaligned, while some retained their denominational heritages. Yu Guozhen 俞國楨 was one early leader, forming the China Jesus Independent Church in Shanghai around 1906,[30] while Zhang Boling 張伯苓 established a group of independent churches in Tianjin in 1910. The Jesus Family encouraged thousands to live communally, although their egalitarian lifestyle and lack of deference to foreigners was strangely unappreciated by the Chinese Communist Party (CCP) in the decades to come. For those from congregational churches, establishing a new church represented the local application of a given model, and destructive splits could be avoided. Other moves were more radical: the True Jesus Church of Wei Enbo (魏恩波, 魏保羅 Paul Wei) was one of the first (ca. 1917) to denounce the mission churches and call on Chinese to leave them, establishing its own brand of sabbatarianism (worship on Saturdays) with Pentecostal tendencies.[31] Ni Tuosheng (Watchman Nee) left his Episcopalian seminary and in 1926 founded the Little Flock church, which grew to seven hundred congregations and seventy thousand members by the mid-1940s (and which continues today as the Local Church from bases in Taiwan and California).

A final thriving sector of the church economy, whose membership overlapped denominational categories, was the revival circuit. Foreign evangelists, both based in China and visitors, had toured China for some years, and Roman

Catholic orators such as Vincent Lebbe filled guild halls for speaking engagements; huge meetings were now addressed by the likes of Yu Cidu (余慈度 Dora Yu), whose career as a Methodist speaker began in Shanghai in 1903 and burgeoned as she transferred to the national arena. She was joined by Ding Limei (丁立美), Li Shuqing (李叔青), and a number of others whose rousing speeches and healing miracles affected many of the younger generation of Christians, some of whom joined this high-impact circuit of independent, peripatetic speakers, including the Bethel Band in the 1930s. These groups were a vital new part of the Christian church in China.

Christian circles were not mutually exclusive early on in the twentieth century, but as the new church initiatives developed and created their own structures and theologies, divergences became more apparent. A range of motivations existed—practical, nationalistic, and theological—for moves among Protestants to create mergers or independent churches. A biblical call to unity inspired Cheng Jingyi 誠靜怡, the first moderator of the Church of Christ in China, while the demand for holiness and separation motivated Wang Mingdao to create the Christian Tabernacle church; theological differences with their Methodist Episcopal mission board led Dr. Shi Meiyu (石美玉 Mary Stone) and Jennie Hughes to set up the Bethel Band.[32] The experience of splits and schisms strengthened many intellectual liberals in their conviction that the way forward for Chinese Christianity lay in transcending Western church structures and in engagement with the world.

THE FOREIGN COMPROMISE

One factor prominent in the theology of the 1920s and 1930s was the relationship between China, the Chinese church, and the church's Western heritage. While historians have recently been reevaluating the notion of foreigners as "cultural invaders" in China, it has been difficult to erase the narrative of post–Opium War Chinese history as "persistent victimization by western imperialism," as expounded by Finance Minister Gu Weijun (Wellington Koo) in 1926.[33] This may have been a partial and a populist view, but its success in mobilizing public opinion meant that politicians and church leaders of all persuasions had to respond to its claims. The pain of the "unequal treaties" (a phrase established by Gu)[34] is still seen today as a stain on the church because of the perceived connection between foreign governments and a foreign church.

There was much for detractors to draw on. As Jing Tsu has noted, injuries by outsiders elicit the most profound professions of sovereignty, particularly when identities are already in distress.[35] There was considerable crossover in practice and in the minds of Chinese observers between foreign economic, church, and governmental activity, ever since Matteo Ricci's generation of Jesuits worked in the imperial court. The first Protestant missionary, Robert Morrison, who arrived in 1807, worked for both the East India Company and the British government, followed by the likes of Karl Gützlaff (missionary translator/civil magistrate) and Peter Parker (medical missionary/U.S. chargé d'affaires). Individual missionaries in the twentieth century may have had nothing to do with their governments—and, as others have noted, the profusion of mission societies from countries from Finland to Ireland problematizes any imperialist narrative[36]—but perception was important and was not helped by certain publications proclaiming a Christian "occupation" of China.[37]

There are interesting parallels in the history of a secular institute like the Maritime Customs Service and that of the church in the late Qing and early Republic vis-à-vis the foreign (including their recent ideological reclamation and physical restoration). These help elucidate why the involvement of foreign money and power in symbolically significant areas of Chinese life forms an important background element to discussion of Anti-Christian movements and Chinese Christian nationalism. The Customs Service was a great source of revenue for the Qing and Republican governments, so it was economically and symbolically important—and a good barometer of attitudes to the foreign. During the second half of the nineteenth century, the "swashbuckling imperialists" who oversaw the Opium Wars were largely replaced with a generation of civil servants, like British Inspector General Robert Hart, whose attitude toward Chinese bureaucracy and colleagues was one of educated respect, acknowledging that the Customs Service was "a Chinese and not a Foreign Service."[38] Like missionary organizations, the Customs Service saw a rapid expansion in the 1880s and a shift in values to sympathy toward Chinese bureaucratic practices and Chinese leadership. As with mission organizations, there were voices of criticism at the end of the nineteenth century that able Chinese were not being promoted to high positions in the organization as well as countermoves to promote Chinese graduates.[39] But the benign common interest did not last. Indemnity payments from the Sino-Japanese war of 1895 and the Boxer Rebellion of 1900, combined with interest payments on loans to Yuan Shikai's new Republic in 1911, turned the Customs Service into "a debt-collection agency for foreign bondholders" and the new Chinese Republic into "a state governed by a man who depended on foreign goodwill and foreign money."[40] The reverberations from the media campaign against foreign control of Chinese debt and revenue lasted well beyond the period of "financial imperialism" itself and resounded through the churches.

In limited areas of China, the foreign presence remained ubiquitous: the Treaty Ports, the concessions, the settlements, the Legation Quarter, and the foreign leaseholds.[41] The concessions were the most foreign districts of all: Chinese were not legally able to hold land there, Chinese troops could not pass through, and local administration was in foreign hands, with the running of the concessions paid for from taxes levied by foreign authorities. Popular depictions of Shanghai concession life in magazines of the late Qing—with its racecourses, electric lighting, golf and drinks parties—reflected something of the new cultural reality. The relationship between the numeric foreign presence in China and the rise of nationalism is far from linear, but the growth in missionary numbers over the late nineteenth century "rekindled suspicion and ill will among many Chinese"[42] and was a factor in an increasingly volatile mix. Growth sustained by treaty protection proved deeply divisive. If rising alarm at the spread of foreigners subject only to their own national laws was a catalyst for secular agitation, and the provocation was magnified toward the end of the nineteenth century by the economic burdens of indemnity payments and the humiliation of territorial concessions, the general unrest was also exacerbated by local violence triggered by droughts and subsequent famines. Chinese Christians understood the angst of their compatriots at the foreign presence, which was compounded for them by asymmetries within their own relations with foreign Christians.[43]

Even if the church was not directly instrumental in the legal and military affronts to China during the Qing, it had benefited from them. The treaties of the 1840s and 1860s remained the basis for diplomatic relations and foreign trade into the twentieth century, not only forcibly opening China to trade but also seeking to redress past losses, including the reclamation of church buildings confiscated during earlier prohibitions. While some governments were unwilling to support their missionaries in demanding the privileges conceded, others, such as the French, who had negotiated—by means both above-board and surreptitious—the most wide-ranging rights of protection for people and property, pursued their legal rights more aggressively on behalf of both their own citizens and Chinese Catholics.[44] As Daniel Bays has noted, it was, with hindsight, "striking how natural it was for missionaries to enlist themselves in a project that essentially put China permanently in a handicapped position of inequality, unable to pursue her own national goals."[45] Foreign citizens carried their extraterritorial rights with them and could not be regulated or taxed wherever, so missionary schools could set their own curricula and appoint their own teachers with impunity.[46] In China, but not of China: the parallels that critics could make with Chinese Christians are clear.

The depth of animosity caused by the use of privilege in establishing and running schools and other organizations is woven into Chinese histories of mission, only recently recalibrated following studies on the positive legacies of higher education and the creation of medical facilities and other institutions.[47] The drive to creating indigenous autonomy and to throwing off foreign leadership in the church from the 1910s into the 1940s parallels the forceful sloughing off of foreign control in national life. The Christian thinkers represented in the following three chapters lived in an elite world proximate to the foreign world of China and mixed with similarly educated citizens of the new Republic.[48] Most interacted daily with the foreign world and were caught between defending friends and colleagues, acknowledging their own privilege, and critiquing the system that treated the nation, and them as individuals, as subordinate. Their theology reflects the pain of this open wound.

THE EDUCATION OF CHRISTIAN ELITES

The flourishing of an indigenous Chinese theology during the 1920s and 1930s would not have been possible without a large, well-trained cohort of Christian seminary and university students—who themselves went on to teach at, and lead, these institutions. The role of the thirteen Chinese Christian colleges, ten Protestant and three Catholic, in precipitating the growth of state universities and in developing curricula for a new China is now widely accepted.[49] Western-style schools and colleges may not have had the decisive role in "modernizing" China that studies once proposed, but the effect of the Christian colleges on their own students is indubitable.[50] The missionary colleges that evolved into universities were mainly founded between 1880 and 1910, and the great majority of church leaders in China, across the church spectrum, had some connection with them.[51] Around 12 percent of tertiary education was institutionally Christian, while a third of all Christian youth were in mission schools.[52] The Western-run colleges and universities promoted models of learning with new emphases: in knowledge content, in expectations of student life and extracurricular activities, and in the understanding of the purpose of education.[53] Their popularity is seen in the quadrupling of student numbers from the end of the exam system to 1920, as the benefits of an English-medium education for employment grew more apparent to non-Christian parents.[54]

One aspect occluded until recently in reports on the debates on language medium in the Christian colleges (should they teach in Chinese? in English?) is the fact that these were predominantly bilingual, bicultural environments.[55] The small core of theologians and intellectual leaders who were the most vocal and active in writing and publishing were urbane and cosmopolitan: where other Chinese students had gone to Japan to study (like Lu Xun) or later to France on work-study programs (like Deng Xiaoping), future Christian theologians went to seminaries and universities in the United States or to Roman Catholic institutes in Rome or Paris. The generation of Chinese theologians from the 1920s and 1930s spoke and wrote near-native English or French and/or Latin, a facility that enabled them to read as widely as their international peers, to study abroad, and to interact easily in international Christian affairs. Wu Yifang 吳貽芳, the first president of Jinling (Ginling) Women's University, was a Chinese signatory to the U.N. charter; Zhao Zichen, professor of philosophy and Christianity at Yanjing (Yenching) University, was an early president of the World Council of Churches (until he resigned in solidarity with China's position on the Korean War). The biographies of Republican theologians exemplify a new internationalist route through school and college, providing lived examples of what Daniel Bays has termed the "Sino-Foreign Protestant Establishment."[56] Roman Catholic Chinese leaders were, if anything, even more closely tied to the foreign establishment. Among Roman Catholic theologians and educators, the Jesuit Xu Zongze studied for his doctorate in France and England. Fellow Jesuit and future dean at Aurora, Zhang Boda (張伯達 Béda Chang; Zhang Zhengming 張正明), received his doctorate from the Sorbonne.

Among the Protestant theologians, educators, and church leaders whose names appear regularly in Christian journals, a significant number had graduate degrees from abroad. Liu Tingfang (劉廷芳 T. T. Lew) followed a doctorate in psychology from Columbia University with studies at Yale Divinity School before heading the theology faculty at Yenching. Xu Baoqian (徐寶謙 P. C. Hsu) studied at Union Theological Seminary and completed a doctorate at Columbia. Zeng Baosun (曾寶蓀 P. S. Tseng) was a graduate of Westfield, the women's college of London University. The Swedish Covenant church pastor Chen Chonggui (陳崇桂 Marcus Ch'eng) completed an accelerated bachelor's degree at Wheaton College.[57] Many of this cohort, including Zhao Zichen, Xu Zongze, and Wu Leichuan (explored in the next three chapters), followed a traditional pattern of study before crossing over to Western curricula; their dual education often meant that facility in composing classical Chinese poetry was matched by an ability to compose in the modern *baihua* language and to write in the scientific English vaunted by the reformers. Their experience, of course, also left them vulnerable to identity insecurity.

If the effects of educational uplift were significant for male graduates of the mission-run colleges, those of mission education on the lives of female students, and on gender relations more widely in society, were even greater.[58] Mission schooling and the modeling of careers for women were strong factors in the new drive for female education. A flourishing female literary culture during the Ming and rising literacy rates in the Qing had not translated into a broader cultural demand for female education (outside elite families employing private tutors) until the late nineteenth century, when female education was linked to the need for educated mothers to raise good citizens. While the relative weight of Christian and local input to the promotion of women's education is contested, the standard narrative that segues from Qing reformers to the feminist movement of the early Republic underplays the Christian component.[59] Protestant missions had earlier played an important role in championing the vernacular in church texts, as well as Romanized scripts for both Mandarin and local dialects, used as a shortcut to literacy for women. While absolute numbers were small, missionary schools continued for some years to educate a significant percentage of girls nationally and pioneered higher education, with the first women graduating with bachelor's degrees from Jinling Women's College in 1919.[60] Just as the secular press debated at great length what the "new woman" should be like, the Christian woman's role was likewise vigorously debated.[61]

Given current debates on glass ceilings and pay inequalities, it is unsurprising that parity in education did not immediately lead to senior positions or the opening of a full range of employment for female graduates, who went disproportionately into the caring professions and into teaching and social work in China, just as elsewhere. Women did publish theological essays and reflections, and their articles appear in mission journals and NCC reports, as well as in the specialized periodical press, like *Nüduobao* (女鐸報 The Woman's Messenger) or *Qingnian nü bao* (青年女報 later *Nüqingnian bao*, China's Young Women, the journal of the YWCA, which exhibited a more marked feminist, and Socialist, viewpoint); but the fact that higher level theological education in seminaries, vocations as priests or bishops, or occupations as university professors were not commonly open to women discouraged careers as theologians or theological educators.[62] Various writers have discussed how women in the independent Chinese churches had more opportunities to lead.[63] Women from the historic churches tended to exercise leadership in para-church fields. Like male counterparts who had been denied promotion by foreign church leaders and devoted their energies to building up the nation, women like Zeng Baosun, Wu Yifang, or Wang Liming 王立明 went into education or politics.[64] Other educated women, like the well-known examples of Kang Cheng (康成 Ida Kahn) and Shi Meiyu, one of the first ordained women in China, were commissioned as medical missionaries.[65] The parallels with male subjugation under foreign rule are clear in the call of Cheng Guanyi (誠冠怡 Ruth Cheng) for recognition of women's place in the Chinese Christian church vis-à-vis men, "not simply the giving of seats in the tram car and the raising of hats," but "sharing with them the responsibility of service."[66]

INTELLECTUAL LEADERS AND SOCIAL ACTIVISM

Christianity may have offered a revolution in social relationships, as girls were educated, free marriage encouraged, and the equality of all before God preached, but the underlying duty to serve society through one's learned capacities echoes throughout Republican-era thought.[67] The primary duty of Christian intellectuals to the community—the wider community—sets Chinese Christian thinking apart from its missionary heritage and is a feature evident throughout this volume. One way for elite Chinese Christians to combine their status with their Christianity was precisely by being socially active. These were Christians in the mold of, and with the interests and moral depths of, China's archetypal intellectuals, accepting roles as the conscience or ethical benchmark of society. It is no surprise that the Social Gospel Movement was widely acclaimed in the 1920s and 1930s by liberal Protestants or that the Roman Catholic leadership in Shanghai in the 1950s saw its role as standing up to political oppression on behalf of the rest of society.

Chinese Christians had to negotiate their social function within the framework of growing secular nationalism. In line with social expectations of the gentry, now transferred to educated elites, Christian leaders expressed a deep concern with the need to shape wider culture. Yet the social imperative raised the question: could Christians ever truly be Chinese leaders—and if not, how could they have an impact on society? In educational terms they could clearly hold their own, but the question of their estranged, compromised relationship with Chinese culture remained unresolved. There had never been a strong role for priestly leadership in imperial China, and the last vestiges of divine authority disappeared with the infant emperor in 1911. As James Legge wrote in the 1890s, "the literati in China do in reality occupy the place of priests and ministers in Christian kingdoms."[68] Few of the authors showcased in this volume could be described as "sacred intellectuals," as opposed to "secular intellectuals."[69] This tells us as much about the standing and role of intellectuals in China as it does about the Chinese church, but it also draws attention to the willful refusal among missionaries and church authorities to promote able Chinese clergy (or women to senior positions). For most Chinese, there was no dissonance with being lay and involved in leadership, or with being Christian and deeply involved in politics: indeed, it was expected. The Roman Catholic

Church was noticeably more lay-led than in most countries, with catechists, lay congregation leaders, and consecrated lay women vested with significant authority for teaching and worship.[70]

The circumscribed lives of Qing Christians highlight the tensions between church and social function with which liberal intellectuals engaged theologically in the early twentieth century. A scattering of Christian lower degree holders in the eighteenth century had provided church leadership and social influence when Christianity was proscribed.[71] Into the nineteenth century, few believers beyond Ma Xiangbo 馬相伯 enjoyed national recognition, but toward the end of the century a small stream of Christian graduates from foreign institutions began to forge careers in medical and educational work and become locally prominent.[72] Scholars have depicted these returnee Qing intellectuals as untapped resources and their lives as thwarted opportunities. Daniel Bays writes of Yan Yongjing (顏永京 Y. K. Yen), a graduate of Kenyon College in Ohio, for example, as someone who "would have made a fine president of St. John's" or an "excellent Anglican diocesan bishop" had he had the chance, and of Ma Xiangbo as someone whose "story was symptomatic of the wastage of indigenous talent by the Catholic church in China during these decades."[73] It is clearly a shaming indictment of church leaders that able Chinese were not promoted, but the valorization of hieratic leadership was not necessarily as strongly shared by the Chinese involved. Intellectuals like Wang Tao (王韜 mission translator, newspaper editor, and columnist) and Ma Xiangbo chose to put their talents and energies directly into social change rather than church building. Their lives warn against underestimating the pull factors of social call or the acuity of contemporary theological debates on social infrastructure as missional activity. In their career paths, the Roman Catholic Ma and the Protestant Wang were following Chinese gentry models of social leadership as well as contemporary missionary activists like Timothy Richard and Young J. Allen.[74] Ma, who was involved in the Self-Strengthening and Reform Movements and joined in the government of the 1911 Revolution, is remembered in secular sources as an educator and founder of three universities, including Zhendan (Aurora) and Fudan—a prominent career by any standards.

Once new opportunities opened up to educated elite in the twentieth century, a driving question became: how best to foster the evolving culture in a way that accords with Christian beliefs? Were energies best channeled into reforming the church itself so it reflected the new national conscience in its structures and leadership, or in broader social work or politics, given the scale of need? And if intellectuals were those whose task was to systematize culture, its symbols and unifying structures, then what exactly were Chinese Christians to systematize, given that "Christian" was still taken as synonymous with "Western" by most? Was nurturing a hybrid Chinese Christian culture the answer? Unlike some of the more fundamentalist believers, for whom Christ was most definitely against culture, the Christian theologians discussed below saw Chinese culture, and Chinese society, as the ground for their work. Some of the most severe cultural clashes during the period were not between missionaries and Chinese, as often depicted, but were internal to Chinese Christians, as they worked to resolve their identity ambiguity and overcome the perception that they were somehow outside their cultural system.

The desire to engage with the world and its problems can be seen in sermon after sermon of the emerging cohort of young leaders. Little fell outside the ambit of their thinking, which was directed not just to matters of theology, church-state relations, and the nature of the indigenous church, but embraced Christian involvement in social and economic action, national education, and the reevaluation of Confucian ethics. A speech delivered by NCC co-leader Cheng Jingyi to a meeting in Shanghai in 1927 set out some of the parameters of the new vision and gives an insight into the task ahead.[75] Cheng himself was heavily involved in ecumenical initiatives and also instrumental in new Chinese-run movements, like the Chinese Home Mission Movement (1918), and was the first moderator of the Church of Christ in China. His 1927 speech to an audience of Chinese and foreign church leaders enumerated key questions of the moment: should Christians speak to political matters? Was religious liberty being violated? Was the registration of Christian schools right and beneficial? Was too much faith being put in the Nationalist Movement?[76] Cheng acknowledged the legitimate aspirations fueling the Nationalist Movement, while arguing that the church should not identify with party politics. The Christian church, he suggested, "is neither a running dog of the political machine nor an institution that lives in water-tight compartments."[77]

DEBATES ON RELIGION AND THE ANTI-CHRISTIAN MOVEMENTS

A final background factor to Chinese theology in the Republican era caused some of the most voluminous responses in print. If Chinese Christian elites were socially committed in the manner of traditional gentry, international in outlook in the manner of modern educated youth, yet also wary of the foreign presence within China, their religious adherence was out of kilter with both traditional and contemporary intellectual leanings. Many early twentieth-century intellectuals and the burgeoning left wing derided religion for its feudal structures and promotion of superstition, frequently singling out Christianity as the religion of colonial imperialists, a narrative that dominated perception over the next half century. At times, antagonisms against religion and imperialism merged, leaving Christians caught between denying their religion and defending the indefensible. The Anti-Christian movements, which culminated in the institution of the Anti-Christian Federation to coordinate action in the early 1920s, had a profound effect on Christian believers and on the environment in which Christianity was practiced.

Anti-Christian movements during the late Qing had ranged from armed responses to foreign effrontery—as in the gentry-inspired riots in Yangzhou in 1868 protesting the presence of the China Inland Mission in the city or the bloody events in Tianjin in 1870 where sixty Catholic believers were killed—to fully considered philosophical rebuttals of biblical miracles and biblical canon formation.[78] Fear was frequently whipped up by seditious tracts, cheap to produce and distribute, such as those that depicted Christians worshipping a pig ("pig," *zhū*, is a near-homophone for "Lord," *zhǔ*) or stealing and eating babies.[79] Some movements were antiforeign and swept up Christianity as part of the nationalist backlash; some were antireligion; and some were specific attacks on Christian ideas from a Confucian perspective. The Taiping Rebellion cast a long shadow into the twentieth century: the abiding legacy of Hong Xiuquan's Kingdom of Heavenly Peace (ca. 1851–1864) was a heightened antagonism toward Christianity on the part of the gentry, who took the not-unreasonable attitude that if this was Chinese Christianity, then even a weak, foreign (Manchu) government was superior.[80] Mission histories often gloss over the fact that the Anti-Christian movements were only one of many forms of protest during this period, where protest had become a way of defining identities, calling for new social structures, and consolidating the overthrow of the patriarchal social and gender relations of feudal China. The Boxer incident around 1900 is the best known and the most deadly of the series of attacks on Christians yet was primarily an antiforeign movement, and the deaths derived as much from the simmering anger against foreign privilege enshrined in the treaties as from fear of Christianity (up to thirty thousand Chinese Christians were killed directly, as well as the foreigners for whom the crippling indemnities were demanded).

Into the early twentieth century, antireligion debates based around scientific progress and human culture took place in the pages of journals, at conferences, and in university theaters when celebrities like Bertrand Russell and John Dewey came to China on lecture tours. The idea that science showed religion to be methodologically suspect, since it was subjective and unverifiable, was common. Debate on religion centered around its value and function in society, rather than the internal perspectives of adherents. Some well-known figures, such as Liang Qichao, did challenge the supremacy of science, holding that society needed the ideals and morals of religion, while others argued that the philosophy of religion was useful for exploring human existence.[81] It was often nonscientists who were most adamant about the omnipotence of the scientific method. Like literature and religion, science was proclaimed the savior of China by its supporters, as in the slogan "science is omnipotent, science saves the nation."[82] Republican-era Christianity has been denigrated for emphasizing social over individual salvation, but the terms of debate were not in the control of the church alone.

The Anti-Christian movements that snowballed into a national campaign in the early 1920s drew on elements of the late Qing Anti-Christian movements, with added tensions. General levels of anxiety about the evils of warlords and imperialism had risen during the 1910s, and nationalism grew as a response to disunity and a sense of powerlessness. The warlords, or regional militarists, who were in control of most of China fomented patriotism with nationalist slogans.[83] Chinese intellectuals were asking searching questions about the ideal relationship of state and religion. Attempts by reformists to institute Confucianism as a state religion in 1898 had met with opposition, as did renewed attempts to do so in 1916.[84] Against this backdrop, two specific incidents catalyzed feelings among educated urbanites: the "Shandong Settlement" agreed as part of the Versailles Treaty of 1919 (despite Gu Weijin's much-applauded speech on China's behalf), which triggered wide-scale protests, including boycotts of British and Japanese goods; and the decision of the World Student Christian Federation to hold its 1922 conference at Qinghua (Tsinghua) University. This seemingly trivial incident led to a series of protests and demonstrations, each more vituperative in its denunciation of Christianity as a tool of imperialism. Coming shortly after the end of the Washington Conference in February 1922, where the Nine-Power Treaty deferred a decision on revoking extraterritoriality, the conference served as a provocative reminder that China did not enjoy full sovereignty over China—and that foreign missions were still educating large numbers of citizens.

As protests proliferated during the 1920s, it was increasingly difficult to separate out anti-Christian from anti-imperialist protest, exacerbating the pressure on Chinese Christians. The May Thirtieth Incident of 1925, when International Settlement police under British command shot at unarmed factory workers, was clearly a political demonstration but led to another outburst of anti-imperialist and anti-Christian sentiment, channeled into protests about Christian schools. The aftermath to May Thirtieth was so serious that it drew many foreign missionaries, previously opposed to any political action, to lobby their own governments to revoke extraterritorial privileges. Protests drew in educators, philosophers, cultural commentators, and politicians. The writings of detractors—including their friends, revered colleagues, and fellow nationalists—had a strong effect on believers. Former fellow travelers, like Chen Duxiu or Lu Xun, joined the ranks of intellectuals for whom the combination of the Russian revolution and the humiliations at Versailles turned passive support into vitriol. The sustained level of verbal attack was shocking, and numerous Christians, including Wu Leichuan, wrote subsequently of a period of severe questioning of their faith.

Into the late 1920s, anti-Christianity protests ceded to government-directed antisuperstition protests, as the Nationalist (Guomindang) government drew together the debates on the role of religion in a modern state that had animated the New Culture Movement and anti-imperialist critiques into a series of campaigns to destroy superstition, with a renewed emphasis on rationality and the wastefulness of temple worship. These included idol-smashing rallies, which Rebecca Nedostup has termed "public, forcible acts of conversion to a secularized nationalism and to the Nationalist revolution."[85] The iconoclastic and antisuperstition campaigns in 1927–1928 and 1929–1930 included an attempted ban on Lunar New Year celebrations; prohibitions on fortune tellers, geomancers, and other "unproductive" workers; confiscations of temples; and an aim to replace religious pilgrimages and symbols with secular, state-based ones.[86] As religious practices were recategorized in line with the premises of secular nationalism (with Christianity as the base model of a "religion") under the Guomindang government, a clear distinction was made between "superstition" and "religion."[87] The freedom of religion that the new constitutional movements had secured was increasingly limited to "real" religions, or modernized, rational ones that would not threaten the state. Chinese folk religions were a major target, but the general tenor of debate also caused much reflection within Christianity and other "acceptable" religions as to how to divest (or defend) their own "superstitious" elements and accord with the new national orthodoxy of strict separation of state and religion.

Scholars have argued that the "indigenous Christian movement was largely a reaction to the challenge of nationalism" and that it was the Anti-Christian Movement that stimulated Christian apologetics.[88] As this chapter has indicated, a great number of factors were at play in the background to the development of Chinese Christianity and its theology, including political reform, traditional values and understanding of the social role of intellectuals, the historical contingencies of missionary education, and changing international views on indigenous church leadership and on the role of religion itself. Nationalism may have been the rallying call and the catalyst for action, but the other necessary conditions cannot be simplistically ascribed to nationalism. Nationalism can only be short-hand for the complex range of identity issues involved for Christians.

By the early twentieth century, conditions favored a Chinese-run church. The historic churches had growing numbers of educated congregants and co-horts of Bible teachers and priests coming through training institutions. There were Chinese editions of major Christian texts, new Bible translations under way, and enough primers, catechisms, and hymnals available for an entirely Chinese-language operation. Urban prosperity and a growing bourgeoisie held out the possibility of self-financing churches. While it is impossible to deny the paternalistic comments and genuine concerns of church leaders about "trans-ferring" authority to individual Chinese, the foreign-run church had created the conditions for a Chinese takeover, even if it was reluctant actually to re-linquish power, by the time the Qing dynasty was in its last throes. A long-held belief among missionaries that foreign mission boards or the Vatican was not best placed to determine policies or structures on the ground came together with the need among Chinese Christians to demonstrate that their churches were not under the authority of foreign managers. The drive for the church to become fully Chinese—in language, leadership, and liturgy—was a shared motivation, despite differences in approach and timing. Nationalist rancor has-tened the process, but the creation of a Chinese church should be seen as a gradual, bilateral process. As the balance of power shifted nationally, to the point where antiforeign sentiment prevailed, there was a simultaneous transfer of power to Chinese within the church: an ideologically longed-for outcome and a political necessity.

A CHINESE THEOLOGY IN A CHINESE PERIODICAL PRESS

The existence of a press and ready communication channels enabled the rapid takeoff of Christian journals and Chinese Christian publishing in the new Republic. The modern press in China had its origins in the Protestant mis-sion press: just as the first Protestant converts in the early nineteenth century had been printers and those involved with mission printing, the first wave of Chinese-run presses came from those with mission links. Wang Tao, for exam-ple, who worked closely with Scottish missionary and translator James Legge, founded the first Chinese daily, the *Xunhuan ribao* (循環日報 Universal Cir-culating Herald) in Hong Kong in 1874.[89] There was considerable crossover of personnel between secular and Christian newspapers, and between English- and Chinese-language presses, with articles translated back and forth. The late

Qing Christian press opened up the notion of a public sphere, thrust scholars to the center of the modernizing movement, and, critically, spread the belief that a better-informed nation was a stronger nation. One of the most famous mission publications, the *Wanguo gongbao* (萬國公報 Review of the Times), established by Young J. Allen, led the way with a circulation of nearly forty thousand by the end of the century. It covered a wide range of topics from international news and economics to science and engineering, with the occasional piece of Christian apologetics.[90] The fact that missionary-editors were publishing both "secular" and "Christian" materials, sometimes in the same journal, shows a broad understanding of their role, as well as the eclectic model they bequeathed to Chinese successors.[91]

The twin processes of institutional and intellectual growth that converged in such a flourishing Chinese Christianity—and of opposition to it—in the 1920s built on parallel textual processes in the nineteenth century.[92] Mission churches had encouraged the gradual sinicization of Chinese Christian texts alongside the slow building up of church congregations, circuits, deaneries, and vicariates. Textual indigenization—in Bible translation, as well as catechisms, educational primers, and hymnals—had reached new levels of sophistication and accuracy in the late Qing. The classical language Bible and Prayer Book translations of priest-scholars like Joseph Schereschewsky, John Shaw Burdon, and their (too often unnamed) Chinese co-workers in the 1870s and 1880s— which were arguably more indigenized in their use of Chinese expressions and thought than the later modern Chinese editions—were not bettered before the language changes of the 1910s rendered them obsolete.[93] The Russian Orthodox Church had also been highly productive in translation work, producing in the 1880s a complete translation of the Sunday *Oktoihon* services and of liturgies for the twelve great feasts.[94] Yet, as with Roman Catholic theology (discussed in Chapter 1), the takeoff point in Protestant writings came when Chinese Christians took over composition—and the means of production.

The periodical press emerged as a natural center of Christian activity during the 1920s and 1930s. Writing and composition was an arena where Chinese Christians had an innate advantage over missionaries and could readily exercise autonomy, and for many intellectuals this was the focus of their evangelistic activities. With no ordination requirements or permission needed from within church structures, it was an area where Chinese in the historic churches could exercise leadership just as the heads of the new independent churches were doing in congregations. (Independent church leaders also sought to spread their message via periodicals, of course; Wang Mingdao's *Lingshi jikan* (靈食 季刊 *Spiritual Food Quarterly*) is a prime example, but for many evangelicals, preaching and congregational work came first.)[95] Critically for Chinese Christians, publishing was a transdenominational activity and did not come with an overlay of foreign division. Like-minded individuals from across denominations and nationalities worked together on projects to define and publicize the gospel. This project was in keeping with the intellectual zeitgeist of the 1910s and 1920s, when literature was held to be a crucial arena for national salvation.

The periodical press was the obvious forum to influence other educated urbanites, as well as to develop a community of encouragement and inspiration in the face of intellectual attack. There are far fewer studies of Christian literature societies and journal boards than secular ones, but it is reasonable to assume that Christian literature societies played a role similar to secular ones (including study groups like those of the incipient CCP) in forming communal identity and expressing social responsibility.[96] The audience for each was their peers: often young, politically and socially engaged idealists seeking to make a difference in the world. It was crucial for Christians to take their arguments into the public sphere if they wanted to influence and ameliorate society as they intended, and the new print culture enabled this. The uptake of Christian ideas can be seen across a range of print publications, and their effect was especially important in the new vernacular fiction, where Christian themes and imagery began regularly to appear in the work of authors like Lu Xun, Ba Jin, or Shen Congwen as well as in explicitly Christian writers like Xu Zhimo or Bing Xin.

Among Protestants, there was a determined push to systematize the production of an "indigenous" Christian literature under the NCC, and writers were encouraged to escape imposed structures of thinking and expression toward more China-centered ways of thinking. By 1922, a comprehensive plan existed to tackle the perceived shortfall in Christian factual and fictional texts. The strategy included creating a readership, nurturing Christian writing talent, and developing print outlets, as well as programs for scholarships and fellowships, proposals for a university school of literature, prize essays, and plans to encourage bookstores to take Christian stock.[97] In calling for a new literature and envisaging the creation of an entire library of Christian works for all walks of life, the 1922 NCC report summarized current problems:[98]

> Chinese Christianity is badly handicapped by its lack of Christian theological books. Tract societies, as their names imply, have concentrated their main energies on the task of helping the outsider and giving him an introduction to the Christian church. In the face of the "New Thought Movement" there is no adequate armoury in Chinese provided for the average Christian minister with which to equip himself for the war. . . . It is not enough for the few

foreign-speaking clergy or foreign missionaries to have access to foreign books. It is essential that the ordinary pastor not well equipped with a foreign language or not equipped at all, should be in a position to pilot himself and his ship though a storm of doubt that only breaks once or twice in centuries.[99]

The paucity of theological works and comparative religion texts for the use of pastors, as well as homiletic and apologetic texts, was raised by the literature subcommittee report of the NCC too, which noted that available works were "too dry and bony" and that only a small proportion of publications was reaching the shelves of those for whom they were intended.[100] Other priorities listed included the need for Christian daily newspapers in the major urban centers, a magazine for preachers, publications for Christian primary teachers and social workers, and a press bureau to supply the secular press with information and the best of Christian thought. The challenges in supplying such a demand were clear and were made more difficult by the changing language, which exacerbated demands on translators,[101] yet by the time of the 1929 NCC report on Christian literature, the list of unmet needs was highly specialized: tracts and ballads for children, a popular periodical for farmers, writings on public health, and religious textbooks for primary and middle schools. One paradox of mainstream Chinese church life was still evident: the urgent need for a literature agency under Chinese leaders, with complete freedom to develop its own contribution to the cause, required financial assistance that "would have to come for the time being largely from abroad," as the report noted.[102]

In an address reprinted as an article in the *Chinese Recorder* in 1925, theologian Zhao Zichen joined the dots between an indigenous Christian literature and an indigenous church. This was, he argued, a question of survival ("whether or not the tree of Christian religion transplanted from the West and still artificially protected under artificial heat and moisture, will continue to live and grow"), as well as one of leadership and of acquiring a spiritual life of China's own.[103] "We need an indigenous ministry and an indigenous group of Christian writers for the church which is now literally starving to hear the truths and to read them on the printed page," he wrote. The hemorrhaging of students from Christianity was in part because "the church has not trained men in the first place that have sufficient respect for their own civilization and that understand the genius of their own culture and heritage." If a lack of grounding in Chinese civilization created an antagonism among those schooled in the Christian colleges, it also inhibited the spread of the gospel in wider society, since the leaders could not articulate their own spiritual inheritance. What was needed, argued Zhao, was not some sort of discredited propagandist literature, but a confident presentation of truths that addressed the Chinese heart and mind. For that to happen, the church needed to concentrate on the expression of its spiritual life as much as on its status in society. For Zhao, Christian literature is envisaged as a preparatory stage for theology, the nurturing of a Chinese Christian sensibility that will begin to produce original theologians who can (re)interpret Christian mysteries and "create doctrines to suit the revelation of Christ in the Chinese consciousness."[104]

Despite the challenges, a plethora of new titles was created to broadcast the Christian message into society. Journals like *Shengming yuekan* (生命月刊 Life Monthly) or *Zhenli zhoukan* (真理週刊 Truth Weekly) were established with editor and assistant editor positions held by native Chinese speakers. Like the late Qing missionary journals and traditional miscellanies, these magazines presented a range of topics and styles within each issue, including editorials, academic articles, sermon transcripts, book reviews, travelogues, and, toward the back, poems, prayers, and short fiction. Church-based magazines like the Shanghai Jesuit *Shengjiao zazhi* (聖教雜誌 Revue Catholique) or the Baptist *Zhen guang* (真光 The True Light Review) might typically also carry a round-up of church news, whether local, diocesan, or international, and biographies and obituaries. Apologetics magazines were intended to appeal to non-Christians, but the wide scope of articles indicates also a theology of integration, an engagement with the world and its politics. Journal articles were often expanded into books, and new book catalogues and mail-order options enabled an even wider circulation of religious texts.

One guide lists more than 450 Christian journals operative at some point between 1914 and 1937; another lists 30 Christian journals active from the 1920s through the 1940s, including denominational ones like that for young Roman Catholics, *Periodicum Trimestre Consociationis Juventutis Catholicae* (中華公教青年會季刊), or the Anglican *Chinese Churchman* (聖公會報); journals for special-interest groups like *Education Quarterly* (基督教教育季刊); organization-specific journals like those of the YMCA and YWCA; Christian seminary and university periodicals like the *Cheeloo University Journal* (齊大季刊); as well as those set up specifically by groups interested in publicizing a Christian message, like *Zhenli zhoukan*.[105] Annualized figures show that throughout the 1920s and 1930s more than a hundred Protestant Chinese-language magazines were in circulation.[106] These included annual journals from national bodies like the NCC and journals created by individual church leaders. Even when institutes relocated during the war against Japan, they worked to set up new journals, such as the magazine of Jinling (Nanjing) seminary "in West China" (金陵神學華西專刊).

A small group of liberal-leaning theologians and writers who edited and contributed prolifically to apologetics journals and magazines defined the core features and values of their theological vision as they wrote. The Christianity they sought to promote was to be truth-seeking, intellectually satisfying, politically engaged, and in dialogue with the world church. It questioned inherited structures, such as theological training methods and the necessity of stipendiary ministers; it reevaluated the relationship of Christianity to Chinese culture, especially Confucian ethics for Christians; it concentrated on Jesus as a human being. The ideological vacuum of the early Republic—not dissimilar to the post-Marxist "spiritual vacuum" of the 1990s, albeit with a strong party-state in power—had encouraged a proliferation of philosophies whose adherents joined in the rash of passion and invective in print. A growing translation industry made a wide range of Western European, Russian, and Japanese writing available in Chinese for the first time, and the wider press showcased competing philosophies from the historical materialism of the fledgling Marxists to the aestheticism of the humanists. Many Christian thinkers welcomed the new freedom to debate wrought by the May Fourth–era activists and sought to utilize the climate of rethinking the past and envisioning the future in the interests of the gospel.[107]

Christian leaders had to engage with the positives of the admixture of political ideologies, draw "objective" sociological discussions of religion into the realm of theological apologetics, and combat the anti-Christian challenges in the realm of science and national determination. They did this in a variety of ways. The Christian writers in these nondenominational journals produced a rational, kenotic theology in keeping with the currents of secular thought of the time. They emphasized notions of self-sacrifice and the egalitarian and nonmaterialistic tenets of Christianity as a rejoinder to Marxist monopolization of the brotherhood of humanity. Theirs was often a deliberately practical apologetics, promoting Christian social action. Building on the thinking (and labor) of the Social Gospel proponents in China like Legge, Richard, and Allen and on contemporary theorists like A. R. Kepler, they sought to build the Kingdom of God on earth. Literacy education and agricultural reform sponsored by the NCC were one expression of this. In the face of calls for a new ethics for society, some emphasized the transformative qualities of Christian life through relationship with God. Others made recourse to a universal Christ, enabling them to integrate traditional Chinese philosophies into a Christian present. In the main, Christian intellectuals pursued a Christocentric theology, with a pared-down version accessible to all audiences giving priority to the life, and humanity, of Jesus. An antimiracle stance was common among theological educators; some, such as Wu Leichuan, went so far as to deny all miracles, including the Resurrection. Soteriologies often combined an emphasis on social concern with this turn from the miraculous: salvation occurred in the present, was played out in one's response to the social need around as well as through Jesus's revolutionary sacrifice, and was collective. God was to be found in quotidian life, in human relations, and especially in meditation on Christ, the most perfect expression of God in humanity.

The desire to produce a reasoned defense of Christianity suffused the vision statements of journals. In a special English-language edition of *The Life* for the influx of delegates attending the World Student Christian Federation conference in 1922 (the one that provoked such a strong anti-Christian backlash), editor Liu Tingfang elaborated on the basic principles of the journal: independence from ecclesiastical control, nonpartisan, and scientific, seeking to encourage Christians to express opinions and discuss their faith.[108] Liu demonstrated how the journal was to act as a two-way channel of understanding between foreigners and Chinese and between Christianity and Chinese culture. The monthly *Life* claimed a simple motivation, publishing authors who had a common desire to "make Jesus Christ known to the Chinese people," who "look forward to the development and formation of an indigenous church in China," and who were engaged in contributing to that goal. Liu summarized the journal's position:

> Within the Christian church there is a rapidly developing consciousness of a Chinese church. The desire for an indigenous church which does not sever its contiguity from the historic churches of the West but takes full cognizance of the spiritual and racial inheritance of the Chinese people, has become the rallying point of many Christians. Along with it there is the insistent desire for a more thorough understanding and a more adequate interpretation of Christian teaching, and a more effective application of it to social and individual life. From every part of the country Christians are yearning for better preachers, better Christian literature and a more thorough Christian program.[109]

A theology that was made in China, for a church in communion with the West, and that was strong on education and social application: this was the vision that this circle of journal editors-cum-theologians set before themselves as they wrote.

The special edition of *The Life* for student delegates exemplified two other facets of the journal's philosophy: first, it tackled head-on the Anti-Christian Movement, reprinting for readers the "Declaration of the Non-Christian Students' Federation" of March 1922 with its diatribe against the Christian church and against the nations attempting to establish churches in China. Besides taking the sting out of the attack through confrontation, the magazine also sought to create a broad forum for debate, through inviting select national luminaries to write on "My Attitude Toward Christianity in China." The names and articles produced show how well-connected the Christian editors were in Chinese society: Hu Shi, Chen Duxiu, and Zhou Zuoren were among those persuaded to offer articles. The attitudes of some of the secular voices included in the journal are particularly illuminating, since they chime so closely with the more radically contextualized versions of Christianity espoused over the next few years by liberal-leaning, Confucian-inspired Christians like Wu Leichuan. Chen Duxiu, for example, in the early 1920s valorized Christianity as a source of European civilization, took the natural sciences to have nullified certain doctrines such as miracles or accounts of creation or the Trinity, highlighted Christianity as a religion of love (contra Friedrich Nietzsche), and directed readers away from theology and ritual toward the character and spirit of Jesus. Hu Shi likewise argued that the future of Christianity depended on throwing off superstitions and the theologies of the Middle Ages derived "from the quibblings of the medieval monks and pedants" and preserving the moral teachings of the "prophet of social revolution."[110]

The emphasis on "truth" was seen in the titles of journals, which included *Zhen guang* (The True Light Review) and *Zhenli zhoukan* (Truth Weekly) as well as the merged *Zhenli yu shengming* (Truth and Life),[111] and throughout editorials, vision statements, and articles. "Truth" was, of course, a wider pursuit in society.[112] When *Zhenli yu shengming* moved from fortnightly to monthly production in 1930, editor Zhao Zichen reiterated its central mission of pursuing the truth.[113] Articles across the spectrum of journals explored this question, "What is truth?" One such article in *Zhen guang* by Jin Bingdao (金秉道 Chin Pin Tau), titled "Truth and Creed," began with Plato, comparing definitions used in science and theology.[114] Another article by Cheng Zhiyi (誠質怡 Andrew C. Y. Cheng), "The Idea of Faith in the Fourth Gospel," in *Zhenli yu shengming* explored different aspects of the meaning of the verb "to believe" in John and its relation to knowledge, arguing for faith as moral surrender rather than intellectual assent.[115] In several of the key apologetic journals there was no unified denominational or Christian position; the debate was what mattered.

The defense of the Christian faith, always intellectually oriented, included positive explanation of Christian thought as well as defensive reaction to printed attacks. The barrage of questioning and derision from anti-Christian factions and perplexed colleagues regarding the supernatural, scriptural veracity of or historical atrocities committed by the church were deflected with a

contextualizing of the past and continued referral back to Jesus. Secular skeptics of miracles were met with an insistence on the character of Jesus and with
historical evidence regarding his existence. Even a magazine like *Dao sheng*
(道聲 The Preachers' Magazine) advised its readers that since the only real
evidence on Jesus in the New Testament is the moral proof of his character,
Christians should foreground Christ and downplay the miracles if they want
to defend against the attacks of unbelievers.[116] Many writers engaged in careful
introspection. In a May 1925 edition of *Zhen guang*, Wang Wenxin (王文馨
Waang Wen-chieu) published a retort to an anti-Christian article in which he
began by acknowledging the fierceness of the movement.[117] The first question
we should ask, Wang begins, is why are they attacking us and war-mongering?
By distinguishing the reasons—Christians as enemies of the state, Christians as
enemies of knowledge and science, or Christians as enemies of society—we can
begin to see whether the attackers are mistaken, prejudiced, or rooted in reality
and respond accordingly. By conceding some elements and analyzing where
the church too was at fault, Wang presented a constructive challenge to readers.
The remedy, he suggested, lay in a greater sinicization of the church—and for
Christians to act more like Christ.

Attacks on Christianity in the national press presented a mix of supposition
and hearsay alongside ideological opposition. The most acute difficulty for
Christians lay in misrepresentation and partial truths, such as the painful accusation that Christians were damaging China. *Juewu* (覺悟 Awakening) was
one Shanghai daily that ran constant articles undermining religion, and it is
easy to see how doubts might assail young patriotic Christians. Christianity was
attacked for instilling a false consciousness, denigrating human effort because
of the expectation of happiness in the next world; for anesthetizing the working classes and making them believe that social inequality was God's will; for
deceiving the colonized into believing that troops were in China to bring the
gospel and education, not plunder its wealth; for duping youth; and for sully-
ing China's reputation abroad.[118] *Juewu*'s ideological battle was explicit, but its
anti-Christian articles sat alongside a wealth of solid scholarship: articles on
new developments in psychology and Western philosophy, on general relativity,
and on the history of sociology that gave the impression of scholarly objectivity.
Some pieces played on a strong subjectivity, such as "A Letter to Friends from
a Church College Student," in which the writer, "Ms. A," inveighs against the
"slave behavior" of those who flatter foreign imperialists.[119] Other articles appealed directly to youth to unite and work to oppose Christianity or called on
writers to demonstrate how religion was incompatible with science, mocking
those "who believe what they are told to believe" in the New Testament.[120]
Tackling the trite assumptions of the naysayers was a continual fire-fighting ex-

ercise. When Dewey lectured, articles soon followed on "Dewey's perspective on religion"; when the legal meaning of public property was contested, journal debates on public property ensued. In one "Open Letter" in 1930, Zhao Zichen set out to rebut the arguments of materialists. His article is a exemplary case of serious, considered engagement with opponents, highlighting Zhao's own core value of individual freedom to pursue truth while concluding constructively that the function of religion was different from that of politics, since its focus was in "soul-making."[121]

The publishing wing of the Chinese church took it as axiomatic that it was part of the world church and saw an important facet of its duty as commenting on international church affairs. As early as 1923 Liu Tingfang and Zhao Zichen had articulated cogently how China "resides in the Church Universal" while at the same time, its own individuality, environment, and national history brought a "synthesis" to thinking about God the Father and Christ the Savior.[122] Following the 1930 Lambeth Conference, T. M. Barker penned for *Zhenli yu shengming* a long report assessing the conference and its implications, showing how experience pushed China ahead of the world curve on women's roles. A report from the conference commending to Nanjing the opinion that "theology faculties should be established in universities wherever possible" prompted a rather caustic response: "Unfortunately Nanking is a far cry from Lambeth."[123] Journals like *Zhenli yu shengming* served to create a sense of belonging by keeping Chinese abreast of developments elsewhere, by reporting on the concerns and needs of overseas Chinese, and by providing practical information on international student mutual aid societies. In the same issue as the Lambeth report, Xu Baoqian began a multipart travelogue detailing his journey around Europe attending Christian conferences in France, Germany, Sweden, the Netherlands, and the United Kingdom. The article presents a digest of meeting reports of church and para-church organizations, along with Xu's comments and scattered travel notes. International comparisons helped readers gain a relative sense of China, and meeting reports gave details on new thinking on mission and evangelization. Xu's comments on the sacrifices needed for church unity were surely aimed at the Chinese situation, offering readers a chance to make their own connections and feel at home with, and engaged in, a world Christianity.

CONCLUSION

As Chinese intellectuals struggled with a conflict of identity between their Chineseness and their Christian faith, with defending their loyalty and their faith to other Chinese and defending both against Western Christian hierarchies, they did what other young activists were doing: they wrote searching essays in the new Chinese language in a modern press. The enthusiasm to create a new theological field during the 1920s was palpable, in keeping with the heady days of the New Culture Movement and the sense of possibility that a break with mission thinking held out. The process of rethinking, or rationalizing, the relationship with the mission churches gave plenty of scope for innovation, and the development of a new consciousness of what it meant to be a Chinese Christian demanded a creative application of the resources of history, literature, and biblical and textual studies. The experiment of being church—of running services and communions, of engaging with local communities, and of aiding in rural reconstruction and mass literacy programs in cooperation with state and nonstate organizations—and of being a community of engaged intellectuals operating through print media and through the university faculties that so many of the Christian leaders were linked to demanded a continual refinement of ideas. The theologians rose to the task admirably; the great loss to the church and to an accurate appreciation of the era has been that their work has remained unread and understudied for so long.

Chinese Christian thinkers and leaders were willing to expend so much energy in developing a broad Chinese Christian literature because they saw it as critical to an indigenous Christianity. A Chinese-language press allowed Chinese to do their theological thinking outside the constraints of Western models of theology or Western church structures and hierarchies. The building of a Chinese Christian literature overcame the worse aspects of missionary domineering and allowed writers to follow Chinese patterns of thought and enable the "interpretation of experience to agree with life," rather than requiring life to fit in with "Procrustean" and "worn out" theories.[124] Parallels between the mission press and the Chinese church are worth noting: missionaries initiated and ran presses and set up publishing houses and periodicals throughout the nineteenth century, but the industry took off when Chinese took the helm at the turn of the twentieth century. Whether in the Roman Catholic Church in the nineteenth century or the Protestant churches in the twentieth, growth in numbers and the social spread of the Chinese church came when Chinese assumed leadership. While other Chinese Christians were preaching to thousands, offering faith-healings and volumes of spiritual guidance, theological educators and leaders within the historic churches were doing their part for evangelism by creating a literature of Christian apologetics.

Reading theology in the journals gives a strong sense of a common theological engagement, nurtured by joint editorships, by authors writing to deadlines and interacting in their various roles across multiple journals. Studying theology in situ in print also gives a sense of the ebb and flow of debate, the web of relations among different publications, and the relative weight of contentious issues—recent research emphasis on "indigenization," for example, gives the misleading impression that this was *the* topic of debate. Theology was not separated out into great tomes to be read only by seminary students and academics (although serialized articles were often republished as complete texts, often by the same presses, and journal articles might be extended into fuller works) but was served up monthly, interspersed among other aspects of Christian life and thought, to a paying audience. Creating a Chinese theology was not in the Republican era a matter of lengthy individual systematic studies, alien in thought-form and application, but bound up with the journals themselves—an interactive discernment of, and speaking into, the relation between the divine and the complex social and political realities affecting believers.

Chinese Christians knew that they had a blank slate in the new Republic to create new structures for the church in its interactions with state and society. While May Fourth activists sought to overturn aspects of feudal culture and its entrenched social roles, the rejection of Chinese culture by certain foreign missionaries in the name of Christian civilization caused much soul-searching. Re-establishing a positive Christian view of Chinese life was a central task. One of the ways in which Roman Catholic scholars could do this was by reassessing the role of the Catholic Church in Chinese history. For others, the "Christ against (heathen) culture" model, which many missionaries had implicitly assumed, began to be challenged with Christian resources. Chinese Christians knew the inner workings of Chinese society from lifelong experience and were acutely aware of the particular difficulties for Chinese in Christianity. Doctrines that contradicted normative Chinese views on humanity or philosophical issues, or which presented stumbling blocks to Christians, were reexamined. Socially, one of the problems many Chinese had with the mission theologies taught to them was the exclusivity of Christianity and the rejection of other religions—the religions of family members and friends. In China, even relatively conservative Christian journals carried studies of the life of the Buddha.

As the 1920s wore on into the 1930s, however, the realities were increasingly prosaic. The ebullience of the early movement could not be sustained, as the sheer difficulty of creating a new theological voice became clear, especially given the social unrest and burgeoning civil war. There was a certain maturity in the downgrading of expectations. It was relatively easy, as Zhao Zichen noted in an editorial, to recognize what was nonsense or subjective in the new thought—but few had the wherewithal to recognize an authentic work, or true experience. Destructive criticism of outmoded old ways was ubiquitous, but the work ahead had to be constructive: "a sharp axe is needed for cutting grass, but planting a forest takes many years of nurturing."[125] Editors began to see their aims in terms of a seeding function: to research the problems and to introduce the fruits of that research as a "prompt" to deeper exploration. The same principles remained in place to guide them as they explained religious life and thought to readers: cherishing the freedom of thought in faith, finding fellowship in the life of the mind, engaging in the scientific study of contemporary thought—but it was now clear that this would be a task that outlasted the Republic and the Nationalist eras.

ZHAO ZICHEN AND A CREATIVE
THEOLOGY: THE *LIFE OF JESUS* (1935)[1]

We want realities. In regard to the doctrines of Christianity, there
are indeed some that we have not been able to understand, some
that we doubt, and some that we cannot and will not believe.
—Zhao Zichen, 1927[2]

It was not as God or the Son of God that Jesus attracted me;
rather, He commanded my attention and interest because
He was a thoroughly human being. To the Chinese sages we
cannot know Heaven without first coming to know man.
—Zhao Zichen, 1933[3]

The Christian intellectuals and leaders who inherited the mission legacy
and its rhetoric and chose to remain within historic denominations occupied
a demanding, mediative position: interpreting Christian thought to China and
on Christ into Chinese modes and bearing the weight of expectation as a new
generation of church leaders. As discussed in Chapter 2, many of those actively
engaged in producing a written body of Christian literature were among the
most steeped of all Chinese in Western ways of thinking, and yet they also
understood the intricacies of cultural tradition and the emotive power of perceived insults against China. Those who were self-consciously reflecting and
writing on what it meant to be a *Chinese* church and how that church should
engage with society often stepped in line with wider Chinese views rather than
church expectations as they took their own stance on matters of theology, governance, and social need.

Zhao Zichen (T. C. Chao, 1888–1979) was at the forefront of those conceptu-
alizing and realizing a Chinese Protestant church. A leading academic in prewar China, Zhao was educated at Dongwu University, a Methodist college, in
Suzhou, where he became a Christian; he then studied theology at Vanderbilt
University in the United States. Zhao started his academic career as a professor
of sociology and religion in Suzhou, and in 1925 he moved to be professor of
philosophy and Christianity at Yanjing (Yenching) University in Beijing. He
penned more than two million characters in his lifetime, including eighty-nine
articles in English. Zhao believed in the power of education—and the power
of Christianity to stand on its own, being one of the few to view with equanim-
ity the abolition of religious studies departments in Chinese universities.[4] Ordained an Anglican priest in Hong Kong in his early fifties, Zhao lived between
church and academia as long as that remained possible in China. An inaugural
member of the NCC, he traveled frequently to international Christian meetings and was an early president of the World Council of Churches. Zhao was,
for much of his life, of the generation that could be openly committed Christians and international academics.[5]

In the midst of civil war, Zhao set aside time to write a biography of Jesus in a
novelistic form. The Anti-Christian Movement was past its heyday, but Mr. Science and Mr. Democracy still held sway in academia and among radical youth,
and many saw the church as backward or even irrelevant in the face of impend-
ing war with Japan. Zhao had earlier drawn attention to the need for a Chinese
literature to nourish a Chinese church, a church that had made its members
"half foreigners."[6] *Yesu zhuan* (耶穌傳 *Life of Jesus*), Zhao's response to his own
appeal, is a tour de force, a literary testament that combines a "scientific" worldview with a passionately Chinese flair in its narrative form and social commitment. His explanation of why he decided to write a life of Jesus when there were
so many versions on the market is revealing.[7] First, he wrote, no Chinese has so
far produced their own original vision, "shedding the conventions of the west."[8]
Zhao also sensed that very few actually knew Jesus, even among Christians, in
part because of the difficulty of reading the Bible, with its "tangled threads and
fabricated, wild tales."[9] Translated Western books, including the lives of Jesus
available, just did not "scratch the itch." Zhao is even more specific in the third
reason: he wanted to do something for Chinese youth during an era of war and
deprivation. The biography was highly successful in this aim, published in at
least five editions by the Youth Association between 1935 and 1948. The final
reason is perhaps the most telling: "it is my own worship of Jesus." The book,
which took Zhao a mere twenty-two days to complete, was a deliberate attempt
at contextualization, an intellectual exercise *and* a personal confession, with

the aim of meeting a pastoral as much as a theological need. It stands as one of the purest expressions of Chinese Christianity, employing its own intellectual forms and interests in seeking to instill, or increase, faith. In turning away from pressing concerns and engaging deeply with Chinese poetic and philosophical traditions and with biblical scholarship, Zhao paradoxically produced a work of great immediacy.

Zhao wrote the *Life of Jesus* almost exactly halfway through his nonagenarian lifespan, during which deeply held views and beliefs were refined and transformed. It would be surprising if someone who had lived through the fall of empire, cultural revolution, war, and imprisonment had not undergone some evolution in thinking; but in Zhao's case, the label from his early, liberal period stuck with him into his neo-orthodox phase, and the early writings have strongly colored perceptions of his theological position—to Zhao's detriment in the wider Chinese church. Zhao's legacy has been contested by those who charge him with being too Christian, not Christian enough (an intellectual idealist, a government stooge), too Westernized, too quick to run back to Communist China in 1950.[10] The *Life of Jesus*, as others have noted, came during a period of brewing change for Zhao, which culminated around the time of his incarceration under the Japanese in 1941 in a modified stance toward his "worship of reason" and a return to more orthodox formulations of doctrines such as the divinity of Christ.[11] The trials of war and his own spiritual experiences during those years played out in a modified soteriology to privilege a transcendent God, a methodological shift deposing science as the supreme model of discourse, and a growing interest in revelation.

By the time Zhao wrote another biography, the *Life of St. Paul*, in 1947, he had come to believe that "the gospel of St. Paul is the unparalleled truth" and acknowledged "the greatest disciple's" views on Christ, salvation, and morality.[12] There is a transformation too in the form of Zhao's writing between Jesus and Paul, which sheds light on the earlier text. As Zhao suggests in the preface to the life of Paul, an intricate connection exists between theological form, content, and expression. A shift in faith position necessitated a different form of writing:

Before the emergency, when I wrote the *Life of Jesus* it was purely a literary composition, allowing the imagination to twist and turn: I was unbridled in penning the lines and applying the ink. Now as I write the *Life of St. Paul*, my methods have changed greatly, my thinking has undergone a polar shift, and what has been refined in the furnace, even if it is not yet gold, has been ridded of much dross. This current book is pure academic research; it takes historical realities as its guide: I hope it is a historical volume, and not a literary volume. Six months in captivity surpasses ten winters of strenuous study, and a thousand days of reading are like experiencing the mysterious darkness oneself. Compared with former times, my faith is deeper. Some say I've turned conservative; I myself feel that I have been renewed.[13]

What Zhao may not have seen so clearly at this point, so close to his work and to the experiences that had challenged his vantage point, was that the richness of the *Life of Jesus*, the multivalence that allows for theological ambiguity, would prove a deep channel for enduring truths.[14] Many would argue that Zhao wrote his best theology in the latter half of his tenure at Yanjing, yet one of the great gifts of his liberal phase, as this chapter explores, was its experimentation with sinicized narrative forms to express the new indigenized theology that he was trying to promote, undergirded by a strong belief in the theological rightness of this path.

At least four book-length systematic studies of Zhao's theology are extant, as well as a recent profusion of articles and essay collections.[15] He has been read as a harbinger of postcolonial resistance,[16] a Confucian-inspired proponent of mystical ethics,[17] an intercultural communicator between "East" and "West,"[18] and a continuing source of inspiration and influence for contemporary social morality in China.[19] There has been, however, little analysis of the literary talent that Zhao displays in his creation of a Chinese narrative out of the biblical accounts, or of the intricate play in the text between skeptical, rational scholar and intense admirer of Jesus of Nazareth.[20] The focus of this chapter is how the theological message is conveyed, including the literary structures and motifs that make the *Life of Jesus* such a generative text. These elements do not survive well in translation, but it is in the very structure of chapters, as well as in figures of speech and expressions such as the "four character phrases" beloved of literary writers, that this reads as a native Chinese text. The mode of narration extends to the depiction of character, as well as to time and chronology. Jesus's character especially is developed through a shifting third/first-person voice common to classical-language texts, allowing for an unmarked move from external narration to interiority. The depiction of Jesus and John the Baptist as *fuzi* 夫子, master, the term used for Confucius (Kong fuzi, master Kong) and other philosopher-teachers, places them in a certain frame of reference for readers. The text as a whole draws on the Chinese tradition of biography as a form of moral teaching, the constructed narration of a moral exemplar.

Three themes stand out in this experimental work and exhibit how Zhao developed his theology within a Chinese conception of the world. The first is the form of the narrative: the structure of the text, its focus on imagination, the use of particular Chinese imagery, and Zhao's distinctive reading of scripture. In the *Life of Jesus* we see a wrestling with both the gospel texts as transmitted and with the lacunae between episodes, while the naturalistic mode of explaining miracles has led many to brand Zhao "humanist" and leave the matter there, ignoring the multifaceted nature of his approach to the Bible. The second theme is a major focus of the work: the nature of Jesus's messiahship. This is central to Jesus's developing self-understanding and to the soteriology derived from it. It is also a prime area where we can see the circumstances of contemporary China at work, shaping Zhao's vision of the political machinations that drove Jesus to his self-realization. The third theme is more localized in the text but gives a Chinese literary vantage point in its reading of the land. Jesus's relationship to the physical land, as he traverses it, climbs up it, kneels down on it, and gazes out over it, is replete with echoes of the literatus poet, seeing where others have seen before. The depiction of the land of Israel displays Jesus's incarnated, localized humanity in a distinctly Chinese form.

FORMS OF NARRATIVE

"Knives are not for children," wrote Zhao Zichen.[21] The imagination is "the living spirit which produces wings that can soar in cloudy skies where there are no pathways; it can latch onto a fragment of shadow and generate a paragraph of literature"—and yet, it must be grounded in historical reality. In attempting to enter into the life of the saints, Zhao selects the two tools of reason and empathy. Those who accuse him of writing a novel, he suggests in the preface, "are right, and not right." Right, because in contemplating writing his own *Life*, he had at first intended to write a novel, and not right, because the *Life of Jesus* was constructed in a historical manner, and Jesus's acts and words are based in critical readings of the biblical texts. In all biographical writing, the author suggests to his implied critics, there is a point at which the imagination soars. Here, the caveat is that "the imagination must have been baptized in the blood of Jesus."[22] Imagination, developed out of the perspective of historical truth, but narrated with an emotional rationale, prompted Zhao to capture such "fragments of shadow" as those limning Mary Magdalene in the gospels and create from them events that appear true to life, even if they are not historically verifiable. It was a move out of kilter with the contemporary literary emphasis on realism, but with strong precedent.

Two significant changes occurred in the writing of biography at the turn of the twentieth century, opening the way for Zhao's work and its questions on imagination and historical truth. The first was a change in the nature of Chinese historiography, of which biography had been a dominant component. Historians became less focused on biography as the core of their work as the notion of history as the record of state and the lives of its officials was transformed with the erosion of Confucian tradition and discourse. This enabled the second change: a more unified life-writing that drew together different aspects of the subject into one text, and an interest in the writing of biography as literature, outside the old rules of historical writing.[23] Zhao drew on the new formal possibilities for biography writing that Liang Qichao, Zhang Mosheng, and others had explored in severing biography from state service, while retaining some sense of the moral exemplar present in the traditional form. The *Life of Jesus* (*Yesu zhuan*) is titled a *zhuan* (傳), a term that traditionally did not connote biography in "the sense of a rounded portrait of a personality in the context of his time and milieu."[24] Traditional Chinese biographies emphasized, rather, "moral, literary, scholarly and official" achievements, while drawing a veil over private lives;[25] their functions were commemorative (recording achievements and personality for surviving descendants) and didactic (providing a positive model for emulation or a minatory one for avoidance).[26] Biographies written by relatives or friends for tomb inscriptions or family histories might, if the subjects were prestigious or had performed their functions as officials or family members exceptionally well, be taken up and honored by inclusion in the standard histories of each dynasty. These formulaic official biographies depicting meritorious actions served as manuals for officials and would-be officials in a belief system where state harmony depended on the virtue of ruler and officials.

It would scarcely have been possible to write a Chinese *zhuan* of Jesus before the historiographical and literary reforms of the late Qing and early Republic. With no official titles or post as a scholar-statesman to write of, and few of the characteristics expected of an exemplar,[27] Jesus and his life subverted the literary form and its conceptions. Writing a biography of Jesus in traditional China would have meant rewriting his life within Chinese norms of social behavior (*li* 理) and within the limited models available for biography (such as military leader, sage, or scholar-statesman). More informal biographical writing styles existed that paralleled unofficial histories and "proliferated on the borders between history and fiction,"[28] but character writing in traditional biography tended toward the ideal. By the late Qing, imported ideas of the Romantic individual and of biography as a life within a social and political context combined with adaptations from within Chinese tradition to form new "biographical monographs."[29] These interrogated their subjects' lives critically, allowed for development and change in the course of a life, and reinvigorated the question of how to depict the spirit of a subject truthfully via anecdote and novelistic techniques.[30] Whereas the great reformer and historian Liang Qichao believed that China needed a revolution in historiography to be saved,[31] Zhao Zichen deployed the revolution in historiography to depict the savior.

There is a fine line, for some critics, between the exercise of the imagination and the writing of potentially blasphemous or heretical fiction. The genius of Zhao's *Life of Jesus* lies precisely in its seamless weaving of the fragmentary biblical narrative together with interludes of imagined background to produce the sense of a greater whole, a narrative of novelistic depth. Vivid characterization and access to the interior musings of Jesus, against the backdrop of the Galilean landscape and Jewish customs, combine to create new convergences, new insights in the mind of the reader. The most extended imaginative interlude in the *Life* is the narration of Judas in Chapter 15, around two thousand characters of Chinese text, which fleshes out an incident that Zhao clearly felt remained obscure in the biblical text. Here Judas is not the evil traitor the scriptural récit might lead us to believe; more in keeping with his Zealot character, he is instead a thwarted revolutionary whose desire for a different type of action from that envisaged by Jesus, and for a more critical, heroic role for himself, led him to make a deal with the high priest's scout—a deal that the temple leaders renege just as soon as it is made. Judas emerges in Zhao's *Life of Jesus* as a gullible firebrand, chastened by Jesus's correction but still strategizing for the outcome of the revolution—an easy target for a scheming high priest.

The eighteen chapters of the *Life of Jesus* are thematically and chronologically arranged such that the reader follows Jesus through his life, but the chapters are formed around gathered material so that, for example, Chapter 5 coheres around liberation, Chapter 6 the law, and Chapter 8 the Word.[32] Zhao's wrestling in the preface with how to write a life sets out the academic and theological fault lines that exercised him. This is both defense against a projected charge of letting fiction intrude into exegesis and an explanation of the way in which Zhao sees God speaking through human responses to a text. If history makes sense of facts and emotions, the imagination is still needed, for Zhao, to interpret those facts—an imagination that causes "creativity to struggle with the truth, becoming indivisible from it."[33] This becomes akin to an explanation of revelation, a means of understanding how humans receive the truths of God. Giving rein to the imagination is not an anti-intellectual stance—Zhao takes umbrage at Christians who use passages such as Jesus "making wisdom unintelligible to the wise but accessible to children" to criticize scholars employed in serious biblical research—but a necessary tool for interpretation, alongside historical data. Without imagination, asks Zhao, how could we ever make sense of passages such as Judas's suicide fewer than twelve hours after selling Jesus or fathom the real reason for Herod killing John? The intellect, insists Zhao, encompasses the imagination, which can be life-giving and faith-stimulating.

The narration of character in the *Life of Jesus* relies on a combination of imagination and emotional common sense. Joseph, for example, is not the absent figure of legend but is emotionally much closer than Mary to their son. Joseph, we are told, is taciturn but full of spirit and hot-blooded — it was he who gave Jesus the name "Joshua," savior, wanting God's people delivered from foreign rule.[34] Joseph has a greater role in child-rearing and character formation than could be gleaned from biblical accounts, and arguably one more in keeping with Chinese father-son relationships, but there are limits to his abilities to raise a prodigy. When Jesus asks difficult questions about God's anger and the retributive aspects of the law, Joseph gives no response, and Jesus drops the questions. Mary, busy with the other children, does not have much time for Jesus but sees that he and Joseph get on well in their shared silences. Characterization is inevitably more novelistic than in the gospel accounts: characters in the *Life of Jesus* voice gospel verses and quote freely from the psalms, but readers are also privileged to their interior thoughts and comments, while narrative flow is suspended from time to time by introjections from the commentating narrator / implied author.

Narration throughout the text segues from commentary to description, from third-person narrator to authorial voices, in a style familiar to readers of traditional literature from the late Qing or of popular low-brow literature. It is a speculative voice, with enough ambiguity to instill a cautious attitude toward historical veracity. Jesus went up to the temple a year early, at age twelve, not thirteen, for example, perhaps because Joseph thought that "he was already tall and man enough, with enough knowledge to take responsibility" or perhaps because several of their friends and relatives were going up early that year.[35] The ambiguity is heightened by slippage between the voices of narrator and characters and by the potential for the implied author to theologize through Jesus's own musings. When Jesus comes out of the waters of the Jordan, for example, and heads off to the desert to think, the transition between his own reflections and those of the narrator is unclear. Likewise, in Jesus's exchange with Nicodemus, the unmarked switches in narration between voices are evident. Nicodemus, who has just addressed Jesus as *fuzi*, master, has taken him literally regarding a second birth and is corrected, in a voice which could be that of Jesus, or the narrator, or his own later recollection.[36] In Zhao's *Life* the secondary reflection is a composite part of the text, in the manner of historians' comment in traditional biographies, and moments of theological insight (those of both Jesus and the narrator/author) are woven into the narrative, producing a more overtly theological text than the gospel accounts.

While Zhao's comment in the preface—"all that Jesus said, and did, was poetry, with the flavor of a novel"—is more a theological than literary statement, an awareness of the particularity of language suffuses the *Life of Jesus*.[37] Chinese sayings and proverbs are scattered throughout, making the text feel like a Chinese-language composition. John the Baptist is "like an unmovable Mount Tai";[38] Jesus understands that the hatred between Jews and Samaritans had to be cast "beyond the ninth heaven";[39] the temptation to call for superficial reform, to crowd-pleasing tricks, is a proverbial one "to change the liquid but not the drugs."[40] Where the setting may be easily sinicized (i.e., nativized, in translation terms), extended sections of Chinese imagery come into play. In describing the banquet scene where Herodias's daughter dances for Herod, the girl is done up "like a spring prunus tree"; her dancing "like a swallow skimming a wave," "a flying oriole catching butterflies"; and her singing like dew weeping on a lotus flower in full bloom, a soughing wind through green bamboo.[41] Such poetic phrases produce the image of familiar, generic banquet scenes from the Chinese past. These images do not exoticize, since these are standard figures of speech, but set the scene of an elegant banquet given for the Galilean hierarchies, with just a touch of the courtesan in the girl's attire and shimmering dance. It is not only the narrative architecture that shows Chinese traces: the temple at the Capernaum synagogue, built by a Roman official, sports eagle mountings alongside Jewish candle stands, with two crouching lions at the entrance and a wide flight of stone steps between, the main door facing south—all of the trappings needed to demonstrate that Jesus is supreme ruler, the rightful (Chinese) emperor.[42]

Each chapter in Zhao's *Life of Jesus* is headed by a phrase from the classical corpus. These provide a depth of layering, another perspective on the biblical texts, a commentary from within the Chinese tradition, and link the story of Jesus's life into that tradition by the resonances created. Chapter 3, for example, begins by describing John the Baptist turning away from his father's profession as priest, on account of hieratic hypocrisy, and initiating his populist movement to prepare for the world to come. The chapter, which moves to Jesus's baptism, is headed by the phrase "[and the mind] in its entire substance and relations to things, will be perfectly intelligent."[43] This quotation, from Zengzi's commentary on the *Daxue* (Great Learning) of Confucius, comes from the chapter "On Perfecting Knowledge," a discourse known to any classically educated child. The *Daxue*, which became one of the canonical Four Books when Zhu Xi published it separately in the Song dynasty, speaks to the rulership of the benevolent and the cultivation of virtue as a mode of transforming the morals of the world, beginning with the emperor himself. The preceding part of the quotation tells how the Great Learning instructs the learner:

> in regard to all things in the world, to proceed from what knowledge he has of their principles, and pursue his investigation of them, till he reaches the extreme point. After exerting himself in this way for a long time, he will suddenly find himself possessed of a wide and far-reaching penetration. Then, the qualities of all things, whether external or internal, the subtle and the coarse, will all be apprehended, and the mind, in its entire substance and its relation to things, will be perfectly intelligent.

As Jesus comes out of the Jordan River in Zhao's *Life of Jesus*, he undergoes an "unimaginable, great enlightenment that gave perfect clarity [/intelligence] to both mind and body," echoing the passage above. The narrative continues:

> The skies were an endless dark, and a brilliant light shone on his head, as if God's heart/mind were opening up toward him. He felt that God had alighted in his heart, like a dove flying down from the skies. He heard a voice say to him, "You are my child, in whom I delight." Whether this was a heavenly voice, a human voice, the voice of his heart, or whether it was the voice emitted by the soul of the universe, Jesus knew that he was God's son, he saw this clearly and understood it without a doubt, his face full of light.[44]

The Buddhist overtones of the "great enlightenment" that Jesus experiences are clear, but Jesus's epiphany at baptism is also linked through the chapter title to the Confucian (Ruist) perfection of knowledge, to the perfect comprehension of all things, and through this, in the light of Zhu Xi's commentary and the reading history of the text, to moral perfection and to the right to rule.

The chapter does not dwell explicitly on the resonances, and no mention is made in the body of the text, but the heading or epigraph is there for anyone who wants to explore the implications, as the chapter moves on to Jesus cogitating in the desert on his growing understanding that if he is God's son, all can be God's children, and all can experience liberation from smoke and fog, sin and evil. Elsewhere, in an essay titled "Jesus and the Reality of God," Zhao muses on why Western theologians have not made more of the "greatest discovery ever made by a human being, the discovery of true humanity as true divinity."[45] Comparing the significance to Buddhists of the enlightenment of Gautama with Jesus's vision at baptism, Zhao writes how Jesus at that moment of baptism grasped "for the first time in the history of human experience, that the thoroughly and utterly human humanity of a true loving man was the Son of God, yea, 'the very God of very God.'" It seems, Zhao inferred, that thinkers in the West "wished Jesus to start into the world as God" and did not think the wonderful discovery of God dwelling among humanity necessary.[46]

Other chapter headings are taken from a variety of source texts—poetry, philosophies, histories—showing Zhao's erudition in the range of referents open to him, but also following the novelistic precedent where allusive poetic couplets begin each chapter to intrigue readers or provide comment on the content. Chapter 4 is headed by a line of poetry from the Tang dynasty wall poem "A Buddhist Retreat Behind Broken-Mountain Temple," by Chang Jian: "The first rays of sunlight shone on the high forest." The poem describes the solitude of this temple, up winding paths, and the silence, broken only by the sounding of the monk's chime. Chapter 5 is headed "The thousand league iron chain sinks to the bottom of the river." The line is half of a couplet from the poem "Cherishing the Past at Xisai Mountain," and the poem refers to the conquest of the Wu state by the Eastern Jin in 280, an event that reunified the nation under the Jin.[47] The great defensive chain of iron across the Three Gorges of the Yangzi River failed to stop the invading Jin forces, whose military intelligence allowed them to send in rafts to burn through the iron before their three-story galleons passed by. Chapter 5 reveals Jesus as liberator, the one who breaks through the heaviest iron chains, who releases a people bound mentally and physically, subject both to Roman rule and to individual failings: "from their various bindings, everyone's heart was struggling to break free—illness, fear, poverty, ignorance— and selfish, self-serving sin, and the precepts of the Law as fine as an ox hair, around their hearts like a chain of a thousand links, layer after layer binding them."[48] The reference in the chapter heading to the iron chains across the Yangzi, the symbolic last resistance to the unification of the country, adds a political angle to the binding. The inclusion of a careful selection of classical references for chapter headings is a didactic as well as literary tool for Zhao: his student audience can appreciate how their own intellectual heritage may be used to comment on and add a depth of response to the biblical text.

READING SCRIPTURE

If Zhao's construction of his biography of Jesus draws on both traditional elements of Chinese narrative and contemporary debates on historical writing, his reading of scripture is likewise informed by critical scholarship and literary creativity. Two aspects of Zhao's reading of scripture are particularly noteworthy and contribute to the overall construction of the narrative. The first is simply the rearrangement of biblical episodes into a single narrative, which creates new resonances and meaning. The second is also in part a function of a continuous narrative but is primarily a theological statement: the downplaying of the miraculous.

In the preface to his *Life of Jesus* Zhao sets out a vision of writing that combines detailed textual and historical knowledge, including that of noncanonical gospels and other authors of antiquity, with an empathy that allows an imaginative transcendence of period and viewpoint. For Zhao, "theology has its own truth," while the subjective position should ideally be avoided in writing history.[49] Zhao regards the gospel of John, for example, of little use as source material for the biography because it was written "so that people may believe" and because its stress on the transcendent ensures that the primary meaning of miracles in the Johannine texts is not to be found in their historicity. The guiding principle for Zhao, in the absence of scriptural detail, was "to assume as a matter of course"—which seems to mean assuming that normal human and scientific relationships govern events unless there is specific reason to believe otherwise.[50]

A characteristic aspect of Zhao's reading of scripture is his creative rearrangement of scriptural units. The imagination is not, here, wild speculation, but re-creating the setting and the sequence in which events took place in a way that makes new and often better sense. Sometimes the narrative scene itself provides the context for linking different portions of scripture. Jesus wends toward Jerusalem through several chapters during the last months of his life. He is worried about the disciples' lack of urgency and chagrined that no one truly understands or is able to share his angst: in Chinese terms, he has no soul mate who "understands the tune" (*zhiyin* 知音). Jesus's interior monologue follows a trajectory from the difference between the disciples' understanding of the nature of the Messiah and his own, to irritation at their jockeying for position in a kingdom they have barely grasped, to an exteriorization in parables:

> the whole way along the road, the disciples had been whispering away to each other, discussing the question of rewards. One said: I came in earliest, so my stint of duty has been longer, and I should get a higher reward. Another said, no, even though I came in later, it was at the most arduous and busy period, and I bore the complaints and the hard work, so I should get greater favor. Jesus couldn't help but be dispirited by this, so spoke to them in a parable: "The kingdom of Heaven is like a master, who went out early one morning to hire laborers for his vineyard. He settled on a rate of one denarius per day with the workers . . ." (Matthew 20:1–16).[51]

Here, the parable where the latecomers are paid just as much as those working the whole day is specifically directed at the disciples, whereas the gospel text gives no immediate context. Jesus continues to muse on the realization that after he is gone, the disciples will be beset by squabbles over their relative contributions to the cause and their leadership standing. Recalling the experience of Herod Archelaus, whose absence in Rome as he went to present his claim to the throne gave the Jews the opportunity to revolt, and who brutally massacred his opponents on his return, Jesus said, "A certain nobleman went off on a distant journey. . . ." The parable of the talents follows, in the Lucan version. The context for the parable is still the disciples' bickering along the way, but the frame of Jesus's recollection of the history of Herod the Great's son shifts the emphasis away from the "master," whose role in this gospel passage (as God) proved difficult for so many later readers.

The style of continuous prose in a coherent narrative, rather than chapters, verses, and individual pericopes, joins passages in new sense units. In Chapter 13, approaching Jerusalem for the Passover festival, Jesus and the disciples are traveling through Hellenized towns where the children think that Jesus looks like the Greek gods in their temple and run over, dragging their mothers, to see him. The disciples try to shoo them off, but Jesus lets them pull his beard and rub his pate, pointing out that all in God's kingdom live as these—as alive as "living dragons and active tigers," not the clay statues and wooden figures their parents have become—and warns that anyone who wants to inherit the kingdom must become childlike.[52] The chapter heading reads "Finds an intimate place in their midst"; the full quotation from the Song dynasty Neo-Confucian Zhang Zai's celebrated *Western Inscription* is "Heaven is my father and Earth is my mother, and even such a small creature as I finds an intimate place in their midst."[53] The chapter deftly combines the question put to Jesus of "what must I do to inherit eternal life?" with a meditation on the nature of riches and the need to be known, to find one's place, on earth and in the kingdom.

In another re-created narrative sequence, we are told that many rich Jews live in the Greek towns, and among them is a "young capitalist" who comes to Jesus seeking life. The gospel quotations are a composite of the accounts in Mark 10 and Luke 18. In Zhao's version, when Jesus tells the man to go sell all he has and come follow him, the rich young man probes further. The man's wealth has put him in danger, responds Jesus: the kingdom and the poor need his help. Anyone wanting eternal life has to take risks.[54] The man reckons up a while, his face first red, then ashen, but he cannot come to any decision and slopes off sadly. Zhao's text continues in the vein of the Marcan account, with the disciples being told they will receive many fold in return for all they have given up, before intercalating a passage in which Jesus muses on the nature of sacrifice. A scribe puts the question a second time to Jesus: what must I do to inherit life? Jesus questions him as to the law and receives the celebrated response: "Love the Lord your God with all your heart, mind, and soul and strength, and love your neighbor as yourself." To the follow-up question, who is my neighbor? Jesus responds with the parable of the good Samaritan.

An extended discussion on the right use of wealth is continued the next morning as Zaccheus appears in the thread. Zhao's reading is psychologically acute: Zaccheus stands up at the banquet he hosts for Jesus that evening and explains, unprompted, why he is about to give half of his wealth away. In his rambling account, Zaccheus tells how no one had ever trusted him before or given him any encouragement or opportunity to repent. Now, he no longer needs to extort wealth: for the first time in his life he had found a *zhiji* 知己, someone who understood him. The chapter concludes with the disciples traveling on from Jericho to Bethany and the well-known scene at Mary and Martha's, where Martha scolds her sister for not helping. Mary understands, as the narrator suggests, that Jesus's need for comfort for his grief is greater than his need for food or rest. Jesus, too, has found his *zhiji*.[55] Juxtaposing texts on wealth with passages on the need to be loved produces here a deft theological commentary.

A noticeable effect of the novelizing of the scriptural text is to downplay the supernatural. The filling in of logical lacunae, of narrative aporia, diminishes the effect of the miraculous present in the spare biblical accounts. This fleshing out of the Bible makes obvious what is self-evident to Zhao in a retroactive writing: that Jesus knew his cousin John; that he was friends with James and John; that when he met up with Peter, Andrew, James, and John long before their lakeside call, he used to tell them about how God would save Israel. Here there is no sudden appeal to unknown youths who drop their nets, mesmerized, as readings of the biblical stories might indicate, but a reminder that Jesus's work as a carpenter took him around the villages and into people's houses to work, an important preparatory time of listening and building up a picture of human needs and hopes. In the *Life of Jesus*, it is talk of John baptizing, and the realization that his siblings are grown up and no longer need him to shoulder the family burden, that galvanizes Jesus's mission. When John says to Jesus, "Why you? You are the motive force for the new era—why do you want to show your repentance and be baptized?"[56] prior knowledge of his cousin helps the text make sense and shows how the truncated biblical narrative renders events more miraculous by the force of terseness.

Making events more concrete also makes the narrative seem more human and less supernaturally divine. When Jesus tells his brothers "No, I'm not going up to the temple," but then goes anyway, the process of very human decision-making that takes him to this point is made explicit.[57] There is nothing deceitful in changing one's mind in Zhao's analysis, no lessening of divinity in the process of reasoned calculation; but again, the authoritative version of events in any one gospel is made more multivalent in the fuller novelistic narration. Just as the narrative context around each of Jesus's parables is reclaimed, aspects that might not be clear in biblical accounts—the injunction to the disciples not to go into Samaria, for example—are clarified in the *Life,* as Zhao creates new patterns and themes through his careful redaction of the biblical narratives.

Natural explanations of miracles abound, in the most prominent recasting of scriptural texts. Zhao repeatedly uses the formula "people said. . . ." As Jesus wanders deeper into the mountains, alone, after his baptism, his mind is filled with questioning. Full of the knowledge of God with him, Jesus "wasn't hungry or thirsty; he didn't eat and didn't drink, didn't sleep yet wasn't tired, because his mind/heart was fixed purely in another realm. Later, people passed on the saying that he didn't eat and didn't drink for forty days and nights as he thought."[58] Zhao undercuts the miraculous but leaves enough leeway in his writing for alternative interpretations. A commotion among pigs, ever herd creatures, causes them to leap off the Gennesaret cliff, and "people said" it was because "the legion" from the exorcised man had gone into them. Jesus remains silent on the topic.[59] It seemed to the disciples, out on the lake one misty morning, as though Jesus was walking on water, not wading along the shoreline, and "people said" that he had crossed by sea. When the people's consciousness is tested through public shaming, in the example of a small boy bringing out his few loaves and fishes to share, "the disciples said that Jesus had used five loaves and two fish, and fed five thousand,"[60] which, in a manner of speaking, he had. The Transfiguration, the great moment of holy communion with Moses and Elijah, in this the "greatest miracle" (Aquinas) is an effect of the trees casting silhouettes next to Jesus under the bright mountain light; natural light rather than a heavenly aura bedazzles the semicomatose disciples.

For Zhao, Jesus's acts of miraculous healing come from an ordered life. It is his sense of mission that gives Jesus unimagined strength; "his healings were originally a most rational, most natural event."[61] In the text there is a subtle interplay between the human and the divine, a permeability between what can be wrought by (a Confucian-style) strength of character and the possibility of transcendent intervention, but all is governed by a principled agnosticism regarding the rupturing of scientific laws. In commenting on the healing of the woman who has been hemorrhaging for twelve years, the narrator notes:

A sincere empathy, a miraculous character, pure faith, a loving touch: what these can bring about is beyond people's expectations. . . . Or is there something else, transcending current knowledge, at work? The universe is truly open and not closed; does it just wait for a divine person to lead people across the boundaries of life? Or is there no such thing, in the end? . . . Can what happened in ancient times really not happen now?[62]

In its discussion of the Word, Chapter 8 develops this theme of the unity in Jesus of word and action that enables a life of unexplainable good, just as words are the interface between the world of spiritual mysteries and what can be seen and touched. A life lived in the impossible demands a deep trust in humans as well as God. This combination of empathy, living touch, and prayerful motivation toward the impossible changes lives. Mary Magdalene is a case in point. A figure to whom Zhao returns in his writings, she is portrayed as a hard-bitten local girl. The seven devils that others see in her include "the lazy devil," "the drunkard devil," and "the crying-and-laughing devil," "but in fact, none of this was true." One day as she is venting her spleen, Jesus listens to others telling him about her:

> . . . he stood still, looking at her amid the others. His eyes alighted on her body, and she saw; she suddenly stopped laughing and crying, opened wide two round, surprised eyes, and shouted out loudly "Enough!" In a trice, she had run back home. She had, in Jesus, in the eternity of that brief moment, obtained what ordinary women cannot obtain, life in the heart of the universe, in a man's heart. Later, Jesus met with her a few times and explained to her his aspirations and his task. At this, she settled down and became an amiable and agreeable person. Because of this, people said that Jesus had cured her, and expelled the seven demons from her.[63]

Jesus's openness acts as a channel of self-discovery and healing for others; exactly where the miracle lies may be determined by the reader.

JESUS AS MESSIAH

The realization that Jesus is the Son of God pounds through the text. It plays constantly on Jesus's mind and is tied to the question of his mission, of how to use his status to save—and of what that salvation means within a limited, human realm. The *Life of Jesus* starts with the people of Israel and their historic sense of mission. Surrounded on all sides, in exile, their temple destroyed, the Jewish people never sold out, never damaged their soul, comments the narrator; scattered, they forged new lives. The Jews had historically lived without the force of arms, yet were united in their revolutionary aim. Political compromise, muses the implied author, is not a religious option.[64] As Jesus grapples with what sort of Messiah he is to be, he turns over scriptural passages as well as contemporary expectations. Early on in the *Life* he has no doubt that he had justice on his side — but being handed over and shedding blood "was not his business."[65] Jesus's developing sense of his role is prefigured in the depiction of faithful Jews holding onto hope in despair and in a quotation from Enoch 1 of the hymn of return (Enoch is a key text for the expression "Son of Man").[66]

The image of a chain binding the people recurs in the narrative, linking different aspects of Jesus's messianic liberation. The first instance comes in the context of Jesus's developing understanding of the divide between the old, angry vision of God, controlled by priestly knowledge, and the new vision governed by love. Jesus's concept of liberation draws momentum from John the Baptist, who acts as a theological fulcrum.[67] If, as Jesus now understood, all could gain God, would this not be the living embodiment of the kingdom? "But there were layer after layer of bindings around the people, an iron chain that a thousand ox-power could not break." John wanted to liberate the people of Israel with a gospel of repentance, which was "like attacking the chain with a thousand-pound hammer."[68] John called the Jewish people "venomous lizards, scorpions" and told of God's anger and imminent punishment, a move that was "rational, but not entirely accurate." It was right that people should repent, of course, but that God would pour his anger on the whole world "was surely a misunderstanding, passed on by the Jewish teachers."[69] Zhao's ventriloquism is at its strongest here in the contested terrain of eschatology, and his vision of the New Covenant comes in strikingly concrete language.

The imagery of the iron chain returns as Jesus walks mountain paths to remote villages, preaching and teaching. Here the bindings are illness, fear, and ignorance. Echoes of the rural reality of China sound as Zhao describes the ghosts and demons that the Galilean peasants fear more than Rome, and Marxist rhetoric in Jesus's awareness of how the liberation of minds was much more important than that of bodies in building the kingdom.[70] The important task for Jesus was to spread the new thought and create a new spirit: the Messiah's role, as Jesus comes to understand it, was to enlighten the masses, fighting against those who have political power, with a consciousness of God's truth. The Kingdom of Heaven *is* the life of the masses. His understanding, underscores the narrator, was different from that of others of his time: the Kingdom of Heaven was to grow from the kernel of hope and develop and change toward an unseen future. The seed lay in people's hearts, waiting. This kingdom was not to be brought about by a ready-made Messiah, coming on clouds from heaven, nor by violent struggle, but in the hearts of the masses.[71] The Jewish people were looking to God to save them in ways beyond human power, a god-sent angel, a Davidian warrior; but Jesus saw that if Israel carried on its inimical stance, it would end up in a bloody battle, with the people wiped out under the "iron-clad horses and the metal spears of Rome."[72]

If Jesus's developing sense of the Messiah's role was based in a pragmatic ethic, the narrow nationalism of the Jewish people remained a problem in the schema. Jesus prayed daily for the salvation of Israel but "felt that God was the God of the whole world; all humankind were brothers" and that Israel "couldn't willfully act as it liked." Jesus's mature understanding is unequivocal: "What was clear was that the salvation of Israel absolutely could not rely on military force . . . the only means of salvation was a new human life, a new mentality."[73] Toward the end of his reflection on the meaning of the Messiah, as Jesus faces up to the "failure" of the campaign in Galilee, he accepts that the failure is not for lack of a strategy or because of idealism; the causes of failure lie in the ac-commodationist policies of Jerusalem—the stubborn adherence to old ways of the Pharisees, the base materialism of the masses. Jesus's failure is Israel's fail-ure. His task is to cause Israel to awaken, and in circling back to Isaiah, quoted at length, he comes to a deeper understanding that failure is also a part of being Christ; that just as Israel's mission is to bear pain and sin, so it is his mission too—salvation lies in the sacrifice of throwing away his own life in order to awaken the masses.[74]

Jesus's understanding of his ministry was far from this kenotic vision at the outset, and much narrative suspense hangs on the transition. When Peter an-swers Jesus's question "who do people say I am?" with the affirmation that he is the Messiah, it is, the text tells us, a revelation so far from the understanding of people of the time (who among the Jews could think of the Messiah being killed? and killed by *priests*?) that it "had to be of God." Jesus symbolically hands over the keys to Peter, "and the key to the kingdom is love, love that gives up itself, gives up life . . . not power, or glory, or any other unfathomable secret or esoteric thought,"[75] but a kingdom built on the very life of Christ. Gradually, cumulatively, Jesus comes to realize that his "white-hot love" for the people brings a willingness to throw his life away.[76]

The gospel of the kingdom liberates the people from the stranglehold of re-ligious professionals, and especially the authority of those professionals to de-termine what is of God. Jesus's first task is to conscientize the people. In the healing of the paralytic, Jesus, psychologically acute, sees into the minds of the scribes and Pharisees and understands how liberation from their author-ity to define sin is critical. His healing of the man lowered through the roof challenges their definitions and power, in this "his first clash with the Jewish authorities."[77] Later, as Jesus watches the whites of the Pharisees' eyes and the downturn of their lips when he tells the story of the prodigal son, the narratorial voice reminds that while the Israelites moan about the Romans, they oppress their own in the same manner. As the Israelites are criticized for looking down on others while themselves being fettered by prejudice, a critique resounds of Chinese oppression of their own in the aftermath of the White Terror.

Because healing and liberation are linked, lengthy discussions of the Sabbath accompany Jesus's ministry. Several healings are gathered in Chapter 5, where the narrator tells readers how the Sabbath was "the most ossified of Jewish systems," where even walking in a field was impossible, since treading on a stalk constituted a mini form of plowing. Keeping the Sabbath had become a matter of class status and pride, as it excluded the common people.[78] This is the crux of the tension for Jesus, always on the side of the *minzhong*, the masses.[79] Liberation is needed from the arrogance of the Pharisees, who believe that the commoners neither understand nor keep the law. One Sabbath, knowing that the Pharisees and scribes are watching, Jesus theatrically heals a man who has a withered hand, revealing himself as "a dangerous element," "a most dangerous, most fearful revolutionary."[80]

The last link in the chain completes the circle. As a child, Jesus had grasped the primacy of love, embodied through the actions of his parents, during his overstay at the temple. Seeing the pain of his parents and their panic at the thought of losing him was formative for Jesus: on witnessing their anguish he felt the "pure love" in their grief. While the gospel narrative focuses on the wonder of the boy genius in the temple and Mary's anxiety and relief, the lesson that Jesus absorbs in Zhao's *Life* is quite different, as he is brought to the subjective center. This experience of love profoundly shapes his ministry and enables him later to cut off ties with his family when they challenge that ministry. "Jesus knew that his family cared about him deeply, but also that they were deeply mistaken. The depths of human tragedy lie precisely in this," laments the narrator.[81] Jesus's life and heart/mind belong to the kingdom and the people of the kingdom. The first deliverance that Jesus must perform is his own, a self-liberation from family ties, which unbinds all else. "The last link in the iron chain, the most solid link, had been broken, and with a clanging noise, fell in pieces on the mountain rocks."[82] For Chinese readers, recently "emancipated" from the bonds of the five Confucian relations, the clanging was sonorous indeed.

While Zhao's Jesus comes to understand that he must turn away from the two prevailing notions of the Messiah — as military liberator, leading the fight for freedom from Roman rule, and as heaven-sent, coming down from the clouds — the vision of Christ's role is colored by the instabilities of a China in the throes of civil war. Chapter 10 focuses on the implementation of Jesus's manifesto: his step-by-step, logical preparation for the kingdom. For Zhao, human strategizing is no less spiritual a mode of discernment and is undergirded by prayer. (Zhao's own project in writing the *Life*, to encourage the youth of China to come to their own awareness and to theologize through their own literary imaginations, is a tested move.) The interior strategizing of Jesus, subsumed in the biblical text, is detailed throughout the biography. In the winter of 28 CE, for example, according to the timeline of the text, Jesus is weighing how, when, and why to return to Jerusalem. The vocabulary is of a strategic retreat, of overwintering in Galilee. The key question now for Jesus is how to get the masses and the people to realization (*juewu* 覺悟, awareness, consciousness)[83] before Herod gets to him. Jesus knows that agrarian families will be inside over winter, and he and his disciples can go from household to household spreading the message. The disciples, who are to be his "embodiment" if he is killed, have met the key people they need to meet and have been once to every town and village in the area; as the network grows, they are now sent out two by two.[84] Jesus, writes Zhao, also sent some disciples to mingle among the receiving groups and re-port back to him how the teams were doing—a credible strategy among survey groups and Nationalist-era leaders, but one absent from the biblical account. Jesus may have excluded a pugnacious role for the Messiah, but his strategizing is highly programmatic, calling to mind the long history of Chinese texts of military advice.

READING THE LAND

Throughout his essays in the 1920s, Zhao Zichen had referred to the need for a Chinese literature to nourish the Chinese church, "a literature that has life, is touched by the throbbing Chinese heart, and can touch other Chinese hearts because it comes out of the subtle life material of the ancient Chinese."[85] In the *Life of Jesus*, Zhao quotes Chinese proverbs and metaphors and alludes to the classics, but one of the most striking features of the text is the character-ization of the land. Early in the text the land is surveyed, like an account from a Chinese local gazetteer, with elevation, population density, and soil quality as-sessed from Josephus and others.[86] Jesus, we discover, reads the land as Chinese literati might: he reads the history of the Israelites into the places that he stands looking out over and is provoked to his own spiritual reflections and insights by the terrain.[87] Travel writers in late imperial China came to respond to place as a web of literary memories. The landscape became a repository of texts: both figuratively, as each writer added a layer to the known set of texts about a certain place, and literally, as poets and politicians alike carved inscriptions onto the rocks at scenic or historically important spots. Jesus's peregrinations in the hills, his prayer retreats on mountains, and his gaze out over the land are described time and again in the biography, taking on a distinctly Chinese form.

The concept of travel, or the journey, is subordinate in classical literature to the greater notion of the landscape. The interaction between traveler, landscape, and textual record is what counts.[88] Travel meant experiencing the famous mountains and great rivers for oneself and *simultaneously* traveling through China's mythico-literary landscape. What sets the Chinese case apart is the frequent inscription of the textual landscape onto the physical landscape. Almost every famous scenic spot has a couplet or literary inscription carved into the stone or engraved on a temple plaque, and part of the reason for travel becomes literary or aesthetic pilgrimage, travel to a certain mountain to see a fine example of famous calligraphy. The landscape is ever changing, because each new pilgrim increases the depth of allusion and thus the beauty of the scene. The contemporary visitor climbing the Fragrant Hills just northwest of Beijing, for example, passes numerous plaques carrying Xu Zhimo's poetic description of those hills; the hills become for the visitor those viewed by a 1920s romantic. As the landscape becomes a repository of literary memories, the pleasure of travel is the pleasure of participating in this ongoing process of artistic creation and memorializing, of forming the notion of what it means to be a connoisseur of the landscape, and therefore of China. In the *Life of Jesus*, the process is a theological sedimentation, as Jesus gazes his way through the history of his people, overlain onto the land surface itself.

Early in Chapter 2 we see the dual possibilities of the landscape: Nazareth nestles on beautiful mountain slopes, its simple houses dotted around like sheep meandering across the slope, but the region also foments banditry and uprising, with Rome swooping down on Judas son of Hezekiah in his base not far from Nazareth, picking off the rebels and leaving troops to burn the rest. Jesus, at age twelve, stands on the Mount of Olives, gazing at the imposing but beautiful "city of peace," his vision caught by a flash of gold—the setting sun reflecting off the armor of a Roman soldier. The landscape provides the contours of theological musing for the child Messiah as he contemplates the mission of God: the Mount Moriah stone, the Holy of Holies at the center of the world, and the Roman soldiers out in force for the festival.[89]

In landscape descriptions are lodged the hopes of, and for, the nation: defending the physical territory was defending the state.[90] China's strong sense of itself as a nation through to the present has been supported by this interaction between physical and literary associations. The landscape operates as gravel pit for nation and individual: through it, memories of the nation are filtered; through it, the individual filtrates his or her past. To revisit a place is inevitably to invite comparisons with one's former self. To visit a place for the first time in the (virtual, or textual) company of former writers is to revisit the place through their eyes, to align one's life and being with the literary traditions and values of those who have inhabited the textual-geosphere "China." As Jesus stands surveying the hills toward the east of the Jordan, the same formulation of the land is in play, both a geopolitical and a historical landscape—a land that comes alive as Jesus interacts with it through the filter of historical memory. At sixteen, Jesus is growing into a thoughtful youth. He goes walking on the Sabbath and talks to God in the silence. As he climbs and looks out over the land, he thinks about the revelation of God in Israel's history; he thinks on Moses and Deborah as he looks toward the sites in their stories:[91]

> Looking East, beyond the plains east of the River Jordan, he can imagine the tracks of his ancestor Abraham, and how he obeyed God's will, traveling to an unknown place. To the southeast, he can see the undulating hills of Gilead. Farther to the south was the territory of Moab, where Moses led the throngs of Israelites, looking to Canaan in the distance. Moses had not fulfilled his dream; to complete a great task, or establish one's merit, it was not always necessary to see the final outcome. Before Jesus's eyes was Mount Tabor; on the slopes of this mountain the prophetess Deborah once did great, startling things. Using the might of Barak's army, who came vertically down the mountain, she sank Sisera's war chariots in the foul mud, as if the constellations were helping Israel in their bloody battle. Looking south, Jesus could see the Esdraelon plain, and, indistinctly, the summit of Mount Gilboa peeking through. There Saul and his three sons Jonathan, Abinadab, and Malki-Shua gave their lives for the people of Israel. Saul, wounded, was unwilling to die at the hand of a Philistine, so fell on his own sword and died. See! Israel had both heroes and prophets. Mount Carmel, like a lion's head, protruded to the west. There Israel had bested the priests of Baal and rescued Israel's soul from freefall. To the north, the ridge of Mount Hermon stood out, blanketed in white cloud. How marvelous was God's handiwork! . . . What, finally, was God's great and eternal will for this sort of a world?[92]

Used as a narrative device to set the scene, and a theological one to retell important stories from the past that condition Jesus's thinking, the land is also a means of casting Jesus's frame of mind. Even when his mind wanders to the goods the lands produce and distant ports provide, he returns to the question of what this all means under God. The themes highlighted by the mountain peaks ranged around are not incidental. Land and the heroes evoked by it are intertwined. Jesus's imagination is caught by figures who obey God unconditionally, by the foreboding of a seemingly incomplete mission, by the possibilities of military power, by sacrifice. These are the triangulation points for his self-understanding as Messiah.

The land itself is also a cipher for morality. The caption heading for Chapter 6 of the *Life of Jesus* is a common poetic expression, "The mountains are high and the rivers long," a phrase that came to refer to the high moral qualities that cause a reputation to last.[93] Chapter 6 expounds love as the greater way, as Jesus teaches his understanding of the law and the prophets to the disciples, with an authority that "causes his listeners' hearts to leap" and understand that this is "a revelation of the heart of God."[94] The passage continues:

> These ideals come both from the quintessence of the law and prophets and their continuity through history, and from the discoveries of Jesus's unique, heaven-given nature, its brand new revelatory strength. A new character, new ideals, a new life: these peaks towered before the disciples: this was the coming of God, this was the Kingdom of Heaven, the new era.
>
> The white mist on the mountains slowly congealed on the tree tips. A tranquility lingered in the skies and on earth. Although Jesus and the disciples had already come down the mountains, the mountains still seemed to be filled with an unimaginable harmony. The path at the foot of the mountain wound around and came out into the open valley, while the other end receded into the green of the hills. In the wide valley, many people were waiting for Jesus. When they saw him coming down from the mountain with his disciples, they crowded around to walk alongside him. Soon they saw the sea, the Sea of Galilee. The seawater was often a tea green color; from a distance it looked like a sheet of crystal, held in a great basin of jade . . .

The passage flows naturally between Jesus's teachings, his exhortations to the disciples to bear good fruit, and descriptions of a landscape in perfect harmony and beauty.

The early philosophers contended to clarify the link between landscape and identity. Confucius is depicted as deliberating on the relationship between the land and the moral character of the nation. In another important passage in *Xunzi*, the sage sits watching the great river flowing east. The extended metaphor compares the attributes of the ideal *junzi* (his morality, aesthetic elevation) to that of one of China's great watercourses:

> Water is everywhere where there are living things, but it does not strive to be, in this it resembles virtue. It flows downwards: if its shores are constrained, it will still complete its course, like righteousness. It sparkles but doesn't overflow, like the Dao; if it is trammelled, it responds without a sound; it passes

through a hundred fathom valley without fear, like bravery. If you measure it, it will be even, like the law. When full, it does not seek to level out, like uprighteousness. It is gentle and submissive, yet humbly reaches its goal, like justice. You enter and exit by it, yet it remains fresh and pure, like goodness. It has ten thousand twists, yet still flows east, like the will. This is why when a *junzi* sees a great river he will gaze on it.[95]

Those who aspire to moral elevation, the basis for political power and advancement in the Confucian worldview, will model themselves on nature, and the act of reflecting on nature will ensure their correct moral development. This link between an appreciation of nature and the recognition of what that appreciation does to someone runs throughout "travel" literature. Confucius is recognized as the source for a maxim that sees different types of character resonating with different types of scenery: "The wise delight in water; the benevolent delight in mountains; the wise are active; the benevolent calm; the wise take delight, the benevolent live long."[96] As Jesus moves effortlessly between the hills and the water, drawing on both for his strength, they reveal him to be both benevolent and a wise teacher.

CONCLUSIONS

The English translator of Ernest Renan's *Life of Christ* wrote in the preface to that work in 1863: "The great problem of the present age is to preserve the religious spirit, whilst getting rid of the superstitions and absurdities that deform it, and which are alike opposed to science and common sense."[97] Following Renan, and in line with other theologians attempting to counter the negative force of the Anti-Christian Movement of the 1920s and 1930s, Zhao emphasized in his writings the rational and socially constructive aspects of Christianity.[98] This was a religion that could build on the humanistic and democratic aspirations of the youth movements, which could engage the intellect as well as the emotions of young Chinese and contribute to national well-being. The twin themes of liberation from political/imperialist oppression and of a rational, morally perfect humanity exemplified by Jesus espouse this approach. While Zhao Zichen was at home in the world church and its debates, he shared the aims and some of the vitriol of reformers. He had written in 1927: "Continued and unavoidable contact with the West with its aggressive and virulent civilization has convinced China of the necessity of a thorough-going revolution. She must at all costs turn away from the solid past toward an imagined future, from her ancient culture toward her new possibilities, which she must realize through her own understanding, determination and achievement."[99] Zhao Zichen's musing on what such a cultural revolution might mean for a Christian writer, and how these "new possibilities" might be realized, produced a work of theological and literary depth that brings new insight to one of the most read and overread texts in history.

Zhao's *Life of Jesus* does more than just counter prevalent criticisms of Christianity: it provides a model for a constructive cultural engagement. Zhange Ni has written of "the demythologization of the historical Jesus and resacralization of him into the Christ of Chinese nationalism" in Republican-era fiction.[100] But this is too extreme a description for Zhao's text and theology, as is the language of "rewriting" the Jesus story. Zhao's biblical hermeneutics are clear: he feels at liberty to rearrange scriptural units to make greater narrative sense and locates reading authority firmly with the people, not church authorities, but his method is to retell from within; there is no overarching or easy nationalist agenda or dissembling, but, as this chapter has explored, there is in the *Life of Jesus* a grappling with biblical texts and a considered inquiry into how theology and the nature of truth are expressed, how Jesus may be conceived in Chinese prose, and how the classical tradition of biography may be appropriated alongside more modern biographical formats and understandings. Certainly, a strong patriotism is at work, but Jesus is not subordinated to the cause of Chinese nationalism. Zhao's prime bequest to his youthful readers is an encouragement to look within their textual traditions for the means of expressing and understanding Christ.[101]

The fact that Zhao wrote this 250-page text in less than a month gives a clue to its composition. The "Chineseness" of the metaphors and allusions or the reading of the landscape was not grafted on from reference works or scholarly reflection, but arose from associations that came naturally from Zhao's recall of texts. This generation had memorized the entire Confucian canon and could still play with its texts at will; Zhao's reading history enabled him to insert Christ lightly yet deftly into a Chinese literary frame. His work fits with the environment of the wider New Culture Movement and its aim to transform literature and historical writing but is firmly rooted in his Christian understanding and vision. His use of the imagination, for example, as a literary and a theological tool was tied to his (then) belief in the primacy of reason as a God-given means to understanding God. The narration of the gospel from within Chinese culture and its textual heritage comes out of a desire to make the text make sense—to express it in a way that appeals to Chinese youth and to demonstrate that it was possible to create that sense within Chinese literary forms, that traditional culture did not need be excised to live and write as a modern Christian. From this structuring of the narrative and from the psychological empathy that Zhao promotes, new insights into the scriptural texts and into Jesus's life are gained, for the benefit of all readers.

In a series of articles Ying Fuk-Tsang has explored Zhao's changing understanding of the project of indigenization, including his vacillating views during the 1930s and 1940s on the relationship between religion and culture, which Ying theorizes as a shift from seeking the "relevance" of Christianity for China to promoting the "uniqueness" of Christianity.[102] Ying traces Zhao's gradual disenchantment with cultural indigenization alongside his move from liberalism to neo-orthodoxy, from a belief that an indigenized church should combine the truth inherent in Christianity with the truth inherent in China's classical culture, to his sense by the 1940s that the implosion of Chinese culture itself meant that there was no longer any point in pursuing the elision of Christianity and classical culture. Christianity then becomes a corrective for Chinese society, a means to redeem the good within the corrupt. Ying's analysis reminds us how valuable Zhao's thinking is, as China reverts now to valorizing its cultural past, and how prescient his diagnosis was of portending social crisis as China discarded its old faith before creating a new one. The *Life of Jesus* does not quite fit, however, with the proposed timeline of Zhao's move from an ethical to a religious Christianity, or his desuetude of the classical. There is still in the biography a desire to undertake that hard process of melding Christianity and traditional culture that Ying places in the 1920s. In his creative writing, Zhao the educator was still trying to do that which Zhao the essayist had already begun to question.[103] The use of Chinese form does not, it should be noted, necessarily imply the privileging of a Confucian message: Zhao selects carefully from tradition, and the dominant theological mood remains rational and liberal. In the postrevolutionary era, the tradition can inspire and enlighten but need not determine ideologies.

What is radical and exciting in the *Life of Jesus* is the mode of seeing, the way a Chinese lens is used to calibrate the gospel; here, Christianity neither completes nor judges Chinese culture: this is a reading in-between, holding onto optimism, a preemptive strike against those who think the old culture cannot speak to present concerns. The spiritual and the literary are deeply connected, with references to classical poetry and philosophy in the *Life of Jesus* creating new resonances in the biblical text. The abrupt insight a reader gains as Zhao gives a worn parable a new twist defies any easy separation of literary from religious insight. The generative quality of the text is difficult to define but lies in the ambiguity, the open-ended possibility of the imaginary. In reverting to his Chinese literary roots and in writing in a style that might be termed "imaginative nonfiction," Zhao exposes quite different thoughts and preoccupations from those of his essays and articles. As his mind rests from active worrying about the education of the young and the economic well-being of China and he engages closely with Jesus's lived life and the accretion of textual scholarship surrounding it, deep currents surface. The land is linked to a sense of nationhood. The tiny, beleaguered Israelite nation under Rome provokes comparison with a weakened China facing imperialist aggression. In turning from China to Galilee, Zhao pens a sharper portrait of the hopes and aspirations of his homeland. In turning to the sacred, he casts more light on the secular, and in writing on a seemingly esoteric topic for contemporary Chinese, he produces a strong rebuttal to his politically engaged critics.

4

THE PUBLIC AND PERSONAL FACES OF THE CHURCH: XU ZONGZE'S *SUI SI SUI BI* AND THE *SHENGJIAO ZAZHI* (REVUE CATHOLIQUE)

The Holy Church is a good mother who protects
her children. . . . The priests of the Church are
spiritual doctors, curing the pain of the people.
—Xu Zongze, 1933[1]

To spread the gospel in a country, the first thing necessary is to
assimilate it with the people's thinking and customs, only then can it
enter deeply among the people and comprehend their psychology.
—Xu Zongze, 1940[2]

For the greater part of his adult life, the polymath Roman Catholic theologian Xu Zongze (P. Joseph Zi, S.J., 1886–1947) edited the premier Catholic journal *Shengjiao zazhi*, or *Revue Catholique*, from the Jesuit compound Xujiahui in Shanghai, the effective center of the Chinese Roman Catholic world.[3] As writer, editor, and public intellectual in an era when print media and social power were closely intertwined, Xu held a position of no little authority and responsibility. The directions in which he guided the magazine and the theological, historical, and social articles he wrote offer important insight into the evolution of Chinese Catholicism during the 1920s and 1930s. Xu penned a good many doctrinal works and textbooks drawing on the articles he published in the journal, such as his *Sheng chong lun* (聖寵論 On Grace: Tractatus de Gratia Actuali et Habituali, 1930) or *Sheng shi lun* (聖事論 On the Sacraments, 1931), alongside works on psychology and social economics—asking such questions as whether capitalism violates the common good and why the church permitted interest on loans[4]—and volumes on Chinese Jesuit history.[5] The dozens of articles and editorials that Xu published during his fourteen years at the helm of the magazine offer the interpretations of a leading Jesuit on Vatican encyclicals and the direction of the church in the new social setting of China.

Another volume offers a more private and personal vision. In 1940 Xu published a curious scrapbook of ideas and comments in the Chinese *biji* 筆記 style of composition titled *Sui si sui bi* 隨思隨筆,[6] or *Pencillus Liber* (A Free Pencil), in his preferred European language of Latin. The book gathers together short entries on a range of topics that Xu had published in the magazine *Shengjiao zazhi* between 1934 and 1937.[7] These jottings, printed in the back pages of each issue, provide tantalizing sparks to illuminate the question of how Christianity, universally understood, could speak into a Chinese situation through the common-sense and the God-sense of a Chinese-rooted, Western-trained Catholic church leader. Public theology appears in a large type font in the magazine, in headline articles; Xu's personal thoughts, rendered in a small font, are slipped in to the journal as postscripts. The *biji* had for centuries been a forum for personal expression outside one's official writings, and these short entries, some just a few lines long, are arguably as revealing as the formal essays and editorials. This chapter sets the *biji*, or "thoughts and jottings," in the frame of the "official" magazine writings to explore any congruence or tension between the two voices and its implication in our reading of Republican-era Catholicism.

A deep social concern unites both types of writing, but while Xu's articles discussing papal encyclicals address broader questions in contemporary Roman Catholic social ethics, such as labor relations or Communism, his *biji* entries respond more to questions being asked by the Chinese press and Chinese society. Here both the content and the form of discussion differ. Xu's official writings addressing the social questions raised by the Vatican are discursive essays, while his *biji* writings tackle topics of local interest that do not fit easily into extant categories of theology, in a distinct Chinese writing form. The second part of the chapter looks at three such issues in the *biji* entries: the role of youth in society, especially in relation to the influx of foreign ideas and ways; the role of Christians in Chinese society; and what it means to be human.

SHENGJIAO ZAZHI AND PUBLIC THEOLOGY

For someone held in high regard among contemporaries, Xu Zongze and his work remain distinctly understudied. Where Xu has been addressed, it is most frequently for his historical research on the Roman Catholic Church in China, rather than his own writings.[8] In this, he fares no worse than a whole cohort of

Roman Catholic intellectuals from the era whose names are no longer common currency, apart from a few, like Ma Xiangbo or Ying Jianzhi, who were later valorized for their patriotic stances.[9] (In terms of gaining renown, it may have been an advantage to die before the PRC and the hard choices of the 1940s and 1950s.)

Xu was from a family numbering several government officials in recent generations, including an uncle who was a priest and editor of *Huibao* 匯報, a direct predecessor to *Shengjiao zazhi*. Happenstance led Xu into the church educational system. Nineteen years old in 1905, Xu was in the very last cohort of scholars to sit the imperial examinations and saw his career plans and prospects disappear with the system itself. As Xu Wenhua suggests, it is difficult to overstate the effects that growing up within an entirely Confucian tradition and worldview and then switching to a wholly Catholic and Western one might have had on adolescents like Xu.[10] Having studied for two years in the Jesuit novitiate in Shanghai, Xu then spent more than a decade abroad, studying in Europe and the United States.[11] He was ordained a priest in England in 1920, returning to China the following year. Xu missed out on the 1911 revolution and May Fourth protests but gained, alongside his education, a sense of global citizenship and an awareness of how societal and industrial problems were being addressed elsewhere.[12] Like the work of many of his Protestant peers, Xu's writing was in dialogue with mainstream society as much as with other theologians, and a prime aim was for the church to influence society, especially in the formation of morals. The series of volumes and articles he wrote or edited during the 1920s show the focus of his social concern, including: *On the Question of Labor* (1924), *Catholicism and the Question of Women* (1925), *Refuting Communism* (1926), and *On Social Problems* (1928).[13] Into the 1930s, Xu's writing concentrates more on doctrinal questions, with volumes or textbooks such as *On Creation and the Four Last Things* (1930) or *On the Lord's Incarnation and Atonement* (1932).[14] There is not as clear a temporal succession in this shift as some have suggested, however, since Xu's response to social issues in the earlier set of works precisely splices social commentary with Roman Catholic teachings.[15]

At this distance, Xu's theological and social writings present an unexpected mix of bold, forward thinking and conservatism. His views on women and education, for example, might be provocative both to women's liberationists and to conservative clerics. His editorials and essays are in direct dialogue with Vatican missives, yet he negotiates by selection and omission. When Xu took over as editor of *Shengjiao zazhi* in 1923, he began to institute a series of changes. The first was a simple modernization, in the addition of modern punctuation, rendering the semiclassical style easier to read. He separated church events and news round-ups typographically from the main articles. His most significant change over time was in the balance of articles and their bid to guide Catholic mores and opinion. Church history, foreign biographies, and Confucianism were cut back, while education, politics, women's issues, and religion all gained in prominence and column inches.[16] Xu also added some newer fields popular in other contemporary journals: travel notes, literary pieces, and the *biji* anecdotes.

An examination of two or three of Xu's "official" articles gives a sense of the scope of his interests and their expression in the journal and allows a comparison with the more personal writings expressed at the back of the journal. Xu published on a diverse variety of religious, historical, doctrinal, and social topics, from the nature of revelation to Western scholars at the Qing court. Throughout his time as editor, he sustained a concern for integrating the quotidian life of marginalized readers into a theological framework. An article titled "Labor Contracts" that Xu wrote in 1932 and one from 1933 titled "How Catholicism Resolves Social Questions" exemplify this.[17] Xu's article on labor contracts, which focuses on employer-employee relations, starts out with a basic explanation of what labor means in the new economic framework of industrial relations, explores Pope Leo XIII's discussion of the condition of work in his 1891 encyclical Rerum Novarum, and follows this with an examination of four types of contractual relations, from hiring and sales contracts to partnership agreements. While framing his discussion in an explanation-and-comment format, Xu triangulates among three constituencies: church teachings, a new language of social science, and Chinese traditional values. Two factors concern him most: the mutuality of relations between employer and employee and the establishment of justice in those relations.

In his article on labor contracts, Xu quotes Leo XIII on justice, on the need for a worker as head of the household to be able to support a family, on the spiritual nature of humanity, and on the reciprocal but different responsibilities of workers and employers (including the responsibility of workers not to use force, harm management's property, or strike). He expands the papal discussion of the spiritual aspects of labor and grounds this in a human-centeredness. The labor contract, Xu argues, is different from other forms of contract because it concerns the labor of a human person, not a thing. Labor as a product cannot be separated from its subject, and a person's labor is both material and spiritual so necessarily involves questions of ethics. In discussing the duties of each party in their mutual need for a business to succeed, Xu reproduces Leo XIII's litany of responsibilities on each side but soon returns to his central theme: that the theoretical relationship between employer and employee is not just built on wages and labor but involves "relations between human and human, and between human and society" and, ultimately, "what it means to be human [為人之道]." Here, Xu overlays a philosophical dimension to the debate, honing in on contracts and mutual relations while scaling back on other aspects of the papal encyclical. Downplayed elements include some fairly fundamental perspectives on society and governance: discussion of the law of nature that accords the right to private property, the "pernicious error" that sees civil government intrude into the family and household, the role of the church in overcoming class conflict, and the world as a place of exile not abiding.[18] (The official Catholic position on such matters is important to understanding the later debates with Socialists and Communists over state-church relations and why the Protestant church could take such a divergent line.)

Xu Wenhua argues that Xu Zongze aims for "safe" views in *Shengjiao zazhi* and that the general tenor of the magazine is to cede the vanguard to a less hasty, more reasoned perspective.[19] There is some truth in this: Xu ends his discussion of labor contracts by listing the drawbacks of the contract form where the capitalists furnish capital and laborers labor as equal partners. Naïve on the bargaining power of the individual in the system, Xu ends on the rather ambivalent note that it does not matter what type of contract is in place as long as it is just. It is unclear whether Xu shies away from tackling Leo XIII's views on the church in the world because of a sense of dissent, a subversive silence, the practicalities of time and space, or a decision to concentrate on what he deemed most relevant to China.

The first epigraph to this chapter, on the church as a good mother protecting her children from pain, opens Xu's 1933 article "How Catholicism Resolves Social Questions," in which he addresses that pain common to workers across the world, the "material pain of unemployment and economic panic" that governments everywhere were failing to alleviate. Xu sets out to present to readers the main ideas of Pius XI's recent (1931) encyclical Quadragesimo Anno, "On Reconstruction of the Social Order," to demonstrate the church's position on social issues. The encyclical that Xu summarizes is an update of Leo XIII's missive of forty years earlier, aimed at "summoning to court the contemporary economic regime and passing judgment on Socialism."[20] If Leo XIII's encyclical led to better labor laws worldwide, as Pius XI suggests, this "more precise application" of Leo's teaching for the current age had several targets in view, including restating the twofold character of ownership, individual and social, and negating the widespread acclaim for Socialism that excessive appropriation of profit by capital had engendered. (The belief that "all products and profits belong by rights to the workers" was even more "dangerous and more specious" an error than that of nationalizing production, argued Pius.) After discussion of the distribution of wealth, workers' guilds, partnership contracts, and such constructive topics, Pius XI inveighs at length against Socialism and Communism. While the Pope favored employees sharing in profits, he lay bare the "impious and iniquitous" character of Communism, with its class warfare, extermination of private ownership, and hostility to the church. Socialism, he concedes, "approaches" the truths of Christian tradition but ultimately cannot be reconciled with the teachings of the church, and "Christian socialism" remains a contradiction in terms.

Given the rising strength of Socialist views across many sectors of society in China, Xu is in a delicate position. He begins his digest of the encyclical firmly in the economic sphere: social problems are, he claims, problems of wealth distribution. A country's wealth needs adjusting into balance between production and consumption; where the allocation is appropriate, there will be no excessive riches or poverty. In an extended architectural metaphor, Xu explores the notion of economic stability as the wings of a courtyard house, segueing into a description of the fine raiment and comestibles of the rich, set against their equivalents among the poor. A society of great inequality is one of violent disorder and chaos, he suggests. Labor questions, notes Xu, are really about the problems of a working life, and these comprise material aspects and spiritual ones. If workers have no real estate and no spare money, they have no means to seek an education or knowledge; without an education, claims Xu, venturing far beyond Pius XI, they are stupid, coarse, and insensible.[21] For Xu, the education of the workforce is the key, and, naturally for Chinese literati of his generation, he holds that education civilizes, just as does the church-infused society Pius is striving for.

Where the papal encyclical is formal and abstract, Xu is concrete and practical; where Pius concentrates on the theoretical ills of Socialism, Xu looks to the (perceived?) realities of workers' lives. He worries about the spiritual pain of those who cannot get to Mass if they have to work six days and have household tasks to complete on the seventh; he sympathizes with the grind of daily existence that leads to protests and strikes. In concentrating on the Catholic response to social issues, Xu offers a more pastoral interpretation, which draws on Leo XIII as much as Pius's teachings and which is directed primarily toward an audience of capital-owning Catholics (links between Catholic capitalists and the Nationalists remained strong throughout the 1930s and 1940s). Xu returns to the question of the rights and duties of capitalists and workers and the notion of a fair wage. He follows Pius's injunction that a wage should allow for the support of a wife and children but adds that it should also be at a level that does not leave a worker anxious. The just duties of capitalists include educating and inculcating moral virtue in workers, whether through education or by example. If justice demands a fair wage, virtue, especially on the part of Catholic bosses, entreats higher standards: the provision of extra help beyond the breadline, support during illness, time off for doctor visits. Virtuous giving, he argues, promotes fraternal relations over class struggle—and accords with the understanding that "poverty is not a shameful thing, and labor is holy work; wealth is not the true source of happiness for humanity, and the rich are not the masters of wealth, but mere managers on behalf of the Creator."[22] Workers' associations are, for Xu, means to implement justice and virtue in labor relations and in apolitical wage negotiations. The combination of gospel insight and practical action allows Xu to assert the superiority of the Catholic response to pressing social problems and highlight the inability of Communism, Socialism, and all other -isms to succeed at the task.

If Xu is fearless in extracting his own message from papal encyclicals, and shaping it to a local audience, he is equally unperturbed in tackling local constituencies with whom he disagreed, in the task of dispensing wisdom and opinion. He took on the traditional ideal of womanhood in an article published in March 1935 on the phrase "Virtuous wives and talented mothers" with the comment that the maxim "is something that modern women do not like to hear."[23] Women think, he continues, that "it implies a humiliation, or, at least, a belittling of them." The path of a virtuous wife and a good mother is, however, that along which each will walk, whether she likes the phrase or not. Some women, Xu concedes, follow a higher reasoning, believing that if they are burdened with marriage and small children, they will not be able to share with men the tasks of society, and for this reason they do not wish to become virtuous wives. Xu praises their noble ideals and accepts that there is logic to the fear of household life. But, he argues, for these educated and knowledgeable women, their mission, or heaven-given task (天職), is not to struggle for the same job or same career as men in a bid for equality. True equality, rather, lies in men and women each fulfilling their duties in their own occupations. History and experience vouch for the phrase "Men rule the outer courtyard, women rule the inner household," he argues, even if New Women do not like to hear it. We cannot legislate, Xu suggests, for a small minority who do not marry because they are following a social calling and working for humanity and on this basis say that being a virtuous wife and good mother are no longer tasks of womanhood.

Xu compounds his position by explaining the importance of the task of womanhood: men cannot fulfill their occupations without a good woman behind them running the household. Xu reverts to his Confucian heritage in rehearsing the notion that a good wife anchors national stability, since a good household leads to a good society, which in turn leads to a good state.[24] The "advances" that some claim for marriage as a friendship that can be retained if it works and exited if it does not, or in communal childcare and dining, are, claims Xu, retrograde. What sort of world would it be, he asks, if marriage and the household were abolished; if the free premarital association that some claim continued into marriage itself, with humans like animals, copulating for a season? Can good parents cast their children off to others to raise? As with so many thinkers of his time, the overriding concern for the good of society and of the state channels all discussion. If Xu's social concern for justice and for the downtrodden does not extend to women, it is notable that he appeals here not to the Bible for justification, but to Chinese tradition and social norms. Justice and righteousness for workers gain biblical backing, but misogyny is underpinned by natural law and common sense. As the essays indicate, Xu was, in his own way, a pragmatic visionary and a trail-blazer in China of Catholic social writings. His thought is not just reactive to the various social movements around him, but contributed to the debates. His work addressing students, capitalists, and the educated elite through the medium of the press placed him in mainstream post–May Fourth life, and the magazine gave him a remarkable vehicle through which to shape Catholic opinion.

In Xu's extended writings, where the journal essays were expanded into short volumes, we can see even more clearly the formal differences between "official" writings and the *biji* writings discussed below. Xu's *On Grace*, one of the series of six theological textbooks he authored in the early 1930s, demonstrates this. *On Grace*, like the essays discussed above, differs from *Sui si sui bi* in language register as well as writing style. Its language is formal, declarative, and precise. Here, the tone is didactic, and the implied reader is not a peer but a student. The logical, step-by-step rationality of the text's structure is striking, especially in contrast with the *biji*: the volume is broken down into parts, chapters, and sections, each labeled and ordered, as the two major divisions of the volume, "Actual Grace" and "Habitual/Sanctifying Grace," are explained. The text appears to be based on Joseph Pohle's 1914 *Grace Actual and Habitual: A Dogmatic Treatise*, but with reference matter—quotations from the church fathers, scriptural texts—omitted and a certain amount of detail condensed. The categories of (Western, Neo-Thomist) Roman Catholic doctrine are followed closely; definitions and terminology form the bedrock to each section. Xu begins, for example, by parsing the term "grace" in Latin and Chinese, looking at its etymology and derivation before proceeding to explain the difference between *grace increata* and *creata, gratia gratum faciens* and *gratia gratis data,* and so forth. He provides a word-by-word explanation of Chinese definitions, in an iterative progression. There is little sense other than that this is a translated text, and translated concepts. It reads as what it is: a doctrinal textbook, a work to transmit, or translate, given concepts into the Chinese language. There is little digression into dynamic equivalence here, and Latin terms are scattered throughout for translation clarity. In form, rarefied language, and tone, it equates to its source text.

"Theology is concerned with the great matters of human knowledge of, love for, and service towards, the Lord of Heaven—and so should not just be studied by theologians, but by church members too," writes Xu in the preface to *On Grace*.[25] This theology, opened up to lay readers, is understood as universal: the "we" in *On Grace* is always we humans, not the "we Chinese" of *Sui si sui bi;* the subject matter is the relation of a transcendent God to human creatures. The only acknowledged adjustment Xu makes to a local audience is signaled by a footnote on the translation/transliteration of "Christ," which he changes to *Jiduo* 基多, on aesthetic and linguistic grounds. (The fact that Xu can institute a translation for "Christ" in 1930, alongside all of his neologisms for the precise Latinate divisions of "grace," shows the fluidity within a seemingly fixed doctrine.) The relationship of the discipline of "theology" and theological discourse to the lived and reflected "Christianity" that Xu writes on elsewhere is not made explicit. His expansion of "theology" to include human love for, and service to, God, motions toward a possible broadening of perspective, but the distinction is only ever implied. As the following section explores, it is in Xu's more personal writings that he grounds the relationship of humanity to the transcendent in the Chinese particular.

SUI SI SUI BI: THOUGHTS AND JOTTINGS

In 1934, Xu changed the cover page of *Shengjiao zazhi*, removing the silhouette of St. Peter's, Rome, which had graced the magazine for years, and replacing it with Chinese calligraphy. At the end of that year, he instituted his popular *suibi* column. Over the next few years of writings, the breadth of Xu's comments on the contemporary world, his exhortations to readers, and the range of referents in these *biji* texts offer rare insight into his unofficial life, his interior worldview, and his theological preoccupations. The *biji* both point to a disjunction between the topics and scope of the official theology of his formal essays and lived life and provide a means to bridge that gap. The entries, which were subsequently collected in the volume *Sui si sui bi* (1940), can be grouped into five main thematic areas: youth; the effect of Roman Catholicism on national life; contemporary proverbs, or wisdom; questions on the nature of a Chinese-style Christianity and inculturation; and writing itself. There are also smaller subthemes, such as patriotism, and a selection of entries that fall into a "self-help" category of pragmatic or business sense for Christians, alongside some eccentric jottings that are a hallmark of the *biji* form, such as statistics on recent suicides or an entry on the astonishing number of offspring a fly can produce in a single summer.

Two points are evident at the outset: the first is that not all of the entries are overtly Christian, or even religious. Xu's thoughts on poverty or Bible translation are interspersed with pithy comments on library holdings, ethics, and writer's block.[26] Aphorisms and bon mots vie with impassioned pleas to youngsters and exhortations to the wealthy to save their souls: this is life, in its multifarious forms, reflected through a Christian lens. Xu absorbs his subject matter from conversations, newspaper reading, and quotidian reflection and responds by observing acutely, then commenting and challenging from his vantage point as an educated Catholic leader. The second point follows: the act of categorizing threatens to make cohesive a literary form that is deliberately not so. It would be hard to find a less systematic form in which to theologize. The *biji* ("pen notes" or "brush notes") finds its closest parallel in the modern blog: a series of seemingly random entries on whatever topic catches the author's attention in the moment. Some short, isolated entries operate as a retweet—Xu passing on to readers a factoid or noteworthy thought that he has culled from a newspaper or other publication. If this makes the work seem trivial, Xu is aware of the charge and, in keeping with literary tradition, is self-deprecating about the form, acknowledging in the preface to *Sui si sui bi* that it is a "minor" stream of literature.

Xu's reproduction of his notes in book form, and his evident delight in this style of writing, begs the question: what could he say in this mode that he could not in any other? Why turn to an outdated literary form in the mid-1930s? These questions ultimately tie in with the broader question of why so few Chinese theologians engage with systematic theology or address cardinal interests of Western theological thought outside of social or ethical issues. To explore why Xu Zongze might have chosen to couch his insights on the church and the world in this particular form, a brief history of *biji* writings serves to introduce Xu's entries. The following sections consider three of Xu's main themes and preoccupations in the *Sui si sui bi*: the place of the Roman Catholic Church in China, youth and education, and the nature of human beings.

The *biji* was one of an array of means of fostering a shared habitus among traditional Chinese literati. The form traditionally provided a vehicle for observation and reflection, including interior reflection on how the self was matching

up to Confucian ideals, and for recording memories of events or passing plea-
sures, as well as an opportunity for flaunting new ideas, or gobbets of news,
when texts were circulated among friends in manuscript or print form. From
its beginnings, the *biji* was an avenue of expression for a tradition of literati
officials "who were keen on recording, commenting on, and cultivating, their
life world."[27] Early *biji* gathered observations of natural phenomena and other
encyclopedic knowledge alongside tales of ghosts and divine beings. Even in
this nonvalorized form of literature—*wen*, literary writing, being contrasted
with the plain prose of *bi* (brush) as early as the fifth century[28]—the formation
of a shared subjectivity was clearly an important part of writing. The "minor
statements" stream of writing had an acknowledged didactic value: in a passage
that could have come directly from Xu Zongze, a first-century commentator
describes the act of "collecting scraps of petty talk, selecting exemplary writings
from close to hand and making short books out of them, with passages worthy of
attention by which we may discipline ourselves and put our family in order."[29]

One of the markers of a genteel lifestyle celebrated in *biji* texts was a shared
aesthetic pleasure in material objects, including books and book collections.
Xu Xongze was a bibliophile par excellence—one of his major day-job tasks
was as archivist of the Xujiahui rare book collection—and his personal library
had a strong religious frame. Most diarists and occasional writers of *biji* jottings
included reading notes among their writings, and Xu was no exception. Some
of these were public-service announcements, such as the many entries in which
Xu alerts his readers to new editions of the classics or the best presses and prices
available.[30] As a true Chinese intellectual, the intersection of bibliophilia and
Christianity is a place of profound enjoyment for Xu. Pointing out even the most
arcane of secular references to church figures, or especially a reference tucked
in an obscure or unexpected text, was both duty and joy. Xu draws attention, for
example, to a text on the geography of Beijing that refers to the astronomical
instruments made by the Jesuit scholars and to Matteo Ricci's status and to his
tomb, both excellent source material for church history, as Xu notes.[31]

In a study of two memoirs of the Sino-Japanese war (1937–1945) that was beginning to shape the Shanghai in which Xu lived, Rana Mitter explores the strategic use of particular forms of writing.[32] One of Mitter's subjects, Xu Wancheng,
documented his wartime experiences through a *biji*, or notebook, and the other
through the medium of journalistic reportage. "By choosing particular modern
or anti-modern genres and styles to write in, the authors expressed a wider sentiment about the war's ambiguous role in modernizing China," Mitter suggests.
To adopt the *biji* form as late as 1946, he argues, indicates "a rather conscious
archaism and a desire to contrast oneself from the now-common modernity

of linear narrative."[33] The disjointed form of the *biji* carried with it echoes of "a culture of disorientation" brought about by the bombings and mass relocations of wartime China, as well as an implicit negation of the grand teleology of certain commentators on the war. While we might not want to go so far in ascribing to Xu Zongze a similar intellectual chariness of metanarrative (although that could be a statement affirming an alternative narrative of life in light of heaven), this reading of form invites a similar account for Xu.[34]

As an extracanonical form falling between the acknowledged categories of writing, there is debate over what texts comprise *biji*, and the nature of the genre before the term came into use as a general literary catchall in the twentieth century (and indeed, the term *suibi* is used interchangeably). As Mitter and others have suggested, writers made deliberate use of the ambiguity. In a study of a well-known Southern Song *biji*, Gang Liu lays bare the deception of the simplicity of the style and argues that descriptions of the genre's "informality" are misleading, since they "may leave us with an impression that the composition of *biji* is often done in a less meticulous or less refined fashion, while in reality it is often exactly the opposite."[35] The lowly genre façade is, he suggests, used by compilers to vaunt their modesty, excuse any inaccuracies in the text, and, more pertinently, offer a more versatile form of reading. The miscellany, argues Liu, embraces a special poetics, a "perpetual dialectic between the text's miscellaneous surface and internal coherence," used in the case of his Song dynasty author to "articulate his literary conception, historical vision, and loyalist concerns of the past."[36] This articulation of vision and retrospection that Liu describes is precisely what drives Xu Zongze's text. The disjointed form of the miscellany, moreover, argues Liu, both forms the "very structure and order" of the text and destabilizes its meaning, pointing to a plurality of interpretive possibilities.

The long pedigree of the *biji* and the use made of the form caution against dismissing Xu's back-of-the-journal musings on account of their lowly genre or unconventional style. In a literature where genre conventions allow for different facets of the self to be expressed in different forms, authors could creatively select the mode of communication to shape the message. The history of reading and experience of shared sensibilities and meaning conventions gives a frame for reading the *Sui bi sui si*, pointing to the author (his self-cultivation, his vision of society, and his comment on the world), his relationship with friends, peers, and an imagined past. Western genres of theological writing simply lacked these same social resonances. Long before the term "contextual theology" became common currency, Chinese theologians like Xu were engaging with the relationship between social setting, economic milieu, and theological thought.

This text is not systematized in terms of either Western philosophical form (a topic in which Xu was well-read, as his *History of Western Philosophy* shows)[37] or writing format or style. The "indigenousness" lay both in form and in the bold move toward redefining theological scope, decades ahead of Vatican II. If the *biji* came with certain historic resonances, publication in the space of the journal, or church magazine, only magnified these by bringing them to a wider audience.

While Xu acknowledges that the snippets of comment and reflection he collates into *Sui si sui bi* have little significance, in their accumulation, and in the context of their reissue in book form, their sum does prove significant. Writing in a Chinese literary form provided a space without the trammels of official theology, beyond the bishop's imprimatur and outside of Vatican expression. This was not theology in any accepted sense, and, as seen above, in writing and translating works of orthodox theology on grace, sacraments, or the Trinity, Xu submits fully to their classification and determination—but these jottings proved insightful and useful for Chinese readers living out their Christian lives. They were developed out of a lived-life and thought-through faith and from reflection on social problems in the light of gospel teachings; they were, it might be argued, fine second-order theology, a contextual theology long before Richard Niebuhr or Stephen Bevans.

A three-sentence entry "On Literary Trifles" elucidates Xu's own view of the *biji* form and debased genres in general.[38] It also exemplifies how the *biji* entries teach by suasion and example, not didacticism. The observation, which involves an extended food metaphor and literary "taste," turns on the conceit that *xiaopin* 小品 can mean both essay or "literary trifle," and small-minded or petty. "Some say," begins Xu, "that the *suibi* is a type of short essay writing and that it is enjoyed by petty people, who because their literary taste is very limited cannot eat rich, nutritious works—and that exotic delicacies can be enjoyed only by great people, or those of military valor." "When I first heard this phrase," continues Xu, "I thought it was well put, but when I thought about it more carefully, it's not quite right, since *suibi* literature is a type of truly aesthetic writing, which can only be understood by those who comprehend true beauty and goodness." Our magazine readers, Xu notes, are all people of true beauty and goodness—and besides, "if you eat delicacies and rich food every day, the appetite will soon be ruined." To the holy-minded, all things are holy—and all things should be taken in moderation. And, as Xu notes in another entry, he is frequently being told that people turn first not to the in-depth research articles in the church magazine, but to the brief *suibi* entries.[39]

A ROMAN CATHOLIC CHINESE HISTORY

One of Xu's clearest aims in *Sui si sui bi*, judging by the number of entries relating to the topic, is to instill in his readers a sense of the positive role that Catholicism had played in national life and to inscribe that history more widely in the public consciousness. The message promoted throughout the mid-1930s is clear: Roman Catholics are an important constituent part of Chinese citizenry, and the Roman Catholic Church has a long and illustrious history within the Chinese cultural world. These are integrated identities, not alternatives. A certain defensiveness of church life is evident in places in the volume, with several anecdotes taking a proactive stance against the criticisms of foreign entanglement made against the church.

Multiple entries discuss historical Roman Catholic luminaries such as Xu Guangqi, valued both by Christians and by secular society. Some examples are drawn from popular culture: in a short entry that shows nothing is sacrosanct, whether in a *biji* or contemporary life, Xu comments on the inclusion of his Ming dynasty ancestor Xu Guangqi among two hundred "great figures of bright cultural achievements" in an advertisement for the Huamei Tobacco company. Xu's use as an exemplary figure three hundred years after his death, is, suggests Xu Zongze, evidence that the commercial world could leverage his effect and shows how he was revered beyond the world of scholarship. Other entries in the volume (e.g., #7) reproduce excerpts on Xu Guangqi from other publications, or from radio broadcasts, for readers to appreciate.[40] The content is of secondary import here; that historical Roman Catholic figures are being valorized is the more important message. The litany of cultural achievements of Roman Catholicism in wider society is a leitmotif of the collection. When a local newspaper, the *Shanghai Evening News*, starts a weekly "Shanghai Firsts" column, Xu creates his own—the first church middle school in 1849, the first school for the deaf and dumb in 1891, the first lithographic press in 1876, all at Xujiahui (the Jesuit residence, seminary, and library in Shanghai)—from which it can be seen that "we Catholics are very sincere about promoting culture."[41]

Xu is keen to show how China has benefited from Roman Catholic scientific work. The Xujiahui observatory, he notes, collated weather data by telegram from the whole country and produced statistics from it as well as readings for weather stations and storm and typhoon warnings.[42] The value of Xujiahui is highlighted for Xu when the national turn toward "real learning" meant that local gazetteers were becoming valued for their historical and geographical knowledge.[43] We stand in the shadow of our towering debt to Matteo Ricci, Xu Guangqi, and the early founders, notes Xu, since the Xujiahui library was one of the earliest to build up a collection of gazetteers, and its collection was second only to those of the National Library in Beiping (Beijing) and the Imperial Palace. Although there is no direct link between cultural impact and mission, reiterates Xu, the effect of the cultural activities such as book collecting that the early Jesuits undertook was instrumental in a positive reception of the church—and so Xu calls on his readers to continue this "cultural mission" to China and collect old gazetteers lying around and send them in. (If readers do not find any, he adds, in pastoral mode, the act of looking still has merit.)[44] Alongside Xu Guangqi, Xu charts the reception of Matteo Ricci (Li Madou) in Chinese secular sources, with some of the longest entries in the volume reproducing reams of poetry composed for Ricci at various events in Ming high society (see e.g. #40). Ricci holds an almost prophetic status for Xu, as a forerunner of Christianity in China, and as Xu documents the continuity of mention of Ricci in texts, the desire to (re)inscribe Ricci into wider Chinese discourse in the minds of readers is evident.

The *biji* is a forum par excellence for personal notes, and several entries in *Sui si sui bi* have a diarylike quality to them, such as when Xu describes a trip out to Songjiang to look for Xu family graves (#88). This is a good example of both the trivial and the meaningful, or how the quotidian means, in *biji* format. At one level the trip does not accomplish much: Xu finds some of the ancestral graves he is looking for but not others; he suggests the former glory of the Xu family residences in his depiction of the chapel and the two compounds; and he notes that the stone columns that had been there a few decades ago are no more. At another level, the trip signifies by inscribing Xu simultaneously into Chinese traditions—both through filial piety and attention to grave rites, and at a more rarefied level, as a member of the literati elite who cared about his image as lineage member, amateur archaeologist, and genealogist—as well as into Chinese Catholic traditions, by reference to centuries of faithful witness. By its very forms and conventions, the *biji* enabled Xu to affirm his Chinese (Christian) identity.

Certain topics in Chinese church history provoke repeated reflection for educated Chinese. For classically trained scholars, the past was an ever-present and a naturally imbued reflection on the present. The style of learning engrained in Xu and his childhood peers—where the classics were memorized by heart, so their mode of textual reading and reasoning was in perpetual dialogue with tradition—meant that historic injustices were constant wounds in the present. In thinking back on the lawsuits of the late Qing that were instigated against church members or missionaries, and those brought by missionaries under the treaty provisions compiled in recent books documenting the cases, Xu Zongze muses on the root cause: the separation of the church from "the people."[45] His criticism of the church goes no further than to open the question up, but readers could scarcely fail to be aware of the anguish in the question.

Another topic of long-standing debate in church-state relations, the Rites controversy, receives a new twist in Xu's hands, as he comments wryly in one entry on the government's institution of a sacrifice to Confucius in August 1934. After quoting from the official text announcing the ritual, Xu suggests that their *aim* in promoting the worship of Confucius in an era of "moral abandonment" was laudable, but a better way would be for politicians to model morality themselves.[46] Living models would be stronger than a dead exemplar, and more effective in their attempt at inculcating virtue. Xu quotes the *Daxue* (Great Learning) of Confucius back at the government, on beginning with the root, the cultivation of the self.[47] While not condemning the sacrifice to Confucius outright (and thus returning the insult made by Pope Clement XI in 1704), Xu offers his readers a better, more practical way of reading the past in the present, as well as an implicit criticism of the venality of contemporary political leaders.

YOUTH AND CHINESE CULTURE

In keeping with the mores of revolutionary and Nationalist China, Xu Zongze places a high premium on youth in the church as the future of the nation: "The hopes of humanity, the hopes of the nation all lie on the shoulders of the young, since the talents and abilities of the young are like spring plants, which when moistened by the dew and rain, shoot up towards glory. Many heroes can come from among youth; the old are already people of the past."[48] For the most part, however, such optimism is tempered by experience, and the dominant reading of youth in *Sui si sui bi* is as a trope for cultural disintegration. Xu constantly prods his readership on the loss of Chinese cultural pride.[49]

For Xu, one can be both Christian and antiforeign, or, at least, against the deleterious effect of an overenthusiasm for foreign culture. Xu comments favorably on the establishment of a new "movement for the construction of a Chinese literature," on the grounds that "modern China" was barely visible in the literary field, and expresses his hope that the movement might remedy a societal weakness:

. . . the intellectual classes strenuously advocate Euro-American culture, resulting in a situation where many young men and women in China can speak Western languages fluently, and can write a literary piece in a fluid Western hand, but they do not know how to write an ordinary letter or a memo in our own language; the names of famous Europeans and Americans are ever on the tip of their tongue: Marx, Kant, Darwin, Gorky, Zola, and so on, but they do not know the great figures of our own history, of our literature and politics. They know Western history as if it were their own family treasure trove, but when you ask them about their own nation's history, even modern history like the Opium Wars or the Taiping Kingdom, they are blind to it, and have no sense of detail at all. This is truly a matter of shame for our people.[50]

Elsewhere Xu excoriates those who flaunt their doctorates or who call themselves university professors but are learned only in foreign things—those "who can teach our students how to become foreign, but cannot teach students about Chinese affairs."[51]

An aversion to Western cultural invasion does not blind Xu to the areas where China could learn from the West, and he advocates Western philosophy or logic repeatedly as a means to greater clarity in thinking,[52] but the balance, in his judgment, is too strongly weighted in favor of the West among the young. This is a particular problem for seminary students, he suggests, who, if they know nothing of China's past and cannot communicate properly with its people, are in danger of serving only themselves by their learning.[53] Xu is clear on his own task, in a rare merging of public and private voices: some say that the editorials in *Shengjiao zazhi* are too "hard," he admits—but "hard" articles foster judgments in readers and strengthen the will; too many soft articles scatter morals to the winds and render the will flabby. Youths who read too much soft writing are particularly susceptible to a diminution of courage.[54]

The need to document a vanishing culture presses on Xu. The rapid pace of change is shown in the fact that he needs to remind his readers of the patterns of life of his own generation. In lyrical mode, he writes in one entry of how his peers began school only at age seven or eight and, having studied eight characters on the first day, continued to build up their character recognition until they had the six hundred or seven hundred needed to read the first primer, the *Sanzijing*, before moving on to the texts of Confucius and Mencius. "As for composition, we used the method of matching characters," he writes. "The teacher would produce a character, say, 'heaven,' and you had to match it with 'earth,'" and in this manner, character by character, children learned to write poetry, but also composition, since in producing parallelisms the pupils were also learning about poetic tones, empty particles, and how to structure writing. As Xu continues the description of childhood pedagogy, it begins to dawn on the reader that the process of learning to write is metaphor for the process of learning to become, and that the becoming Xu is describing is becoming Chinese. The pride when a child has learned well and "makes a name for itself, bringing glory to its parents" is immediately followed by reference to the patrimony. Although the old method of learning was not very scientific, admits Xu,[55] the people brought up in this system "knew a little of Chinese books," unlike modern youth, who can barely write and are proud "as a crane among chickens" when they know a smattering of "foreign pidgin." The change in childhood learning, implies Xu, has brought about a profound change in culture; the loss of an ability to read and write Chinese is a loss of Chineseness. What one reads, as Xu adumbrates, trains one's writing (and thinking).[56] Since reading is constitutive of the person, the fact that youth are not making the connection between reading more and being able to write well is highly disturbing for an educator.

In the self-appointed role as guardian of culture, Xu frequently takes it upon himself to make up for cultural ignorance among his younger readers. In one entry, he explains what preceded the new bachelor's, master's, and doctoral degrees; how the national examination system worked in imperial China; and the special titles conferred on the top three candidates at each stage from provincial to capital exams.[57] Xu does not mention the Christian colleges, their curricula, and the educational debates directly. In the *biji* he does not, in fact, mention foreigners much at all. Xu addresses the aftermath of the Anti-Christian Movement only tangentially. This form of writing gives him the space and the permission to address his insights and concerns about life and meaning to a Chinese audience. The ethno-nationalism that suffused the essays and newspaper columns of the 1930s as the rallying cry against imperialist encroachment shifted to anti-Japanese sentiment is found in more subtle form in Xu's *biji* writings, where many entries begin with "we Chinese," "in our recent history," or some form of reference to a bounded community.

There are exceptions, however, and over the period of the entries, 1934–1937, Xu's writings become more acute on the question of the nation. The link between language learning and nationalism is brought home forcefully to Xu one day when he meets a young student now engaged in business. Xu probes why the lad had not continued studying ("boring"), and a discussion of the relative merits of English and Chinese literature follows. Xu is soon alarmed by the turn in conversation, as the boy comments that Japanese literature will be useful in the future, "Now that Japan has taken the two northern provinces, in the future Japanese power . . ." the boy begins, before Xu cuts him off: "And so you want to study Japanese, to prepare to be the slave of a foreign power?" asks Xu, incredulously. "No, no, no," stutters the boy, eliciting Xu's final word to his readers: "Youth, if you do not wish to be the slaves of a foreign power, you must realize the importance of our national literature, and read more of our own books."[58] Fifteen minutes later, Xu reports in a separate entry, a teacher came into his office grumbling at the exorbitant price of foreign-language books and the difficulties of affording reference material. Why the need for foreign texts?, asks Xu; "why should we promote demand for other people?"[59] His interlocutor concedes the point but adds that "if a university doesn't use Western books as textbooks, students look down on it, saying Chinese textbooks do not have an equal standing with Western ones internationally." "When I heard this, I knew that students were happy in their hearts to be foreigners . . . I'll say no more!" expostulates Xu.

On occasion Xu attacks directly the confusion and hypocrisy of youth. "To-day's youth," he notes, "are steeped in atheist thought, and all say that religion is a form of superstition, that it's for women and those with the intellectual ability of children—but when something momentous happens, like a death, an illness, or a family misfortune, their hearts are awakened, and they go into temples to pray to the gods, and burn incense and ingots, and do all of the things that they habitually regard as heresy."[60] The reason for this, Xu proffers, is natural theology: the innate good nature of humans indicates to them that there must be a Creator who should be worshipped. It is right, he notes, that they express this religious faith, even if its object is misguided. In another gripe about youth (#19), Xu moans that they do not use the traditional church vocabulary; instead of saying "the Lord's Day" for the Sabbath, for example, they were wont to use "Sunday" (禮拜日); they used *xintu* (信徒 believer, used by Protestants) instead of *jiaoyou* (教友 church member); and so on. Their reasoning, notes Xu, was that these terms were "more widespread" and "sounded better." "How wrong-minded!" he retorts. Xu frequently laments that the church has not yet unified its scriptural vocabulary, with multiple versions of proper names and nouns in use, but he does not elaborate: perhaps the value of Catholic tradition and traditional terminology were so self-evident as to render discussion pointless.

The links between education, social fabric, and church teaching exercise Xu frequently. On some matters, he is surprisingly modern in his thinking; on others, a rather more hard-core conservatism emerges, especially on moral issues. The provocation is often a text. In one instance, a textbook that Xu chanced upon in a Shanghai bookshop prompted him to pen the entry "On Erroneous Sayings on Marriage." The second chapter of the textbook in question discussed the household, but Xu deems that the social science studies presented, debating the origins of conjugal life and polygamous families, are lacking in evidence. What is the gain, he asks, from filling minds with so many incorrect perspectives? Youthful minds are easily unsettled, Xu suggests, and the sort of writing—of which the textbook was replete—that presents one alternative and then offers a contrary reading by another expert is potentially damaging, leaving the young without any sense of fixity. The shift to a more evaluative pedagogy rather than a model based on knowledge transfer was clearly a move too far for Xu. It is best, he concludes, for church schools to use church-published textbooks, since they are more trustworthy—and it is difficult to correct erroneous thinking later.[61] The damage to youth caused by writers not considering the effects of their words in an age of proliferating texts, and the confusion that results from the series of grey shades presented, is focal to several entries.[62] The continuation of classical thinking into the Republican era was alluded to in Chapter 3 but is rarely more apparent than in Xu Zongze's implicit equation of textual and moral probity and in his strong emphasis on fostering good reading habits, and therefore good citizenship, among Chinese youth.

ON BEING HUMAN

If some of Xu's jottings address trivial subjects, others cut to the quick. Life, death, and how to live well—to live well as Chinese—are recurrent foci of reflection. On death and dying, Xu takes an orthodox Roman Catholic line. Death and illness are a product of humans being a union of material body and spiritual soul: viewed from a transcendent perspective, illness can be seen as God's grace and can be used as a warning from God or to dampen an excessive delight in things of the world. For pious Christians, God may allow illness to enable them to gain merit and reduce the time spent in purgatory. Xu points out that the next life will be completely different from this life—and if people want to live a good life in the life to come, they should start preparing for it now.[63]

Matters of death are often inspired by secular newspaper sources. The plight of people who commit suicide and the statistics on suicide rates were constant concerns to Xu. In entry #108, for example, Xu relates government statistics on urban suicides for the year, calculating the daily and hourly rate of death, to shock readers into an appreciation of the scale of the problem. He sees root causes in economic pressure, family problems, or a world-weary pessimism, yet argues emphatically:

But human life is not something one bestows on oneself; it is a gift of the Creator God, and so human life is not a person's own, humans do not have sovereignty over their own lives. Humans have but the right to enjoy the use of their lives, and so suicide violates the sovereignty of the Creator Lord. If it is a sin to violate human sovereignty, how much greater is the sin that violates the Creator God's sovereignty, suicide.[64]

The mysteries and marvels of God's command of life and death are noteworthy, if not fathomable. Xu tells of a recent trip to Songjiang (#89), where a moribund patient had been brought into St. Joseph's hospital by a third party, not affiliated with the church, who did not want the sick man to die in his home. Xu sees the hand of God in the hopeless decision to take an incurable man to a hospital. The woman in charge of the ward urged her patient to convert; the patient assented to each of her questions, was baptized, and died not three hours later. "How marvelous is the Lord's wisdom and planning," concludes Xu, the act of soul-saving of overriding import in his theological thinking.

Xu draws on Confucian philosophical material, biblical texts, and folk wisdom interchangeably in proffering advice on life. Several of the *biji* entries are explicitly modeled on proverbial or wisdom literature; others echo the moral guidance of Chiang Kai-shek's New Life Movement in its injunctions against overeating ("the one who eats much will be ill much") and other vices. The value of wisdom literature in shaping human life is clear to Xu, and he sees his role as a Catholic publisher and church teacher as promulgating biblically based and commonsense wisdom in society. A couple of extracts illustrate the point:

> The greatest virtue of the elder generation in treating the younger is to tolerate their failings. The young generation finds many things difficult, and there are matters that only the elder generation can understand. If the elder generation does not foster a heart of tolerance, the younger will not be able to endure!

> If you want to gain people's affection, you need to accommodate yourself to others, to help others, be modest, not seek your own advantage, not be selfish, and not judge others.[65]

Xu's rewriting of household codes for a contemporary China includes many suggestions for intergenerational harmony, as well as exhortations to play down one's own abilities, not publicize oneself too widely, and not damage others' reputations. Xu's theological anthropology presents an accessible, Christian-inflected humanism. He divides humanity into two groups: those who care about you, and who therefore admire whatever you do and cover over your faults, and those without any affection toward you, who will criticize whatever you do.[66] The trick is getting people into a relationship so that they are well-disposed toward you; this is achieved by being empathetic, acknowledging others' mentalities, and getting to know their quirks. All should make their behavior as amenable as possible to others—a policy ultimately encapsulated in the Confucian version of the Golden Rule, "What you do not want done to you, do not do to others."[67]

Xu is well aware of the dangers of dispensing wisdom and comments wryly on the fact that most people who seek it do not really wish to avail themselves of it:

> People like to say very many things that are not heart-felt. To take an example: sometimes people say: please teach me, or please guide me, or correct me, but if you really give guidance to them, or correct them, they are not very happy! . . . To be human we need to be sincere; if you do not like something or someone, the best thing to do is keep your mouth shut. There is no need to go overboard in praising people, since this is fake.[68]

A central area of wise living is wealth, which Xu links both to death and to fullness of life. Xu characterizes the lifestyle and attitudes of those who are "slaves to money" and contrasts their material wealth with the fearfulness that the need for money brings. "You rich need to see through the wealth of the world," he exhorts; "no matter whether rich or poor, all are God's managers of wealth and possessions, and not the owners of it." All will have to give an account to God after death, "and the report of the poor will naturally be simpler and easier," he advises, pointing out that this was not a matter in which one would want to have regrets.[69] In "On the foolishness of accumulating money," Xu points out the paradox that people are willing to go without food and clothing and suffer for their children and grandchildren but unwilling to lift a finger for others ("if plucking out a single hair would benefit the world, they would not do it"). Can people take their amassed wealth and property with them? he asks.[70] Xu is consistently negative about the possibilities of good among the wealthy or worldly. As Xu writes, he can relate the importance of holy poverty only from his own experience, and a monastic outlook is evident both in his regarding the simplicity of "holy poverty in the heart and holy poverty in actions" as the best way and in a repeated emphasis on the freedom that poverty brings, in distinction to the entrainment of wealth.[71]

A social commentary links individual concerns to wider societal problems. In one entry (#44), Xu tackles the high interest rates that are crippling the agricultural economy. His comment is based on a newspaper report from the Tianjin *Dagong bao*, explaining what seemingly low percentage rates on loans equate to in compound terms. An interest rate cap is needed, Xu argues, to stem this major cause of rural poverty. The Bible prohibits usurious rates, he notes, and financial gain made through such transactions violates the seventh commandment. Xu hammers the point home: the principles of church teaching should not be neglected as a means to remedy the countryside. In another entry (#65), he points to a further drain on the national economy that Christianity battles against: superstition. The best way for Chinese to reduce their expenditure is by getting rid of superstition, especially incense and paper burning at temples, "which not only does no good, but actually harms children and grandchildren" by reducing the family estate. In line with much contemporary rhetoric, Xu also argues that luxurious weddings, funerals, and other such ritual spending to save face should be cut back.

The question of what it means to be human receives metaphysical and practical treatment in the *biji*. In several entries, Xu discusses how all humans should have a goal, an aim in life. We all need to know where we have come from and where we are going, he suggests. Not knowing, or not realizing the need to know, leaves one a "wanderer." If a student were to go to school without attending class or reading books, people would question whether he were a student; likewise, if we do not head toward our goal in being on earth, then are we really "human"?[72] We need, Xu implies, a purpose, for life to be fully human. Xu melds examples from history and legend with Christian ones and uses them to strengthen his point. Philosophers throughout the ages have not managed to explain "the riddle of being human" because they have been unwilling to admit that heaven and earth have a ruler, suggests Xu.

For Xu, faith is a means of living well, a pattern for life and a motivating force. In an entry titled "Human life needs a guiding rule," which presents a somewhat stark contrast in its portrayal of Christians and others, Xu expounds on the notion that all humans, and all thought, speech, and action, need principles and standards. Life without a compass to guide it "floats wherever the waves and current take it, and is controlled by the tides of the times"; people living such a life are "sacrificed to circumstances," lacking ambition and courage.[73] The true pattern for life, however, is to be found in religious faith and belief in a Creator God, and particularly the Ten Commandments, which form the standard for life. The Ten Commandments enable Christians "to have riches without greed, to meet poverty without complaining," and to be self-possessed at all times. By contrast, those without faith, and without the bindings of the commandments, "if rich and noble, become arrogant, in times of poverty, may injure their own interests, when facing disaster, will harbor grudges and hatred, will regret, lose hope, and when things are at their most negative may even end their lives."[74] Many of those now killing themselves following business failure share this malady, notes Xu: without religious faith to sustain them or comfort them, they can see no other route through in extremity.

In a more humorous reflection drawing together two of the cardinal Republican-era themes of science and ethics, Xu expands on the thought that scientific progress has meant we now have anemometers for testing wind, barometers for testing weather, and machines for gauging earthquakes—but no one has been able to devise a machine for testing the thoughts of the human heart. The complexity of human thought and its myriad twists and turns has so far defied science. "I suspect that this too is the Creator God showing consideration for us," writes Xu, "otherwise, if people's thoughts, good and bad, were laid out bare in front of people, how could they retain any face at all?"[75] Xu draws the thought out further elsewhere, when he points out that "modern" people all have thermometers and barometers, but that our bodies can also sense changes in the weather before they occur and experience a certain unnatural feeling before seasonal shifts. Moreover, we also have an internal conscience-ometer, a tool that can test our daily thoughts and actions. A kind act or good word leads to peace and calm whereas crude words or bad deeds lead to chaotic times or turbulence in the conscience-ometer.[76]

Xu explores the changeability of human nature in another meteorological metaphor. Given that he returns repeatedly to the theme of the unsettled times under the threat of occupation, his musings can be read in a political frame as well as pastoral:

> The weather varies from cloudy to bright, from windy to rainy, thunder and lightning to cold and hot, and people are just the same. Gloomy equates to cloudy; happiness to bright; an unsettled heart and will to the wind; distressed spirits to the rain; a disturbed conscience to thunder; excitement to lightning; impulsivity to heat; insensibility to cold. In the midst of these changes, humans are particularly susceptible to a variety of influences that can cause all sorts of confusion or havoc for an individual. The best way to inhibit these changes is to keep a calm state of mind, be patient, not allow "the heart to caper like a monkey and the mind to gallop like a horse," and not change one's purpose. After a while, the situation of the heart will change again, and so—you should train your mind.[77]

The general applicability of Xu's wisdom is notable, given that the audience for the *Shengjiao Zazhi* was preponderantly Catholic church members. The golden mean he advocates is both monastic and Zen. In Xu's writing, human wisdom is neither confined to Christians nor applicable only to them, just as theology cannot remain in a distinct, intellectual sphere of life.

In an entry that turns on two meanings of the character *ge* 格 as a rule or pattern and as character or personality in the compound *renge* 人格 (literally "human pattern"), Xu links human morality with the state via its etymology and the early philosophical text *Guanzi,* as recently reinterpreted by Chiang Kai-shek in launching the New Life Movement in 1934.[78] The entry in its entirety reads as follows:

> There is a rule for learning to write characters, and so the characters them-selves follow a rule. There is also a rule for being human, and so we speak of human character. There is also a rule for establishing a state, and so we speak of national character. If there were no rule for characters, and they could be written in any old higgledy-piggledy fashion, then the characters would not be characters; if there were no rule for humans, no "propriety, morality, modesty and sense of shame," then we would lose the way by which humans are made human. If there were no rule for the state then the strong would intimidate, and the weak be demeaned, and opportunism and artifice abound, and the order of a civilized state would not be achieved. And so "rule" is an important character.[79]

The pattern for being human that Xu quotes is a common phrase: the four cardinal virtues in *Guanzi*'s version, from "On Shepherding the People."[80] The first section of Chiang's 1934 speech promotes "a regular life guided by the four virtues" and notes that "a nation that neglects them will not survive."[81] The New Life Movement aimed at regenerating China through promulgation of a code of behavior based on these Confucian virtues, intended to be applied in all practical areas of life, from food choices to action, under the belief that a pure or clean life would lead to social order and individual morality would transform society.[82] Xu's entry thus locates the pattern for human life, without which one is not fully human—just as badly written characters are not charac-ters—in a traditional and contemporary Chinese sensibility and anthropology. The *Guanzi* text itself (attributed to Guan Zhong of the seventh century BCE but compiled after the Warring States and reaching us via a Han dynasty edi-tion) is discussing the relationship between the actions of the ruler, the morality of the people, and the flourishing of the state. Propriety (or ritual), morality (or righteousness), modesty (or integrity), and a sense of shame are the "four cords" or "four guy ropes" that stabilize the state.[83] The metaphoric association of the state and the virtue of the ruler and people is absolute: eliminate the virtues and the state falls. The *Guanzi* has been used and accepted to a degree by Confucianists, legalists, and Daoists alike. It sits between the hard-core legal-ists in their insistence on the rule of law and the more idealistic Confucianists of the Mencian variety[84] who promoted rule by virtue; the *Guanzi* allowed for both regulation and ritual, both feudal rule and clan law, and both the rule of the virtuous and the voice of the people (where in the latter it coincided with Confucian norms).

The rule, or pattern, for being human is here inextricably linked with the stability and continuation of the state. This relationship between state and people is mutual: a well-managed state provides the conditions for the flourishing of the people, constrains immorality, and promotes good behavior among the people. This tight connection and understanding of the formation of a state, problematizes the objections of contemporary missionaries and later writers to the "nationalism" of many elite Chinese Christian writers in the Republican era. Nationalism could still be, for a writer like Xu, less a promotion of this state against another state (although in the anti-imperialist and anti-Japanese war periods it took this on as its primary hue) than a focus on statecraft and that right rule which produces the optimal conditions for human flourishing. By the early years of the PRC, the term *aiguo*, "love the country," had begun to shape the discourse of nation and nationalism, but, especially in the writings of the classically trained, the fount of nationalism was still a benevolent source—and entirely compatible with Christianity.

CONCLUSIONS

Xu Zongze's *Sui si sui bi* illustrates, perhaps most clearly in this period, how distinct forms of written expression can shape Christian discourse. Xu's manifest ability to compose in different styles illustrates his multicultural education but also provides a commentary on the issues of what theology is and what Chinese theology might be. The adoption of the *biji* form provides for a different range of expression than writing in a non-Chinese literary form and brings into play a different persona, valence, and set of cultural assumptions. The literary miscellany, as one commentator wrote, presents "a more balanced picture of society than that offered by official history and biography."[85] Here, Xu can address a different set of topics and interests than in his essays and editorials and expect them to mean differently. The entries in this medley of jottings allow us kaleidoscopic glimpses of an entire worldview and trace the links between intellectual, political, and spiritual visions.

Both Xu's "official essays" and his *biji* writings elucidate core issues of Catholic social teaching: the life and dignity of the human person, the rights of workers, the needs of the vulnerable, participation in community and society. The abstract and intellectual discussion style of the essays in the journal may be contrasted with the *biji* jottings, which work Christian thinking into the fabric of everyday life and thought. The *biji* bridge any disjunction between the theological underpinnings of ethical thought and the lived life of readers and also act as an entry point to Christian thought for Chinese observers. Xu's examples and philosophical citations start out from, and accord with, Chinese understanding; their mode is not declarative or didactic, but observational and acerbic.

The social-centered nature of Xu's thought is immediately noticeable across his writings: his wisdom is practical, combining Catholic moral and spiritual values with a more humanist, commonsense perspective. As Li Lili points out, the focus of Xu's work was to "churchize" the new discourses and new currents of thinking that were circulating among intellectual groups and influencing the educated young, rather than to propagate the gospel.[86] Li argues that Xu's Roman Catholicism was central to all of his writing, that his writing was not simply directed toward society but was based in his Catholic theology—whether he was responding to such issues as the women's movement, where his comment "assumed Catholic doctrinal traditions as the basis, to defend the Catholic official position," or was drawing on Catholic traditions "for the principles and standards for resolving China's social problems."[87] It would be impossible to argue that a Roman Catholic lens did not set the focal length for Xu's writing, as it did for his personality, but it would also be hard to deny that in a work like *Sui si sui bi*, it is Chinese society that is his horizon. This chapter has taken its cue from Xu's writing and considered his reading of social problems not just in terms of Roman Catholic theology, as might be appropriate for a specifically social text like his *On Labor* or *On the Women's Question*, but in terms of how Xu writes and thinks through specific forms and how those forms shape the theology that emerges.

The collected volume of Xu's *biji* entries speaks to individual and family formation in the modern world. Its themes overlap with the interests of contemporary Protestant thinkers, in an emphasis on the education and development of Chinese youth, caught between an influx of Western ideas and the demise of Chinese learning; but they also diverge, particularly over aspects of moral ethics and in a focal interest on the role of Roman Catholic history in secular life. Xu's work and occupations imprint his thinking: as rare books librarian at the Jesuit compound, Xu's bibliophilia is everywhere evident; as the overseer of a new girl's middle school, Xu's concern for all matters educational is clear; as spiritual director, his care for moral growth is apparent. The integrated nature of life and thought is also clear: Xu's miscellany promotes a scholarly generalist, or renaissance, version of life. Even in the 1930s, Xu was still living life in the mode of a late imperial literatus, commenting on the world and taking an interest in everything from science to morality.

As the chapter has explored, while there is overlap in matters of social concern—poverty, well-being, social justice—between Xu's essays in the magazine
Shengjiao zazhi and his *biji* writings, there are also differences in both style
and content between Xu's formal writings and his personal musings. Unlike the
rational, Latinate deliberations of his textbook theology, *Sui si sui bi* presents a
cacophony of voices, sources, and ideas. Public articles are for general Catholic
dissemination and reflection; Xu's personal writings evidence a more Chinese-
centered sensibility and more catholic appeal. In Xu's *biji* writings, a concern
for the text, the nature of writing, and the Roman Catholic historical textual
legacy is a constant theme. As someone who grew up in the old-style learning,
Xu still relates to texts (whether biblical, theological, or Chinese philosophy)
in a mode of classical scholarship. Reading and ingesting texts forms the moral
self: this is seen in the *biji* writings in Xu's concern for school curricula and his
insistence that students read more Chinese texts. Texts have a didactic role for
the young but are also, as in traditional understanding, formative of communities and a major source of spiritual joy. Xu's Christianity is deeply entwined with
his textuality.

Through Xu's *biji* entries we see that contextual theology cannot be about just
social and economic context, since there cannot be a textually noncontextual,
or decontextualized, theology. That is, the text itself must be understood in its
textual context, not just in the cultural or sociopolitical context of the author.
The importance of Chinese textual forms has too often been underplayed in
reading and understanding Chinese Christian writings. Writings may be dependent on, or integrated with, particular literary forms in ways not apparent
when viewed aside from those literary categories. To limit debate and interaction with Chinese theology to those texts that fit some "traditional" pattern of
theological writings limits theology itself, as well as contemporary interaction
with Chinese theologians.[88] The extreme case of these *biji*—a "trivial" writing
form capturing topics of this-worldly concern that on the surface bear little or
no resemblance to systematic theology—points toward the need to look beyond
received doctrinal texts and forms in assessing Chinese theology. Few Chinese
theologians of the Republican era have chosen to study or articulate anew di-
vinely revealed truths of God, especially in their inherited philosophical structures. In Xu's *biji* a broad wisdom is revealed in creaturely things, and the truth-
value in Chinese wisdom, a long way from the binding dogmas and infallible
teaching authority of Rome, offers a subversive comment on what theology
means in, and for, China.

5

WU LEICHUAN, *CHRISTIANITY AND CHINESE CULTURE*, AND THE KINGDOM OF HEAVEN

The aim of religion is to improve society, and so all who believe
in religion must directly or indirectly take part in political activities. Humans are political animals—if people want to improve
society, how can they have nothing to do with governance?
—Wu Leichuan, 1936[1]

Religion was not primarily something to be believed, or felt; it
was something to be done, a life to be lived, a principle and a
program to be incarnated in character and built into a social order.
—Sherwood Eddy, 1927[2]

Religion, for Wu Leichuan (1870–1944), is a motivating force for progress in
human society. It propels individuals forward and upward: from the material to
the spiritual, from the individual to the communal. So begins *Christianity and
Chinese Culture* (Jidujiao yu Zhongguo wenhua 基督教與中國文化), a book
that has had a notable effect on Chinese Christian thought since its publication
in 1936. The question of what a Christian China might look like has attracted
scholarly attention in the debates since, and numerous studies have considered Wu Leichuan as a "Confucian Christian"[3] or engaged at length with his
form of contextualized Christianity.[4] This chapter builds on these studies in
exploring contextualization in Chinese culture and Wu's negotiation between
classical Chinese culture and an emerging modern culture, particularly in his
reading of scripture. But to read Wu's work solely in terms of "saving the nation" or as an exposition on contextual Christianity is to overlook the theological vision behind his state-building project. Wu's vision of the Kingdom

of Heaven, molded by the writings of the Social Gospel theologians, is central to his call to build a Christian China. This chapter reassesses Wu's reconciliation of Christianity with Chinese culture by foregrounding the centrality of the Kingdom of Heaven in his thinking. The chapter draws greater attention to the theologians with whom Wu is in dialogue: the British, German, and American Social Gospel proponents whose writings on the kingdom had such a critical effect on Wu.

Wu's introductory principles in *Christianity and Chinese Culture* set the frame for his thinking: religion is a close cousin to philosophy, it shares its roots with science, and its function is to guide the individual to transform society. A strong view of progress, with humanity governing the narrative, is combined with a social salvation: there is no distinction, in the end, between individual salvation and the transformation of society, since the latter is the purpose of the former. The implied question running through Wu's book is, how can religion benefit society? This question is a Christian version of the New Culture Movement quest (how can literature benefit society?) and a reflection of the zeitgeist of the revolutionary generation. Wu's work functions both as an apologetics to rebut the continuing fallout from the Anti-Christian Movement of the mid-1920s and as an exploration of the new meaning of culture and its relationship with religion in a changed world. As Rebecca Nedostup has written, dispute about "the proper place of Christianity in nationalism and modern civilization" was a major cultural debate in 1920s China.[5] It was also two-pronged: the question of the role of religion in the modern state entailed a dialogue with government and society and a dialogue within the church. Wu is writing in the light of Nationalist debates on secularism and on instilling a faith in the party-state to combat the dangers of religious "superstition," but also in response to contemporary Christian thinkers such as Ni Tuosheng, for whom "the Kingdom of this world is not the kingdom of God."[6]

Like Zhao Zichen and Xu Zongze, Wu Leichuan was of the generation whose formative years and adulthood were spent in two different worlds. He came from a minor official family in Xuzhou, growing up in near poverty, although he studied the Confucian canon in its standard late imperial curriculum. In Chinese terms, Wu was one of the best educated of all converts, having obtained the highest degree possible (the *jinshi* 進士)—and entrance to a life of elite state service—under the imperial examination system in 1898. By the time Wu wrote *Christianity and Chinese Culture* in the 1930s, however, China had come through to the other side of a cultural revolution. Language had been modernized and the old genres of writing, in which Wu had excelled, had been overturned; education had been westernized; dress, social mores, interpersonal relations, and all sorts of cultural certainties had changed beyond recognition. The "culture" aspect of Wu's title required almost as much explanation as "Christianity" to his readers, and Wu tackles the two separately in the volume, rather than engage in "endless comparisons" between them. Any relationship with the classics might seem to sit uneasily alongside the forward-facing, transformative ethos of the postrevolutionary generation, but Wu frequently explores what might be Chinese about the kingdom in China through relating Jesus to the concepts and mores of traditional culture.

The pressing imperative for Wu's generation, who had lived through the overthrow of native and foreign imperial rule, and the question that galvanized the minds of the elite across the political and religious spectrum, was to work out *how* to reconstruct the nation. Threaded through Wu Leichuan's work on the relationship between culture and Christianity is one answer: by envisaging the Kingdom of Heaven on earth. It is an answer that is at once both attractive and repulsive to alternative Marxist utopian visions and that frames debate on a question of central importance to both the Christian church and the Nationalist Party, and later the Communist Party: the relationship between church and state. What can the church do to bring about heaven on earth? Where does Christian allegiance lie: is taking part in building the new China a Christian project? This question was to split the historic churches once again in the late 1940s, as those who answer in the negative secede to build their own enclaves, leaving a remnant to negotiate an incipient national church and build its relationship with Chinese society.

If the Kingdom of Heaven is the cornerstone metaphor of Christianity for Wu, it is a description both of the reign of Christ in the present world and of the salvation of all humanity. Others have written on Wu Leichuan's nationalism, and Philip West makes a convincing case for the development of different stages in Wu's views on national salvation, in line with changing events during the 1920s and 1930s[7]—yet nationalism for Wu is also inseparable from his theological construction of the kingdom. The strength of his mature writing on the topic in 1936, long after the most turbulent period of damage and doubt both to faith and to views on the nation at the height of the anti-Christian attacks, goes some way to answering West's question as to why Wu "hung on to the Christian faith when it appeared to be largely meaningless among the students in whom he placed his confidence."[8] To read Wu's nationalism purely in terms of the debate over gradual change in society versus subitaneous revolution neglects the architecture of the kingdom in the construction of *Christianity and Chinese Culture* and Wu's understanding of how the nation was to be saved. In terms of his general argument, it is striking that in *Christianity and Chinese Culture* Wu did not draw on his long experience in public office or university administration to frame the vision of the kingdom. He makes few references to the present as he writes in 1936, even as the Japanese threatened to remove all Western teachers from his university. On the surface, Wu writes of the kingdom solely in terms of the biblical text, as interpreted through philosophical Confucian writings.

LAYING THE FOUNDATIONS

Wu Leichuan was no stranger to the workings of earthly kingdoms—or republics, at least. Throughout his early career he had combined the roles of educator and civil servant, putting his scholarship to the use of the state as befitted a Chinese degree holder. From being superintendent of a provincial college and concurrently a councilor in the local assembly in Zhejiang during the early 1900s, he rose to work in the Jiangsu governor's office while a school headmaster. When Hangzhou declared independence from the Qing government in 1911, Wu was briefly a magistrate in the city's military government. A stint at the Board of Education in Beijing, first as secretary and then senior assistant to the minister of education,[9] set him up in excellent standing for his later task ensuring the registration of the mission-sponsored Yanjing University with the Beijing and then Nanjing governments and its constitutional compliance with new regulations, including that of installing a Chinese national in a leadership position.[10] Wu taught in the Yanjing School of Theology from 1922, and as chancellor of the university from 1929 to 1933 was de jure head of the institute, even if in practice many regarded the American John Leighton Stuart, the president, as its leader.[11] The awkward division of labor—Wu tried to resign in 1931 but was persuaded to remain for two more years—was emblematic of the continued compromised position of Chinese Christians and their struggle for full recognition in Christian establishments. Wu served two masters: the Chinese government wanted educational institutions to have a Chinese president or vice president; the American funders and mission boards wanted one of their own as leader.

The boundary lines between social reform or revolution and the Kingdom of Heaven are highly permeable in Wu's thinking. The kingdom is not an eschatological event, as some "foolish" people surmise, he writes, but a reality, an architectural feat that requires long-term planning and effort in its construction. When Christians pray "your kingdom come," they are not praying for another world beyond this one and certainly not for some paradise after death, but for this world to be rid of everything that does not accord with God's benevolent love and justice.[12]

Wu is writing constructively, but we might assume that his framework also targets influential evangelical thinkers like Ni Tuosheng. It is instructive to set Ni's views alongside Wu's at the outset, given that Ni's interpretation of the biblical kingdom in the 1930s was diametrically opposed to that of Wu. For Ni, the world was created to be led by Christ, but "Satan set up a rival system known in Scripture as 'this world'—a system in which we are involved and which he himself dominates."[13] The first creation, the old creation, remains under Satan's rule; God's prime concern is now with "a new and second creation." Contra Wu, this new creation and kingdom was a rival realm where "nothing of the old creation, the old kingdom or the old world can be transferred to the new."[14] The point of contact between Wu and Ni was a shared belief that God needed to renew God's people to bring in the new kingdom, but their divergence on how this was to happen is emblematic of the widening gap opening up on the entwined questions of the Christian experience of salvation and of church-state relations. For Ni Tuosheng, the work and responsibility of the church is spiritual warfare, and the kingdom represents a cosmic restoration of God's loss at the fall, as well as the fulfillment of humanity's purpose. The kingdom, for Ni, is brought about by human weakness and an acceptance that God in Christ has already fulfilled the task, in a kingdom theology that draws strongly on Revelation; but for Wu, the kingdom is something that humans participate in, plan for, and realize.[15]

In Chapter 2 of *Christianity and Chinese Culture* Wu Leichuan sets out his introduction to the kingdom by categorizing Jesus's actions into seven types and his teachings into six classes. It becomes clear that Wu's exposition is not merely an analysis of Jesus, but also a blueprint for readers' responses, as the life of Jesus exemplifies revolutionary action. Jesus's life is a model, and the actions are stages in revolutionary action.[16] Just as Lu Xun had issued a clarion call to the nation in his short story collection *Nahan* (呐喊 Call to Arms) more than a decade earlier, so Wu's paring down of the kingdom to its essential building blocks charges the Christian community to go out and reconstruct the kingdom themselves.

The first of Jesus's actions is preaching the kingdom, his "sole mission." As Jesus invests the old Jewish term with new meaning from his own knowledge of God, he laments the disparity between Roman management, Jewish evils, and what should be and takes up his mission of reforming society with the phrase "love one's country, love humanity" (a phrase later echoed by PRC Christian leaders). Jesus uses the phrase "Kingdom of Heaven" as a caption, a heading, suggests Wu: whenever the gospels employ the phrase, they are in effect elucidating Jesus's ideas on the ideal society.[17] The second of Jesus's actions is to debunk empty or superstitious customs, an act that enables the ideal society to begin to grow (and an emphasis entirely in keeping with the spirit of the Nationalist-led "campaign to destroy superstition" of 1927–1937, which was intended to facilitate the building of the political kingdom, if not the heavenly kingdom).[18] The idea that tradition can be jettisoned is a timely one: for Wu, the "clear message" that new patches are not put on old clothes "indicates the principle for social progress."[19] No matter how often Wu is characterized as a Confucian, he is scarcely averse to revolutionary thinking. However, the revolution for Wu is within: the paring away of the bad and the irrational and striving toward the ideal do not entail a separation of religion from politics, as Nationalist rhetoric proposed and contemporary theorists like Zhang Zhenzhi were advocating, but precisely their combination.[20]

Once foolish customs are eradicated, the next step for Christ is "to repudiate all those obstructing progress" toward the new kingdom.[21] Reading rather like a political manifesto intent on keeping all on board, Wu's work describes how, in the great task of revitalizing the people, Jesus was willing at first to work collaboratively with the people and their leaders but was stymied by the intransigence of the Pharisees, who were keen to protect their own territory. Throughout *Christianity and Chinese Culture*, Wu returns to the need for careful selection of personnel and to the qualities of leadership that selectors should be looking for, as attested amply in the Confucian classics. Grasping that those current leaders who will not go along with his vision present "the most serious obstacle" to the initiation of the kingdom, Jesus has no choice but to "expose their sins" and bypass them.[22] The fourth action in the sequence of kingdom construction stems from the effects of worldly power and sin: to save the suffering. Once Jesus has come to understand how he will save the suffering, he can turn to training his disciples.

Jesus's decision to concentrate on training his disciples was premised, for Wu as for Zhao Zichen, on the failure to build the kingdom directly. Only "after Jesus understood clearly that his ideals could not be implemented in the present time" did he travel through the border areas of Galilee, "pouring all his effort into training his disciples."[23] Jesus's aim was that his disciples should understand his *xin zhi* 心志, the will or intent of his heart/mind; but since they could no more accomplish his great intent than he had been able, he provided two model actions for them to be proclaimed throughout history as the standard for being human. These two actions, which Wu brackets as equal, are the foot washing of the Passover eve and the breaking of bread and drinking of wine.[24] Their message, and Jesus's enduring legacy, is that leaders must serve the people and that only in losing themselves can the disciples commemorate

their master. The corollary, sixth action of Jesus is "going to his death unflinch-
ingly." A stoic obstinacy informs Jesus's final act ("he did what he could, knowing clearly it could not succeed, yet doing it"),[25] aware that there was no way
to complete his true task, yet driven on by his love for his country, society, and
humanity. It was this steadfastness, in Wu's estimation, this strength of character
that elicits the empathy of all later people of integrity and virtue, *zhishi renren*
志士仁人. If there is to be a revolution, it is an upturning of the old ways and a
pruning of regressive traditions and those who uphold them; there is no militant
revolution. Jesus's ultimate choice of self-surrender dictates, for Wu, the terms
of the kingdom.

The seventh and final category of kingdom-building action leads into Wu's
most controversial connection of biblical and classical Chinese motifs. Wu rejects any trace of supernatural power in Jesus's actions. In Chapter 1, Wu has
already established that Christianity is, at base, about teaching people how to
be human and that the miracles were added later to sweeten the message.[26]
Of Jesus's healings, Wu writes: "These are things people of the time thought
important, and things that ordinary Christians later liked to commend," without which Christianity would seemingly lose its "religious factor"—a position
he dismisses as a "great misunderstanding." Wu quotes Mark 1:33–39 in support of his contention that Jesus understood his primary task to be preaching and that he "refused requests" for healings, aware that miracles were "just
a medium for transmitting the gospel."[27] It is hard to see this as an entirely balanced reading of the passage: Jesus does escape to the desert from the crowds,
but only after healing many who were sick and ill—and his motivation for leaving was that others elsewhere should also hear. When he did heal, notes Wu,
it was to lead people to faith, because he understood the ways of their hearts.
When he expelled demons, Jesus would likewise often say that it was by the
power of the Holy Spirit, and "what the New Testament calls the Holy Spirit,"
argues Wu with a flourish, "is what is called *ren* [仁 benevolence, or virtue] in
the Confucian texts." It was through Jesus's steadfastness of will, through the
power of his perfection, that Jesus healed demons, "and not some mysterious
thing."[28]

The equation of the Holy Spirit with the Confucian virtue of *ren*, which Wu
returns to later in his discussion of Jesus's teachings, invites further consideration. For Wu, the Holy Spirit is not transcendent but immanent, and innate
to all humans. Using a methodology that proceeds by juxtaposition, Wu draws
inferences about Christian theology and Chinese terms from reading each
against the other. A close examination of two of his list of "reasons" for why the
Holy Spirit and *ren* are identical shows his mode of thinking:

1. We can pray to receive the Holy Spirit. Jesus taught his disciples that prayer would be fulfilled when he said "If you, then, though you are evil, know how to give good gifts to your children, how much more will your heavenly father give the Holy Spirit to those who ask him?"[29] We may know that the sole aim of prayer is to gain the Holy Spirit, exactly as Confucianism teaches people to seek benevolence (*ren*). Confucius said "They sought to act virtuously (*ren*) and they [Bo Yi and Shu Qi] did act virtuously."[30] He also wrote "I wish to be virtuous (*ren*) and lo! virtue is at hand."[31] Mencius said "Benevolence (*ren*) is the human mind (*xin* 心). The great end of learning is nothing else but to seek for the lost mind."[32] So let us imagine: benevolence can be sought, it can be desired and obtained; there is nothing to learning but the seeking for the lost mind (*ren*): is this not saying that benevolence seems to be a living thing, and, moreover, the one thing needed for humans?

2. The one who blasphemes against the Holy Spirit will not be pardoned. Jesus warned the scribes of his day "All sins may be forgiven, but the one who sins against the Holy Spirit will never be forgiven." This seems rather arbitrary. But if we examine the views of Confucius and Mencius on those who are not benevolent, we find that, for example, the rites and music were a necessary part of training in ancient China, but Confucius thought that those who were not benevolent could not perform the rites or music.[33] . . . Mencius also frequently took *ren* to be the most honorable nobility conferred by Heaven,[34] and, as for those who cast away the "nobility of heaven," he says "The issue is simply this: that they must lose that nobility of man as well."[35] From this we can see that the Ruists' bitter rebuke over a lack of benevolence is just as grave and that Jesus's words should not be explained as complaints.[36]

In the next four points, which proceed by similar analogy and quotation from the classics, Wu explains how the Holy Spirit is always connected with forgiveness, just as the Confucian *ren* is linked to *shu* (恕 forbearance); how those who possess the Holy Spirit are deemed able to judge others, just as is true of the benevolent; how the Holy Spirit brings about the kingdom of heaven, just as there can be no progress in the world without *ren*; and how the shock of Jesus's death provoked an awareness of the Holy Spirit among the disciples.[37] The parallels Wu finds in these six points between the scope of the Holy Spirit and that of *ren* lead him to posit that they are "different names for the same reality"[38] and that the teachings of Jesus align with those of Confucius and Mencius.

It might be surprising to us at this distance that anyone could make the leap between the Holy Spirit and *ren* with the felicity that Wu does, but the move allows him to draw on this key term in Confucian morality in limning the kingdom. The leap shows a manner of reading the Chinese classics and a depth of investment in spiritual development as a Confucian that have been all but lost in China since the Republican era. It is also a move tied to a deep sense of the universal. Seeking resonance appears as a form of Scriptural Reasoning, developed out of a familiarity with one's own scriptural heritage (here, Wu's youthful study and ingestion of the Chinese classics). In this instance it is clearly more of an exegesis of those Chinese classics than of the Christian scriptures. Making the Holy Spirit into a motivator for the kingdom allows Wu to draw parallels with classical passages describing rule through benevolence. In Confucian terms, only through the virtue of rulers can true leadership be exercised. By showing that the truly virtuous must be those who are "full of the Holy Spirit," Wu elides the concepts. The reasoning is simple (if tautologous): benevolence is innate to humans, the Kingdom of God is "among you," therefore the Holy Spirit promotes the kingdom. This style of dialectic is not limited to the discussion of the Holy Spirit but forms the basis for comparisons between various aspects of Christianity and Confucianism. In a later discussion of prayer, for example, Wu links prayer with the perfection of the self, demythologizing a Christian reading by reference to the Confucian and understanding Christianity by the translation, or transfer, of attributes from what is already known to him. He is unapologetic about the directionality of his approach, arguing, for example, that when we understand the meaning of prayer from a Song dynasty Confucian perspective, "then we can examine Jesus's teachings on prayer."[39] Wu frequently lifts phrases from the Confucian classics out of context, and he is equally lax with Christian scripture, often unwilling to accept an obvious reading where it does not suit his case.[40]

The question of miracles raised in the final category of kingdom building is linked to a broader pattern of scripture reading. In Wu's analysis, although Jesus responded with compassion to requests for healing, his feelings on miracles are seen more by his "groaning at people's stupidity" in asking. This is a rather artful reading: that particular response (in Mark 8:11–13, as footnoted in Wu's text) is to the Pharisees who ask for a sign, not to those seeking (miraculous) healings for the sake of being well. Wu repeatedly stresses the fallibility of textual transmission and the need always to assume later additions. In Wu's discussion of the Mark passage, Jesus was not willing to brag or perform miracles, but "because the gospels were written several decades after Jesus died, what was passed on in them inevitably gained some far-fetched interpretations in line with common thinking, so there were many events which no longer corresponded to their original truth."[41] Close textual analysis is precluded by such a strong sense of textual corruption. For Wu, as for Zhao Zichen, the presumption in reading the gospels should always be a nonmiraculous explanation. The example of the five loaves and two fishes is common to both, as is the explanation that those present were moved by Jesus's words and offered the food they had brought to the gathered masses: "and lots of the miraculous events recorded in the gospels can be seen like this." Wu takes his experience in the Chinese textual tradition and applies it to a very different history of biblical oral and textual transmission. His unremitting deconstruction of the text makes short work of Jesus's testing in the wilderness, for example, where "a symbolic manner of speaking" is used by writers steeped in oral traditions, leading some later readers to mistake the event as some sort of spiritual experience or "mysterious phenomenon."[42] Throughout *Christianity and Chinese Culture*, there is a distinct lack of recognition of the literary power or value of symbolic readings.[43]

The kingdom, in sum, is founded on Jesus's actions of preaching, debunking superstitions, and neutralizing those in power who oppose it. It is premised on the painstaking training of disciples, for whom the most important lesson is that of service. The miracles and healings that Jesus used to draw people into the kingdom were mainly a sop to the people's expectations, enabled by Jesus's supreme realization of humanity, and their interpretation has been greatly influenced by later writers' belief in the centrality of miracles to religious meaning. Since the Holy Spirit and *ren* describe the same entity, our understanding of how the kingdom is to be built can be much enhanced through tracing the role of *ren* in Confucian thought.

THE KINGDOM OF HEAVEN IN BIBLICAL
AND THEOLOGICAL THOUGHT

If the Kingdom of Heaven can be drawn from analogy with the Confucian virtue of benevolence, it is also described directly in scripture. The parables show that the kingdom is the greatest treasure on earth, but, more importantly, that it takes visionary individuals to see the value of this pearl, this hidden treasure—individuals who are prompted to jettison everything to buy it, who become aware of their own dissatisfaction with society and strive to change the environment.[44] Such fervor for treasure, for changing the environment, can never be contained but imbues everything, writes Wu. The treasure is only treasure when someone discovers it and is willing to share it with others who are also working for the well-being of all.[45] The Kingdom of Heaven is not built overnight, but a significant amount of human effort is required in its construction, and those engaged in this "must possess a range of moral qualities, and only then will they be qualified to take part in building the kingdom of heaven."[46] Rooted on earth and turned toward heaven, as any Confucian edifice should be, the kingdom takes shape through the Holy Spirit in its guise as the quality of *ren*, without which there is no progress in the world.[47]

Wu Leichuan's thinking on the kingdom is strongly influenced by his reading (in translation) of the writings of various Social Gospel proponents of the 1910s and 1920s. Wu quotes directly, and at length, from Bishop Charles Gore's Halley Stewart lectures of 1927, where Gore argues in his call for peaceful revolution that "salvation," in both the Hebrew scriptures and the New Testament, comprises a social element and reminds that the early church worked on a voluntary system of communal ownership;[48] and from Sherwood Eddy's *Religion and Social Justice* (1927), in which Eddy explores how the Social Gospel embraces social justice in the commercial world and the economic sphere.[49] Wu draws extensively on the thinking of Gore, Eddy, Walter Rauschenbusch, and others in his understanding of the relationship between stewardship and property ownership; of the need for a small vanguard whose ideas would transform wider society; of the construct of the early church; and of the relationship of the kingdom with society and with the eschaton. In the Social Gospel writers, Wu found an echo of his own sense of deep unease with present society and a quest to clarify what a Christian life expended in shaping the kingdom should look like in the present time. Eddy wrote of the "growing dissatisfaction with 'things as they are'" and the "desire to find a way that leads to 'things as they ought to be,'"[50] while Gore quipped that "society as it now exists it may be taken for granted is a parody of the divine intention."[51]

One of the chief points that Gore made at the outset of the lectures from which Wu quotes was that the "evil we deplore in the present society" is not an inevitable result of human nature, but that "a fundamental change of the spirit in which we think about and love our common life" was needed—a change made possible by the fact that Christ really is the savior and redeemer of humanity "in its social as well as its individual life."[52] It is unsurprising that Wu found common cause with writers like Rauschenbusch. They were facing similar social evils—in the United States, as a result of industrial unrest and the widening disparities in urban living that capitalism was producing, alongside racial injustice and a new awareness of social revolution in terms of gender— and were thinking through them in a manner that was not typically "theological" but embraced scientific thinking and rational method. Rauschenbusch saw common cause with the Chinese philosophers in positing society as the locus of human relationship building and therefore of kingdom building. Where theology had, for Rauschenbusch, overplayed sacramental activities and priestly importance, it had downplayed righteousness, mercy, and solidarity,[53] the same cardinal forces of traditional Chinese ethical life. Rauschenbusch's earlier challenge to the church had delineated a Kingdom of God that chimes in almost every respect with Wu's construct throughout *Christianity and Chinese Culture*: divine in origin, the church establishes a community of righteousness; both present and future it manifests humanity organized according to the will of God, a social order in which humanity is enabled to have its highest and freest development; it is the purpose for which the church exists (and not vice versa!); it is not confined to the boundaries of the church.[54]

Teachings on the kingdom form a substantial part of Chapter 3, which is captioned "Essentials of Jesus' Teachings." In a concise passage, Wu weaves together disparate biblical passages with his own interpretations to build up the Kingdom of Heaven as a project, a task. The kingdom is a call to action, predicated on the moral fiber of the called. (There is an interesting convergence between the governmental New Life Movement, evangelical theologians, and liberal voices like Wu on moral renewal as the prerequisite for state/kingdom building, derived from early Chinese philosophical thought.) As Wu reminds us, only those who do God's will enter the Kingdom of Heaven, and many will call on his name in vain.[55] Given that "the main condition of the new society is the equal distribution of wealth,"[56] it is unsurprising that solidarity with the poor and a determination to suffer for righteousness are conditions for Wu of participation in kingdom building. Only if a person is born again can he or she enter the Kingdom of Heaven: all evil practices, the practices of the old times, must be washed away.[57] If only children can receive the kingdom, this shows us that the task requires humility. No one puts the hand to a plow and looks back: there cannot be any procrastination once the aim is clear. The one who makes a profit in business is a loyal servant and will be rewarded in the kingdom, while those who do not prepare, or miss the opportunity, will be thrown out. Those who bury their treasure—who do not care for the common good, who are evil and lazy—will be punished. The transformation of society is key, as parable after parable shows—and *all* have to work at reforming themselves.

The Kingdom of Heaven has clear institutional characteristics. Since it is a new society, much of the old must be dismantled. In another close biblical reading—of the sort that Wu often mistrusts as a basis for theology in others, particularly in passages like this from John that he has already noted were written decades after Jesus's death, with considerable leeway for memory lapse— Wu discusses how Jesus's talk of bringing division, and the pains of a woman in labor, show his disdain for the family structures of the era, or lack of any great investment in their continuance.[58] There will be revolution in political structures and in economic systems as the kingdom is built. The very fact that people will come from north, south, east, and west proclaims this: there will be no national boundaries or ethnic divisions in the kingdom. Jesus's ideal, the Kingdom of Heaven, is, Wu reiterates, a reformed, new society—and not an otherworldly, postmortem destination.

THE ECONOMICS OF THE KINGDOM

The cornerstone of the kingdom is economic reform. Since the most acute inequalities cause the most pain and division, transformation into the kingdom starts at the base. In the economics of the kingdom, getting rid of inequality enables peace, and the first task is therefore to remove private property. A world where the majority cannot meet their daily needs affords no prospect for the human happiness that characterizes the kingdom. It was a misunderstanding of later readers, argues Wu, drawing on Karl Kautsky, to think that Jesus looked down on material goods: he did not, as the Lord's Prayer shows—but any serious attempt to get rid of the class distinctions of wealth must reject private property ownership.[59] As Charles Gore explains, in exploring how "something has gone very wrong with our tenure of property" in England, the biblical doctrine of stewardship holds that God alone is the "only absolute owner" of things or persons and that human ownership is always "relative and dependent." It was no longer conscionable that the right to self-fulfillment should be afforded only to the leisured few, and a new ideal of property, regulated by society and predicated on "use" not "power," needed to accompany the realization that the self is always brought to being in community.[60] Situating morality in terms of property ownership and a willingness to work for the public good seems a radical move now but may have been less startling to someone raised on classical Confucian ethics. Wu envisages a truly egalitarian society with no room for human calculation of greed or gain, when needs will be met from equal allocation. The justification is again biblical: the parable of the talents, for example, is about the management of public property; the parable of the workers in the vineyard also makes clear the principle that "each works to the best of their ability, and each receives what they need";[61] the late workers receiving the same pay works on the same principle. Those who were hired for just an hour in the evening had no opportunity to work earlier in the day as no one would hire them: their needs remain the same as those of others. When property is held in common, all are property owners, and there is no need for a system of taxes (and so Jesus pays none, finding his in the mouth of a fish).

When viewed through Wu's internal logic, so many of Jesus's parables speak to the economics of the new kingdom. The parable of the lost coins shows how most people think about property. The prodigal son's enlightenment comes after he has squandered private property and becomes a hired laborer, acknowledging that everyone is a worker in society.[62] Those who refuse to attend the wedding banquet all do so to pursue their own private interests, whether selling an ox or seeing some land; they are unwilling to join in the transformation of society and take no responsibility for the public good. A social understanding of capital precludes individual greed or gain: "you received without payment, give without payment," quotes Wu, explaining to his audience that everything humans have is given, all are born with nothing.[63] Like Gore, Wu links property to the proper functioning of society. All are dependent on society—not only wealth and external property, but intelligence too is nurtured by society, and it is only natural and proper that it should in return be used for society. "It's a pity most people don't get this," Wu notes laconically.[64] In an adroit move, he links Jesus's "new commandment" to the social. How can "love one another" be a new command, he asks, since it is one of the two planks of the Jewish law?[65] The novelty, Wu argues, lies in the fact that the commandment is aimed at the community. Jesus knew that if his disciples were to maintain group cohesion and fulfill his mission after his death, they would need to love each other, hence the "new" command. Social love is the key to building the kingdom.

Wu's conclusion that without change in the economic system, there will never be any progress in morality in society, and so economic reform must be placed at the heart of transforming society into the Kingdom of Heaven, is a natural outcome of rooting the kingdom in personal moral transformation. A liberative theology, redistribution of wealth is here seen as a means of fulfilling the kingdom promise that all shall have daily bread. In drawing together so many parables that have frequently not been read in an economic frame, Wu gives new impetus to Jesus's words and builds out of them a clear blueprint for kingdom life.[66] For Wu, sin is structural. It has economic and postcolonial properties, and it is overcome by Christ and in Christlike lives. As one of the few Chinese theologians of the era not to have studied abroad and not able to read foreign languages, Wu was relatively immune to accusations of peddling foreign theologies, whether Social Gospel or Marxist in leaning, although it is clear how closely he drew on them. Where Joseph Ratzinger was later to argue with regard to the Marxism of Liberation Theology that "it is difficult, and perhaps impossible, to purify these borrowed concepts of an ideological inspiration which is compatible with Christian faith and the ethical requirements which flow from it,"[67] Wu had no such qualms in his Chinese, nationalist, Confucian—and quite possibly also Marxist—reading of the Bible, since the outcome was his yardstick. The "purification" Wu aimed at was the return to Jesus's central task, reforming society and building the Kingdom of Heaven, whose real meaning was lost as the disciples—even as they held a common table—spread a message of individual salvation and as the environment, inherited beliefs, and fall of Jerusalem affected the gospel writers in their transmission of Jesus's real intent.[68]

THE KINGDOM OF HEAVEN AS LINKED TO THE NATURE OF THE MESSIAH

If the Kingdom of Heaven is preeminently a matter of economic justice, its realization is brought about through Jesus's perfected, messianic nature. "The center of Christianity," argues Wu, "is Jesus's character, and Jesus-as-Messiah is the center of Jesus's character."[69] The gospels, laments Wu, fail to make clear how "all that Jesus did in his life, and his being killed and becoming a perfect human—are all deeply connected to his being Christ."[70] Theologians, with their emphasis on events in Jesus's life being foreordained by the Father, are even more useless for the study of Jesus as a human. Jesus's character saves because in modeling self-sacrifice, and in his confrontation with evil, Jesus shows others how to do the same, and his spirit of courage is replicated. The quality of Jesus's life and his vision for society together bring about the Kingdom of Heaven. Although Jesus's life and his vision can be listed as separate bullet points in the summation of the kingdom, they are necessarily linked: it was Jesus's exceptional human qualities of "self-knowledge, of choices made, of self-determination,"[71] coupled with heaven-given wisdom, that enabled him to implement his vision—and that process of implementation that leads to his death and models the act of self-sacrifice as the means of bringing about the kingdom.

If "Messiah" means "anointed one," explains Wu, three sets of people were anointed in ancient Israel: rulers, prophets, and priests. If we combine these three categories together, we end up with the figure of the Chinese Son of Heaven, or emperor, the "one who rules all peoples, transmits the will of Heaven in teaching the people, and represents the people in his sacrifices to Heaven." Christ's role, implies Wu, likewise embraces all three anointed roles. The Messiah must necessarily be a person of the highest morals, a moral exemplar, if he is to lead or rule others. Wu's understanding of the Messiah is framed by his base understanding of the personhood and function of a ruler in the ideal Chinese past, combined with his reading of the social vision of the gospels. In pointing to the inner anointing Jesus received, Wu quotes the *Shu jing*, or Book of Documents: "The sincere, intelligent, and perspicacious one becomes the great sovereign."[72] The role of a benevolent ruler in teaching all to live rightly (whether out of moral compunction or legal coercion) is reiterated in a second reference taken from Mencius, through which Wu reminds of the role of the prophets in Israel, decrying failures of governance when "superiors violate the laws of righteousness, and inferiors violate the penal laws."[73] This is the state that occurs, as Mencius shows, when the ruler lacks benevolence. The Israelite prophets, Wu notes, had much cause to complain about their country's leaders, who concentrated too much on heavenly things and not enough on earthly affairs—to the point where their negligence saw the people carted off into exile and the capital city captured.[74] Notwithstanding Wu's lack of direct reference to contemporary circumstances, it is clear that human affairs and governance are central to the building of the kingdom.

The first role of the Messiah was to fulfill the longings of the Israelite people for a wise and benevolent ruler. Being the "ruler Christ" that the majority of Jews longed for had been Jesus's original plan, argues Wu, honed some twenty years earlier when at age twelve he realized that there was no greater "father's business" to attend to than the coming of the Messiah. For Wu, John the Baptist's question "are you the Messiah, or should we expect another?" was evidence of that planning and a ministry shared with John. Early in Jesus's ministry, when the disciples were sent out in twos to preach and when Jesus told them that at the revival they would be judging the twelve tribes of Israel, the disciples clearly believed Jesus would be "a ruler who would revitalize the nation." Their failure to grasp Jesus's evolving understanding of the role of the Messiah is evident in the fact that they were still asking for higher positions in the kingdom even as Jesus was explaining his death.[75] Even as he planned to be the ruler Israel was waiting for, Jesus's main aim was still to reform society, Wu avers—but without indicating how to reconcile the two. While the Jewish people were looking for rapid military extraction from a foreign yoke and a declaration of independence, Jesus's investigations led him to conclude that thoroughgoing reform was the better way forward. Only when rotten elements within society had been removed, a truthful administration established, and the people's hardship relieved—only then could a new state be established.

It is hard not to read a commentary on the Chinese situation into Wu's writing, and we can presume this was intended. Military uprising versus internal reform, the relief of poverty versus the creation of a new state: it is difficult to say whether Wu uses his Bible reading as a blueprint for reform in China or whether his ideas of what China needs influence his reading of Jesus. Wu's logic is reinforced, as ever, with Chinese philosophical expertise: Mencius's statement "When the ruler of a state loves benevolence, there are no enemies under heaven" shores up the contention Jesus had grasped that when a state is internally strong, belligerent neighbors will reappraise their positions.[76] Without internal reform, any overcoming of an enemy will produce only a temporary reprieve. Theologically, the people's good is the highest blessing: working for the good of the nation is God's work, building the kingdom. Given that the most important of the internal reforms is the economic system, the first issue that the messianic ruler must address is the people's livelihood. Jesus shared with John the slogan "repent for the Kingdom of Heaven is near." John's answer to the question "what should we do?"—share your garments and food, don't extort, be satisfied with what you have—which was intended to correct the people's attitudes toward property, was surely Jesus's too, Wu contends. When Jesus tells his disciples not to take money or food on their preaching trips, he is again foregrounding the economic system.[77]

Jesus's twin aims, to fulfill hopes for a Messiah who would revive the nation and to implement plans to build a new society, were predicated at the outset on gaining political power. In Wu's schema, Jesus never wavered in the second aim, but the means had to be reconsidered: indeed, abandoning the first became the only way to secure social reform. The pragmatic reasons for Jesus's thinking were simple: the original plan, according to Wu, had been to split the task with John, with John preaching in Galilee and Jesus consulting with the Jerusalem leaders. When John was imprisoned, the loss of his colleague was "like having an arm cut off," and the subsequent rethinking saw Jesus concentrating on preaching, with the plan to gain political power postponed. The second reason for Jesus's change of mind was the result of experience: it was evident that neither the peasants nor the Jerusalem leaders were sufficiently persuaded by his ideas to provide a route to power—and if power was the sole aim, the means would then require turning stones into bread and leaping from the temple roof, which Jesus had already determined he could not do. The first aim thus had to be sacrificed to protect the second. If plan A had been to build the country up in truth and model the ideal kingdom for other nations, the circumscribed plan B was to sacrifice life and struggle with the forces of evil in order to spread the seed of truth among humans and let it grow into a universal blessing.[78] Jesus's moral choice was in line with the Mencian philosophy of "not debasing oneself and thereby ruling all under heaven."

The sacrifice of Jesus's life is not here to be construed as a restitution or ransom for sin, but as part of the plan to model the kingdom. Wu builds up a clear inner vision for Jesus of his messianic role. This is not the ex post facto or orthodox imputation of theological reasoning to Jesus but comes, it seems, out of his own experience of a beleaguered and war-torn country, with its political factions and occupying forces, and a scientific or rational mindset. As Jesus comes to realize that the Jewish state could not act as a model for the world, he reasons that he can fulfill God's mission another way—by sacrificing himself for the truth and so guiding others to act similarly. If the initial task had been to create a model state (along the pattern of the Zhou state?) that prefigured and enacted the Kingdom of Heaven, as that option is closed down by circumstances, Jesus accepts that if Israel cannot collectively model the kingdom, he can at least personally model his life as a means to bring about the kingdom. The pattern of self-sacrifice is an object lesson in how to bring about the Kingdom of Heaven, a theological move rather than a soteriological one. It is a practical, life-changing move, to eradicate the evil that promotes sin. Ultimately, there is little difference in Wu's view between a soteriology of redemption and what he is describing: Jesus's struggle with evil and self-sacrifice as the way to bring about the kingdom, which is the reign of blessedness for all.

Illumination for the disciples came more slowly. They had grasped, Wu notes, Jesus's teaching on eradicating private property but could not slough off their inherited patterns of thinking on matters of human rule and pomp, as seen in their quest for honor in the kingdom or attempts to fight in Gethsemane. Although their thinking on the kingdom changes after Jesus's death, when they come to recognize Jesus as Messiah, they are still constrained, and their failure is nothing less than a new betrayal. Although Wu cannot allow himself to attribute this "great change" to the (supernatural) power of the Resurrection, he shows how it is manifest in their speeches explaining Jesus as the Messiah, in which "they place the guilt of Jesus's death on the Jewish people, and say nothing about Jesus's great plan to transform society—which shows that their recognition of Jesus as Messiah was informed by another inherited concept of the Messiah, and that they had not understood its true meaning. And so when the church spread the gospel, they always emphasized individual salvation and neglected the transformation of society." The recovery of the true meaning of the Messiah, Wu exhorts, "awaits the present generation's searching and investigation."[79]

Given the disciples' misguided response to Jesus's vision for his role as Messiah, Wu Leichuan, like Zhao Zichen, is much more understanding of the disciple Judas's reaction. Since, for Wu, Jesus has originally planned to be a ruler-Messiah and Judas was a Zealot, whose cherished aim was precisely the restoration of the country and who had placed all of his political hopes on Jesus, his disconsolate and angry response is an understandable one. When Jesus had explained to his disciples that he must die, Judas alone fully believed and understood the absolute change in Jesus's vision for how to bring about the kingdom. Compared with those who fled in the garden, or to Peter's denial, isn't Judas's response more excusable, posits Wu?[80] It, at least, arose from a patriotic zeal. The insights, or creative explanations, that both Zhao and Wu present for Judas suggest that they may have seen his face in the responses of too many colleagues and comrades during the civil war.

THE KINGDOM IN THE WORLD

As Li Wei points out, Wu Leichuan was not the only person of his era to write a book titled *Christianity and Chinese Culture*. Both Zhao Zichen and church academic Wang Zhixin did too, and numerous others produced articles on the topic. Li links the flourishing thought on religion and culture to the "golden era" of church development in the first two decades of the twentieth century, when Christian input into politics was at a height (with sixty Christian members of the 1912 interim National Assembly), and to the subsequent backlash during the 1920s when the influx of Western -isms (liberalism, anarchism, scientism, etc.) coalesced around attacks on Confucianism and on Christianity as antiscientific. The attacks gave Christianity, as theologian Liu Tingfang noted, the opportunity to right its own house and a reason to explain to outsiders how Christianity brought out the best in Chinese culture.[81] A signal change in thinking on culture was marked by the shift from a missionary-era accommodation to Chinese cultural practices and needs (as seen in church architecture or gender separation in pew seating) to a wholesale theological and ideological defense of the project of Chinese Christianity itself, by Chinese and for Chinese.[82] As Li suggests in using the term "contextualization" over "inculturation" for these developments, the understanding of "culture" here goes beyond the dominant modern one of the high arts.[83] Wu's understanding of "culture" is in some senses a classicist one—he separates out the "small minority" who understand the higher precepts of Daoism and Buddhism from the majority who see the religion in temple practices and rituals, and discusses these as a contradiction, for example—but his discussion of the relationship of religion and culture deliberately encompasses the whole realm of cultural life, including economic affairs and industrial relations.[84]

If the Kingdom of Heaven is to be established in a minority Christian country like China, it will necessarily be through the wider apparatus of the state, and in a manner that accords with broader Chinese self-understanding. One of the interesting questions that Wu's work raises is that of whether the relationship of culture and religion is fundamentally different in a convert nation or culture. In Chapter 5 of *Christianity and Chinese Culture* Wu discusses the relationship of culture and the state, noting how, in its attempts to popularize, early Christianity lost its reforming social mission. Initially, the church was oppressed by governments and looked down on by society, so its spread was supported through the strong cohesion of the believers, irrigated by the blood of the martyrs. The nature of Christianity inevitably changed when it became a state religion, when the degenerate freely entered the church, and when, under the influence of political models, the church installed popes and bishops and such hierarchies—when power rather than spiritual formation became its task. As the church concentrated on maintaining its status, dissenting voices were silenced, and theologians obscured Jesus's teaching.[85] By contrast, Wu goes on to elucidate the central role of the Christian church in world history and, using the American J. W. Williams's work, to list some of the many practical, social contributions the church had made in recent times, from the Red Cross to prison reform. In Chapter 9 of the volume, Wu compiles his own corollary list of what China needed to do. The vision is entirely social and political, but for Wu, entirely Christian also—there is no distinction. "Like a doctor curing illness," he writes, "we must first be clear about our weakness, and then apply medicine."[86]

Wu's strategy for kingdom-building in China is highly pragmatic. The cultural vision, he argues, must deal with three pressing problems: the people's livelihood, education, and the relationship between the individual and the social collective, or between democratic and autocratic rule. Wu sets out four areas for immediate social reform: land reform, economic control, rural construction, and moral education. The equalization of land ownership had been on the statute books since 1930 but was not yet achieved and was, in Wu's view (quoting Sun Yat-sen) a key factor in the people's livelihood. Greater economic centralization, or a controlled economy, was needed to support agriculture and industry and to deal with foreign capital flow and control.[87] Rural construction, which included education and hygiene projects, offered roles for both governmental and nongovernmental organizations and also required the reallocation of land.[88] The two prime questions of the future that Wu detects are the relation of the spiritual to the material and that of the individual to society. Wu was clear about the barriers to reform, prime among them foreign economic encroachment and military burdens, but even if we accept a certain lack of expertise in his political or economic program, the theological imperative to act, to act for the cause of economic justice and empowerment and social well-being, remained strong. Wu argues that moral education cannot wait until after these social reforms have worked, as others were suggesting, but must occur in tandem. The problem was not the principle of encouraging moral education, but the fact that if the leaders of the country (including those from the Guomindang) were not themselves modeling such behavior, there is no incentive or reason for those below to do so, as Mencius wrote "in an apt portrait of the present."[89] In understanding culture, just as in reading scripture, Wu looks to the classics for comparison, clarification, and authority.

The relationship of Jesus and Israel (and of Israel and China) provides a link between Wu's reading of the relationship between the work of the Messiah and the coming of the kingdom in the world. In a few brief paragraphs early in *Christianity and Chinese Culture*, we travel from Abraham through the twelve tribes to the divided kingdom and on into exile and successive occupying conquerors and Jewish self-rule under the Hasmoneans. The tale of rulers and ruled continues to Jesus's time, when the territory is split into the Tetrarchy, with Herod Antipas and Philip getting on happily with their smaller share of land, but brother Herod Archelaus incurring the wrath of the people and Rome and seeing his territory revert to direct rule.[90] Wu sets up the background to Jesus's final days by describing the workings of local Jewish councils and explaining how Roman involvement with the ruling council in Jerusalem occurred when the death penalty needed ratifying. Ethnic tensions are introduced, as army and troop composition are given and we are introduced to the Samaritan people and the possibility of collaboration. Throughout Wu's work there is no sense that the Chinese people are to be grafted onto the Jewish nation, as in a New Testament or traditional Western Christian reading; the Chinese people remain a separate, parallel case. As in the Jesuit era, when the Chinese case necessitated a different set of mission strategies, the Chinese case, for Wu, is to be read through its own historical and cultural lens.

Wu frequently directs his readers' attention to links between political history and identity formation, repeating the notion that "the Jewish strength of consciousness as a people group is unrivalled."[91] The subtext to the introduction to the Jewish land and division of territory is a reflection on the situation in China. Wu carefully prepares for a salvation message through historical parallels with the downtrodden Jews. Territorial division, warlordism, the Japanese occupation of the Northeast, and the establishment of Manchukuo were all high on the minds of Chinese readers, for whom a description of conquest and colonialism might produce immediate resonances. Wu continues his argument for the strength of identity awareness among the Jewish people with an account of the humiliations a merchant people experiences abroad and concludes by reiterating the staunch belief in their chosenness. "Their golden era is their future ideal," he writes, when "they believe God will cause a Messiah to come down to earth and revive [*fuxing* 復興] the people."[92] The implied parallels between the Jewish people and the Chinese culminate in the need for revival, or rejuvenation. Bringing about national rejuvenation or regeneration (*fuxing*) through a moral code of (Confucian) behavior was the central aim of Chiang Kai-shek's New Life Movement, launched in 1934, and here, Wu links social revival directly to salvation. Against the odds of foreign rule, the failure of multiple revolutions, and an increase in the troubles of daily life, the Jews maintained their hope, Wu notes: indeed, it was precisely during such troubles that their hope was strongest. Wu's historiography errs toward traditional Chinese notions of history here, rating the moral message more highly than strict accuracy; in any case, the message is clear: social salvation will come to China, a country as beleaguered as ancient Judea, and it will be ushered in as a messianic kingdom.[93]

A single incident in scripture provides the source for a lengthy exposition on nationhood. To his youthful audience, Wu explains that only one event in Jesus's childhood appears in the gospels, which he repeats verbatim from Luke 2 in the Chinese Union version, before adding four comments, which are essentially applicable lessons for China. Jesus arguing with the temple priests during his Passover visit to Jerusalem teaches how the Hebrew race valued education for the whole populace. The most important lesson of education, apart from learning letters, mathematics, and geography, speculates Wu, was the scriptures, in which the Jews could find the entire history of their people. Wu imagines what was being taught in the temple when Jesus visited: the past glories of Israel, its hardships, and prophecies relating to the nation. Such rousing teaching would, he conjectures, illuminate present humiliations and concentrate the Jewish people's attention on God's promises. The parallels here with the classics and their role in community life are evident and leave a reader wondering what role exactly Wu sees for the Chinese classics vis-à-vis the Bible in his cultural vision.

The narration of Jesus's childhood experiences provides a template that may go some way toward an answer: scripture reading inculcates patriotism, which leads to action, involving both strategizing and community-building. The inferences that the twelve-year-old Jesus makes are decidedly political: "Although Jesus was still young, he already had a good grounding in history, and coming to Jerusalem now for the Passover, and seeing firsthand compatriots from all over come to the temple to worship together, he must have felt that there was such strength in unity among the people—why should they still suffer being trampled on by a foreign people?"[94] It is at this point that salvation, as a some-what political act, is implanted in the mind of the young Jesus, who "felt that he should . . . bear the duty of saving the people." Wu's reading of scripture engages as imaginatively with the text as Zhao Zichen, but without the acknowledgment that this has as much akin with fiction as biblical exegesis. Wu draws on the 1919 Union translation of Luke 2:49, which can be re-rendered as, "Why were you looking for me? Did you not know that I would have my father's matters in mind?"[95] English translations of the Greek are almost equally split between "Did you not know that I would be in my father's house?" and some version of "about my father's business." Wu takes the latter, without any discussion of vari-ant readings, and builds the phrase up as a focal moment in Jesus's career:

> But we can see that the events of Jesus's entire life were deduced from what he said in this one sentence, and we can know that after this outburst of emotion he really could hold to this, and let it become his firm will. The sayings "he who chooses what is good and firmly holds it fast" and "whenever he got hold of what was good, he clasped it firmly"[96]—this is what Jesus spent his energies on in his teens.[97]

Although eschewing a version of Christianity that needed Chinese culture to affirm it, Wu shows his classical training in his inability to omit a relevant refer-ence or two from the classics to substantiate any given point—and in so doing, creates a Chinese Jesus as role model. In describing Jesus though classical refer-ences and in terms of Chinese ideals and mores, Wu intertwines holy scripture, *shengjing* 聖經, and the classics, *jing* 經, to inscribe the Jewish youth into a Chinese perspective and to allow the young rabbi to comment on the Chinese situation.

At twelve, Jesus's "great purpose" (*dazhi* 大志) was set, and his preparation work for national liberation began in reading the scriptures. There is more than a touch of didactic encouragement to Wu's young audience here, but it is an encouragement that embraces a specific religious identity. Jesus's prepara-tion involved experiencing the truth that God had revealed and reading more widely in the prophets and histories, using them "to solidify his loyal patrio-tism."[98] This reading, argues Wu, must have also drawn Jesus to think about how he "absolutely could not rely on his own individual potential, but needed to examine the social situation, and fully understand the people's suffering." The deep social concern that was fostered and stored up in his trips to the local town during breaks from carpentry was complemented by time up in the hills, surveying the land and its famous sites, and by his annual trips to Jerusalem, where he saw the stubbornness and corruption of the Jewish leaders, which "caused his desire for reform and revitalization to grow stronger every year." Jesus, the political malcontent, the social activist, the young prophet steeped in the scriptures and in the suffering of his people, lacks just one thing in Wu's fertile mind: accomplices. As every reader of Chinese fiction knew, as well as anyone who followed recent events in China (the decisive Long March had begun just two years earlier), "to succeed in a great affair requires gathering together a band of disciples."[99] This was, naturally for Wu, something Jesus attended to well before depictions of the beginning of his ministry. Following Zhao Zichen's logic, and claiming gospel support, Wu explains how several of Jesus's disciples were people he already knew and that he had been careful to recruit youth with force of will, among whom was his comrade and soul mate Cousin John. Their strategizing in Wu's version comes close to undermining the gospel account:

> At the time, Jesus must have talked often to John of his aspirations, and of how it would be very difficult for someone without status, wanting to engage in activities in society, to get any attention if he didn't have anyone telling the crowds about him. So in due course John came out first to do the propaganda work, and when John had gained the trust of the people, Jesus went out, when the crowds had massed, to receive his baptism from John. John solemnly told the crowds that Jesus's ability was greater than his, that Jesus was the Messiah the whole people had been waiting for. When Jesus later came out to preach and used the slogan "the Kingdom of Heaven is near, repent!" it was precisely the same slogan that John had used, and we may assume all the more that the two of them shared a full understanding, which had undergone a period of close planning, and which was put into practice according to their pre-understanding, to make sure that Jesus's first steps in his activities in society would be accomplished smoothly.[100]

A deep grounding in scripture, personal experience of life under foreign control, and collaborative mission-planning prepare Jesus—and Wu's readers—to begin building the kingdom as envisaged.[101]

CONCLUSION

Wu chose to tackle "Christianity" and "culture" as two separate entities in his volume *Christianity and Chinese Culture*, but it is clear throughout that a reconciliation of the two is Wu's aim, or rather, the application of Christianity as a transforming agent for Chinese culture. Through its moral message, through its motivating force, through the example of Jesus, Christianity was to serve and save China. This is a kingdom message, however, not a simple nationalistic message: Christianity is the means to bring about the Kingdom of God on earth in China, which is the fulfillment of China and Chinese culture, as for all nations. Those who have criticized Wu for "secular" interpretations of the gospel have both missed and nailed the point: the gospel is precisely for the world, to be instantiated in the world. Paul Tillich argued that the Kingdom of God has an inner-historical and a trans-historical side, participating in the dynamics of history and questioning those dynamics, manifest respectively through Spiritual Presence and Eternal Life—and that the Social Gospel Movement was one of the forces that had caused the kingdom to lose its power as a symbol.[102] But in many ways, Wu contests the prevailing nationalism of his era with a deeply Christian vision built around this symbol. The loss of the trans-historic was a necessary corollary of the need to mitigate the conflict between science and religion, or between Christian theology and the theory of evolution, and to rebut the damning charge that Christianity represented a retrograde, antiscience culture. It was also in keeping with Wu's belief in the continuous evolution of religion, away from primitive miracles and eschatological motivations for action.[103]

If there was no need for miracles in the kingdom of Republican or Nationalist China, the church was not essential to its construction, either. After the propaganda of the Anti-Christian Movement rocked his faith, Wu no longer felt he could believe in inherited explanations or creeds and sensed that liturgies and church regulations were not vital to Christian life: the character of Jesus was his sole refuge.[104] It was the power of Jesus's character that modeled salvation, Jesus who "taught us that to be human was to take on the task of improving society."[105] In this, Wu stood with many other Chinese of the period. Chen Duxiu had written in 1920, the year before he cofounded the CCP, that the creation, Trinity, and miracles were "mostly traditions of the past," which had been nullified by social and natural sciences and which should be discarded in favor of new beliefs, beliefs "embodied in Jesus's wonderful personality."[106] It is worth recalling that Wu was in his mid-forties when he came to the Christian faith and that he did so through his own reading of the Bible. If his theology is light on the transcendent, or detail of theology or tradition from the church fathers onward, it is closely grounded in a reading and textual interpretation, within Chinese textual traditions, of the New Testament. Wu's writing embodies the transitional nature of his generation: *Christianity and Chinese Culture* is written in essay format, with a rational and social scientific perspective, and yet the citations are predominantly from the canon and the textual world of the classics. The influence of translated Western works is noteworthy and shows the successful transmission of Western theological texts in China alongside biblical ones.

It would be hard to argue that Wu's life, fears for the nation, and ingrained sense of social duty did not affect his reading of the Bible. If Wu's initial motivation for reading—as Wu explains in the introduction to *Christianity and Chinese Culture*, he read the Bible *before* coming to faith while searching, unsuccessfully in Confucianism, for a way to cultivate his own self and do good to others—was linked to his Confucian ethic of service and desire to save others, as Liang Hui has suggested, then the mode of reading and interpreting the kingdom also revolves around the theme of salvation.[107] The ideal society, the Kingdom of Heaven, was the collaborative effort of those who were being transformed by Jesus's vision. Where Gore and others had warned against utopia-building, or the anticipation that a change in human conditions could ever eliminate human selfishness, Wu remains deliberately naïve, holding onto the (Confucian) notion that the right conditions would produce moral goodness, which would lead to and ensure good governance.

The Kingdom of God, for Wu, is fundamentally a matter of how we treat others. The economic ordering of society to the benefit of all, as described by Jesus in multiple parables and discussed at length by Wu, is critical to its establishment. Much of the fault for the failure to build the kingdom that Jesus envisaged lies with the disciples and the early church: although Jesus set the revolutionary kingdom clearly before them, and the early church began along the right track in practicing a common table and common means, it was not the message that the church chose to spread. A gospel of individual salvation took over the Christian movement, and Jesus's great plan of reforming society sank without a trace. The Kingdom of Heaven—the ideal society—was Jesus's true task, thwarted in his day by his inability to gain a leadership role or popular following and after his death by the incipient church veering away from its task and Christ-given commission, to concentrate on ecclesial matters. The task of the present, Wu contends, is to recover Jesus's original vision and set the Kingdom of God at the center of the gospel.

6

The Church and the People's Republic of China

When I was writing the diary, what I first thought of was not
what had happened today and whatever noteworthy thoughts I
had had, but those events and those thoughts that I could not
under any circumstances note down. The society we lived in
at the time did not permit anyone to have individual, private
thoughts. Everybody's every private thought had to be "handed
over" to the Party, including personal diaries. The leaders used
the degree of private intimacy of the thoughts handed over
to determine the degree of a person's loyalty to the Party.
—Zhang Xianliang, novelist, ca. 1961[1]

I didn't know whether to laugh or cry at his words. They were
accusing me of a very serious crime that carried the death penalty. I then made a firm resolve that if I ever got out alive I would
never keep any more letters. In the 29 years from my release in
1982 until today, I have not kept a single private letter. . . . After my
release, I never kept a diary again. A diary is written to be read by
oneself, but one's private thoughts are better kept in one's heart.
The past is like smoke; to what end should one write it down?
—Bishop Jin Luxian, describing events of 1955[2]

If the early twentieth century saw great growth in the Chinese church, the
first decade of the second half of the century saw a mass falling away from the
church. By the end of the 1960s, when public religious activity in China had
been shut down for several years, the rest of the world wondered whether a Chinese church still existed. The threats to the flourishing church of the 1920s and

1930s—the anti-Christian polemics centered on Christianity's imperial links and its supposed antiscientific outlook—must have seemed trivial in the 1950s when the clamps of the security apparatus began to tighten. There are no outstanding theological tomes to turn to from the 1940s through the 1970s. The theology of this period is, in keeping with the era, either activist or quiescent. The church had a hard enough task responding to political decrees and keeping track of its members; few had the institutional setting or the inclination to contemplate more systematic theology. It is no coincidence that the authors discussed in this chapter and the following are primarily church leaders and secondarily theologians. What was produced in abundance were strident editorials in new church publications exhorting the faithful to serve the people and resist imperialism and equally hardline pieces in mission bulletins excoriating the Communist overseers. To many in the persecuted sectors of the church, it seemed that the defensive war of the early 1940s and the civil war of the late 1940s had segued directly into a spiritual war in the 1950s.

Despite a lack of original writing, this era is far from theologically uninteresting or unimportant; rather, it is deeply fascinating, as well as profoundly moving and troubling. But it is a period hard to make sense of in retrospect, which may be why histories and narratives of Christianity often gloss over the early decades of the PRC, eager to compare the revival of the 1980s with the vibrant 1930s or look to the uplifting stories of the martyrs. In the years after the establishment of the PRC in 1949 we find some of the most engaged grappling with the relation of church and state and with the nature of an indigenous church, as well as truly pathetic accounts of resistance. The acute experience of challenge has much to say to the universal church: questions about the nature of faith, of what it means to witness, of whether martyrs are called or created, of how the responses of different faith communities can be held in an affirming tension, of how to manage a divided and riven church. The Chinese church regularly quotes Tertullian in assessing these years: the blood of martyrs is the seedbed of the church. The tearing down, both figurative and literal, of the church during the 1950s and 1960s preceded, as we now know, unimagined growth. The polemics and the pain of those years are not easy to read, but that makes it all the more important to attempt to do them justice.

BACKGROUND AND OVERVIEW

The major political events and intrigues of the 1950s and 1960s are relatively well-known: from land reform and constitutional reform in the first years of the PRC to the relaxation of the Hundred Flowers campaign (1956); the purges of

the Anti-Rightist campaign (1957); the industrial mania of the Great Leap Forward (1958) and the famines that followed it; the rises and falls of Mao Zedong;
the Red Guard era and the seismic events of the Great Proletarian Cultural
Revolution (1966–1976) with its attendant deaths, incarcerations, labor camps,
and struggle sessions. Beyond this lay the Lin Biao affair (1971), the death of
Mao (1976) and fall of the Gang of Four, and then the rise of Deng Xiaoping
and rehabilitation of civic life in the Reform and Opening Up period from
1978 onward. These shape the climate to the events of this chapter but are not
rehearsed in detail here. Church life during these decades follows the broad
sweep of the influence of national events, as did all sectors of society, but also
suffered in the micro-climates of particular policies and campaigns directed
against religious ideology or religious links with the outside world. Given the
effective curtailment of church activity from the early 1960s to the late 1970s,
the key decade in church political history was the 1950s, and particularly the
policies and events of the first years of that decade, which form the focus of
this chapter.

   In an era of concerted government action to shape society, reactions by individuals in institutions were decisive in directing church history. As the government mobilized citizens through campaigns and sloganeering, church bodies also responded in print and by mobilizing signatures on manifestos, giving
power to editors and activists. Clerics whose authority was recognized could
disperse a crowd protesting arrests outside a Shanghai church compound or
motivate a prolonged sit-in. The directives of Pius XII had a critical and lasting
effect on the line of the Chinese Catholic Church; time and again reports of
lay Catholics speak of their dismay at church leaders who reneged or signed
documents in prison acceding to views different from those they espoused before arrest. The writings of Wu Yaozong (Y. T. Wu) on the Protestant side or the
actions of an independent church leader such as Wang Mingdao, who stood
against prevailing Protestant views, could likewise turn the course of events.
Relations between individuals were important for another reason, too: they
proved to be key to the success or failure of the church under trial. Once relations between those of opposing views broke down into open slander and public
rebuke, it mattered relatively little how faithful individuals were to their beliefs:
a future of mistrust and division was ignited. The most serious threat to the
church catholic in the 1950s turned out to be internal disunity. The extreme
provocation and terror and the very real sufferings of many faithful are not in
doubt, but a lasting mark was left on the church by a lack of charity in dealing
with each other's responses to the provocation. The martyrs, ever a minority,
whose stand did so much to inspire future believers, were not just those singled

out by the government or led by the faith of the church, although both those conditions were necessary; in most cases they were those who chose death over breaking friendships and relationships in the body of believers. It is clear from accounts of the era that choosing one's own death over betraying another was a real choice; death was accepted on behalf of other, imperfect individuals and not as an abstract call. The living martyrdom of long imprisonment seems more often to have been borne for principled resistance, or defense of an article of faith. People might remain in prison for twenty years for a principle, but they died for others.

The division of the church occurred as unity was imposed from outside in the 1950s, when the Three-Self Patriotic Movement (TSPM) came to represent all Protestants and as the Chinese Catholic Patriotic Association (CCPA) was brought into being, following protracted opposition, in 1957.[3] The institution-alization of the Protestant church in China as a para-state organization came about to a greater degree through the church's own hand, although it was en-gineered by the demands placed on the church. Both bodies led eventually to the creation of alternative "underground" churches by those who rejected the official churches. The division, and the ongoing rejection of coreligionists within the Catholic/Protestant churches, has in some cases persisted into the twenty-first century, and the vehemence of the language of exclusion can be quite shocking to outsiders, especially now.[4] The rejection of believers by be-lievers was predicated on the sense of betrayal among those who believed that they could not compromise their faith and work within the religious framework created in the newly established PRC—and on a sense of frustration on the part of those who chose to work with the state to develop the church. The question of how to bring about reconciliation between these groups is still occupying successive pontiffs as well as Protestant church members.

The different responses of the Protestant and Roman Catholic churches to the CCP, both before Liberation in 1949 and in the New China, mean that the two churches followed quite different practical and theological trajectories during the 1950s, as traced below. Questions raised by accounts of this period include why the TSPM saw optimism in the CCP's religious policy, where Catholics did not. How much was treatment by the Communists a self-fulfilling prophecy—the Catholics bearing the brunt (especially in Shanghai) because of their expectation of, or provocation of, ire? There is a tension between sym-pathetic Roman Catholic accounts of the terror wrought on individuals and congregations and the analysis of certain historians who maintain that the Mao government largely stuck to the United Front agreement on religion until the Cultural Revolution.[5] The views are not irreconcilable, since terror and accommodation were both practiced, but the question remains as to why some groups experienced greater persecution than others.

One notable difference between the Catholic and Protestant churches was that devolution to the decision making of the local church and its own intellectual autonomy in matters theological was the aim and goal of most Protestant missions of the early twentieth century, even if reality lagged behind ideals; whereas Catholic missions had tended to generate priests whose intellectual rigor was shown more in their loyalty to, and development of, theology in line with their religious order and the trammels of Vatican thought. There has been a tendency in modern Chinese academic studies to underplay the indigenizing that happened before the twentieth century and the common interest among missionaries and Chinese in promoting a Chinese church in the first decades of that century;[6] but even so, the transfer of authority to Chinese Catholics happened more slowly than among Protestants. French Jesuits handed over control of the Shanghai Diocese to the new Chinese bishop and his confrères only in 1950, for example. Differences in ecclesiology between the two churches come out in moments of crisis, such as in February 1951 when Zhang Boda (Father Béda Chang) spoke up passionately for the patriotism of the Catholic Church, arguing contra Protestant and government detractors that no patriotic Catholic could accept the proposed "Three Self" or "Three Autonomy" formula. Catholics, he claimed, are "unswervingly faithful to their faith and to the Church of Christ, while Protestants went through an initial reform, which allows them to form themselves anew according to their own wishes."[7] Through the actions of a figure like Zhang, one of the most impressive exemplars of faith of the era, we can see how being steeped in church formation and dogma since childhood both framed and constrained moral and political choices.

The absolute Vatican rejection of Communism through the 1950s—and the existence of a supranational entity to pronounce that rejection—meant that, unlike for Protestants, where differences made (merely) for rancor and mistrust among different groups, accommodation to or collaboration with the Communist government in any form brought with it for Catholics the ecclesiological and soteriological implications of excommunication. (The bitter irony here is that during the decades when priests, nuns, and lay members of the Roman Catholic Church in China were incarcerated or denied education or a livelihood for their stance vis-à-vis the government, the Vatican changed its policy on cooperation with Communist regimes. Those in prison remained largely unaware that they were suffering for an outdated principle.) The nature of the universality of the Catholic Church was a critical difference with the Protestant churches, for whom the existence of a national church did not contradict the universal. Pope Pius XII iterated the point in his 1954 letter Ad Sinarum Gentum (To the Chinese People) in which he condemned the false patriotism of those in China who "adhere to the church thought up by them," explaining that a "national" church would no longer be Catholic "because it would be the negation of that universality."[8] The same letter shows how the universality of the church in its pre–Vatican II instantiation and the issue of indigenization were intertwined: "But—and it is absurd merely to think of it—by what right can men arbitrarily and diversely in different nations, interpret the gospel of Jesus Christ?," the Pope wrote to his diminishing Chinese flock. Even recent writers have failed to grasp the importance of agency among Chinese Protestants, as when a commentator asks, "Why did so many Protestant churches quickly acquiesce to the CCP?," suggesting that the CCP exploited their weaknesses in doing so.[9] At least one leading group of Protestants actively chose to work in consort with the CCP, with whom they initially shared many social ideals, including poverty alleviation, land reformation, and reclaiming national sovereignty. The theological legacy of the Social Gospel and indigenous theology movements, central to the formation of the intellectual wing of the Protestant church, bequeathed the right to make this choice.

Differences between the two churches are not uniform, and ideological alliances emerge between Roman Catholics and Protestant evangelicals (who were also absolute in their rejection of Communist oversight), but divergences are evident in the histories of the two state organizations established to oversee religious congregations, and in the forms of the emerging underground churches. Into the 1960s, experiences were more similar, both as wider social issues prevailed—Christians suffered in the famines that followed Mao's Great Leap Forward just as everyone else did, and those of bad class backgrounds were swept up alike in campaigns against the bourgeoisie, intellectuals, and other social undesirables—and later as all religious personnel in China, no matter how left-leaning or pro-Socialist in their theology, came to be demonized. The chaos of the high period of the Cultural Revolution, around 1966–1969, further eroded distinctions among Christians and between Christians and others: all suffered.

It is unsurprising that relatively little academic theology and few personal sermons and writings survive from this period. During the war years (1937–1945), seminaries in areas of Japanese occupation, like universities, relocated west, sometimes multiple times; and during the purges of the 1950s, some church institutions, such as the Legion of Mary, burned their own holdings to prevent incriminating evidence of church membership or thought crimes reaching the security apparatus. In the ultra-Maoist years of the late 1960s and early 1970s, nothing was secure (not even the Public Security Bureau: when the Catholic bishop Jin Luxian was released from prison in 1982, he was told that his confiscated belongings, including the only photos he possessed of his parents, could not be returned because the location where they were stored had been taken over by Red Guards and all records lost).[10] From the mid-1950s, all print media came under the various channels of the Propaganda Department, and editors of books and journals had to "warmly love socialism" and "implement the party's line, principles and policies,"[11] meaning that any material still extant was state-approved. What is perhaps more surprising is that a theology of the Cultural Revolution does not seem to have emerged subsequently in post-Mao China. There is "root searching" and "scar literature" in secular writing, early accounts of camp life and death such as those of Zhang Xianliang, comparable in their terse power to the writing of Elie Wiesel, but no body of works theologizing on the forces of destruction.[12] The two streams of writing to emerge on the Protestant side from the 1980s onward, theological reconstruction and Sino-Christian theology, are either in tune with, or tangential to, government narratives. Possible reasons for this absence are explored further in later chapters.

RUNNING DOGS OF IMPERIALISM, HIDING UNDER THE CLOAK OF RELIGION

The years immediately following the establishment of the PRC were critical to the life of the church for the remainder of the century, since during them the major policies governing religious life were formulated and the ideological direction of the state was gradually determined. Religious bodies had some input into these, but an ever-decreasing one, and between 1949 and 1951 the situation evolved considerably. Western Christian commentators who had been pleasantly surprised by support for the continuation of church life in the early months of the new Republic were left stranded, applying for exit visas. Protestants and Catholics negotiated the gradual hardening of policy very differently, in part because of their divergent ideological starting points. It is fair to say that the church was more acted on than acting during the 1950s and 1960s. Those who were physically handed over to the authorities had ample opportunity to experience a Christlike passivity under trial. If the external political environment was the single overriding factor affecting church life and theological development, three broad movements that shaped church experience can be isolated: nationalism experienced as anti-imperialism, the aftermath of the war against Japan, and the legacy of the investment in "inculturation" in the 1920s and 1930s (particularly on the Protestant side). The most heinous factor in government eyes was imperialism, but the three are all related, in some form, to China's sense of self. The reaction of Chinese Christians to anti-imperialism and the war legacy displays a complex mixture of responses derived from church education or formation, and contemporary sentiment.

The war against Japan (1937–1945), and China's experience as an ally of the Western powers during World War II, affected the political climate in China in multifaceted ways. While the war "marked a vital step in China's progression from semi-colonized victim of global imperialism to its entry, however tentative, on the world stage as a sovereign power with wider regional and global responsibilities," it also created a society that was "more militarized, categorized and bureaucratized" than before, with devastating consequences as the 1950s wore on.[13] What the May Fourth era had begun, in its intense questioning of Chinese identity, and the civil war of the late 1920s and early 1930s had put on hold, the War of Resistance against Japan channeled into a defiant, vulnerable nationalism. The war had allowed the influence of the CCP to grow as it resisted the Japanese, and the anti-Japanese sentiment it fomented raised the anti-imperialism, which had earlier driven Jiang Jieshi (Chiang Kai-shek) and the Nationalists to ever higher levels of vitriol under the Communists. It suited the PRC government to elide the experience of Western imperialism in the extraterritoriality of the Shanghai concessions and Treaty Port life with that of Japanese occupation. The church was caught between its historic foreign ties and the exigencies of current political ideologies, and the crunch came with the rhetoric of the Korean War, which began in June 1950 and preoccupied the Chinese media for the next eighteen months.

Moderate Chinese Catholics like Zhang Boda, who understood the CCP well, argued strenuously that the church must avoid at all costs being labeled imperialist or antipatriotic. Zhang sought a middle way: unswerving loyalty in matters where the faith was at stake, and a concessionary attitude on matters of secondary importance (to no avail; Zhang died a martyr in 1951, his wisdom unheeded by superiors).[14] As a group of Chinese Protestants acknowledged in a "Message from Chinese Christians to Mission Boards Abroad" in 1949, an epistle that tried hard to balance the unpalatable message with gratitude for what missionaries had accomplished,

> there does exist some deep-rooted feeling on the part of the communists that the Christian church has been intimately related to imperialism and capitalism. It is a fact that the Christian church in China in the past has been entangled with the unequal treaties imposed upon China under duress, it did enjoy special privileges accruing from them. It is also a fact that the churches

in China have had close connections with the churches in Britain and America in personnel and financial support. It is also a fact that the church life and organization here in China has been modelled after the pattern in Britain and America. Traditions of denominations have been imported and taken root here. Much of the church administration is still in the hands of missionaries.[15]

While explicitly countering the suggestion that mission work had ever been in direct relation with foreign governments, and affirming that many missionaries had done what they could to promote an indigenous church, the writers were clear that change had to come.

In retrospect, it is clear that the degree of foreign influence in the church—or "imperialism," in Communist terms—came to seem more invidious than many Christians, both foreign and Chinese, had understood at the time. It can be seen in trivial things, such as in the Peking Union Church bulletin of June 1940, where we read of a new undertaking as part of the manse building fund, a bilingual guild cookbook, "consisting of recipes of foreign foods translated into Chinese for the benefits of our cooks":[16] the norms of ex-pat life carried on, notwithstanding the war, and one's servants were expected to step up to the mark. It can be seen in personal slights, such as requiring the "brilliant" Jesuit Wang Changzhi, with doctorates in philosophy from the Sorbonne and in theology from the Catholic University of Paris, to teach Chinese literature and edit a children's magazine.[17] It can be seen—for good and ill—in the fact that Zhang Boda wrote childhood letters in French, that Jin Luxian wrote his personal diary in Latin, and that Zhao Zichen wrote as beautiful English as Chinese.

It can be seen in the crushing litany of arrogant and offensive misjudgments over the political situation and the capacity of Chinese Christians to run the church, which are spattered throughout mission press writings and recorded in the memoirs of Chinese believers. Those who had grown up in a bilingual atmosphere, and who had appreciated the forms of liberation that the missionaries had brought—from illiteracy, foot-binding, famine—were less able, or had less need, to see some of the downsides or hypocrisies of what missionaries had once termed the Christian "occupation" of China. Or, as Helen Djang wrote in her self-confession in 1951, "the fish seller doesn't know that he stinks of fish."[18]

Anti-imperialist rhetoric drove much early PRC policy on religion. An early edict in December 1950 governed the control of funds from foreign sources. Any group receiving foreign funds had to register, utilize the funds in the location where they were received and reported, and produce biannual reports; anyone violating the reporting rules was to be punished.[19] A further directive on the

"Method of Controlling Christian Organizations That Have Received Financial Help from America" was delivered directly as a speech to Protestant leaders in Beijing in April 1951. Following a statement from Vice President (and noted writer) Guo Moruo that "all religious institutions should be self-supporting" and that the government "would assist them in this movement," Christian churches and organizations were told to sever all ties with U.S. mission boards and U.S.-financed missions. Self-supporting churches could continue charity service projects, but church-financed schools, hospitals, and such had to be separate from the churches themselves. Foreign mission boards were permitted to turn over property to Chinese churches. Nonnationals were permitted to stay if they were not deemed "reactionary" but could no longer hold administrative positions. Restricting financial support was, as Communist leaders emphasized, a central tactic in the struggle "to wipe out the influence of imperialist cultural aggression against the whole world and against the new China."[20] Beyond making sure church funds were wholly Chinese, the patriotic duties of Christians included taking part in the Resist-America-Aid-Korea war effort, facilitating agrarian reform, and actively suppressing counterrevolution.

The problem for the church was that demands on the government side became progressively more stringent, shackling what had been considered legitimate church activity. A church that had gone along with the early initiatives, out of support for anti-imperialism, was in danger of acceding to new directives merely because it had complied with the last. Decisions were presented as the church's own agreement, creating a pattern so that when more radical measures were enacted, such as the unification of worship in 1958 and the effective dismantling of denominations (that "relic of the Mission Boards' aggressive policy by which they tried to divide and rule"),[21] they still seemed in line with church aspirations.

Moderation, of sorts, still ruled in 1950, the first full year of Communist governance. Although the legitimate footprint of the church was shrinking, there was still enough room to operate, in most minds. A New China News Agency dispatch of November 1950 titled "What One Should Know About the Question of Catholic and Protestant Religions" still spoke in the language of separating legitimate religion from illegitimate imperialism, religion that arises out of its social circumstances from "the weapon with which imperialists have invaded China."[22] The new government had done its homework on the church and collated accurate statistics on membership, numbers of priests and members of religious orders, and the proportions of foreigners among them. The time line was propagandistic ("since liberation the imperialist influence received a severe setback"); the representation of foreigners' aims was inaccurate (foreign priests managed the finances of both churches and hoped to retain authority); and the Marxist line was hopeful (since Liberation fewer "sought relief" in religion and its influence had waned)—but coexistence was still possible. Although materialists and believers could never be allies, they could be "fellow-workers" in the defense and reconstruction of the fatherland, or, as Mao proposed, in the building up of an "anti-imperialist battle front." There were gestures of conciliation: as long as churches were "entirely free from foreign domination" and did not impede land reform with their activities or influence, they and their enterprises would be accorded the protection of the law.

A vocal section of the Protestant church had taken on board the anti-imperial message, which chimed with its own growing sense of unease at inequalities in church leadership and life, and was quite content to promote this aspect to government thinking. What came to be known as the Christian Manifesto, a document of May 1950 drawn up by the founders of the Three-Self Movement in conjunction with Zhou Enlai, addressed head on the question of the Chinese church's historic relations with "imperialist" countries. The manifesto was eventually signed by upwards of four hundred thousand Protestants.[23] Given the background of the missionaries, the manifesto asserted that Christianity was "consciously or unconsciously" related to imperialism and that imperialist countries used Christianity to stir up dissent and create "reactionary forces" in China. Church members proclaimed their support for the government's opposition to "imperialism, feudalism and bureaucratic capitalism" and pledged to do all they could to teach church members "to recognize clearly the evils that have been wrought in China by imperialism; recognize the fact that in the past imperialism has made use of Christianity; purge imperialistic influences from within Christianity itself; and be vigilant against imperialism, and especially American imperialism."[24] A second aim of the manifesto was more constructive: to take measures to cultivate a patriotic spirit and move forward as rapidly as possibly toward self-support and self-propagation.

The message of anti-imperialism continued to be reinforced in government directives and initiatives. It soon transpired that nothing less than an active promotion of the Three-Self principles (self-governing, self-financing, and self-propagating) was required: those such as Zhao Zichen who were deemed to have taken a "passive attitude" toward the Three-Self Reform Movement were censured, and in Zhao's case, required to rewrite unsatisfactory self-criticisms before being dismissed and given time to "ponder his crimes."[25] It is clear that concerted attempts to create a certain history of mission were being advanced as part of the overall public relations strategy. The strategy was simple: to ensure that Christians and others associated the history of mission with the history of imperialist aggression and believed that the two were deliberately and inextricably linked. The message was taken to the heart of the Christian establishment and kept at the forefront of attention for well over a decade. An "Anti-Imperial Exhibits" display at Jinling Xiehe Seminary (Nanjing Union Theological Seminary) in 1962, for example, included "confessions" of colonialists and imperialists which "proved that the missionaries were really the vanguards of aggression" and that imperialists had used Christianity as an "ideological weapon."[26]

Anger and incomprehension are evident in much English-language (especially Catholic) writing from the early years of the PRC, stemming from a belief in the absolute right to mission and to nonnationals residing in the country of their choice to spread the gospel as they saw fit. One can have much sympathy with missionaries' anger at the Chinese government for confiscating church property and destroying church institutions, and that the genuine, faithful religious sentiment and intent on the part of missionaries was being tarnished by the conflation of mission and imperialism; but one can also see how those who were conscientized by their Marxist teachers felt that they had been duped into believing, and living within, the ideological framework of the prewar era. Chinese Christians had a more acute sense of how the foreign was viewed, when in their message to mission boards abroad they stressed how the missionary from now on would "be living in an economical environment" where "austerity" would rule and that the role of the foreign missionary would in the future lie in special projects and not administrative oversight.[27] In retrospect it is clear that the degree of transfer of leadership and authority to Chinese within denominations correlated with the degree of ideological awareness and desire to effect change.

The views of those European and American missionaries who denied or minimized the degree of imperialism, or indeed colonialism, in the church in China can be contrasted with less accessible local voices. Henrietta Harrison's recent account of life in Shanxi Catholic villages shows why the Vatican and the Shanghai Catholic hierarchies' views of life were not monolithic in the 1950s. Harrison's highly readable narrative of three hundred years of village history presents a different hue, detailing how resentment at missionary actions and attitudes in the early decades of the twentieth century contributed to a desire for reform among many Chinese Catholics. (As Harrison shows, the understanding of Chinese Communists of Catholicism as a "foreign religion" was also diametrically opposed to local understanding.) Anomalies in the post-Boxer world created lasting resentments, injustices that had a power to affect later generations through their continuous oral transmission and that influenced local priests' responses to the Communist cause. Areas of contention involved money, land, water supply, authority, and power. In Taiyuan, for example, the provincial capital of the area Harrison studied, the diocese had invested local Boxer indemnity payments in itself, rather than disbursing them to the families of the dead, making the diocese rich.[28] There was tension with local villagers over such matters as water supply and its diversion into the production of communion wine.

As in other localities, foreign missionaries were used to intervening with the local government in matters such as the tax burden on Catholics, inevitably creating local resentment. "Payment" for conversions continued into the 1930s when food shortages brought in outside villagers looking for aid, with some contemporary Catholics aware of the exact price of their ancestors' conversions.[29] Cracks in relations between Chinese Catholics and foreigners were seen as the revolutionary ethos affected understandings of power dynamics, among both progressive foreign priests (influenced by their great mentor Vincent Lebbe) and Chinese clergy. Low levels of spoken Chinese among foreign priests, and a lack of incentive for them to improve, were an ongoing point of contention, especially as foreign priests with weak language skills used local priests as their chaplains and intermediaries—clergy "who did the work but would never be promoted" and whose resentment at their overwork, as Harrison notes, "comes through even sixty years later."[30] Tensions that had surfaced in the late Qing when missionaries returned and reassumed control were echoed in Taiyuan when foreign superiors arrived and sent local sworn virgins out to work as evangelists, a task they had not anticipated when they took their vows.[31] The reduction of vocations in Europe had nudged the Vatican toward ordaining more Chinese clergy—but foreign clergy were not obliged to work under them. Stresses in working relationships became more intense during the 1930s and 1940s; in Taiyuan the predominantly Italian missionaries actively supported the Italian government and its ally, Japan, defending the Japanese invaders on the grounds they were fighting Communists. (This was one of the complaints the Communists had against the Vatican that were rejected as "preposterous" by correspondents in the *China Missionary Bulletin*.) When Chinese priests gathered in Taiyuan in 1947 and petitioned to take control of their own diocese, the motion was rejected. As Harrison concludes:

> After so many years of tension between the Chinese and Italian clergy, it is not surprising that when the new government insisted that the priests of central Shanxi reject the era of missionary control they were willing to do so. In 1951 all the priests in Taiyuan diocese subscribed to the creation of what is generally known as the official Catholic church in China. In later years they would

accept a bishop whom they themselves had elected and who was consecrated by the head of the official church. That did not mean that they were rejecting membership in the global Catholic community.[32]

Such actions were, however, anathema to Rome.

In 1951 the first batches of self-confessions also appeared, a genre that became widespread later in the Cultural Revolution. The confessions, which signaled the onset of a political climate change, were demanded of a variety of reprobates, not just religious ones, with the first Ideological Reform campaign initiated in universities in autumn 1951. That campaign illustrated the centrality of "struggle" to Communist methodology and the commitment to repentance and reform in the new thinking. The plethora of self-confessions in print media added significantly to the general insecurity and lack of ability to trust—since the accounts of colleagues and acquaintances should tally—as can be seen in the quotation from Bishop Jin Luxian at the start of this chapter. (Jin grieved during his own imprisonment the collateral entrapment of others through brief mention in letters, or even in single meetings, since he had to report to the Public Security Bureau those whom he had met only once, meetings of which he naïvely thought the bureau would have no knowledge, leaving him to note wryly, "In later life, should I regain my freedom, I should be careful to know fewer people in order to avoid implicating them.")[33] The rash of self-confessions also created a longer lasting problem for the church, in the later association of "repentance" or "confession" with state-demanded self-criticisms and their attendant fear and confabulation. Anecdotal evidence suggests that the elision of "confession" and "church" put many off religion for decades after the Cultural Revolution.[34]

While the Catholic mission press printed several self-confessions culled from *Renmin Ribao* (The People's Daily) to document the trend, the examples selected show not just template confessions, as the article suggests, but the possibilities of more subversive, or subsurface, readings. The confession of Qian Duansheng, dean of the College of Law at Peking University, is a case in point: practically the entire document could be read against itself. In a passage redolent of Zhang Xianliang's advice to think one thing and write the opposite, Qian admits, "My contact with both the students and my colleagues was always inadequate"; "I did not make a success of rallying my colleagues." "Handicapped" by his capitalist education, Qian thought he had only to read up on Mao to improve himself but "was completely mistaken." No overburdened academic could take the apology seriously when Qian states that he was "confused" about his reasons for resigning as law dean and adds, whatever the motive, "it was completely inexcusable of me thus to disrupt seriously the work of the College of Law through my determined refusal to assume the post of Dean."[35] One assumes that fellow intellectuals could read between the lines—if not the low-grade Communist cadres dispatched to elicit the statements from those with "feudalist" family backgrounds or who had studied abroad. Jin Yuelin, dean of the College of Arts and chair of the philosophy department at Qinghua (Tsing-hua) University, displayed an equally careful negotiation between what he was expected to say and what faults to expose, but the admission of a metaphysical philosopher to "an incomprehensible state of confused thinking" has a certain parodic value.[36] While the confessions of elite intellectuals display a healthy self-awareness, there are parallels in the process of negotiation even with the simple statements of apostasy of village Catholics that Henrietta Harrison documents.[37] The confessions did not save all of their authors: Wei Yisa (Isaac Wei), son of Paul Wei and leader of the independent Protestant True Jesus Church, was purged in 1952 despite the publication of his self-criticism in *Tian Feng* just months earlier.[38]

PROTESTANT DIRECTIONS

Meanwhile, many Chinese Protestants truly viewed the establishment of the PRC as liberation. These may not have been a numerical majority, but they were a vocal and influential minority. For those coming out of a Social Gospel mindset, the fact that the Communists, it seemed, had wrought a social liberation—salvation—for the people changed the religious and theological landscape in China. As an August 1949 editorial in *Tian Feng* (天風 Heavenly Wind, the Protestant magazine that later became the main voice of the TSPM) stated:

> Since Spring 1949, great swathes of land to the north and south of the Yangzi have in turn gained liberation and freedom, turning a new page in Chinese history. This People's liberation is greater than any previous revolution— whether the Taiping Revolution or the 1911 Revolution—because it is a true victory of the people. The liberation of the Chinese people is comprehensive, and entirely new. . . . Of course the church in this new situation wants not only to welcome the new heaven and new earth but also to be of use in the new society, and make the greatest contribution it can to the country, offering its fullest service to the people.[39]

The editorial continued by expressing its hope for the unique contribution Christianity had to make to the new society and a belief in the status that Christianity could enjoy in the new regime if it cooperated with the new democracy. In overtly Christian language, the editorial called on all to offer their whole "heart, soul, mind and strength" to the task. The editorial writers also commended to readers the Communist practice of self-criticism as a useful tool for Christians to learn more about themselves during reform, and as a practice akin to Christian repentance and redemption but centered on more positive and constructive aspects.

Wu Yaozong was among the most prominent of those who welcomed the establishment of the PRC and lauded all that the Communists had begun in their program of social transformation. He was also one of the more optimistic voices, believing that freedom of religion was such a basic universal principle that it would be maintained in China, and he proclaimed in articles in *Tian Feng* that the CCP authorities had acknowledged this principle both publicly and privately. To those Christians who questioned whether this was not just a tactical ploy, Wu opined, "my own answer is that Communist Party advocacy of religious freedom is sincere and permanent."[40] A former leader of the YMCA, Wu was involved in the initial negotiations with Zhou Enlai regarding the formation of the Three-Self Movement and was an insider with much invested in the successful integration of religion in the new regime. Since materialism anticipates the evaporation of religion under the right social conditions, the existence of religion, argued Wu, demonstrated that society has not yet reached that normal state; dealing with the resulting religion, and not the causes, he warns, would be self-defeating and cause religion to thrive. Wu was the main force behind the Christian Manifesto, and *Tian Feng* magazine regularly documented the number of signatories in the growing campaign.

Not all liberal-leaning Protestants were satisfied with the Christian Manifesto and its anti-imperialist message. The Anglican bishops and General Synod issued "A Pastoral Letter to Fellow Christians of the Chung Hua Sheng Kung Hui" (Zhonghua sheng gong hui) in July 1950, a carefully worded document (in both Chinese and the official English translation) that set out the church's position on the salient issues in a manner that was designed to be as acceptable as possible to government readers without joining in the defamation of foreign missionaries. The church, acknowledged the document in the language of Maoist propaganda, was "unable to compromise with imperialism, feudalism or bureaucratic capitalism" but also took issue with the notion that these were automatically opposed to the faith of the church.[41] The church had always, the bishops reiterated, "regarded alliance with power and prestige and the exploitation of the common people" as contradictory to the spirit of Christ. In distinction to any official Roman Catholic wording, the Anglicans stated that

they "rejoice greatly in the liberation that has come to the people of our nation" and that "with the utmost sincerity uphold that freedom of religious faith
which is guaranteed in the 'Common Political Principles.'" The document is
a decidedly Anglican weaving of encouragement and exhortation toward the
government, defense of the Anglican church's own actions (pointing out that
it "had already made real achievements" toward becoming self-governing, self-
supporting, and self-propagating),[42] and coded warning to believers (proposing
that all pray for a few minutes each day at noon "to strengthen our church, and
to prepare ourselves to overcome difficulties"). The document seeks to carve
out a Christian space that is both authentic and serves the state, arguing that the
church is there both to cultivate spiritual life *and* to promote productive labor
in the service of society.

The time from the issue of the Christian Manifesto in 1950 to the establish-
ment of the "Planning Committee of the China Christian Campaign to Resist
U.S. Aggression and Aid Korea" was, argued Wu Yaozong, the embryonic period of the Christian Reform Movement.[43] At an NCC meeting convened in
October 1950, the delegates signed up to the Christian Manifesto and to the
Three-Self Reform Movement. After this the NCC effectively ceased to exist, as
Protestant activists began to develop the new Three-Self organization.[44] Wu was
at the center, but the group was (initially) a broad ecumenical coalition, with
the evangelical Chen Chonggui on board, as well as Jing Dianying 敬奠瀛, the
leader of the Pentecostal Jesus Family; YWCA and YMCA representatives; and
intellectual leaders from the academy, such as Wei Zhuomin (韋卓民 Francis C. M. Wei) and Zhao Zichen. The voice of the Three-Self Movement, given
wide circulation through the magazine *Tian Feng*, presented a unique synthesis
of Christianity and nationalism, as can be seen in a selective reading of articles
from 1951. Some issues were (relatively) innocuous, as the editors of *Tian Feng*
operated as agony aunt to new theological and practical questions in the new
era. "Should we hang our leaders' portraits in church?" began one discussion
thread, after a reader from Guangdong wrote to say that the local church had
been criticized for not hanging a portrait of Mao in church.[45] The question
provided the opportunity for some model reflection, with an answer that would
have fitted Zhang Boda's maxim of protecting the core and accommodating to
the maximum elsewhere, as the editors remind readers that the People's Government respects the freedom of religious belief and that believers who love
their church ought also to love their country—given which, it would be wise to
distinguish between the public areas of the church and the sanctuary. There is
no tradition of hanging portraits other than of Jesus inside the worship space,
but lots of churches have taken the decision to hang a national flag inside, and

"we hope you might choose to do the same," they respond. If, on the other hand, a governmental organization borrows the church for a meeting, the sanctuary becomes an ordinary meeting place, and portraits may be hung—but it should be returned to its former state afterwards.

The year 1951 was pivotal for the church Protestant and Catholic, and most press coverage was of more life and death matters. The wholesale militarization of society and language is evident in a series of articles on the Korean War. The lead article in *Tian Feng* of 7 July 1951 is titled "Christians! Hasten to Donate Arms to Defend the Country!"[46] State-church boundaries are warped as the church is urged to do its part in an era of competitive nationalism. The link between defensive nationalism and Christian duty is made clear:

> Over the past few days we have heard the reports of the goodwill mission to North Korea that have warmed the hearts of every one of us. Every single person's blood has seethed and this has raised our level of political awareness and deepened our sentiment of love for the nation! How we must be clear about the enemy, oppose imperialism, and love our country! How we must embrace the government's appeal, and each play our fullest part! We must quickly arise, act in unity, and contribute to an aeroplane and cannon, to provide for the Chinese people's volunteer army, so that all enemies, with America at the forefront, are sent into the depths of the oceans!

The Three-Self Movement, continues the article, had responded to the appeal through its Planning Committee to Resist U.S. Aggression and Aid Korea and was now calling on all Christians to unite and donate an aircraft named "Christian Innovation" (!) to the cause. Yesterday the Japanese imperialists, today the American imperialists. This, proclaimed the article, was a test, a chance for the church to put its words into action and demonstrate its love for the country. On a practical level, ten thousand yuan per person was suggested as a target: perhaps congregations could donate one or two Sundays' collections to the war effort to show their patriotic intent.

The following article in the same issue, "Young Believers, Sign Up for Military Cadre School!," commends the examples of Wu Yaozong and the Baptist minister Rev. Li Mingda, whose cherished children had sat the exam for military cadre school and taken up the opportunity "to repay Mao Zedong for his loving kindness." The nationwide appeal to patriotic youth was, the writer suggests, also an appeal to Christian youth who "love the country, love the church." This phrase (*aiguo aijiao*) was fast becoming a rallying call. Another article in the same issue provided a fuller ethical treatise on the war, analyzing different types of war in the Old Testament "that the Lord permits, and not only that the Lord permits, but also encourages, and not only encourages, but that also, under the Lord's support, achieve great victories": wars of liberation (text for exegesis: Exodus 17:8–14), wars of resistance against incursions (1 Samuel 17), and patriotic wars to defend the nation (Nehemiah 4).[47] As Raymond Whitehead points out, during the Korean War the polemic was ratcheted up on both sides of the Pacific. The language used in the U.S. press was as partisan as anything seen in China: *Christian Herald* editorials for 1953 that discuss support for a congressional investigation of those clergy who called for recognition of the PRC speak of the spread of "Red lies, red murder, red rape, red slavery" and of "this sadistic, obscene, atheistic Red Scourge" destroying minds and souls.[48] The anti-Communist rhetoric emanating from the United States was inevitably seen by many of the internationally savvy Chinese Christians as anti-Chinese, a continuation of the same imperialist attitude that had criticized previous Chinese regimes. In these circumstances, defending the Communists was proxy for defending China against renewed imperialist depredations.[49]

Although the Korean War was the center of fierce propaganda, it was not the only focus in mid-1951, and the thirtieth anniversary of the CCP was heralded with much celebration and reflection. Wu Yaozong published a lengthy article, "What the Communist Party Has Taught Me," one of a series of post-reeducation autobiographies that ran in *Tian Feng*.[50] Wu's was notable for its eloquence and passion. Theological and political, the article shows how the question of the relation of church and state was a personal question for Wu as the CCP challenged and reformulated his Christianity. Like other examples of the genre, it traces a changing view and a process of reevaluation in the light of CCP doctrine. It was, as Wu knew, a retroactive evaluation for propaganda purposes, a constructed tale of enlightenment and confession of sins to encourage others, in the manner of the desert fathers, but the article also has an authentic ring. What the CCP had done for China over the past thirty years, wrote Wu, was inestimable.

Wu's article on the CCP is a prominent source for understanding the transformation of a group of liberal, Protestant intellectuals between the 1930s and the early years of the PRC (the events of the late 1950s and 1960s would challenge anew the views of all but the most die-hard sympathizers). Wu describes his journey from opposition to the CCP, through his awakening in 1931 (following the September 18 incident, the pretext for the Japanese invasion of Manchuria) and gradual appreciation that the ideological line of the CCP was the only route forward for the salvation of the country. In lauding the successes of the CCP a bare year into office, Wu offers his thanks on behalf of the entire nation. He goes into considerable detail in documenting the shifts in his understanding brought by Communist teaching: on the true meaning of "love your enemies," on recognizing the true face of imperialism, on the meaning of revolution, on grasping the class nature of Christianity, and on perceiving the true relationship between theory and practice. On the first, the role of the war in bolstering nationalism is clear in Wu's explanation of how the Japanese incursion shook his Quaker-inspired pacifism and his worship of "Gandhi-ism and Tolstoy-ism." Wu came to see that he had misunderstood Jesus's teaching and that loving one's enemies ought not to mean indulging evil, but attacking it. The CCP had shown true love for its enemies in its treatment of prisoners of war and in its desire for the Japanese people to gain freedom and democracy. Now, concluded Wu, he understood that pacifism was imperialist propaganda used to anesthetize invaded and oppressed peoples. Each of the five areas of new understanding repeat the same narrative pattern of consciencization and enlightenment. Wu came to understand, for example, how imperialism is what Christians call "the devil," and how those whom he formerly admired, such as Sherwood Eddy and "the imperialist spy" John Mott, were among the chief instigators of the use of Christianity for global aggression. Wu's testimony is important because of his role as a Protestant leader, for the insight it gives into the roles that war and the CCP played in drawing intellectuals toward Communist ideology (whether in reality or in the careful construct of a confession following ideological reeducation), and as an example of the internal negotiation between inherited faith and societal reality.

The slogan "love country, love church" remained with the church throughout the 1950s and into the late twentieth century. By the time of the National Christian Conference of July and August 1954, the guiding direction for the church had been firmly set and "much success" declared for the first four years.[51] The national conference, attended by 232 delegates representing sixty-two Protestant church bodies, combined worship sessions with reports from governmental representatives and small group discussions on the new constitution and produced agreed statements on embracing the constitution, censuring the United States' imperialist aggression and welcoming the cessation of fighting between India and China. In 1954 the Three-Self Reform Movement officially became the TSPM and was placed under the oversight of the Religious Affairs Bureau, an agency supervised by the United Front Work Department.

The magazine *Tian Feng* continued to combine "church" and "political" themes. An Easter edition in April 1954 was devoted entirely to Christian reflection (although with a certain political edge: the leading editorial, "Feed My Lambs," asks each reader, "Will we use our hearts of love for God to love our sisters and brothers?") while a double issue in July 1954 was filled with discussion of the new constitution and its relevance for the country and the church, including articles by the evangelical preacher and TSPM vice chair Chen Chonggui

("My Feelings on the Constitution") and feminist YWCA leader Deng Yuzhi ("Welcome the Promulgation of the Draft Constitution"). While imperialism still filled column inches, the issues had broadened, including opposition to nuclear power and, increasingly, a call to "strengthen unity." This began as a coded discussion of the evangelical preacher Wang Mingdao and his separatist theology and reached a crescendo in 1955 of open hostility and denunciation of Wang and other "counterrevolutionaries," that is, those not acceding to the new TSPM-party line.[52] This debate, or breakdown in dialogue, which is taken up in the next chapter, deepened the fissure between various Protestant groups, creating a rift that has yet to be bridged.

Protestant accommodation to the new regime had bought six or seven years, but little more. Good relations with the state had also thrown a protective mantle over some foreign church activity of friendly nations. As one letter home from a Scandinavian member of the Peking Union church noted in 1954, "The Protestant churches can continue, but the Catholics have a hard time." The English service at the Union church had by this point declined to a dozen congregants, but it still existed. The Chinese side was thriving and included outside university Christian groups using the Union buildings for Bible studies and services as well as retreats (靈修會) that gathered students from cities across the region; "thus our witness continues in a way that was never planned, with a power and outreach that was never dreamed of, and in an environment many thought hopeless," wrote one member.[53] The lull did not last. By 1958, denominational "unity" of worship was imposed on all, willing and unwilling. The Socialist study that Christians had been engaged in through the 1950s as part of the Socialist Education Movement had enabled (some of) them to see how combining churches might free up pastors' labor and church estate for the good of the nation. To some, when Nanjing Theological Seminary was brought into being from the various denominational colleges and seminaries as a combined theological education center, the breakthrough seemed as much God-given as governmentally dictated. For others, including those Protestant groups that did not agree with the new party line, disestablishment came rapidly. The last foreigners were hastened out of the door, and by 1961 the last students to enter an official seminary for two decades began their studies.

ROMAN CATHOLIC EXPERIENCES

A long-standing Catholic anti-Communism, combined with a belief in the church's absolute authority in matters of both theology and moral conscience, set the Roman Catholic Church on a collision course with the CCP long before the 1950s. Paul Mariani documents the antagonism beginning in the early days of Marxism, from Pius IX's insight in 1846 that Communism would "destroy society itself" to the Fatima visions and prophecies about the Soviet Union in 1917, Leo XIII's description of a "fatal plague," and Pius XI's condemnation of a "false messianic idea."[54] Mariani, a Jesuit, reads the situation in China as a struggle for survival between two religious groups—the Maoist Communists and the Roman Catholics—pointing to shared traits and values, such as hierarchical organization, belief in social harmony, support of family values, and a desire to perpetuate their own lineage. While the comparison may give an inflated impression of the role and status of the church in China, it emphasizes the fundamental nature of some of the clashes. As Richard Madsen once noted, the very existence of an independent Catholic Church challenged "the quasi-religious claims made by the Maoist state."[55] If a strong anti-Communism predisposed the Roman Catholic Church toward a problematic relationship with the new state, its transnational vision, politically as well as spiritually centered in Rome, and emphasis on heaven as the true kingdom of Christian belonging threatened the new national narrative. The ideology of absolute allegiance and the militaristic language promoted by such allegiance had the potential to be viewed by the CCP as a genuine threat to its rule. Given the bitter treatment of Nationalists after the Communist victory, it is of little surprise that religious personnel who had had close relations with Nationalists, such as Cardinal Yu Bin, came under fire.

The gradual tightening of foreign financial support for the church was more of an ideological barrier than a fiscal one for the Roman Catholics. Intelligent and more mild figures in the CCP hierarchy like Zhou Enlai understood something of this sensibility in spelling out that Catholics would be allowed to maintain religious links with the Pope, but not economic ones. The new regime demanded a willingness to see things in a new way: those who were willing were (initially) fine. The concession was not appreciated by most Catholics, for whom the link to the universal church was the very definition of Catholicism. There is much fodder for those who wish to see "war" developing between the CCP and the Roman Catholic Church; language on both sides during the 1950s and in subsequent discussions of the era has been highly partisan and denunciatory. Chen Zhemin, the secretary of the papal nuncio Antonio Riberi, drafted a response to the calls for an independent church, which stated that those who "willingly separate themselves from the Holy See also separate themselves from Jesus and from the Catholic church," calling any "national" church schismatic.[56]

Mariani elucidates the theological lines drawn here: since the Pope was Christ's representative on earth, "a Catholic could not sever ties with the Pope and still remain a Catholic."[57] It was precisely this type of thinking that was negated by the creation of a Chinese Catholic Church, but that very term is oxymoronic to Vatican traditionalists. Like Madsen, who documents the self-contained "world of God" in which many rural Chinese Catholics grew up and lived,[58] Mariani points to the "integralist" vision of life within which Shanghai Catholics existed, where the church was engaged in all aspects of life (an ideology close to that of the evangelical Protestant groups that also bitterly resisted Communist ideology). The combination of anti-Communism, fierce loyalty, and a belief in the heavenly kingdom of the church triumphant promoted a climate of martyrdom.[59] As with Protestant evangelicals like Wang Mingdao, who thought at length about the Christian's duty to an "unrighteous" state, the tension for Catholics came when the CCP became the lawful government, since believers recognized their biblical duty to obey authorities. As early as July 1949, the Vatican moved to deny the sacraments to anyone who so much as read Communist propaganda or allowed their children to join the Youth League.

Although some Catholic personnel were imprisoned or died in the late 1940s, regular church activity continued during the first couple of years of the PRC, with ordinations, including the translation from Suzhou of the new bishop of Shanghai, Gong Pinmei, and the continued transfer of mission property from religious orders to local diocesan control. There was, however, a palpable sense of loss among missionaries. One "Méditation du Missionnaire prisonnier" in the *China Missionary Bulletin* of October 1950 lamented the loss of what had represented the mission: the material power of its buildings, the well-being of body and mind formed in the schools that had kept going right through the war with Japan, the spiritual capital of the monasteries and seminaries represented by its ministers, catechumens, and adult baptisms—"maintenant tout cela est bien fini." The churches were occupied or destroyed, the trees in the garden had been cut down, tombstones were broken, and the central residence had become "an anti-Christian college."[60] The time lag in reaction to local events in a country still recovering from war, and in communication with the Vatican and the press, meant that normalcy continued in print for longer than it did in reality. The papal nuncio, Mgr. Riberi, was still writing a long article to priests in 1950 discussing the extent of, aims for, and problems with lay participation in evangelism in China and recapping previous pontiffs' attitudes to the lay apostolate. These were not the instructions of a man who believed he was about to be imprisoned.[61]

A sense of gloom and fear was widespread among Catholics by 1951. One French missionary wrote of the immense effort being put into propaganda, calling the creation of the Organization of Propaganda "a New Year present from the Communist Party to its adherents" and describing the "bitter and bloody fruit" that provinces, towns, and districts blindly brought forth in response.[62] Mariani in his study makes much of the intent of the CCP to divide and rule Christians by using "patriotism" as a tool to play off those who would put God's kingdom first against those who were willing to obey the CCP. There was certainly dissent in the ranks over the response to government directives. Some Chinese Catholics, like their Protestant counterparts, believed that their loyalty need not be divided between two absolute kingdoms, that it was possible to be anti-imperialist *and* Catholic. The Korean War brought these tensions out into the open when five hundred Catholics in Guangyuan, Sichuan, issued an anti-imperialist manifesto in late 1950, followed by others in Tianjin, Nanjing, Chongqing, and elsewhere.[63] The Catholic hierarchy was now fighting on two or three different fronts simultaneously. Hardliners, including those who were still expecting the Nationalists to return to power, saw no reason to make any compromises, while others understood the import of maintaining unity, like Bishop Gong Pinmei, or tried to find a middle way, like Zhang Boda. The Nanjing manifesto called on Catholics to separate themselves from the imperialist Vatican, a move swiftly denounced. The lead signatory, the vicar general of Nanjing, was one of the few actually excommunicated by Rome. Externally, the Korean War was proving problematic for the church, which was expected to encourage its youth and the students in its schools and colleges to sign up for "volunteer" forces. Church-funded organizations, such as the Catholic universities, were also finding themselves the subject of attention; foreign-financed universities were told in January 1951 that they would be nationalized, and some, such as the flagship Catholic university Aurora, were labeled "reactionary."[64] Worse still, the national campaign to suppress "counterrevolutionaries" began to draw Catholics into its dragnet.

Once regulations on church financing existed and expectations on patriotic allegiances began to be codified, those who pressed the case for the church catholic and universal in the face of a new, Chinese Catholic Church became suspect, and those in leading positions were threatened with the damning counterrevolutionary label. Thousands of citizens were arrested in the move to suppress counterrevolutionaries, Christians among them, and CCP figures suggest that a thousand were executed in Shanghai alone for plotting to overthrow the regime.[65] The church began to understand how vulnerable its reliance on foreign leadership left it.[66] Legitimate religion was protected under the interim constitution, the Common Principles, but imperialists were fair game, and "hiding under the cloak of religion" became the catchall term for removing any undesirable or recalcitrant citizen from active participation in society. The church's response was overt and covert. In Shanghai, Bishop Gong dedicated the diocese to the Immaculate Heart of Mary, with a program of prayer, renunciation, and Masses. A secret Jesuit novitiate was set up to train successor priests, with Yan Yunliang as master of novices, and an underground convent formed under a French spiritual director.[67] Sermon series, with daily teachings, were initiated at the bigger churches to equip parishioners with greater knowledge of their faith. Two youth organizations were developed that came to play a critical role in events: Marian sodalities and the Legion of Mary. The former, encouraged by Zhang Boda, gathered students in Ignatian exercises and training in apologetics; the students ran catechism classes for others and strengthened themselves through retreats. "Special militants" were recruited — young Catholics committed to supporting the faith whatever the cost, who worked alone in secrecy or in groups that utilized many of the same techniques as the CCP had during its clandestine guerrilla days.[68] The Legion of Mary, which had been drawing in elite students over a few years, had the backing of the envoy Riberi and Bishop Gong. Its name proved a drawback: the "Holy Mother Army" (Shengmu jun 聖母軍) became a government target, along with the Catholic Central Bureau, staffed mainly by foreigners and set up by Riberi.[69]

By late summer 1951 around two-thirds of Beijing's Catholic churches had been sealed shut. In Shanghai, Riberi was under house arrest and Zhang Boda imprisoned, but life for others carried on: Jin Luxian recalls spending time that year setting up a new printing outfit to build up a Chinese theological library for lay teaching.[70] The Legion of Mary was declared a counterrevolutionary organization in October 1951, and its young members were required to register in person their resignation from the league or face punishment. The declaration of resignation involved an admission of involvement in counterrevolutionary action against the government, and many were unwilling to sign a statement they felt was neither true nor fair. Some parish priests, and many parents, fearful for their offspring's future, advocated signing. Fifty students wrote a letter in blood, a statement of no compromise. This, and the death of Zhang Boda in prison, strengthened Catholic resistance to the formation of a "Chinese church" and enforced a split with Rome.

The official Vatican response to events was, in early 1952, still conciliatory. The apostolic letter of Pius XII Cupimus Imprimis dated 18 January 1952 was addressed to the ranks of priests and the people of China but was clearly angled toward government readers as well as church members. It set out an explanation of why mission was still necessary, combined with a denial of imperialist aggression. "Those who adhere to the Church cede to none in their love of fatherland; they obey public authorities out of a duty of conscience and in accordance with the norms of God's law," the epistle states, adding that the church loves all, and "it cannot be affirmed that she serves the interests of any particular power," in a deliberate rejection of CCP rhetoric on the loyalty of Christian citizens and on imperialist intervention.[71] The Pope's words on the missionary presence were more open to ideological challenge, reiterating that missionaries were sent only to care for the religious needs of the people and "offer their aid to the native clergy, which is still numerically insufficient for those same needs." A defense of the slowness of transfer of authority might be read into the words "as soon as the Apostolic See saw the possibility of entrusting your Dioceses to Bishops who were your countrymen, it did so willingly," but the paternalism underlying the basic stance is evident when the Pope notes that the forced departure of missionaries would be "not only distressing but also most injurious to the growth of your church," since it was clear that the church was "not yet at that full maturity where the aid and collaboration of foreign missionaries will be no longer necessary." Events soon proved this line of thought to be behind the times, politically and ecclesiologically. Even Mariani notes that there was a revival as the foreigners left.[72] Where other denominations had planned for such an outcome, the Vatican held on to the vision of an integrated universal church and to the structures that perpetuated it.

The pastoral words of the Pope, which enjoined the faithful to be strong through the grace obtained through prayer, commended them also to "offer to God as a sweet holocaust your hardships, your sorrows and your sufferings," so as to enable all to see that the church "does not seek earthly things but those of Heaven," striving to bring all of its followers into "the true fatherland in Heaven." As Madsen's alternative cosmic hierarchy theory suggests, the restatement of a church separate from the world, whose real citizenship is in heaven, sets up an alternative fatherland and country, fostering theological martyrdom.[73] By mid-1952 a significant number of articles in the *China Missionary Bulletin* were concerned with the arrested and the imprisoned. A "Mission Chronicle" in successive editions of the journal lists those expelled, under arrest, or under house arrest. A four-page article titled "Church Hierarchy in Communist China" in May 1952 tabulates diocese by diocese those "in residence" (fifty-nine), expelled (forty-two), deceased (eight), imprisoned (twenty), and under house arrest (eight). While those expelled or unable to return to their sees were almost all foreigners, the other columns record a mixture of Chinese and foreign names.[74] Interspersed among the chronicles of arrest and prison diaries were stories of resistance, such as the case where 150 orphans at a Shanghai Catholic orphanage tried to prevent the arrest of a French Jesuit priest by locking him in safety and chanting at the police, "We are the people—we are the government." (Two months later nine of the orphans, a lay teacher, and the Jesuit were arrested, but still, a "properly stamped summons" had been rendered defunct by slogan-savvy children.)[75]

It is clear that among the positive stories, there were also breakdowns and suicides of priests, religious, and others who could not bear the pressure to denounce others.[76] The language of the foreign mission press became increasingly shrill as official expression became increasingly absurd. The death of the moderate Zhang Boda was a tragedy for the church, but not without some macabre humor. The veneration of Father Béda was revealed by an official outburst that deemed it "counterrevolutionary mental bacteria" of a type that would "contaminate the purified minds of the patriotic Catholics." Priests were summoned to state their attitude toward Zhang, with one priest told that the police "would hold Bishop Kung responsible for any miracles which occurred through Catholics praying to Beda Chang."[77] The Catholic press might not have laid its religious folly out quite so openly as Communist officials, but the language it used to refer to the CCPA newspaper discouraging the veneration is equally extreme ("the violently anti-Catholic Communist 'Catholic' newspaper").

A resumption of anti-imperialist crackdowns in 1953 was accompanied by a growing lack of trust within the church. Fear was a motivator for both sides. The Roman Catholic Church had been regularly refusing communion to the "schismatics," but there were also suggestions that some CCPA members were being sent into Roman churches to cause difficulties for officiants.[78] Stand-offs between police and worshippers continued as churches were shut down. In Shanghai, authorities targeted the seminary at Xujiahui, although most seminarians had already been transferred to the Philippines, and Christ the King church was labeled a "center of espionage." Tactics were getting nastier as time wore on and the Catholic resistance in Shanghai was preventing the government's intended church organization, the CCPA, from taking up its role nationally on behalf of all the faithful. By 1955, the year when the "Gong Pinmei counterrevolutionary clique" became a major target of propaganda campaigns in line with the countrywide suppression of counterrevolutionaries, it was clear that the local police were not above planting evidence. A coordinated sweep on 8 September 1955 saw all in contact with Bishop Gong arrested across the country.[79] CCP and Catholic sources suggest that around twelve hundred leading Catholics were arrested at this point, and several hundred of these would remain in labor camps or prison for much of the next two decades. Some were strong in prison, others less so. Jin Luxian's account of his own treatment gives some insight into conditions and the tactics interrogators used. Jin is understanding toward those who made full and frank confessions, including handing over names and details that incriminated others; his incomprehension is retained for those like the French Jesuit superior Fernand Lacretelle, who denied his confession (of eight hundred pages and countless taped hours) to fellow church leaders afterwards, prolonging the harm to church members.[80] For those on the outside, the Socialist Education Movement was cranking out discussion sessions and struggle sessions to persuade the remaining ideological laggards. By 1957, when the CCPA was formally brought into being out of the Catholic Three-Self Renewal Committee, priests in areas without bishops (that is, bishops loyal to Rome) were already being granted certain episcopal powers. When the CCPA began its "illicit" ordinations of bishops in 1958 and was denounced by the Vatican, the framework of an alternative "underground" church was firmly in place.

CONCLUSIONS

This chapter has traced the interaction between external forces and internal responses in setting the direction of the church during the first decade of the PRC. It is clear that there was no inevitable connection between these; faith did not suppose a given response, and individuals within faith communities came to strongly divergent positions on the same issues. The acute challenges and high penalties for certain responses to political provocation meant that faith itself had a high value and overriding prominence in believers' lives during the period.[81] What is evident is that the highly visible sector of Protestant leadership and that of the Roman Catholic hierarchy were operating in two different rhetorical worlds during the 1950s.

Through the 1950s and into the 1960s, as the CCP was engaged in envisioning and engineering the ideological transformation of the nation, there was much overlap among Protestant activist-theologians regarding their hopes for China and its transformation. If imperialism was the cardinal sin against the state, Protestants could point to mitigating circumstances and show what they had been doing to sinicize the church and slough off all foreign influence (which was itself ironic, since the Catholic Church was far more embedded into Chinese life and generations of history). Protestants made patriotism acceptable in religious language much earlier than Catholics. Given their rejection of a dichotomy between God and the world, and their embrace of the social good that the Communists had achieved, the question for liberal, elite Protestants was how to order the church's affairs and foster a good working relationship with the state without compromising core beliefs. There was little precedent or outside help for them in this; as Raymond Whitehead writes, "Chinese Christians in the 1950s were very much on their own in the task of discerning where and how the western fear of socialism functions as a cover for imperialist goals that had nothing to do with the gospel."[82] Christians found that the ideological anti-Communism of the Western church had misled them, and they needed to find their own path to create and affirm their own faith and "break with the public presuppositions of western Christianity."[83] Enthusiasm for the vision of improvement and an investment in the three "selfs" led some to welcome the dismantling of denominations and the imposition of a unified church. Other Protestants, whose belief in holiness set Christians apart from the world, found a theological common ground with Roman Catholics at this juncture. Their leaders found genuine common ground in prison and in labor camps.

The question of whether the Roman Catholic position of absolute refusal to acknowledge or work with the CCP was vindicated or not is a difficult one. Their mistrust in 1949 and 1950 proved correct; crackdown came, and decimation followed. But if the church had not taken such an antagonistic line, might the terror have been avoided? The hard questions that remain—questions as to how wise, or godly, it was to create martyrs—may be offensive to those who suffered for their faith. But the Catholic martyrs were nurtured within a Constantinian theology, where religion held sway over all civic life, and were guided by a Vatican whose demand for absolute allegiance was a theoretical position for those in Rome espousing it. It is difficult not to agree with Madsen in his stress on Vatican responsibility, since it was the foreign bureaucrats who demanded that the church take a "maximally provocative, aggressive stance against the Communist regime," and, unlike in Eastern Europe, where a degree of accommodation was reached, "Vatican officials seemed more rigidly concerned with the purity of their principles than with the fate of the Catholics."[84] Certainly, some Catholics who lived through the period and imprisonment, like Jin Luxian, rethought their positions subsequently; tragically, Jin was to pay twice, once to the Communists in two decades of prison, and once to the church that disdained him for participating in the official church on his release. Their stories highlight the provisional, human nature of history. Raising stakes by such signs of dedicated and absolute resistance as guerrilla tactics and sleeper cells in Shanghai allowed the CCP to regard Shanghai Catholic groups as legitimate targets and retroactively justified the case that the imperialist foreigners were using religion as a means of attacking China. It is possible both to admire greatly the martyrs and those who suffered during this period and to feel immensely frustrated, especially when mediating Chinese voices, like that of Zhang Boda, were not heeded.

As Henrietta Harrison's research is Shanxi shows, however, those who signed up to the CCPA early on still suffered for their faith, with ugly "living exhibitions" of religious personnel, processions, and ritual humiliations, as well as incarcerations—so there may have been little gain in succumbing to governmental pressure, especially when an individual believed that such an action might compromise faith.[85] In Shanxi it was not the pressure of the 1950s that threatened church members or divided congregations, but the unrelenting force to leave a "feudal" and "capitalist" religion during the mass movements of the 1960s. With all Catholic religious activity banned, with militias surrounding villages, and with constant criticism and investigation most villagers did eventually succumb and apostatize. What divided the church in a province like Shanxi was not the creation of a state church and the tarnish of compromise in the 1950s, but the return of priests in the 1980s who had capitulated in the 1960s. Here, an institutionally separate "underground" church was created only at this point, where communities did not want to be led by, or receive sacraments from, priests who had betrayed their faith.

There has been no truth and reconciliation commission in China and no framework for religious believers who denounced each other by which they might come into any structured reconciliation.[86] The conflict for the most part is not open now but may be staged at symbolic sites, such as Sheshan, the Catholic pilgrimage site outside Shanghai, where underground church members continue to kneel and pray in groups outside at the shrines, while official Catholics stream past them, coming out of Masses in the basilica. The narrative of resistance has remained so important to Catholic communities and to the inculcation of faith that one suspects little short of a papal visit will bring change. As Giles Fraser writes in a different context, "The daring deeds of a few undoubtedly courageous men and women are often used as the lens through which we view political reality."[87] There have been conciliatory moves in the period since 1979, allowing some non-CCPA priests to practice, and in the institution of a national conference of bishops separate from the CCPA, as discussed in Chapter 8. More than a third of CCPA bishops whose ordinations were technically valid, but unsanctioned, have been retroactively approved by Rome. But the division of the church over several decades has created an institutional tangle as well as deep pain, with double bishops (underground and CCPA) for some sees, situations where congregants are not always clear whether their bishop has been approved by Rome or not, and unknown numbers of "black priests" ordained by underground bishops, whose situation during the period of rapprochement counseled by Pope Benedict in 2007 is not entirely clear.

Although the divide between TSPM and unregistered Protestant churches has also been bitter, the separation of congregations may have cushioned the damage. In Protestant congregations the majority may be new worshippers or converts, and there is not the same historical sense of injustice at priests having "betrayed" the faith. Within the TSPM churches many accepted the government line early on; those who did not moved to form the "house churches," but there is no compulsion to see these as fragmented parts of the same church in the way that there is for the Catholic Church. Since a high heaven was needed, and ideally, a purgatory and a hell too, for a strong climate of martyrdom, Protestant liberals with their Social Gospel theology of a Kingdom of Heaven on earth had much less incentive to die to secure a place in a perfect heaven; the legacy of the martyrs lives on among unregistered congregations.

It is difficult at this distance to see the wound inflicted on the church during the 1950s as anything other than some sort of visceral revenge for all that imperialists were perceived to have inflicted on China during the nineteenth century. The church was a major foreign presence; businesses were leaving, the diplomatic world a more tricky adversary. The church formed no military threat; any hostility lay in the power of an alternative ideology to challenge the Communist narrative on which its power was based. The church's strength lay in the proclamation of a variant worldview and in the fortitude demonstrated by its stubborn and unreasonable submission to this alternative ideology—a faith that undermined the proclamation of rational ideology by not acceding to its methodological premise. The "reasonable" faith of liberal Protestants did not offer the opportunity for martyrdom in quite the same way, and their subsequent theologies have yet to deal fully with this period.

DING GUANGXUN: MAINTAINING THE CHURCH

Must the church follow a path opposed to our nation? Did the
Lord say that we must hate what the people like, and like what the
people hate? Is it a sin for the church to see eye to eye on some
matters with the people? Can the church only glorify God by placing itself in opposition to the nation and its people? Absolutely not!
—Ding Guangxun, 1954[1]

It is lamentable that many Christian leaders use the principle
of obedience to man's rules and submission to man's authority to cover up their cowardice and failure. They thus deceive
many believers and don't fully understand the truths of the
Bible. This results in the faith of the church and the ministry
being subordinated to the rule of men and man's authority.
The truth then becomes obscured, the Bible misinterpreted,
the foundations of the church undermined and the flock scattered. . . . These foundational and precious things are so
lightly surrendered by some so-called servants of God! How
can such Christian leaders then escape the wrath of God?
—Wang Mingdao, 1954[2]

Ding Guangxun (K. H. Ting, 1915–2012)[3] was heralded during his lifetime as
the premier church statesman of the PRC era, a figure whose leadership of the
authorized Protestant church and its national seminary spanned five decades
and whose theological thought guided the church through much of that period.
Ding's effect as a church leader was arguably greater than as a theologian, but
his theology is highly pragmatic in orientation, and the two cannot be readily
separated. This chapter does not attempt to provide a comprehensive study of

Ding or his writings: separating the man from the myth was already a problem for historians in the pre-Internet age (the question of whether Ding was ever a CCP member, for example, has stubbornly persisted, despite disavowals), and a single chapter devoted to this preeminent leader could barely sketch out the contours of his thought—his emphasis on the Incarnation, on God as love, on the Christlikeness of God—let alone integrate these with Ding's complex biography, which was so singularly intertwined with the postwar history of the Chinese church.[4] Ding's funeral in 2012 encapsulated two core aspects to his life in a notably Chinese manner: for the official media the coffin was draped in a national flag, with a portrait of Ding in a suit, and the funeral was attended by such dignitaries as Politburo Standing Committee member Yu Zhengsheng; for Christian remembrance Ding was enveloped in a white shroud with a cross and portrayed in his bishop's vestments.[5] For someone who sought to serve both church and state, Ding may have preferred a greater unity of symbolic identity. As a member of the National People's Congress and vice chair of the Chinese People's Political Consultative Conference for two decades, Ding had earned his national standing. Yet it was this association with the state—and the impression among some Christians that Ding was too close to the government, or worse, that his theology was an act of appeasement—that formed a source of contention throughout his decades of leadership.[6]

This chapter concentrates on the early writings of Ding Guangxun from the 1940s and 1950s. It does so to create a base understanding of his theological position in the first years of his ministry, which may act as comparator for later developments, and because this period encompasses intense debate on the relationship of church and state, debate that accompanied and precipitated the effective split of the Chinese Protestant church and whose ramifications are still ever-present. Given the scattered nature of Ding's sermons and essays, and the lack of any sustained writing or dogmatic treatise, it is not possible to take a single text for detailed study, so the argument here is woven from various sources. The first section considers the central themes of Ding's early publications: mission, evangelism, and Christology. Ding, who was ordained in 1942, worked in Canada and Switzerland from 1946 to 1951, and the broad theological foci of this period of relative stability provide a base for assessing how Ding's thinking shifted as PRC governmental policies came into effect and Marxist-Leninist-Maoist thought began to mold the social context.

As the chapter explores, the tone and focus of Ding's work shift distinctly during the period after Ding and his family settled back in China. Much of his early work is in English, and the content and style differ markedly for different audiences. Ding may have wished to distinguish himself from the ideology of the earlier generation of theologians, and from schoolmates "so imbued with the comprador mentality and lack of patriotism as to be discussing which was the best world power for China to be colonized by,"[7] but his upbringing had much in common with the bicultural Republican-era theologians explored in previous chapters. Ding is the first of these theologians to grow up with texts in modern vernacular Chinese, and while he might quote Laozi in his early writings to make a point, he is just as likely to quote T. S. Eliot: he was educated at the prestigious (English-language) St. John's University in Shanghai as well as Columbia University and Union Theological Seminary in New York. A close reading of his early texts suggests a marked change in language use and style around 1952–1953, in keeping with national shifts in language and rhetoric.[8] Little remains of any writings between 1961 and 1978, so this early period is separated from Ding's mature work by the aftermath of the Anti-Rightist campaign and the spectacular folly and destruction of the Cultural Revolution.

The central resonances that emerge from Ding's early writings may surprise, such as the strength of his evangelical beliefs and his creedal orthodoxy: there is very little to separate Ding theologically at this point, for example, from conservative nemesis Wang Mingdao. When by 1955 a bitter and very public debate ensued between these two pastors, the passion on each side was so strong that the theological becomes interlaced with the personal. This debate, which revolves around the relation of the church to the world, forms the second part of this chapter. The terms and fallout from the debate were critical to the immediate future of the Chinese Protestant church, and the chapter considers a possible Barthian solution to the impasse. A final brief section looks ahead to the development of Ding's thinking in the era of economic reform and theological reconstruction.

GOD HAS NOT ABANDONED US

An anecdote about Ding's route to ordination tells us a surprising amount about his righteous stubbornness, his humility, and his priorities in wartime China.[9] When his principal at St. John's University in Shanghai, the American F. L. Hawks Pott, plotted out Ding's future studies and first chaplaincy position for him before he had completed his undergraduate degree, Ding recoiled at the presumption and the history of missionary arrogance it signified. He refused the offer and rethought his ordination plans, at which point Hawks Pott demanded the repayment of the university fees Ding owed and the return of his theological books. The latter caused him to weep, alone in his room, before complying. When Ding restarted the ordination process (in the Sheng Gong

Hui, or Anglican church) some four or five years later—and had to write to Hawks Pott to resume his studies at St. John's—it was as a candidate to work with the YMCA and Student Christian Movement, underscoring the political edge and educational vision that drove him. In one of Ding's earliest publications in 1937, a piece in a parish youth magazine, he wrote that the most important aspect to religion was "its effect on our lives, for religion is a way of living that is related to every action we take."[10] From the beginning of his ministry, Ding's faith was an active one, sustained by an integrated vision of community and church life. He did share one trait with his classically educated predecessors: his activism embraced voluminous writing.

Ding's lifelong interest in education is evident at the outset, as is his focus on human growth and development. His message to both secular student audiences and Christians in the late 1940s was that no one lives in an ivory tower—that during wartime no one can be neutral and that all have to consider what cause they are serving and face "the tribunal of our conscience,"[11] a stance consistently reflected in Ding's views on church and society. The prophetic role of Christians during wartime, viewing the world "optimistically and with hope," is predicated on the Incarnation, the "sign that God has not abandoned us."[12] In an early meditation, "Reading the Bible at Christmas," the sense of how hard it is to struggle against sorrow and suffering is palpable, yet Ding counsels that the time ahead, though it will be one of even deeper suffering, will precisely be a time when "Christians learn from our Lord." The only antidote to pervasive fear, argues Ding, is love: the self-sacrificial task of "participating in the great work of building up the Kingdom of God on earth," which alone creates a kingdom devoid of insecurity.[13]

EVANGELISM, WITNESS, AND INCARNATION

Ding's commitment to evangelism was expressed practically by his taking up a post as missionary secretary to the Canadian Student Christian Movement in 1946, and his theological commitment to evangelism remains strong even as his repudiation of the asymmetry of international mission hardens. Evangelism is "the life-blood of the church," wrote Ding in 1948; it is the means by which the church remains vital, since "nothing can really kill the church until the church is induced to forget its missionary task."[14] The desire in a Christian that Christ should mean all to all corresponds to "the eternal hunger in the heart of God," longing for all to return to God. The "conquest of the world by love" is "the nearest humanly possible vocation to that of the incarnation itself," Ding avers, reiterating the heights of the apostolic task. Ding lists the gains to the "younger churches" from missionary input, gains that include experience, links to the universal church, youth training—and the benefits to the sending churches from the inspiration of new Christians. While Ding wants Western Christians to see that they cannot keep mission stations permanently running, he cautions at this point against idealizing the younger churches and allowing "romantic discussion" about their growth and strength to blind one to their needs, commenting that he wished "it had not created abroad the notion that the younger churches are really mature enough today to dispense with western personnel help." These views, expressed in English in a Canadian student publication in 1948, and close to those expressed by many missionaries within China, may be compared instructively with Ding's views on the role of foreign missions in China, written in Chinese just a few years later.[15]

In a short article produced during Ding's stint at the headquarters of the World Student Christian Federation in Geneva, he reflects on the tension of proclamation and conversion, arguing that evangelism that forces religion on another is not evangelism. Genuine evangelism consists of bringing about the "voluntary offering" of a person to Jesus Christ "with the full and honest participation of one's intellect and emotion and will." This true form of evangelism respects the integrity of others and their existing personhood, "recognizing and appreciating all healthy and sublime aspirations and struggles for the good, the beautiful and the righteous" in others, and gives inquirers enough encouragement and information to enable them to know what is involved in a decision for Christ.[16] As throughout his ministry, Ding combines a genuine respect for others and their worldview and affirmation of their good, God-given humanity with a genuine desire that they come to know Christ. Ding's broad church Anglicanism is evident here, as is his orthodox language, with the inflection of the *Book of Common Prayer* coming through in his phraseology.[17] Forcing a religion on anyone is, Ding reiterates, a self-defeating task and cannot be done "without making yourself a nuisance and a cultural imperialist." Ding believed strongly in the need for mission and the role of evangelism in maintaining the vitality of the church, but not at the cost of integrity. On balance, he warns, "the church erred more often in forgetting its missionary vocation altogether than in imposing the Christian religion on others."[18]

In an unfinished second part to this article, Ding muses on the criteria involved in choosing a religion, arguing that these cannot ultimately be rational ones, since rational criteria privilege faith in one's own reason, and evaluative terms like "better" involve using a person's own moral system to judge a figure like Christ. Comparative religion can be done only from within one's own reference frame, while Christ "challenges the very basis from which we make all our judgments."[19] The development of the argument shows the strength of Ding's Christology: unlike predecessors Wu Leichuan or Zhao Zichen, or even his mentor Wu Yaozong, Ding has a robust faith in Christ as "the unique fact in the history of God's dealing with humanity," a Christ in whom "all of history gains coherence." The radical otherness of Christ informs a bias in Christians "towards that Truth to which objectivity is self-deception and neutrality moral cowardice." This uniqueness and wholly otherness precludes Christians from a relative position on other religions (if Christianity "is only relatively better," then the ideal would be to create a religion out of the best elements of all religions, Ding submits) and is the basis for Ding's strong impulse to mission. Importantly, Ding suggests that those who resort to argument to evangelize and justify their actions do so out of a want of experience: people who have been "captured by Christ" naturally tell others about their experience, "once they recover from the shock of the encounter."[20] Just as Christ chooses people and not vice versa, the question of what right we have to preach to others is misdirected, Ding argues, since this is actually a question of God's prior love for humanity: speaking of the "right" of God to choose to love, or rescue from sin, is palpably absurd. The analogy shores up the link between mission and soteriology but critically places love at the heart of all evangelism. The love of God in Christ is not a new theme in Ding when it reappears in a Communist setting, but it is central to his early evangelical, and strongly Christological, view of mission.

Where witness fails, the church bears a responsibility. Too many people, suggests Ding, encounter Christ only in familiar stereotypes. The tendency of humans to picture Christ "in images that best suit their selfish views of what he should be like" is overcome only by Christ's breaking through and self-revelation.[21] As God works out the realization of God's loving purpose in tandem with human history, Christians participate in God's act of reclamation by recognizing Christ and proclaiming the gospel in the world. God relies on the church to bring about "the ultimate triumph of his purpose." Evangelism, salvation, and the Incarnation are inextricably linked, since "to behold the incarnate Christ is to see with eyes of faith his unique position at the center of history."[22] Christ, who is both continuous with humanity via Mary and discontinuous in the new act of creation whereby humanity was taken into God, is "the realization of the true nature of the destiny of us all." This Christ cannot be grasped without distortion in human language and can be proclaimed only through an act of the Holy Spirit and in terms of the listeners' environment.[23]

One of Ding's responses to his own insights and claims about the need to witness was highly practical: he produced in the mid-1950s a series of short essays aimed at individuals and church study groups titled *Zen yang du shengjing* (怎样读圣经 How to Study the Bible), reissued in the early 1980s.[24] This short text, some forty pages long, which reaffirms the centrality of Christ and the key-note of love, is intended to present worked examples of good reading practices and to encourage readers to ask questions of the Bible. The principles of reading are described in the essay headings (such as "Let the Whole Bible Speak," "Make Comparisons," "Let Personalities Come Alive," and "Listen to the Tiny Voices")[25] and in exhortations to readers to put their confidence in Christ, to pay heed to the silences in the text as well as what is said, and to find what God has in store for them.[26] Ding introduces in simple lay terms three key issues to explore in the text: its historical-critical context, its applicability to current context, and the need for self-awareness in understanding one's own purpose and motive in addressing the passage.[27] The Bible must become, counsels Ding, "a letter with my name on it which I myself receive from God each day" and personally open and read.[28]

The principles Ding outlines in his Bible-reading guide are given force by the exquisite quality of the insights in his own example readings, asking why, for example, the bliss of Bethel came before the wrestling of Penuel for Jacob, or what it means that Adam's first words expressed fear. Ding's reading is personal, and his appraisals are honest (he explores, for instance, the selfishness of Jacob), but much of the insight comes from a close textual reading and attention to literary style. In this we can see elements of Chinese text reading alongside Western biblical exegesis: in Ding's examination of parallelisms in the eleven sets of paired opposites in Matthew 7; in a reading of Ephesians as showing a central movement in the Bible from unity to disunity and back to unity (同归于一); in the (Confucian) emphasis on self-examination as integral to reading; in the attention given to the overarching shape of the biblical narrative (such as extensive detail of the symmetry between Genesis and Revelation, or the significance of the Psalms of praise being the exact midpoint of the text), just as the structure of a classical Chinese novel would be parsed.[29] There was also a critical edge to the writings: these emerged at the same time as Ding's debates with church leaders opposed to the TSPM (see below), and the interspersed reflection and comment are consonant with Ding's beliefs on the action of the church, and God, in the world. In this respect, Ding suggests that the silence of the book of Esther on "God" implies that what God cares about far surpasses our notions of religion, while the lesson to read the Bible in its totality and not isolated verses—since even the devil quotes from the Bible—provides a veiled comment on his opponents in the debates; the message of Penuel tells us that we cannot separate ourselves from the world or live in sweet eremitic isolation, just as Jacob's wrestling shows how God wants to create not automatons "but a new kind of conscious co-worker."[30]

Across Ding's early writings, Ding deals only tangentially with the Kingdom of God in relation to mission, and although he rivals his theological predecessors in China in his commitment to the construction of a Socialist state, his more orthodox eschatology precludes an immediate, human-driven utopia. While God yearns for the return of all humanity, and "what stands between now and the final culmination of the Kingdom of God is but the completion of the evangelistic task by those who are already members of the new humanity," the initiative for this task, so central to "the forward march of history," remains with God.[31] The center of the church's mission is not building the kingdom, but witness. Witness is the command and the duty of every Christian. We neither know when the kingdom will come nor should plan for its coming, argues Ding: all we know is that there is a close relation between the coming of the kingdom and the witness of the church.[32] This shift from a kingdom-building emphasis of theologians like Wu Leichuan in the 1930s to witness itself is an important marker—an acknowledgment of the failure of Christian state-building under the Nationalists. The kingdom may not be imminent or the primary duty of the church, but Ding does see a role for Christian leaders in challenging perceptions of the realities of the world. In 1947 Ding questions in a Canadian journal whether missionaries could preach a gospel of peace and reconciliation when maintaining unquestioning support for the U.S. policy of military aid to the "reactionary Nationalist one-party dictatorship"; it was, he argues, "an insult" to suggest that Chinese were not capable of making their own decisions in working toward a modern democratic nation.[33] Elsewhere, Ding sets out statistics on agrarian reform and land redistribution to demonstrate why there was such support for the Communists and to suggest to a North American audience the need to engage with the policies, and politicians, of the majority populace in China, as well as limning why CCP solutions differed from Eastern European or Russian Communist policies.[34]

Ding's theology operates as an organic whole: Christ's nature at the center of history and of the Bible compels the church to witness, and the incarnate Christ provides the model for the church's role vis-à-vis humanity. Christ's two natures qualify him to be a mediator between God and humanity, since "Christ is human, completely and truly human. And so he can represent humankind before God. Christ is also God, completely and truly God. And so, he can represent God to humankind."[35] Christ has entrusted his role of reconciliation to the church, whose "task is to represent God in the midst of humankind and to represent humankind to God." In this way the Incarnation models the role for the church in its witness and in teaching the church how to *be* in the world. Christ identifies with humanity in the Incarnation to redeem humanity, and so the church too must identify with humans in their needs—but be separated from them in their sins. The nature of Christ, as identifying with but separated from humanity, is thus the pattern for how the church should relate to the world: "If it [the church] were completely to identify with the world, then the powers of the world would be only too glad to acquire ecclesiastical sanction and blessing for their desires. But if the church were to seal itself off from the world—as the hermit is confined to 'spiritual' things—the world would again be overjoyed, because then church and world would each be 'minding its own business.'"[36] Ding's position on the church's role in the world, derived from his Christology, predates by several years his arguments with Chinese separatists.

CHANGING EXPRESSIONS OF FAITH

In 1951, delayed by the Korean War, Ding Guangxun and his wife Guo Xiu-mei (Siu-may Kuo) returned to China to find a church in the midst of negotiating new ecclesial structures and in the thralls of the Denunciation Movement. This latter campaign, coordinated by government officials, aimed to separate the church from any remaining imperialist forces within—whether foreign missionary personnel, funding, or lingering ideologies.[37] It drew church members into making increasingly divisive and inflamed criticisms of each other, in the manner of secular mass campaigns of the period. Ding, who was yet to be fully reintegrated into or appointed to a leadership role within the church, did not take part in the Denunciation Movement, nor did he sign the Christian Manifesto being circulated at the time, with its strident critique of the missionary past and its call for an independent future. Ding's support for New China is not in doubt, but as Philip Wickeri's study of the period details, much care is needed in tracing the different factions in church politics at this point and in not assigning the views of the more radical, or leftist, TSPM leaders to all.[38] On his return to China, Ding was clearly exercised emotionally and theologically about the disparity between the contemporary reality of Christian witness and the truth of what the church was. Although the church is entrusted with the great task of reconciling humanity to God, he writes, whenever "church" is mentioned, it is merely a reminder of "events which have caused our people and our nation unhappiness for over a hundred years."[39]

Ding's language, at least in articles published in the official church magazine *Tian Feng*, begins in the early 1950s to be suffused with the phraseology of the period, and his thinking takes on a much more sino-centric focus. Moments of optimism—such as those expressed in a 1948 article in the *Canadian Student* when Ding discusses how the simplicity of the truth of the gospel strikes those outside of Christian-inflected language and philosophical systems most freshly, or how India, China, and Japan would soon be communicating their experience of the power of the gospel to the Western world[40]—cede to a predominantly negative assessment of foreign interference. Whether to accord with publication expectations or fashioned subconsciously by the lexicon emanating from directives all around, Ding's language begins to adopt the slogans and formulas of the time. "Under the protection of the People's Government, we have been able to shatter the shackles of imperialism and truly become a church," he writes in a 1953 article on witness.[41] On the need for separation from the Western churches, he laments in 1954: "For one hundred or so years, under the control, manipulation and corruption of imperialism, the Chinese church was most unworthy of its name. It followed along behind Western churches, modeling itself on them, not knowing what it believed, hoped for, or loved. Its situation was truly painfully bleak, broken and foul."[42]

Ding was not alone in this line: David Paton's 1953 *Christian Missions and the Judgement of God* shocked many by its litany of mea culpa: the "paralyzing professional clericalism" that the missionary church had brought to China; the "sterility" of the organization, exemplified by its exalted sacramental system but scarcity of priests and bishops to deliver such; disparities in salaries between Westerners and Chinese and "bourgeois" healthcare provision; and its failures in nurturing a theological literacy among Chinese priests.[43] In terms of Ding's language, the ideological language during the period of the Korean War was shrilly offensive in both Chinese and U.S. media (see Chapter 6), and this is the context for interpreting the tenor, and content, of some of Ding's more effusive responses to his new, and quite revelatory, understandings of some of the failures of the mission church with which he had been associated. Retrospective analyses have not always allowed any leeway: Tony Lambert, for example, explores Ding's discussion of "revolutionary Marxist heroes" in February 1952, when Ding claims that "ordinary people are producing extraordinary results" in the New China and quotes in his assessment of their travails Hebrews 11:34 and 38; Lambert writes, "this extraordinary exegesis has clearly crossed the borderline between Biblical Christianity and full-blooded Marxism."[44] Other commentators have taken a more pugnacious line and accused Ding of not just crossing a boundary, but being thoroughly and primarily a fully fledged Communist. Li Xinyuan, for example, contends that "Ding's thought is merely the product of a politico-religious figure that emerged from a particular environment, for the purpose of 'accommodating' God's word to human Communist 'ideology'"; and that Ding's "'accommodation' is heartfelt [but] thoroughly misleading because in actuality, Chinese Communism is his 'basic belief' and 'ultimate concern.'"[45]

A new situation demands a new assessment, and Ding places his trust firmly in God's prompting in the circumstances. The result is a combination of pragmatism, maneuvering around the bounds of new political rules and expectations, and theological reflection. The article on witness continues: "If we admit that huge gatherings for evangelism and revival may not be God's choice for today, we must then understand that we need to withdraw a little in order to learn lessons in Christ. Because of the deep influence of imperialism on our thoughts, we need to discipline ourselves to learn to love the country; we dare not act rashly or be self-willed."[46] The first lesson in sloughing off "imperialist" habits and learning to love the country was to learn to love the people. In becoming increasingly convinced of the damage to the Chinese church of the period of foreign leadership, Ding channels this sentiment into a counterbalancing affirmation of the nation and the TSPM.

"The Lamb of God" (1952) begins with the question "what would Christ feel about a new country such as ours?" and goes on to critique those who will not rejoice along with the people and whose indifference is an impediment to the spread of love. "If we cannot love what Jesus loves, how can we claim to love Jesus?," Ding asks pointedly.[47] Taking the cue from the people, rather than seeing them as the subject of evangelism, signals a change of emphasis, if not perspective. The justification given is biblical, but the difference between a contextualized message and a Maoist understanding of "the people" is rhetorically blurred: "As citizens of China we should love our country and be at one with its people. To be worthy of the trust of the gospel we need to think what they think, love what they love, hate what they hate. Our Lord Jesus acted thus; Paul acted thus. . . . If there is no common ground, how can the gospel, no matter how beautiful it is, make any sense to whose whom we want to reach?"[48] Ding calls on believers to set aside differences and "enter into the midst of the people" so that their witness will be a living one and not merely "religious slogans, sounding gongs or clanging cymbals." Anticipating the next phase of political campaigns, which culminated in educated youth being sent down to the countryside for reeducation from the workers, Ding calls for a "true joining of hearts" with the people, whether in lifestyle, work, or study. The education of the saints in the community was to equip them to become "Christians who love God, nation, people and church" and who are at the same time "staunch supporters" of the TSPM. The growing awareness of the effects of the "imperialist" past prompts a searching reassessment of the mission years too, as now Ding notes, "when we ought to have been angry, we lacked the conscience to bear this kind of witness."[49]

The alignment with the people, a reorientation necessitated by the guiding direction of the party but also one for which biblical justification could be readily garnered, had a corollary effect on Ding's theology, one that put him on a collision course with great numbers of evangelical Christians to the present. On more than one occasion Ding argued that one of the twin dangers of overexaggerating justification by faith was that it could lead to a denigration of the achievements of ordinary people and be used as a weapon against the people (the second danger was that of underplaying the sins of the church).[50] Although Ding was adamant that "justification by faith is a crucial doctrine" and Christians erred only when they emphasized this to the exclusion of all works, his detractors have read this stance as an undermining of the doctrine, not a corrective to it, and the issue has proved an ongoing thorn in relations with non-TSPM Protestant Christians.[51]

It is easy to see at this distance how any theological innovation or any attempt to speak to the language of the times could be interpreted as a deviation from traditional ("biblical") faith, although Ding's thought might equally be characterized as strict orthodoxy with some censor-appeasing additions having to do with loving the people and the country. What is clear is that a rhetorical strategy develops across the 1950s that seeks to minimize the differences among Chinese Christians and maximize the importance of external threats. Ding is critical of imperialists for an array of evils, from nuclear proliferation to taking pleasure in the fragmenting ranks of Chinese Christians, but his ire is directed as much at those in China who would divide the church.[52] By this point, the questions of theological orthodoxy and TSPM membership are intertwined, and both are defended vigorously. Unity is for Ding both a Christian and an ideological goal, but it becomes an increasingly fraught test of belonging. "What exactly are these differences?" he asks. "We believe in the same God and the same Bible; we have all been saved by Jesus Christ." The TSPM, argues Ding, is built on the principle of respect and guarantees the preservation of the faith of each group: Christians should be finding joy in each other's company, not exaggerating their differences and destroying their unity "in faith and anti-imperial patriotism."[53]

Christian beliefs, national pride, and Socialist conviction all combine to persuade Ding of the rightness of his stance on relating to society and on the strength of goodness outside of the church, as well as the fact that "Christians have no monopoly on the truth."[54] A combination of the necessity of relating to society as a minority voice within and the great heritage of Chinese social and moral values, together with a view of God at work in the whole of creation, persuades Ding of the fundamental need of valuing and working with outsiders.[55] An evolving sense of how Jesus related to his country adds to Ding's depth of conviction and strength of defense. The social changes in the New China fill Ding with excitement and allow him to say in so many things, including patriotic love, "I was blind, but now I see." "In the past we thought that Christians, being spiritual, should not be concerned about national affairs," Ding writes. "In this way many patriotic exemplars in the Bible became 'a garden locked, a fountain sealed' (Song 4:12). Indeed the Bible does not directly mention the term patriotism. But the sentiment of love for one's native land is everywhere apparent. The strange thing is that we were blind to it in the past."[56] He then engages in a lengthy exposition of examples from the prophets, showing their impassioned concern for the nation. Jesus was no different in this, Ding concludes: "The Lord Jesus loves all humanity and gave up his life for all humanity. But this did not lessen his fervent love for his own nation," as shown in his exchange with Nathanael or his weeping over Jerusalem. Paul too shows us how "only those with such deep love for their own people are capable of being preachers."[57] Simone Frutiger Bickel, who worked with Ding in Geneva in the late 1940s, comments helpfully on the comprehension gap over use of the term "patriotism": "Many find it difficult to understand that the 'patriotism' which animates the China Christian Council and the Chinese Catholics is experienced as a dynamic of solidarity and with a profound love for the people, not in an arrogant, chauvinistic manner which in the West is characteristic of conservative, nationalist movements and which is rightly denounced."[58]

It is those who cannot see the good or respond to "the grand scale" with which God is spreading his word and understanding in China who frustrate Ding, not any antigovernment convictions or separatist instincts per se. In an article published in January 1957 in the *Student World*, the magazine of the World Student Christian Federation, Ding sought to explain the current situation to those outside of China and to defend the direction of theological thinking and policy of self-sufficiency.[59] This article is a fairly comprehensive summation of Ding's theological-political position in the mid-1950s and one that drew attention at the time, as seen from reaction in the North American press.[60] The various themes described above are gathered into a cogent defense of, and advocacy for, the uncharted track that the Chinese church was forging for itself. China finds itself in a new situation, without a route map, writes Ding, facing "the bankruptcy of all pragmatic Christianity and the subsequent emergence of a Christocentric theology."[61] Past formulations of Christianity as a ticket to heaven or a means to save the country are no use, he asserts, implicitly repudiating the Christianity of the late Qing and of the Republican era; publications from the West are of little help to contemporary China as well, since their authors were "in bondage to the political atmosphere of hatred current in their own society," and their writings were "just theological buttressing of their own political views."[62] As the Chinese church reassessed its past, a period when it "did not realize the extent of our own alienation, from God and from our own people," it was forced to move from a pragmatic Christianity to true faith, from foreign financial and political backing, "protected by discriminatory treaties," to self-support. The church had to face new standards for self-assessment, but it had also come to see, as it moved metaphorically from Laodicea to Smyrna, that "Christ's strength is perfect in our weakness."[63]

If these views collectively seem to suggest that Ding was a wholehearted supporter of the Socialist cause and presage the Theological Reconstruction program two decades later, it is important to note that he also challenged CCP orthodoxy, even at the height of the ideological campaigns, and drew clear ideological lines that indicated: beyond this, no farther. An address delivered at Nanjing Seminary in 1957 stands as an important apologetic in this regard.[64] In it, Ding discusses two of the great Marxist critiques of Christianity as an opiate and as a falling on the wrong side of the materialist-idealist divide, as well as addresses the existence of God, structural and social sin, and whether a nation can be inherently Christian/atheist. The speech attempts to strengthen his students and shore up their belief in the face of strong ideological attack (1957 was the year of the Anti-Rightist campaign), but its thinking addressed a wider audience too, and the text was singled out in criticism of Ding both in 1959 and during the Cultural Revolution.[65] Philip Wickeri regards the section rebutting charges of Christianity as an opiate as particularly important, not least because it was the only essay by a Christian challenging this dictum before the Cultural Revolution, and its conclusions on how religion might be understood by science were two decades ahead of their time.[66] Reclaiming the methodological ground on Christianity as opiate was important, as Wickeri notes, but Ding's challenge to dialectical materialism as the basis for all knowledge, and his promotion of the Christian understanding of revelation as an alternative, was perhaps a more courageous and dangerous move.

Any support for idealism was a direct challenge to Mao's writings (or writings claimed for Mao), such as the essay "Dialectical Materialism" (1938), and to the foundational Marxist-Maoist belief in the ongoing struggle between materialism and idealism predicated on class divisions in society. In "Dialectical Materialism," Mao argues that idealism was reactionary, representing the thinking of the oppressor, not the revolutionary class. Ding Guangxun was not the only thinker to challenge anti-idealist views; philosopher Zhang Xin in his 1956 article "Liberate Idealism," for example, had defended such views during the more relaxed atmosphere of the Hundred Flowers campaign, claiming that many Chinese were materialist in public and idealist in private and that idealism should be carefully analyzed and not rejected in toto—but the danger of Ding's doing so when the prevalent Marxist view interpreted the whole of human history as a struggle between the two concepts is clear.[67] In his calm analysis, Ding discusses positive examples of idealists, such as the historically safe Wang Yangming, as well as counterexamples of Christian materialists like Ivan Pavlov.[68] He challenges both Christians who attempt to claim Christianity as materialist (and therefore politically progressive) and the binary categorization and Marxist framework of argument itself. Christianity, Ding suggests, may be in form a product of history but is not in essence an ideology, nor is it a structure built on an economic base; the substance of Christianity is (extra-historical) revelation, the Incarnation, and it cannot be reduced to an ideology, since it "moves in a different orbit from any system of thought."[69]

Ding's recognition of the nature of the era as pivotal in the history of the Chinese church gave him the courage also to challenge outsiders who thought they knew what was best for the Chinese church. Historical circumstances, he claims, force a reevaluation of priorities and assessment of enduring truths; for Ding, the outcome is a push for internal unity and an unwavering stand on the need for an independent Chinese church, achieved through the structure of the Three-Self Movement.[70] The church needs to be reconciled before it can reconcile the world, he reminds. In his own Anglican denomination, Ding notes wryly, the fourteen dioceses use eight different versions of the *Book of Common Prayer*. Self-support is a God-given experience, and the Chinese church now understood that it "is less a financial than a spiritual necessity," as well as a prerequisite for greater evangelization. (Given this, it is easier to see why Ding and TSPM leaders rejected the influx of Western missionaries concerned to spread the message to a Communist people when China opened up again in the 1980s.) The Three-Self Movement, Ding notes, is often represented in the West as a sign that the church had yielded to Communist pressure, whereas in reality it "represents God's act of great mercy in giving Christians a new chance in China"; Liberation and the new Socialism were not "God's punishment or judgment, but an act of God, showing God's love for China."[71] If the West understood how backward life had been in China, it may have more sympathy for the CCP's actions. We may not agree with the Communists on religion, argues Ding, but their spirit of humility and self-criticism has much to commend it.

Ding takes a side-swipe at Chinese intellectuals who under colonial influence fell prey to a cult of the West but denies some of the more outlandish claims put about, such as the one that Chinese seminaries no longer used Western materials. Western Christian visitors, explains Ding, often expect the church to focus on contextualization, but evangelization through love, in the awareness that God loves all, was the key.[72]

THE CHURCH IN THE WORLD: DING GUANGXUN AND WANG MINGDAO IN DEBATE

The complex negotiations over political directives that an individual enters into with the government, the CCP, family, colleagues, conscience, or the passage of time cannot be underestimated. There is an expectation in Western media that individuals in an authoritarian state will be either dissidents or sympathizers, but this is a simplistic and weak response to the quotidian realities of living and working in China. When the 2012 Nobel prize for literature was awarded to Mo Yan, a barrage of articles in the world media asked whether someone who no longer seemed to criticize his government "deserved" the prize, analyzing the trajectory of Mo Yan's writings from his subversive novels of the 1980s to his accommodating silence on incarcerated fellow Nobel winner Liu Xiaobo, his support for state-authorized boycotts of writers, and his participation in the project to commemorate Mao's "Talks at the Yan'an Forum on Literature and the Arts."[73] Jia Zhangke, the director and winner of best screenplay at the Cannes Film Festival in 2013 has similarly been a regular critic of government censorship, yet he pulled out of a film festival where exiled Uighur leader Rebiya Kadeer was due to speak. For theologians and artists alike, the choice during the most pressured times—whether during the mid-1950s or after 1989—has been to find an adequate form of accommodation, or to contemplate exile. For a community builder and priest, the cost of exile in the cessation of work may be even greater than for the writers who struggle to retain their critical edge outside of China.

Ding's early ministry in mission and broad theology, combined with his developing vision of the scope of the church in the New China, set the scene for the specific debates that arose on the relationship of church and state. Recent examples show how these debates still matter in the present and the complexity of the issues and campaigning involvement of diasporic voices in the debates, voices that Ding sought to problematize in the 1950s. (Ding, who rarely resorted to French critical theory, came to understand that postcolonial emancipation of the Chinese church necessarily involved a de-westernization of personnel and of the terms of engagement, a reclamation for which Maoist rhetoric proved ideal.)[74] To take an example: ChinaAid is a campaigning and support organization run by Bob Fu, a well-known U.S. advocate of the Chinese church. The ChinaAid 2012 report documented at length government abuses of house churches and their members and claimed that it was state policy to "wipe out" the house churches within the next ten years.[75] The same ChinaAid article, meanwhile, pointed out some of the ways in which the government is trying to manage the transition to bringing house churches from being semilegal organizations to registered entities, part of mainstream church and social life in China. Whether this action constitutes a "wipe out" or not depends on perspective. ChinaAid favors bombastic rhetoric in its headlines, but the analysis points to a more balanced view, one which effectively concedes that the state cannot continue indefinitely to condone illegal activity. There is room for healthy debate on how much religion should be regulated in any country, and what role there might be for national clergy training bodies, but the history of state regulation in China has made many wary of any government contact, and views on the formation of the state church have tended toward polarization. Current debates echo those of the 1950s, captured in the epigraphs to this chapter from Ding and Wang Mingdao. In electing to work with the government, Ding justified the project theologically over the six decades that he led the TSPM and China Christian Council, while Wang Mingdao spent most of the first twenty years of Communist rule in prison for his stance.

Wang Mingdao remains one of the best-known figures in evangelical Chinese theology and church leadership, both in China and abroad, and his life epitomizes the vicissitudes of twentieth-century Chinese religious history for those who held out against state registration. Wang's preaching reached many through his articles in the *Spiritual Food Quarterly*, the magazine started in 1926 that Wang edited. Wang was never ordained, and the church he led ran along puritanical Reformed lines—no choir, lest it distract, and straightforward biblical teaching. Wang's church was steadfastly self-supporting and self-propagating, keeping its distance from foreign missionaries even before Communist ideology required such things. His theology foregrounded holiness, repentance for sins, and mission. Holiness meant separation from the world and a steadfast persistence in doing what one believed to be right. Wang was never afraid to be a lone voice; before his imprisonment he wrote: "There were four hundred prophets who flattered Ahab but only one prophet who did not value his own welfare, who did not care that others slandered him, because he was determined simply to be faithful to God. The situation in the nation of Israel in those days is parallel to that in the church of God today."[76] Where Ding draws on the Hebrew scriptures for his position on loving one's country (*ai guo*), Wang was to call on them for his understanding of holiness. The difference between the two pastors was predicated on the role of the church in interpreting those scriptures and its own life. For Wang, Christ held authority over all temporal things; for Ding, Christ had given his authority to the church. Wang's sermons are primarily exhortations to godly living, textual expositions on some aspect of a life lived to please God and not other humans, whereas for Ding Christ's salvation restores relations between humans as well as with God.[77] The principled division of life into the spheres of God and the world had spiritual and political ramifications. Ever strict with himself in his personal life of faith, Wang was clear how the church should proceed when the PRC was established. He refused to sign the Christian Manifesto condemning the church as a tool of imperialist powers and attesting loyalty to the Communist cause. He denounced all forms of compromise, including the establishment of the Three-Self Movement and those involved in the initiative, and in 1955 was given a fifteen-year prison sentence for "antirevolutionary" activities.

In a poignant sermon from the early 1950s, Wang explored how incremental concessions or accommodation lead to irreparable damage, a stance against which Ding's views need testing. China had before it at this point the examples of other East Asian churches that had faced the question of compliance with authorities: over Shinto shrine rituals in Christian schools during Japanese occupation in Korea, or over ritual compliance with the state in Japan itself. In the latter case, the national church was shamed and forced to repent in retrospect. For Wang, the strength of reaction came from a sure sense of what was, and was not, of God. Keeping the peace by agreeing to call black white is, Wang holds, a major sin. Agreeing not to make a big issue of a matter in order to coexist happily with others and retain opportunities to witness is *"completely wrong."*

> Spiritual victory is obtained by being faithful in small matters. . . . Maybe someone will say, "If I should say that a white sheet of paper is black, at most I myself only speak a lie. This will not hurt anyone nor disgrace the name of God. On the contrary," they reason, "if I agree with their false statement, it might remove people's dislike of me. Then I can live in closer harmony with others and be able to help them because I bear no ill will against anyone nor they against me. God will be glorified. Wouldn't that be wonderful? I can't understand why you insist on saying that if I do not agree with them it would be such a very serious sin."[78]

Agreeing to a small lie today in order to avoid offense will lead to denying the Lord tomorrow, holds Wang. In a sermon exposition on Romans 13:1, Wang argues that Christians should be exemplary in their obedience to rules and regulations, giving details of how that obedience might play out in various professions and walks of life; but where regulations conflict with God's commands, the duty is to obey God. The matter was simple: "if the regulations and decrees of men come into conflict with God's demands, then we have no alternative but to disobey men and obey only God."[79] The overriding example here is that of Peter and the apostles and their response to the authorities when forbidden to preach: "We must obey God rather than men." Like many, in order to be freed Wang was coerced into signing a public confession of guilt, which he later recanted and came to regard as a moment of weakness. (Wang was resentenced and remained in the prison/work camp system until 1980.)

As one of the living martyrs of the church in the most repressive years of Communism, Wang inspired many believers in China through his stance and example of strong faith and suffering for the gospel. But his condemnation of those who did not take the same faith line, who were willing to work together with the state to build a legitimate church within China, inevitably caused friction with other Christians—and became a point of tension later when it was time to reconcile those who had been imprisoned, and those who had not, into one church. In an article printed in 1987 in the *Chinese Theological Review*, Jiang Peifen called on Wang Mingdao to come back into the fold and accept that God had been at work in the state church. Jiang contrasts Wang with another church leader who thought that he was suffering for the sake of the faith but who later recognized he was "foolish and proud and seeking suffering" himself. Jiang's article implies that Wang's imprisonment was entirely because of his antigovernment activities, and he accuses Wang of dishonestly suggesting that Three-Self leaders had put him behind bars. Jiang's argument shifts subtly the terms of debate and plays into Wang's denunciation of state-church relations by arguing that "a nation bullied and enslaved by others" had become independent and free through the actions of the CCP and that God had built up a church in China that was both biblical and Chinese.[80] For Wang, the end never justified the means. Indigenization was less of an issue for Wang than holding to what he saw as a biblically based lifestyle.

Ding Guangxun consistently took a contrary view on working together with Communists and atheists. He wrote many variants of the following in debates over the years, but always held to the same principle: "It is the conviction of many of my colleagues that, as long as there is space for Christian witness to be borne and for dialogue on issues to be carried on, we must for the good of the church refrain from adopting confrontation and martyrdom as church policy."[81] In different times and places Ding has expressed rational, intuitive, personal, and historical reasons for his stance on the church. One of the difficulties in reading Ding is the preponderance of later articles expressing his views on the situation in the 1950s, and the relative dearth of contemporary writings. The historical context in which Ding and other intellectual leaders of the period saw themselves as operating is clear: the overriding issue for the Chinese church was the ongoing resolution of its colonial legacy in China and the institution of a "Chinese" church and Chinese theology. Part of this Chinese identity was an identification with the fate of the Chinese nation, expressed in terms of hopes for good governance for all, the alleviation of poverty, and social well-being. There is genuine admiration for what the Communists have achieved in the areas under their occupation, and hope for what Liberation and the "New China" might bring. As the timeline of documents relating to the establishment of the TSPM shows, a positive unification movement and postdenominational ideal in the church was coupled with a challenge from outside for Christians to demonstrate their love for the motherland, but the scope for theologizing was drastically reduced after the imposition of a single state-endorsed body for each of the recognized Christian denominations.

In his 1954 article "Why Must We Still Be Preachers?" Ding answers his own rhetorical question to explore why he continued as a priest when his friends saw the church as "unclean" and "unlovable."[82] In the article, Ding combines his conviction of commission to preach the truth and belief that "people of all times and places need the gospel" with the beginnings of a systematic response to the moral and theological niceties of whether to work with the Chinese government. An assertion of the deep truth of the gospel is followed by a critical assessment of "the very wrong road" taken by those who spend their time finding fault with unbelievers, or who hold that everything outside the church is false or bad. Our own worthiness to preach is irrelevant, argues Ding: we preach because we have been moved by the love of God and are sanctified to do so. In a reading of Isaiah 66 and the ascent psalms, Ding argues that love for one's nation, especially during times of suffering, is a thoroughly biblical standpoint. As China progresses, preachers have a "glorious mission" to make the church a good church and to match progress in other areas of society: the church should not be the only weak link in society. In subsequent writings, Ding expanded both his sentiments on those who could not work with the (state) church and his positive theological vision for China.

If Wang Mingdao and Ding had been able to hold their differences in an amicable tension, the church history of the period would not read as it does. But, as in wartime, the early years of the PRC did not permit neutrality, and the ratcheting up of government demands on the church forced a confrontation. In an article in *Tian Feng* in March 1955, Ding expressed some of his frustrations

at those who were publicly denouncing anyone who worked with the government or TSPM. He described as "heart-rending" "the fact that some Christians
have gone so far as to label others arbitrarily as unbelievers" and asked, "who
are you to judge the servant of someone else?"[83] By August 1955, Ding had
done away with the nicety of anonymous critique, publishing "A Response to
Wang Mingdao" in *Tian Feng*. Ding's language betrays his turbulent feelings,
but the article provides an object lesson in holding one's tongue and not writing reactively; however right Ding may have been, this was not a well-timed
or constructive criticism. That Ding plows on indicates what was riding on the
outcome of bringing the church body of believers alongside. "We would not
object to Wang publicly," Ding writes sardonically, "if he were really supplying
food to believers. But he is clearly filled with hatred for China and is absolutely against rational assessment."[84] Ding is rankled by what he characterizes
as Wang's insistence that the ideas of Christians and those of ordinary Chinese
differ on every point and the rift Wang is bent on causing between Christians
and the "New China."

Ding takes umbrage at Wang's unwillingness to give any credit to what is
good in the new society and at Wang's proclamation that the PRC is oppressing
believers, a point he rebuts by pointing to a speech that Rev. Chen Chonggui
was invited to give to the Chinese People's Political Consultative Conference,
subsequently published in the state newspaper *China Daily*. Ding's language
stretches toward hyperbole, reacting to the way both Wang and Ding are being
constricted by the state. Wang's dislike of the New China ("the more freedom
of religion there is the higher rages the fire of hatred inside him") is matched
only by his dislike of the TSPM (which "he hates, to the very marrow of his
bones").[85] On a seemingly more substantive point, the accusation that Wang
refuses to acknowledge that "Imperialists" used the church in their aggression
against China, when Ding was demanding that a clear line be drawn between
imperialists and the church, is blunted by the fact that Wang merely "avoids"
the question. Given all that is at stake, Wang brings out a shriller voice in Ding
than in his usual writings, whether in defending the labors of the TSPM as
"the work of God" or in mocking symbolic readings of Revelation "by some"
in which the Soviet Union and the United States are represented by red and
white horses, respectively. Ding calls for mutual respect among Christians and
(correctly) implies that Wang is not adhering to this in denouncing certain
Christians as unbelievers, but then he slanders Wang and the "disaster" he has
brought on the motherland and the church.

There is a theological side to Ding's argument, as he points to richness in
diversity (cf. the four gospels) and the fact that unity need not equal a unity
of belief and could be a unity of love, but Ding's main theological work has

been done earlier, in coming to the position he cannot, through any amount of rational dialogue, persuade Wang to see. Philip Wickeri argues that this was "not really a theological debate but a highly charged polemic shaped by the struggles of the times" where "Wang Mingdao was rejecting Ting's theology, while K. H. Ting was criticizing Wang's politics."[86] Wickeri asserts that there is no doubt that Ding's criticisms of Wang were "part of the government-initiated struggle against separatist religious groups" and that the debates "cannot fully be understood as a conflict between two Christian leaders with radically different theological and political positions."[87] It is undoubtedly true that both were subject to external forces that they may have only partly recognized, but the theological element, and the definition of theology itself, is critical. At issue is Ding's encompass of "worldly" politics in the remit of his theology, whereas Wang held that it was possible, if one tried hard enough, to keep religion separate, in a sphere of lived life untouched by politics. Raymond Whitehead notes that throughout Ding's writings he "is careful to segregate theology from politics,"[88] but this needs nuancing: while Ding is perfectly capable of adhering to a professional role in a political capacity and maintaining a working distinction, his theology precisely cannot be viewed separately from his politics, since that would negate his understanding of theology's all-encompassing nature. That there cannot be a separation of "church people" and "world people" is central to Ding's critique of Wang; theology likewise cannot be contained in a bounded discipline or related only to certain in-groups or to certain spheres of life.[89] Ding's political vision is rooted in his theological doctrines; the difference between how he relates to the different spheres of church and world/government is one of strategy, not of kind.

Ding's rhetoric against the separatist or holiness groups grew stronger and more flourishing in later iterations: in a speech at Doshisha in Tokyo in 1984 he comments on the "theological but highly political" arguments used to negate Liberation and the New China:

> The world is the realm of Satan, they said, condemned to imminent destruction. The Christian is not to love the world and whatever is in it, even that which is lovable. . . . Human beings are evil and a person who does not confess faith in Christ can do nothing good, and the better his or her conduct, the more truly he or she is Satan masquerading as an angel. The animal with two horns and the red horse referred to in Revelation are actually representations of the Communist Party. . . . The doctrine of the security of the believer ensures those elected by Christ the freedom to do anything, while others are condemned no matter how good their work is. . . . That is antinomianism and,

in the early fifties, was the main theological weapon used by those in church circles who were determined not to be reconciled to the fact of new China.[90]

The "antinomian reactionism" that sought to persuade people to "work against the people's liberation movement with all its goodness and beauty" was "an ethically indefensible alternative," concludes Ding. Elsewhere, he laments of those who cannot work in the world or with the (Communist) government. "To them, God has lost the world he created to Satan," he argues, demonstrating why this cannot be a theologically acceptable argument.[91] In speaking to Christians, Ding employs defenses from the three spheres of the Chinese classics, the Bible, and theology to argue that humanity is not utterly depraved, that the created world is God's sphere; to revolutionaries he explains how Socialism has restored human dignity but has not removed human spiritual poverty.

A BARTHIAN MEDIATION

The close relationship between the events of the 1950s and the subsequent journey of the church, including its "period of darkness" and reflection during the late 1950s and early 1960s, means that the task of reassessing this historical period remains essential to present development. One way of reconciling the positions of Wang and Ding might be through a reading of another theologian of the era who thought long and hard about the transition to Communism. It does not take a great leap of the imagination to see how two of Karl Barth's best-known and most courageous acts speak incisively to the situation in China: the declarations against Hitler and the role of the German church, and his later refusal to condemn Communism, or, as his son Markus Barth wrote, his refusal to "give religious sanctification to the superficial or hysterical condemnations of communism."[92] In Barth's short letter "How to Serve God in a Marxist Land" the most striking note is the pastoral wisdom of reticence. In speaking to the pressure Christians in East Germany were facing, Barth cuts into the debates between Ding Guangxun and Wang Mingdao with his understanding that the situation is impossible to assess from outside. There is no simple answer to give to those under Communist rule: "One would need to have spent all these years with you, to have experienced in one's life the growing pressure under which you stand," he began his response to his East German correspondent. Barth's situational ethics articulates a rare empathy for his Communist neighbor, which extends to moral exigencies, since "one would need to have tried out personally the various possibilities of withstanding it [Communism] in order to avoid coming up with some kind of wisdom which because of a deficient knowledge of the facts, situations and persons, might be totally irrelevant to your questions," he continues.[93] Given the overwhelming tendency to partisan condemnation in the debates surrounding "Red" divisions wherever in the world—divisive precisely because of the power of the belief invested and the huge effect on life of implementing faith decisions in the circumstances—Barth's honest ignorance is profoundly helpful. Faced with the unwillingness of a Wang Mingdao to call black white, but also Ding's perception of a calling to keep the church going and save others through continued preaching, who is fitted to impute right or wrong?

In a move that is powerfully affirmative of Christians in the Communist East, but also prescient of the direction of the West, Barth condemned not only the "spirit, and the words, the methods and the practices" of the East German government, but also the distortions and "creeping totalitarianism" of the West too, alongside its tyrannous press, its systems of private enterprise, and its "snobbish presumption." All regimes, implied Barth, are potential "prowling adversaries" and demand resistance; identifying Communism as the "lion" of 1 Peter might prove to be "the trap of a dangerous optical illusion." The church has "a gift and a task" to fulfill even when it is under an alien power: God reigns over socialism too, and even "an alien power" can be God's instrument.[94] The West may yet have its own "purification," Barth argues, "perhaps at the hands of Asia and Africa."

In words that chime with the voice of Ding Guangxun, Barth affirms that God is sovereign over atheism too—that much of atheism has itself arisen "from misunderstandings caused by the prevailing teaching, attitudes and practices of the Christian Church" and that the way to counter the unbelief of atheists is "with a joyous unbelief in their attempted atheism" because "what is certain is that God is not against them, but for them." The "sound basis"—which God is for Christians—on which they can live together with the "enemies of Christ" is the basis to witness to them also.[95] A contextual wisdom is called for, since at times the church will be called to confess its faith openly but at other times to "maintain an eloquent silence and stand aside." Barth is ever-willing to expand God's reach and direct attention to God's capacity for regeneration. "Can Christianity truly fulfil its task only in that form of existence which until now has been taken for granted?" he asks, pointing out that there is no conditional link between God's cause and national churches or freedom of action. In a move that threatens to undermine much of Wang Mingdao's argument, Barth suggests that loyalty does not signify approval of a particular government ideology and opens a way to a conditional recognition where acknowledging the validity and authority of the state, to the degree that is possible for an individual, does not preclude retaining the "right of freedom of thought, right of opposition, even resistance" in particular instances.[96]

Ding's iteration of the cosmic Christ finds much support in Barth's "The Christian Community and the Civil Community," where Barth is insistent that it is the purpose of the church community to serve all within its geographic range, just as much as it is that of the civil community.[97] Barth, like Ding, is adamant that the existence of the Christian community is itself political and that a Christian decision to be "indifferent" or "nonpolitical" is "quite impossible."[98] The church must be attentive to its own particular task — both Wang and Ding concur that preaching the gospel is their raison d'être — but, critically, it shares in the task of the civil community in as much as that fulfills its own task, a point Ding addressed in "Why Must We Still Be Preachers?" Trusting in God's presence in the outworking of the historical church is a task that requires a dual focus, according to Barth:

> . . . to see and understand that which is effected by God, the Church, in its true reality, we have not to lose sight even momentarily or incidentally of the occurrence of the divine operation, and therefore concretely of the divine work of upbuilding the community by Jesus Christ. The Church is, of course, a human, earthly-historical construct, whose history involves from the very first, and always will involve, human action. But it is *this* human construct, the Christian Church, because and as God is at work in it by His Holy Spirit. In virtue of this happening, which is of divine origin and takes place for men and to them as the determination of their human action, the true Church truly is and arises and continues and lives in the twofold sense that God is at work and that there is a human work which He occasions and fashions.[99]

Barth's clear antistate movements in Germany place him alongside Wang Mingdao in Wang's resistance to and denunciation of evil and wrong, yet the theology of community and affirmation of possibilities in the Communist state place Barth firmly next to Ding Guangxun. The difficulty remains assessing to what degree, and how to assay, whether the actions of the Chinese government in the early 1950s should, or could, be seen as akin to those of the Nazi regime in their totalitarian nature, and so whether denunciation or cooperation was the truer response. Both Ding and Wang seem to be sure of the guidance of the Spirit/revelation/conscience in their own decisions. The problem with Ding's position is the nature of the gradual descent into tyranny (which can be traced through the TSPM documentation of the era) and the difficulty of saying "not now" and "stop." Barth's warning that it is impossible for an outsider to make those distinctions seems sound, but our only conclusion here might be that it is not our task to reconcile these positions: that task is for historians, not theologians. How such a stance might help the ongoing process of reconciliation in the Chinese church between the house-church proponents of Wang and the TSPM inheritors of Ding's legacy is a separate question, but through Barth we can affirm both the power of demonstrating the difference of kingdom values through twenty years in prison *and* the value of working together with the state to keep Christ present in the civil and church communities.

LOOKING FORWARD

The Reform and Opening Up period that began in 1978 was a time of gradual normalization, of increasing economic stability under Deng Xiaoping's policies, and of the resumption of aspects of civil life such as organized religion. Ding remained at the helm of the church as it was reinstituted in society, and he was at the forefront of the movement of Theological Reconstruction, or building a theology in line with "Socialism with Chinese characteristics" (discussed in Chapter 8). In 1978 a Centre for Religious Studies was created at the University of Nanjing, and Ding became a vice president of that university. Ding regarded this reintegration into society and the presence of a religious studies faculty within the secular university system as a breakthrough, a vindication of the years of support for an independent church within an independent China.[100] The cycles of relaxation and repression so integral to Chinese history had not ended, however: in 1983 the Anti-Spiritual Pollution campaign brought a swing back to fear and crackdown, followed by another stint of growth and respite until the post–Tiananmen Square clampdown in 1989. Key events in the life of the church under Ding's leadership included the reopening of Nanjing Theological Seminary in 1981, with Ding Guangxun as dean (as well as head of the TSPM and chair of the new China Christian Council); the establishment of the church-related nongovernmental organization Amity Foundation and Amity Printing Press by Ding in 1985; and the consecration of two Protestant bishops in 1988 in a new Chinese mode where these were not diocesan but administrative appointments, with spiritual authority rather than governing oversight.

With a reestablished stability and strength, the church leadership also in the late 1980s began to question anew the relation between church and state oversight, the role of the Religious Affairs Bureau, and the status of the TSPM. In an address to TSPM leaders in December 1988, Ding Guangxun spoke of the historic value of the TSPM in creating and sustaining a Chinese church, in uniting Protestants in China, and in modeling church development but questioned whether a new path was not now needed. Neither the Religious Affairs Bureau nor the TSPM was the church, and the time had arrived for a greater separation of church and state, with a lighter monitoring touch, he argued. Theologically, the experiences of the second half of the twentieth century did not change Ding's fundamental allegiance to a God of love or to Socialism as the path for China—a better alternative to "feudalism, colonialism and capitalism" for the masses of poor, since people in endless suffering "cannot easily recognize God as love."[101] In the Reform era, a concentration on the Incarnation and the "divine yes to creation,"[102] a move away from the belief-unbelief dichotomies that Ding saw as derailing discussion, and a Christology that proclaimed the "Christlikeness of God" were central to Ding's developing thought. Once theological resources were again available and Ding was able to catch up with theology in the outside world, he suggested that the three schools of Western thought most consonant with those of Chinese intellectuals were liberation theology, process theology, and the work of Pierre Teilhard de Chardin. Many speeches, sermons, and articles were to expand on Ding's embrace of the "cosmic Christ." The universal nature of Christ's care and Christ's ongoing role in creation were fundamental to his later writings, emphasizing, as he had throughout the 1950s, God's loving embrace for all.

CONCLUSIONS

The authors of several of the English-language volumes of collected editions of Ding's works may have done a disservice by gathering his articles thematically. It might make it easier for a reader looking for dogmatic connections, but such anthologies threaten to make coherent what is not coherent. Ding's theology, as an accumulation of sermons and short articles, is closely tied to the moment. By dint of its sermon format and Ding's pragmatic and activist inclinations, the theology is particularly context-oriented. As cultural contexts shift and history progresses, Ding's theology undergoes marked shifts; gathering his reflections and advice from very different periods into a thematic whole undermines this contextual nature. Unsurprisingly, while Ding was working as a mission representative for the Student Christian Movement in Canada and then for the World Council of Churches in Geneva, mission and the rights and wrongs of evangelism were the subjects uppermost in his thinking. Immediately after his return to China and into the mid-1950s, the New China and the Christian role in the nation were foremost. Ding's writings of the 1980s take on another hue, as the restoration and renewal of the church became the pressing tasks for its leaders.

It is hard for an outsider to see how Ding squared his years in the international church and international student bodies, and a theology of interdependence and integration, with his absolute insistence on Chinese self-determination—to the point of the exclusion of all foreign ties. The only way to do this, in light of the heritage of Ding's anti-imperialist predecessors of the 1930s, is to understand the prior need for redress—and the determination to be equal partners in any world gathering: to be both independent and integrated. Ding maintained good relationships with international church bodies as long as he was allowed to travel, into the early 1960s,[103] and reprised his international connections as soon as was possible; a political stance was distinguished from personal friendships. Some of the most fascinating insights into Ding's thinking have been glimpses into the shut period of the church. Both Whitehead and Wickeri note that during the Cultural Revolution Ding envisaged a future Christianity in China without a strong institutional form: without paid clergy, possibly without formal ordinations, with little institutional theological education. A decade of house-based Bible studies, and separation not just from the missionary church, but from any institutional church, had given Ding a vision that looks surprisingly like that of the unregistered church of the past few decades; and yet, Ding reverted to his role as an institution builder when the call came. The grinding back to life of the Chinese state in the late 1970s and early 1980s brought an increased institutionalization and oversight to the church, not a less formal regime.

Ding Guangxun surprises because of his blend of leanings from all theological walks, from stances usually identified with conservatives (on matters such as church unity or mission and evangelism) to those more readily seen as liberal (God's universal love and church-state relations). This chapter has traced the integrity of Ding's thought from his early days as a missioner in Canada to the arguments and divisions over the proper role for Christians vis-à-vis the state— an atheist, autocratic state—in the mid-1950s. If, in the light of Karl Barth's wisdom, we accept that only those in a given situation can discern its rights and wrongs before God, the more important task for the Chinese Protestant church now might be first to reevaluate honestly what Ding, Wang, and others actually said and wrote through study of the texts of the 1950s, and then to set these aside in the attempt to bring a genuine unification based on the present situation and present concerns in the church.

8

STATE REGULATION, CHURCH GROWTH, AND TEXTUAL PROFUSION

The period since Reform and Opening Up began in 1978 has proved to be one of the most exciting, diverse, and unpredictable in the history of Chinese Christianity. The great growth in the number of religious adherents and of churches and temples in China has forced the government to respond and adapt continuously. The scope of Christianity in China—with probably eighty million believers regularly attending worship services[1]—means that it is increasingly difficult to generalize about what constitutes "Chinese Christianity." From the old populations of Shandong Catholic villages or Lisu minority towns where generations grew up in entirely Christian surrounds, to the new urban house churches challenging the status quo; from Wenzhou "boss Christians" running their city's politics, to Korean-speaking congregations worshipping in lavish tiered sanctuaries in northeast China, the oft-repeated statistic about Chinese Christians being old, female, and poor has long needed modifying. The experiences of Christians are correspondingly disparate, and depending on the constituency—or the website visited—an observer might gain a sense of renewed persecution and defiant resistance or of thriving worship, civic integration, and a commitment to charity work among the new underclass.

This chapter analyzes some of the burgeoning categories of Christian writing and thinking that have emerged in various media across this period of growth. Although we can distinguish four broad types of church profession in contemporary China (official or open Chinese Catholic; unregistered or underground Roman Catholic; official Three-Self Protestant; and unregistered or house-church Protestant),[2] Christian writings fall more neatly into three categories: the essays and expositions of official church theologians, the writings of other Christians and pastors, and the scholarship of academic Christianity.[3] The three have prospered in separate phases and in different institutional settings, often with quite distinct readerships. The writings of state-sanctioned seminary professors have received more attention than either unofficial publications or the recent academic theology movements, and so this overview is followed by two chapters examining writings from the Sino-Christian theology movement and from recent Protestant house-church leaders.

To provide a context for the development of theological writings during the Reform era, the chapter begins with a review of recent church directions and religious life focused through the lens of religious policy and regulation. Much of life in the PRC has been highly regulated, but religion has been among the most constricted of all spheres, with regulation eased less rapidly. Christian writing has naturally grown in tandem with the church, with the rise of an educated middle class and technological advances, with government funding of university departments, and with trade growth and publishing agreements with foreign presses; but it has been affected throughout, both directly and indirectly, by government policy on religion. All sectors of the church have been subject to the same legislation, but the legislation has been tailored to differentiate among the various sectors and has mediated their development in different ways, providing the three broad categories of official church writings, unofficial church writings, and academic writings. The regulatory framework provides a window into the ideology behind religious policy in China and a sense of the constraints under which churches operated, offering a proxy for government thinking on religion while telling us relatively little about the actual church history of the period or the theological responses to social and political developments. The survey of Christian writings that follows aims to flesh out the Christian narrative, including its varying responses to, or disengagement from, the government vision.

The relationship between church and state is an inescapable datum in Chinese Christianity, both for those who have invested much thought in the question of how to align the two and among those who made a faith-based choice to side-step the question. The legacy of policies that provoked the splits in the Roman Catholic and Protestant churches in the 1950s has been a significant factor in church development since the reopening of churches and seminaries. The questions of how, or whether, the Chinese Catholic Church has negotiated its status as a Chinese rather than Roman church and how Protestants have lived into their official identity as a postdenominational church are central to the narrative of late twentieth-century Christianity. The pattern of Christian writing and publishing does not correlate exactly with the history of state legislation any more than it maps neatly onto church belonging, but the correspondences between ideology, theology, and regulation are important to grasp in an era of great growth but also of deep division in the church. Theology may drive ideology, especially among the underground Roman or resurgent Calvinist-leaning churches, with regulatory consequences accepted as a cost of faith, but ideology also shapes theology: official church theologians may have been free to publish on any topic they like in accord with China's aims and policies, but in practice many have been guided in their work by specific policy drives, such as the concern during the 1990s to adapt religion to Socialism.

Recent commentators have shown how models of church-state relations that assume a pattern of state control and religious response are overly simplistic and unable to account for the interactions between different players in the Chinese religious sphere.[4] This has helpfully reframed the debate, but more work has still to be done in clarifying the role of church bodies in shaping policy (and especially more recently in the positive noncompliance of some unregistered groups) and in examining regional and sectoral differences in the implementation of legislation.[5] It is evident that regulation needs to be treated with caution as a guide to the forces shaping the church, given the fact that the strongest sector in the present church economy is that of unregistered Protestant churches, which have been the target of much legislation and currently are still "extra-legal."[6] (Meanwhile, the publication output of this sector has been relatively small, both because of a concentration on person-to-person evangelism and because of controls on religious publication; even today, leading house-church and underground Roman Catholic voices are published in print by presses in Hong Kong or Taiwan.) While legislation has not curbed growth in the targeted sectors—and leaves us to ponder the question of why legislation on religion has failed so spectacularly—it has served to differentiate between groups within the church and reinforce the theological and ecclesial divisions.

A series of policy and administrative documents issued by the State Council from the 1980s to the 2000s shows their central areas of concern with religion. The main tenet throughout legislation over this period is that religion should not be allowed to threaten the state. The major avenues anticipated for this are civil disruption, jeopardizing national "unity" or "stability" through negative ideologies or action (articles aimed at Muslim or Tibetan separatists as much as Christians), and the potential for foreign subversion of China's aims through religions' links with international organizations (the Roman Catholic Church and underground Protestants are targets here). Regulation during the 1980s and 1990s was thus aimed at reducing and controlling the flow of money and religious literature from outside China, at ensuring adequate means of supervision for believers within China, and at raising up a new generation of religious leaders and pastors whose thinking and teaching would promote the well-being of the state as envisaged by the CCP. The results of this legislation were the close supervision of the official churches and the effective creation of an unregulated zone subject to sporadic sanction and punishment. A more positive attitude toward religion in the 2000s coupled with more flexible local attitudes toward regulation seemed to presage better relations between church and state, but new directions under Xi Jinping still surprise.

ECONOMIC REFORMS AND THE REGULARIZATION OF (OFFICIAL) RELIGIOUS LIFE

It is easy to forget that the tale of China's rise as an economic and global superpower—its sustained double-digit growth figures, entry into the World Trade Organization, purchasing of foreign companies and land tracts, and corresponding soft-power initiatives to stake a place in the world's imagination—was far from accepted or assured even into the 1990s. The market liberalizations begun under Deng Xiaoping that spurred the transition and that aimed at bringing a moderate level of economic well-being to all (*xiaokang* 小康; rather than rampant consumption, high social inequality, and corruption) entrained a political shift that necessarily brought with it a degree of social release.

Religion has often been viewed in isolation as an example of regime oppression or, more accurately, as the subject of a tradeoff where greater freedom and autonomy were given in return for political loyalty and quiescence,[7] but religion cannot easily be disentangled from the entirety of the Deng-era reforms. In retrospect it is clear that economic, ideological, and policy reforms worked in conjunction in the early post-Mao period and that change in any one affected the other two. Collectively, the reforms worked to chip away at, and then dismantle, the integrated identities that individuals-in-community had held under an all-encompassing state system. Until the 1990s, for example, graduating students were allocated an employment sector and a job; that job came with a work unit that provided housing and furnished all of the basic necessities of life. Work units enforced the supervision and regulation of life in areas mandated by the state, down to such detail as the fitting of female contraception or the recording of individuals' association with foreigners. Religious belief was one among many aspects of life that were highly determined, especially for urban residents.

The new policy directions of the late 1970s forged the way for the return of organized religion. As the ongoing place of religion in society was accepted by the CCP in an ideological concession to reality, confiscated church properties began to be returned, with (most) priests rehabilitated. As Deng Xiaoping's "Four Modernizations" were blazoned across newspapers, along with his new guiding slogan, "seek truth from facts," the path toward "Socialism with Chinese characteristics" began to gain in definition. Some churches preempted the wider restoration of worship, and certain house-church members have looked back on the few years preceding the 1980 reestablishment of the patriotic bodies as their best years—a time of unfettered and relatively legal evangelism.[8] Academic institutes were the first to regain their status nationally. By 1978 the Institute of World Religions was operating within the reopened Chinese Academy of Social Sciences (CASS), and an Institute for Religious Studies was founded within Nanjing University, based at the former seminary, Nanjing Union Theological Seminary. In 1979 the Religious Affairs Bureau, the state unit of religious oversight, was revived (later to become the State Administration for Religious Affairs [SARA]), and in 1980 the TSPM and CCPA were reestablished nationally, allowing the resumption of clergy training and the reissue of religious literature. New church-focused committees to complement the political bodies of the TSPM and CCPA were established in the Catholic Bishops' Conference and the China Christian Council. The national Protestant seminary in Nanjing reopened in February 1981, with Sheshan Roman Catholic Seminary opening in 1982, soon followed by the National Catholic Seminary. The church's growing social role was highlighted by initiatives such as the Amity Foundation, begun in 1985.[9]

New regulations followed the resumption of civic life. The most significant, charting the course for the next two decades of church life, was the 1982 "Document 19,"[10] which codified the parameters for the "respect for and protection of religious belief" until such time as Socialism was attained and religion died out naturally.[11] While asserting that religion was a result of helplessness and fear in the face of an oppressive social system, Document 19 grudgingly accepted that because people's consciousness lagged behind reality, "the long-term influence of religion among a part of the people in a Socialist country cannot be avoided."[12] It was, moreover, "entirely wrong" to try to end religion through coercive measures; the task was therefore to manage religion well (Section I). The document as a whole is fairly balanced and pragmatic in tenor, as long as the basic premise is accepted that religion is subordinate to the needs and central aim of "building a powerful, modernized socialist state"[13] and that the first duty of citizens is their responsibility to the state. The document urged the redress of injustices against believers, at the same time as setting out the measures to be taken against "criminal and antirevolutionary" activities. These included the heinous crime of "infiltration by hostile foreign religious forces,"[14] with the "imperialist" Vatican and Protestant foreign mission societies singled out as foremost among these (Article XI).

By detailing the distinction between "normal" and abnormal or illegal religious activity, and arrogating to governmental organs the right to judge between these, Document 19 effectively continues the policy of dividing the church(es) and opened up the dangers of local decision making in its implementation.[15] While there are clear gradations of severity between the actions listed—believers may not interfere in public education or solicit foreign funds for their church work, for example, but colluding with foreign religious bodies that wish to establish their own church work in China is a much more serious offense—there is evident scope for local difference in working out the balance between sanctioned practice and criminalized activities. A significant point of contention for Protestants, for example, was whether the gatherings of Christians in homes, which had been continuing prior to the reopening of churches, were now illicit.[16] The 1982 document permits practices that by custom take place in believers' homes (Article VI; the list includes prayer, Bible studies, Mass, and baptism) but adds that "as for Protestants gathering in homes for worship services, in principle this should not be allowed, yet the prohibition should not be too rigidly enforced."[17] The policy seemed to suggest that supplementary religious activities could take place in homes, but not a main worship service. It is clear that the document intended that adjustment should be made to circumstances—many rural congregations still did not have houses of worship—but this highlights exactly the problem many Protestant Christians faced in practice throughout the 1980s and 1990s: some zealous officials prohibited gatherings in homes, even where no church was available for believers. Given the emerging problem of decidedly heretical Christian sects in rural areas, such as the Shouters or Eastern Lightning, some legislative attempt to determine the boundaries of orthodox (and compliant) worship was perhaps inevitable, but the interpretation of Document 19's wording, often local and inconsistent, was to play a significant part in the negative experiences of thousands of well-intentioned local ekklēsia.[18]

Throughout the 1980s two features of nationwide life affected religious communities. The first was cycles of repression and relaxation, a component aspect of religious experience since at least the Tang dynasty, and the second were structural adjustments in the economy that caused a creaking of the entire system and tested the limits of political and religious freedom. The brief Anti-Spiritual Pollution campaign of 1983,[19] aimed at curbing some of the Western, bourgeois, and degenerate values creeping in and threatening Socialism—ranging from individualism to pornography—was the first post-1978 salvo and caught the church, with its foreign links, in its ricochet. In 1988 and 1989 social unrest among Buddhist and Muslim Uighur populations in Tibet and Xinjiang, respectively, led to periods of martial law in each, highlighting the complex conflation of religious and ethnic identities for authorities. A meeting of Roman Catholic (non-CCPA) leaders in Shaanxi saw some prelates imprisoned, an event that coincided with the issue of a new confidential circular by the Central Office of the CCP and the State Council: "On Stepping Up Control over the Catholic Church to Meet the New Situation."[20] Some have suggested that Chinese perception of the Vatican role in the fall of Communism in Eastern Europe was instrumental in this particular round of suppression.[21] Elsewhere in the country, liberals and intellectuals were making use of the environment of greater freedom that came with economic liberalization to test out imported ideologies, including a rethinking of China's place in world history.[22] Such forays were brought to an abrupt halt by the army massacre of students and workers in and around Tiananmen Square in the summer of 1989. Just as the flowering of creativity among intellectual elites in 1956 was met with a campaign of terror in 1957, the student protestors at Tiananmen—who had been agitating for unions, a freer press, and political representation and protesting against the corruption that economic growth had unleashed—were, after a summer under the daily beam of the world's media, labeled counterrevolutionaries and subjected to a systematic crackdown.

For the generation in high school or university in Beijing in the late 1980s, Tiananmen deeply marked their worldview and led to a prolonged introspection over the direction of the country. The flight of participants abroad had a secondary, unforeseen effect, engendering a stream of high-profile U.S.-based Chinese Christians.[23] In the aftermath of Tiananmen, religious life was regulated anew with the publication of a series of documents intended to improve the management of religious venues, registration processes, and foreign citizens' religious activities. These were a natural extension of the aim to regularize religious activity and bring it under greater control through administrative and legal means.[24] "Document 6" of 1991 tried to suggest a scrupulous balance between affirming the rights of believers and warning what might befall those who failed to fulfill their obligations to society, but the balance fell toward curbing "lawless elements" and "hostile forces."[25] Important aspects left ambiguous in 1982 were clarified: religious sites were to be registered "in accordance with the law" and administered by the local patriotic associations. In this way the role of the official religious organizations was strengthened, and activities operating in a previously grey area beyond their purview were now forbidden. The document spells out what this might mean: "illegal" Bible colleges, seminaries, and convents active since the beginning of the Reform era were to be closed and "self-styled preachers" firmly curbed (Section II). The institutionalization of sanctioned and unacceptable religious groups naturally served to deepen suspicions and divides within denominations.[26] It also ushered in a testing period of struggle and sacrifice for those outside of the official organizations, a period that seems to have stimulated as much as contained evangelism.

Commentators have suggested that it was the sheer growth in religious adherents that prompted the tone and content of Document 6 and further regulations in 1994 on venue registration and foreign nationals; this is made more plausible by the sense of self-criticism hovering in the final section of the document, which enjoins the strengthening of political and ideological work by CCP committees in inculcating a scientific worldview among citizens and educating the young in dialectical and historical materialism.[27] As Pitman Potter and others have noted, the regulation of religion is linked to Chinese domestic issues of authority and the legitimacy of the party. Too much control brings into question regime legitimacy: regulation essentially depends on compliance and voluntary acceptance.[28] A corollary of this has been the need to maintain the distinction between good and bad religion—and to persuade people of the validity of the distinction, if not the CCP's authority to make it—a strategy that has required making sure that only a small minority are censored or imprisoned for their religious activities, leaving the impression that the treatment of the majority is wholly reasonable. Into the late 1990s and early 2000s the balance of power had ostensibly altered, with the greater acceptance of religion in society—national leaders had openly commended Christianity's social ethic and lauded more "scientific" religions—and with the force of huge numbers of unregistered churches; and yet significant numbers of priests and pastors were still under surveillance or imprisoned, and the foreign press regularly reported on churches being bulldozed. The saturation of Internet and social media usage among students and urban residents has meant that cases of harassment or breaches of the rights of believers are internationally logged and quickly publicized, but this has rarely led to authorities backing down.[29]

A second burst of "administrative rationalization" between 2004 and 2007 produced a series of new ordinances and a significant volume of local legislation. A generally more positive baseline for religious work had been indicated in 2002 by "Document 3," which proposed, inter alia, that "doing religious work well affects the strengthening of flesh and blood relations between the Party and the masses of people" and was therefore important in maintaining unity among different ethnic groups and preserving social stability.[30] The comprehensive "Regulations on Religious Affairs" of 2004/5 provoked much debate, with Ying

Fuk-Tsang calling them a "legislative milestone."[31] Some commentators have seen a clear deviation from the status quo in these regulations, while others have been more skeptical as to whether they signified real change, including experts testifying to a U.S. congressional hearing on the topic in 2005.[32] On the surface the regulations seemed to provide a positive corrective in areas both ideological and pragmatic—with a relaxation on administrative issues such as annual recertification for worship venues or donations from foreign donors and with the legal institution of routes of appeal to bureaucratic or judicial decisions against congregations and individuals[33]—but much of this pertained only to registered congregations.

A more significant critique has begun to be voiced by scholars and lawyers regarding the churches' position within the whole gamut of legislation. As Wang Yi notes, there are now four types of regulation in play in China: constitutional clauses, administrative laws, administrative regulations, and regional laws and regulations.[34] The dichotomy between the party-state overseeing administrative regulation and legal bodies (and ultimately the National People's Congress) determining the meaning and enforcement of legislation has ensured an ongoing tussle in religious affairs. Beijing house-church pastor Jin Mingri calls it "absurd" that the authority of the party-state has trumped the constitution over the issue of registration.[35] Scholars and Christian activists have pointed to numerous contradictions in the present legislation, both between national regulation and regional clauses and between the constitution and national legislation.[36] (Among examples Ying Fuk-Tsang gives: the Russian Orthodox Church is a legitimate entity in Heilongjiang but not elsewhere; foreign citizens in China may adhere to religions that Chinese citizens may not; the freedom of religious belief in the constitution is potentially at odds with legislation in limiting religious belief to the private sphere and in administrative restrictions which mean that, in practice, only adherents of the five originally authorized religions can obtain approval for worship venues.) The Regulations on Religious Administration were themselves, as Ying and others have argued, an evasive response to the calls from church leaders and legislators from the late 1980s onward for a religious *law*, in line with the government's own trend toward rule by law.[37]

The volume of regulation does show, however, heightened government consideration of the importance of religion, and toward the end of this phase of regulation in 2007, the cumulative weight of new thinking on religion is evident. For the first time, a statement on religion appeared in revisions to the party constitution, urging the "comprehensive implementation of the Party's basic direction on religious work, uniting the masses of religious believers to contribute to the economic development of society."[38] That Christians might contribute positively to society was a novel position. Experts were gathered for a Party Political Bureau study session on the religious question for the first time since 1949, and Hu Jintao reiterated to participants the (positive) mass nature of religion. "Religious relations" were made one of the five important relations in the "harmonious society" and so were built into strategic thinking nationally. The short-lived nature of the effects (Roman Catholic relations, for example, which reached a high point with Pope Benedict's letter to Chinese Catholics in 2007, later fell to a nadir over unauthorized episcopal ordinations) shows the jagged nature of gains and the need to differentiate between sectors of the church economy.

This is the real insight that the history of regulation gives us: it defines a broad channel within which regular religious life, as interpreted by the state and managed by religious bodies, enjoys an increasing acceptance and normalcy within everyday life. Those attending registered churches, small devotional groups, or Bible study groups and living as Christians in their workplaces are now able to integrate their faith and lives in ways unimaginable even as late as the early 1990s, as long as they are not CCP members—and even here, there is evidence of some tacit acceptance. But for Christian groups whose presence or actions are not contained within the boundaries of the regulation, a different type of existence and relation to the state pertains. A prominent new category is that of Protestant political and legal activists who challenge the basis of the regulatory order itself and are inspired by their faith to press ahead for democratic change or greater civil society.[39] A longer-standing group is that of underground Catholics, where external political events and relations with the Vatican have as much bearing as internal policies, given China's emphasis on "foreign infiltration." For both of these groups, the Marxist ideological vision enacted in legislation has acutely shaped their experiences of faith and suffering. While there is a startling lack of correlation between regulation and church history in terms of the numeric growth and strength of the target groups, there is a precise correlation between the groups targeted and the effects of the law on their expression of faith.

There are some general reasons why the growth and strength of the unofficial churches has confounded the authorities' intentions, particularly in the past decade, aside from any theological arguments believers might posit. One is the Internet and its capacity for allowing the creation of real and virtual communities and discussion beyond immediate state control.[40] Another is the changing relationship in society to rules and the law itself. In the 1980s and early 1990s rules ruled, and any irregular activity was strongly curtailed; but with the increased easing of restrictions on economic and social life, a more phlegmatic and flexible approach to legislation has returned, especially in its local application. This period has coincided with the strong growth in the urban house churches. The more flexible attitude to the law by local officials is in keeping with the principle at work among higher echelons that Communist Party state constitutions are subject to decision-makers, not vice versa.[41] Various case studies have documented the processes of negotiation and the manipulation of social and cultural capital that unofficial church leaders have engaged in locally to be allowed to continue prohibited actions, such as distributing gospel leaflets in public areas or employing foreign preachers; the same studies have shown the flexibility on the part of the authorities to ensure the greater good of social harmony.[42] Other scholars have considered the variables at play in the "dramatic variation" in relations between unregistered groups and the authorities.[43] As Yang Fenggang notes, a "shortage economy" of regulated supply leads to a "vivaciously dynamic" religious demand[44]—and many have wondered whether growth will cease once oppression is removed.

In the more specific case of the dance between China and the Vatican, legislation has naturally lagged behind relationship peaks and troughs. While China has wanted to assert its sovereign authority and protect internal stability, Rome's agenda has focused increasingly on the difficult and painful task of promoting reconciliation and unity among Catholics.[45] Significant moments outside the track of legislation included the resignation of surviving "Chinese" bishops who were foreign nationals in 1987;[46] tentative steps toward establishing diplomatic relations in 1996, when the papal representative, Archbishop Claudio Celli, met representatives of the Beijing government; and Vatican preparation to drop diplomatic relations with Taiwan in 1999 in return for securing its own candidates as bishops, which was foiled by the ordinations of five bishops by the open church without Vatican approval and reciprocated in the spectacular (and highly offensive to Beijing) canonization of 120 Chinese martyrs in Rome on Chinese National Day, 1 October 2000. Pope Benedict XVI's well-crafted twenty-page letter to Chinese Catholics in 2007 marked a high point in relations that did correspond with general policy shifts by the Chinese government.[47] Since then, however, the issue of episcopal ordinations—and the power plays they represent—has continued, with relations nose-diving in 2010 as the CCPA deviated from recent protocol and ordained a new bishop without Rome's approval. Another dramatic incident came in 2012, as Thaddeus Ma Daqin was ordained with full pomp auxiliary bishop of Shanghai but immediately announced that he would no longer remain a member of the CCPA. (He has since been stripped of his episcopal title by the CCPA, an act whose authority is naturally contested.) The year 2015 saw new high-level delegation meetings between Vatican and Chinese officials and intimations of progress on stumbling blocks.

If the philosophical problem for the CCP in the 1950s was the continued existence of religion, its ideological headache in the twenty-first century has been the continued resistance of religion to conform to its expectations and policy requirements. Despite concerted effort in the legislation outlined above, the Roman church in China has not severed foreign contact, and the portion of the church in close communion with Rome has remained resistant even to Rome's calls for reconciliation and unity; meanwhile, the Protestant church has neither become fully postdenominational nor united under one patriotic body. The less robust correlation than one might imagine between legislation and church history has to be traced through individual church sectors, particularly in the cases of the targets of much of the legislation, Protestant house churches and the Catholic Church in communion with Rome, where alternative and/or external bases of authority contest the legality and morality of that legislation. But if a divided house cannot stand, the CCP's bequest to the churches is still a first-order theological problem.

CONTEMPORARY THEOLOGICAL WRITINGS

As the churches began to engage in the business of reestablishing congregations, training clergy, and developing national church structures in the 1980s, church leaders were once again able to access and read theological materials. The Chinese Catholic Church had to catch up on global changes since Vatican II. Protestants and Catholics alike had to take stock of liberation theologies, feminist theologies, and new contextual theologies, as well as heed developments in biblical studies, ethics, and related fields. The 1980s offered potent days of possibility, when clerics released from prison such as Jin Luxian and Fan Zhongliang in Shanghai or Protestant leaders like Ding Guangxun in Nanjing began to gather up the threads of their earlier theological training and work out which could be woven into Reform-era life. (Ding enjoyed his most prolific decade of writing in the 1980s, producing a stream of speeches and essays for church audiences as well as for intellectual and governmental consumption.)[48] Journals like the *Jinling shenxue zhi* (Nanjing Theological Review) published the writings of sanctioned church leaders for Protestant priests and students, while church magazines like *Tianzhujiao* (Catholicism) or *Tian Feng* spread an authorized message tailored to congregations throughout the country. There were, however, few theologians active and as yet scarce means of training new ones to a high academic level within China; extant leaders were mostly aged and preoccupied with the demands of re-creating ecclesial life. Given the history of legislation and religious containment, publications outside of the official church sector were still rare or not widely distributed. Meanwhile, the academic study of Christianity in state institutions was beginning to enjoy an unexpected resurgence and form its own center of theological thinking.

Zhuo Xinping 卓新平, the director of the Institute of World Religions at CASS, has argued that theology in China forms three separate streams: Chinese theology, Sino-Christian theology, and academic theology. Chinese theology here indicates the theology of the church, while academic theology describes the Christian part of the discipline of religious studies, a "faith-neutral" subject. Along with other commentators within mainland Chinese officialdom and academia, Zhuo regards denominational and church theologies as peripheral in China, arguing that they receive "little attention from either society or Chinese intellectuals" because of their lack of academic rigor and limitations on the interaction of the church in society.[49] Zhuo's category of Sino-Christian theology (*Hanyu shenxue* 汉语神学) refers to a broad movement of academic study of Christianity that has developed since the mid-1990s, which Zhuo separates from academic theology proper because it may include confessional elements or approaches. The distinction demonstrates the perceived need to maintain a clear separation of the academic from the dogmatic, faith being regarded as concomitant to superstition for most of PRC history. Given that the leaders of the Sino-Christian theology movement are major intellectual figures at leading universities, the boundary of the "academic" is a little arbitrary. In a system where "theology" (*shenxue*) is not regarded as an academic discipline and seminary degrees are not recognized by secular institutions, a clear scale of progression exists in Zhuo's thinking from faith-based church thought through Sino-Christian (faith + knowledge) to the higher pursuit of academic thinking (neutral, cognitive knowledge).

The speed and scope of the growth of academic theology in the late twentieth century are noteworthy, as is the role it has carved out in the humanities and in broader society and the changing nature of Chinese Christianity toward which it contributes. This chapter regards Sino-Christian theology as a subset of academic theology but creates a separate category of unofficial church writings. The very different experiences of faith and of being church, as well as the publishing limitations on unregistered believers over the past several decades, suggest that the writings of underground or house-church thinkers should be addressed separately. In the (near?) future we can only assume that these distinctions will subside, but until the political tide turns and civic society embraces greater freedom of religious expression, or cooperation between church sectors overcomes present divides, the category division still has force. The publishing record suggests, in fact, that while registered and unregistered, or open and underground, church publications follow different routes and media, there is much more cross-over between church and academic theology than is usually allowed for in discussion: in personnel and in subject area.

OFFICIAL CHURCH THEOLOGIES

The severe toll on the church that the purges of the 1950s and the Cultural Revolution inflicted, together with the residual generation gap from the lack of training of new leaders over that twenty-year period, has meant a slow recovery for theological education and the development of new, creative thinking. A dearth of priests relative to congregation sizes and the administrative demands of re-creating church structures spared few for sustained writing. On the Roman Catholic side, this has been compounded by continued uncertainty over leadership, dual incumbents for certain sees, and the removal of leaders from office over disputes between the CCPA and Rome.

Official Catholic theology is readily found in the journal *Zhongguo Tian-zhujiao* (中国天主教 Chinese Catholicism), which, as the full name suggests, takes a sino-centric view of its place within the universal church. The acceptability and broad promotion of this publication are seen in the facts that the table of contents for each edition is available on the CASS website, and individual articles may be downloaded from SARA webpages. Articles range from local CCPA committee reports to essays on church history, wisdom, or morality pieces (such as "Holy Mother Mary: Receiving and Putting into Practice the Divine Word" or "Warnings on Staying Away from Avarice");[50] translated articles on the implementation of Vatican II; and essays explaining current church policy. A 2013 retrospective of ten years of the institution of "Three Documents and Systems" and its guiding policy of "Running Church Affairs in a Democratic Way" shows how the policy framework has been expected to set the agenda for theological thinking. The desire to link running the church democratically with national good and a sense of global Catholic belonging are evident in the titles of articles in the magazine, such as "Consistently Raise High the Flag of 'Love Country Love Church': Firmly Develop the System of a Democratically Run Church" by Li Shan 李山, or "The Local Implementation of a Democratically Run Church Is a Development Trend in the Universal Church" by Shen Bin 沈斌.

When originally instituted, the Three Documents were hailed as the culmination of fifty years of an independent Chinese church. (To outsiders, they seemed to bring church management—including the election of bishops and formation of clergy and religious—back more tightly under CCPA control.)[51] At a workshop to mark the tenth anniversary of their promulgation, Jiang Jianyong 蒋坚永, the deputy director of SARA, explained the thought behind the policy: "Running Church Affairs in a Democratic Way" is a management model that adheres to the basic "love country" and "anti-imperialist" framework of Chinese religious life while being fully in keeping with Vatican II trends on local autonomy.[52] As Jiang outlined, the four key traits of the policy are "collective leadership, democratic management, mutual co-operation, and common decision making." For SARA, all good theology is by definition autonomous and collective. The top-down nature of SARA thinking and its understanding of the relationship between policy and theological thought is clear in Jiang's plaint that no one has as yet created a theological system to complement this model of democratic management. Catholics should, he argues, learn from the "theological reconstruction" movement of their Protestant counterparts and pay a bit more attention to developing a new theology in line with policies, to truly creating a theological system "with Chinese characteristics."

Beyond publications directly linked to the CCPA or SARA, three significant Roman Catholic presses are operated by diocesan or church authorities, including the Shanghai diocese Guangqi Press (光启社, reestablished in 1984) and the Beijing Sapientia Press House (上智编译馆, reopened in 1997), and publish a range of church texts such as missals, original works in Chinese from outside mainland China, and translated theological texts, dictionaries, and commentaries. The presses also supply translations of great reference tomes like *The Modern Catholic Encyclopedia*.[53] The Guangqi Press runs academic activities such as workshops on indigenization and publishes the quarterly *Catholic Research Compilation*, while the director of Sapientia Press, Rev. Dr. Peter Jianmin Zhao 赵建敏, also edits the *Journal of Catholic Studies*.[54] A third press, the Hebei Faith Press in Shijiazhuang, publishes the magazine *Xinde* (信德 Faith Weekly), with a postal circulation through most provinces, and also hosts a dynamic website. Peppered with pictures of Pope Francis and news flashes, the website includes both topical items, with a church news discussion board, and in-depth reports. Special features include reports on liturgy and inculturation and on vocations, and a focus on migrants and evangelism (with an interactive map). The website promotes a public apologetics, countering, for example, common negative beliefs regarding the history of the church in China and reproducing articles from other Christian or ecumenical sources. A rich site for church news and applied theology, the *Xinde* website also encourages and supports practical action and charitable donations.

The existence of more a lively and progressive website within the open church points to the broader church economy that is operating but also exposes some of the fault lines for which outsiders chide the official churches. Reading reams of articles in CCPA and TSPM magazines, written in line with committee-agreed agendas and buzzwords, can on occasion seem farcical; and there is a legitimate question over the degree to which articles on policy-oriented theology prominent in the official magazines are a front, a signal to authorities that minds are working on these questions, or whether they are really intended to have a decisive effect on pew life or local preaching.[55]

To a greater degree than in the Roman Catholic Church, Protestant thinkers in China have attempted to create a "theology with Chinese characteristics." Bishop Ding Guangxun in 1985 admonished foreigners who peddled the notion that Chinese theology was "political" or "biased"; such accusations were condescending, he argued, and implied that Chinese congregations lacked the wherewithal to recognize false teachings when they heard them.[56] Chen Zemin 陈泽民, former vice principal of Nanjing Union (Jinling) Theological Seminary, has called for acknowledgment of a "Jinling School" of theology, which promotes the adaptation of Chinese Christian theology to China as a Socialist society.[57] For Zhuo Xinping at CASS, one of the defining features of church theology in China has been its awareness of the need to adapt to contemporary society in China.[58] As in the Roman Catholic Church, expertise in the main Protestant seminary in Nanjing was devoted initially to theological education and writing textbooks for the new Reform era, with scholars producing several volumes in the late 1980s and early 1990s on biblical studies, including commentaries on 1 and 2 Corinthians, the Song of Songs, and the Pentateuch, as well as texts on church history and pastoral ministry.[59] Four new publication series were launched from Nanjing Seminary, including a "Correspondence Compendium" for the church's high-demand correspondence course to educate church workers, a "Nanjing pulpit" sermon series, and the Chinese Christian Theological Education Series, under editors Shen Yifan 沈以藩, Chen Zemin, and Wang Weifan 汪维藩.

Parallel to the Roman Catholic Church but slightly earlier in time, the Protestant church worked under the slogan of "running the church well" during the 1980s, a maxim supported by Bishop Ding, who linked the idea to reflection on the universal and particular nature of the Chinese church. As the church continued to discuss how to develop its patriotic, self-governing, self-supporting, and self-propagating message, various avenues of thought emerged, from Shen Yifan's incarnational theology to the better known "unceasing generation" theology of Wang Weifan and to Ding Guangxun's own "theology of love" and emphasis on the cosmic Christ.[60] As we have seen, the "theological reorientation" (神学再思 *shenxue zaisi*) that Ding espoused in the 1980s drew on Teilhard de Chardin, liberation theology, and ecumenical thinking, and his writings returned time and again to the theme of God as love, healing and redeeming both in and beyond the church.[61] Wang Weifan meanwhile argued that a "theology with Chinese characteristics" for a postdenominational Chinese church needed to look back to the older generation of Chinese theologians, more deeply into the Bible, and into Chinese cultural texts and philosophical concepts (such as Great Harmony 大同, or the Great Ultimate 太极); his own work on "unceasing generation" or the God "who gives birth to life" (*sheng sheng* 生生) draws on the Chinese classical canon and also elements of mystical Daoism.[62]

A common thread through much Reform-era Protestant theology is expressed in Chen Zemin's oft-repeated quotation "theology is the church thinking": theological reflection must be founded on real, contemporary experience—and so closely tied to, if not starting out from, Chinese society and social and political life. This can be seen in the emphasis of Shen Yifan and others on the Incarnation and related affirmation of the material, and of the consecration of secular life, including a critical identification with Chinese culture and its positive aspects, such as the valorization of relationships. It can also be seen in numerous articles on *aiguo aijiao* ("love one's country and love the church") and church-state relations or on how Christianity intersects with "harmonious society," a buzzword of the 2000s. And it can be seen in the high proportion of articles and theological reflections that take the nature of Chinese Christianity as their subject, including more recently pieces on women's identity in the Chinese church,[63] but more often on Chinese identity as defined vis-à-vis Western theological thought or the house churches. Although this is constructive theology, a certain defensiveness is also at work, whether in articles that hark back to the cultural imperialism of the missionary heritage[64] or in articles on mission that point—rightly—to the sacramental and teaching elements of the Great Commission yet use these to criticize the dangerous work of "self-styled evangelists" outside of the official church.[65] Even a thoughtful and interesting essay such as that by Gao Ying 高英 on eschatology and continuous creation, using Jürgen Moltmann to challenge traditional dualities of earth and heaven, is interspersed with a standard condemnation of the perils of house-church preaching on the eschaton.[66]

In a 1992 retrospect of forty years of church publications in the PRC, Ding once reflected on the parameters in which postliberation theology had developed in China—an article that elucidates the constraints on church theology from an insider perspective.[67] While Chinese theology was shaped by the historical and ecumenical church, its thinking had to be its own work, a reflection by Chinese Christians as they faced squarely the problems of the Chinese church, wrote Ding. The Chinese church was unlikely, he noted, to be producing articles on women's liberation or ecological questions when these were not pressing issues in its congregational life. What the church had to contend with was, from the beginning, the question of unity. Ding reminds that the postliberation church was a broad union, and the principle of mutual respect and tolerance was a necessary baseline in a newly integrated church, even if it stymied theological creativity. (When Nanjing Union Theological Seminary came together in 1952, it was a merger of twelve seminaries with a great range of theological viewpoints; the seminary initially even ran twin-track classes for fundamentalist and modernist students).[68] If sapidity and novelty were a sacrificial cost of unity, Ding was keenly aware of other constraints on theological thinking that promoted the same end: the minority status of Christianity in China and the educative role of the church. From his perspective as leader, Ding felt a strong responsibility to building up the church and encouraging gratitude for freedoms gained rather than inciting martyrdom, and to proclaiming a message that went beyond personal salvation and reached into society. At that stage in the early 1990s the concept of the cosmic Christ was a natural point of coherence, and other scholars followed Ding in amplifying how Christ as co-creator, revealer of God's love, and sustainer of the universe might be a relevant model for China, and for drawing all people—including Communists—into Christ's universe and beyond Western theological debates on such matters as Christ's human and divine natures.

By the late 1990s, the Protestant church, guided by Ding, had collectively embarked on a program of "Theological Reconstruction" (神学思想建设): the deepening of the Three-Self program and of running the church well, together with the deliberate aligning of theology to life in a Socialist China. (In his remarks at the end of the Ji'nan meeting of the TSPM and China Christian Council in 1998, during which Theological Reconstruction was adopted by those bodies, Han Wenzao 韩文藻 spoke of "adjusting" theological views not compatible with Socialism.)[69] Though much talked about, the concept of Theological Reconstruction has remained somewhat elusive. Chen Yongtao 陈永涛 has described the process as "through a new interpretation of our universal common faith, to establish a uniquely local contextualized theology,"[70] while Cao Shengjie 曹圣洁 reverted to the text of the TSPM/China Christian Council standing committee report: "to integrate our national ethos and culture in explaining basic Christian faith and moral principles in this context."[71]

It describes, in essence, the moves outlined above to derive theology from lived life in Socialist China, alongside the attempt that Cao alludes to, to protect "basic Christian faith" (i.e., the traditional or creedal faith of ordinary Christians) while allowing for more radical interpretations among the theologically educated. It is perhaps a comment on the nature of Chinese theology that almost every senior figure in the TSPM or Nanjing Seminary leadership has written on Theological Reconstruction (including Cao herself, Chen Zemin, Han Wenzao, Ji Jianhong 季剑虹, Wang Aiming 王艾明, and Ding Guangxun), but relatively few others. While Protestant church theology has been addressing a range of theological and ecclesiological questions—deserving of much greater treatment than afforded here—the more interesting avenues of thought have tended to be those that speak to these questions from within theological or Chinese thought, rather than those refracted through state dictates.

ACADEMIC THEOLOGY

From small beginnings in philosophy and history departments, secular Christian studies programs began to be introduced in Chinese state universities. By the late 1990s and early 2000s thriving master's (and doctoral) programs in Christian studies emerged at dozens of Chinese universities, specializing in various aspects of Christian philosophy, intellectual history, literary criticism, and cultural studies, with occasional offerings in the more controversial areas of biblical studies and church history. A range of Chinese academic journals was founded to support and publicize this inquiry, with one of the earliest being *Jidujiao wenhua pinglun* (基督教文化评论 Christian Culture Review), published by the Guizhou People's Press, whose editors included the "church fathers" of Sino-Christian theology Liu Xiaofeng 刘小枫 and He Guanghu 何光沪. Universities' own publishing houses began to publish academic journals in the field of religion, such as *Youtai yanjiu* (犹太研究 Journal of Jewish Studies) from Shandong University and *Jidujiao wenhua xuekan* (基督教文化学刊 Journal of Christian Culture), started by Renmin University Press in 1998. Individual academics (here Fu Youde 傅有德 and Yang Huilin 杨慧林, respectively) have acted as editor and guided the journals through the processes of official acceptance and ongoing censorship.

The CASS hosts a list of some two dozen current journal titles in religion; those that publish articles on Christianity include *Zongjiao zhexue* (宗教哲学 Philosophy of Religion), *Dangdai zongjiao yanjiu* (当代宗教研究 Contemporary Religious Studies), *Zongjiaoxue yanjiu* (宗教学研究 Research in Religious Studies), and *Zhongguo zongjiao* (中国宗教 Chinese Religion), as well as the two church publications of *Tian Feng* and *Tianzhujiao*. Journals published under the auspices of a SARA-related press such as the Religious Culture Press are also readily available; these include both church-academic journals like the *Tianzhujiao yanjiu lunji* (天主教研究论辑 Journal of Catholic Studies) and more specialized academic titles like the *Journal of Comparative Scripture* edited by You Bin 游斌 of Minzu University in Beijing. These journals each have their own ethos, from more pragmatic discussions of the work of religion and how it might benefit society in a journal, like *Zongjiao yu shijie* (宗教与世界 Religion and the World) or *Dangdai zongjiao yanjiu*, to a spectrum of academic questions covered in *Zongjiaoxue yanjiu*. Recent 2014 articles in the latter—showcasing the breadth of research on Christianity in Chinese higher education—have included essays on Marcion and Gnosticism, Cardinal Newman's conversion, missionary hospitals in Guangdong, John Calvin's concept of conscience, medieval Conciliarism, and Mary in Ming/Qing poetry.

The academic sector has enjoyed more publishing leeway than church publishers, but it too has benefited from the ideological shifts and greater openness of recent decades; nonetheless, there is still a vibrant censorship industry even for academic articles (particularly those by foreign scholars appearing in translation). A flourishing circuit of workshops and conferences addressing all sorts of topics in Chinese Christian history and cultural exchange now feeds into academic publishing, and proceedings from workshops and annual conferences, such as that hosted by the Institute of World Religions, are published by university and research presses. E-networks like the Google group run by Xiao Qinghe 肖清和 (a specialist in late imperial Catholicism) circulate announcements of new articles on Chinese Christianity almost daily, keeping subscribers abreast of the proliferating research. Secular academics in state universities have been pivotal to the greater acceptance of Christianity in China by politicians and officials as well as in academia, and their teaching of a new generation of scholars of Christianity and academic theologians has provided the foundation for the broader development of Chinese Christianity—and ultimately for the strengthening of academic Christianity in the church too.

One of the most intriguing developments in Chinese Christianity of the past two decades is the unabashedly academic Sino-Christian theology (*Hanyu shenxue*, literally "Chinese-language theology") movement, which initially circled around the philosophers Liu Xiaofeng and He Guanghu and came to public attention in the mid-1990s in China.[72] An outgrowth of the Reform era, the Sino-Christian theology movement as it developed has brought together scholars working on disparate aspects of Chinese Christianity who sought to carve out institutional space for Christian theology to become an academic discipline in China—and succeeded. The question of what that discipline was (whether "a kind of philosophical expression of personal faith," as Liu's thought has been described,[73] or something closer to its systematic or dogmatic cousins) has evolved in the process. An early aim of the movement was to bring theology into public discourse, utilizing Christian thinking in areas such as values and ethics for the benefit of Chinese society and providing a disciplinary methodology in the humanities to complement monovalent Marxist methodologies.[74] Sino-Christian theology has not assumed a theological basis for itself or taken the church as its source or audience but has repeatedly offered the explanation "from academia, for Chinese academia, facing the church and society" as the rationale for its existence (a stance challenged in some recent writings, as more professing Christian academics join in the debates).[75] Sino-Christian theology is deliberately contemporary, addressing current sociopolitical realities in China; its focus is to articulate a Chinese theology in line with Chinese thought and intellectual priorities.

Early writers within Sino-Christian theology included Liu and He, Yang Huilin (whose work is the subject of the next chapter), and Zhuo Xinping at CASS. Many such academics came to the field of Christianity through their study of philosophy, theology, or literature rather than encounters in the church, and this has influenced their understanding of the material and the shape of the Chinese discipline. Several of the scholars, including Liu and He, have invested much time in translation projects to bring the works of German- or English-speaking theologians to a Chinese audience.[76] Defining early works of the movement included Liu Xiaofeng's 1988 *Zhengjiu yu xiaoyao* (拯救与 逍遥 Salvation and Easy Wandering, also translated as Delivering and Dallying), which considered afresh the possibility of comparison between Christian and Chinese concepts (whether Daoist, Confucian, or through terms like *Tian*, Heaven), and He Guanghu's essays of 1995 examining the basis for and methodologies of Sino-Christian theology.[77] More recent compendia of articles in the field run to several volume-sets; and even an English-language anthology of Sino-Christian theology shows how the disciplinary sweep is of similar breadth to the "academic" studies described above, with articles on topics from the phenomenon of "cultural Christians" in China to the function of theology in the humanities, or the notion of Dao 道 as word and Word.[78]

While much subsequent research has been comparative (discussing Christian-Buddhist dialogue or Christian-Confucian interactions), the location of theology in the academy has inevitably given rise to continued questions about the nature and purpose of the discipline: a strong thread has been the exploration of the construct of Sino-Christian theology itself, including a reassessment of its historical trajectory in China, and debate on what role Christianity should have in contemporary China. Discussion has included the relation of Christianity to culture and the locus of Chineseness (residing in language, territory, or cultural traditions?) in the "Sino" part of the term, and questions of revelation and the interaction of Chinese theology with historical and contextual theologies in the "theology" half of the term. He Guanghu's early work on mother-tongue theology, which gave primacy to the language medium, broached questions of indigenization and contextualization and stimulated much debate with Hong Kong theologians. (He, Liu, and Yang Huilin have all been critical of Republican-era debates on indigenization, objecting variously to the terminology used, the May Fourth framework, and misguided attempts at sinicization, arguing that Christianity should retain its otherness.) Much debate has occurred between mainland and Hong Kong scholars over the questions of what theology is, who it is for, and its relation to the church. Initial debates, and rebuttal of Liu's and He's writings on the Christ event and indigenization, were gathered in an edited volume published by the Institute of Sino-Christian Studies in Hong Kong in 2000.[79]

As the younger generation of academics develops their careers with fewer restraints on subject area and with a greater confidence in bringing theological questions to bear within the academic study of religion, and as Liu Xiaofeng's generation moves on to other areas of study and into retirement, the distinction between Sino-Christian theology and neutral academic study is likely to lessen further; or perhaps the term "Sino-Christian studies" will expand to its broader definition and encompass all Chinese Christian research. New avenues of research are developing all the time, such as work on Christian-Islam affinities in China or the creation of a Chinese form of Scriptural Reasoning, as discussed in the next chapter. The pressing question for the future is how this resonant sector of the Christian economy will interact and integrate with church thinking and development.

HOUSE-CHURCH LEADERS AND WRITERS

The church sector that has experienced the most dynamic growth over the past few decades has been the independent or unregistered sector of the Protestant church, despite being targeted by legislation. Its growth, predominantly in rural areas during the 1970s and 1980s and in urban areas from the 1990s,[80] has been the subject of several popular volumes predicting the "Christianization" of China and welcoming the entry of China as a major force in global Christianity.[81] Urban house-church pastors, many of whom are highly educated and technologically savvy, have utilized a variety of media to spread the gospel and connect with their congregations, from micro-blogs to webcasts of services. Gerda Wielander's pioneering study of online church congregations and web-based church magazines and journals gives a sense of the breadth and reach of these publications, as well as the ephemerality of some.[82] Although the rural churches and new urban churches of the 1990s and 2000s are often elided, there are good grounds for regarding them as essentially different categories.[83] While many would acknowledge that the latter could not have developed as they did without the former, and while the two are bound by a common evangelical heritage, experience of suffering, and mistrust of the government and the TSPM, their liturgical styles, target audiences, and theological stances may be quite different, in line with greatly different educational levels and life experiences of congregations and pastors. The scope of publishing also represents a clear difference, as discussed below. There is a sense, verbalized by émigré writer Yu Jie 余杰, that while the "lifeblood" of the house church had been kept alive in rural locales, urban house churches have now taken over the baton in China.[84]

Rural house churches in general in the Reform era have been characterized by a relatively simple biblical faith, by an anti-intellectualism or distrust of theology, and by patient suffering, fervent prayer, and testimony to miracles and healings. A wide spectrum of rural house churches exists, from mainstream ones—including those providing their own leadership and theological training and organizing regional networks of likeminded fellowship groups[85]—to more hybrid forms of Christianity imbued with folk religion, to outright sects. Recent research has analyzed the spectrum of church groups between independent indigenous movements and sects and considered Christianity itself as a folk religion. Lian Xi speaks of the "sustained phenomenon of the cultic thrust in Chinese Protestantism" in the late twentieth century, which "featured dire apocalypticism, opposition to the political order, tight underground organization, and deification of spiritual leaders."[86] Folk aspects incorporated into rural Christianity more broadly have included ancestor worship practices and a strong emphasis on healings, with illness the highest reported factor in conversions,[87] as well as a variety of superstitious and talismanic practices. A dearth of education and theological training for leaders, as Lian Xi, Dan Bays, and others have noted, combined with the sense of spiritual battle against governmental repression have encouraged the proliferation of splinter groups and cults; Lian Xi's work traces the interconnections and lineages of many of these groups.[88] Government crackdowns have targeted the more evidently cultic churches, but it has not always been obvious to local bureaucrats which were which; a safe policy erred toward suppressing all unregistered churches—including those mainstream unofficial church groups of the late twentieth century that grew out of the independent churches of the pre-1949 era.

By contrast, house-church pastors and intellectual elite like Wang Yi 王怡 (b. 1973) in Chengdu or Jin Mingri 金明日 in Beijing have been engaged not just in spiritual battles, but in legal challenges to authorities over their religious policies and implementation, and in struggles to articulate theologies of power and patriotism. It would be a great mistake to think of the Chinese house-church sector as a nonintellectual variety of evangelicalism. There are, of course, a variety of urban congregations, just as there are rural ones, including concentrations of business people, of student returnees from abroad, or of migrant workers, often subdivided into language or regional groups, and there is dissent among groups over theological views; but the existence of a body of house-church leaders who are also public intellectuals has changed the nature of the debate and its public profile.[89] Leaders like Wang, a former law professor at Chengdu University, or Jin, a graduate of Peking University with a doctorate in New Testament studies from the United States, are joined by a growing contingent of graduates from key universities who have set aside academic pursuits to lead congregations. Their theologies are often far from the eremitic or world-denying beliefs of predecessors like Wang Mingdao or Ni Tuosheng—whom they may nevertheless admire for their steadfast faith—and display a strong engagement with the world, in contradistinction to much mainstream house-church belief. They are often extremely well-connected abroad, usually with U.S. church organizations and with networks of mainland Chinese Christians living abroad. Services in the larger new urban house churches may be barely distinguishable from TSPM liturgies in format and style, and as Wielander has noted, they might cater to quite narrow strata of social background. Many of these leaders, alongside those of congregations serving intellectuals like the Fangzhou (The Ark) congregation in Beijing, regard their churches as "above ground" and open to all.[90] These are not concealed spaces (Jin Mingri's church on Beijing's fourth ring road seats two hundred) but may be hidden in full view—they do not register in the landscape in the way of church spires.

Three examples of writings to have come out of the Protestant house churches are discussed in Chapter 10: the hymns penned by Lü Xiaomin 吕小敏, the essays and reviews of Wang Yi, and the biographies edited by Yu Jie. These offer an insight into the range of publications emerging from beyond the official church and state academia in the past two decades, their creative interpretations of the gospel message, and the struggles that individuals within unregistered churches have experienced in the living and writing of their faith.

CONCLUSIONS

During the Reform era both state and nonstate agencies had to negotiate the transition from the high Communist years of authoritarian state control toward greater freedoms in social and individual life. Because religion is so ideologically fraught for a Marxist state, and because of the worrying ability of religious groups to mobilize adherents (as in 1999 when ten thousand Falun Gong supporters suddenly appeared outside Zhongnanhai, the state and party headquarters), religion has been kept on a tighter rein than other spheres of society and administered largely through regulations rather than the law. As the brief history of regulation at the beginning of this chapter showed, the policies throughout the 1980s and 1990s differentiated increasingly sharply between authorized and unauthorized expressions of religion, and the state fared poorly in divining a workable solution for religious groups that did not threaten social stability yet were not within the state ambit. Government regulation is, as it transpires, a surprisingly poor indicator for many aspects of contemporary church life, including growth rates, and yet the promulgation of a Marxist ideological vision did significantly affect the experiences of faith among the various church sectors. Throughout the Reform era, just as during the Nationalist or early PRC eras, church types were effectively determined by their relationship to the state, and that relationship conditioned the scope of Christian life and its theological reflection. Both state-aligning and state-decrying groups found positive, or reinforcing, theological narratives in their choices and their outcomes.

Through shaping the categories of religion, in a combination of ideological and pragmatic ways, policies shaped discourse also. This too had ideological and material components: for example, the availability of publishing routes was determined by whether an author was affiliated with a church that was sanctioned or not. More surprising, perhaps, the categories of religious affiliation have also affected the form and format of writing. Official and academic church publications over the past three decades have focused almost exclusively on the essay or the journal article, with some collections of individual's writings, but very few long studies. These "SARA-approved" writings, both essays and policy documents, appear in the burgeoning number of academic print journals or in official church journals that may be accessed via links from the CASS website. As the brief summary suggested, a good deal of official church theology has revolved around ecclesiology and church-state relations, while (secular) academic essays have frequently concentrated on examining the nature of theology as a theoretical construct. In contrast, while there has been a smaller volume of published writings from unofficial Christian sources, there is a much greater spectrum of types of writing. Theology, here, is still being produced as original, creative pieces of writing in a range of literary forms, but outside of mainstream publishing, often via Taiwanese, Hong Kong, or U.S. presses or on the web. Examples of these are discussed further in Chapter 10.

The sharp delineation of religious groups has militated against an atmosphere of reconciliation. As in the early years of the PRC, state policy has been more imposed on the open Catholic Church than embraced by it; and despite encouragement, directives such as the Three Documents and Systems and its management ethos have failed to find many takers as the basis for formulating a Chinese Catholic theology. Vatican relations have proved a better indicator of Roman Catholic trends than domestic legislation, and Rome continues to act as a theological fulcrum for the open church as for the underground, if in different ways. Meanwhile the positive choice of Protestant leaders and theological educators centered around Nanjing to adapt and align theological thought to Socialist values has produced a body of work which continues to define a Chinese Christian theology that is independent from outside influence, embraces the entirety of the Chinese people, and seeks the good of the nation. As the voices of unregistered church thinkers and writers begin to be heard and publicized more widely once again in the new century, state-aligned theologies are being openly challenged and scrutinized. This challenge appears poised to upset the status quo in terms of both discourse and church relations in a new phase of greater diversity and equality in the church economy. As a wise Roman Catholic has written, the submission of the churches to government control brought the "danger of putting the integrity of the faith at some risk and, as a consequence, of jeopardizing authentic Christian living."[91] In the more open and aware present society (notwithstanding Xi Jinping's apparent reversal and tightening of religious life and Christian worship in the 2010s), the time has come for a clearer, and less acrimonious, evaluation of the consequences of both engagement with and prophetic challenge to the government.

There are hopeful signs of rapprochement that presage a more generous and self-reflective position toward Christians who have taken a different stance, in good conscience, on the defining question of relations with the state. The younger generation of churchgoers knows little of the personal animosity their elders may feel, having not experienced the same level of fear or suffering. For Roman Catholics, the strengthening of the Bishops' Conference vis-à-vis the CCPA, and measures that allowed for the recognition of the Pope as the spiritual leader of the church, much reduced the grounds for division between the open and underground churches in the 1990s. The rapid growth of Protestant Christianity has primarily been through conversion, which rarely comes with a family solidarity to one group of the other. In cities, many people now attend a TSPM church on a Sunday and a house-church group during the week. Studies show that for many urban Protestants, church choice is a practical as much as theological decision.[92] Another important fact that recent data highlight is that it is becoming increasingly acceptable to be both Chinese and Christian. Christianity is at last shedding its reputation, among the populace if not politicians, as an alien religion, which will change the nature of the debates and antagonisms over links with the Vatican and foreign-mission organizations.

If political relaxation and technological advance have conjoined to strengthen unregistered church growth, the third sector of academic Christianity has also seen remarkable expansion and progress over the past two decades. Academic Christianity is now a significant force within Chinese Christianity, especially for its training of students and researchers, its translation of classic and modern Christian texts into Chinese, and its role in public and governmental evaluation of Christianity both Catholic and Protestant. A final point of note here is the specious nature of much argument on the separation of church and academy. It is clear that despite an ideological desire to insist on an a-religious, neutral academy, there is considerable, and increasing, convergence in research interests, shared publishing routes and readerships, and cross-over of personnel between academy and church. Whether state-funded academic Christianity might yet play a part in ameliorating relations between church sectors through its analysis of theological debates and historical differences remains to be seen; it is an intriguing possibility.

Yang Huilin: An Academic Search for Meaning

Christian studies in secular universities, especially in the interdisciplinary studies of humanities and social sciences, have been
obviously more influential to the Chinese spirit than those in
the church-based theological seminaries, and also more influential to Chinese society from a long-range perspective than
religious practice, to be frank. So when it is contested whether
academic or collegial Christian studies can be still categorized as "theology," the true question is rather whether and
how to have a "non-religious interpretation of Christianity."
—Yang Huilin, 2011[1]

Among scholars of Christian theology and philosophy working in universities
in China are card-carrying CCP members, many of whom do not profess any
personal faith or denominational allegiance, yet whose thinking and writing on
Chinese Christianity and culture have proved significant in and beyond academia.[2] Their work is one new stream of Chinese thought, appearing in monographs and academic journals and existing alongside the writings of seminary
priests and professors and the thriving online and print publications of house-
church leaders and Christian commentators. While far from representative of
the church, their academic scholarship, which has been termed a "third force"
in China,[3] is valuable for its theological insights and assertions, as well as for the
institutional presence of its practitioners. Academics have created journals of
Christian theology, fostered translation series, and nurtured graduate students
in Christian studies, and their status as public intellectuals enables their work to
have a broad impact on society. Like the pragmatists among church members

in the 1940s, these scholars are social insiders, often with high-ranking profes-sorial or administrative posts in Beijing or Guangdong universities, and their opinions can carry an influence well beyond the Christian sector reached by church theologians. Their work, as the epigraph suggests, has often proved con-tentious, especially among the traditional guardians of theology in the church, but the sheer volume of academic articles currently being produced in Chinese Christian studies demands attention.

This chapter considers the writings of Yang Huilin (b. 1954), a key figure in the Sino-Christian theology movement and a professor of comparative litera-ture and religious studies, whose work triangulates between philosophy, literary/ critical theory, and theology. Yang's research focuses on textual interpretation, and he himself acts as an intercultural interpreter, introducing the likes of Job, medieval theology, and Western literary theory to Chinese readers and inter-preting theological methodologies for Chinese academia, while explaining Chinese Christianity to an English-speaking audience. Yang's work has played an important role in the reinterpretation of China's disparaged Christian his-tory. His writings traverse various eras and disciplines and a vast range of think-ers, demanding of readers a giddying grasp of intellectual fields. Words and the Word; interpretation, translation, the ineffable, the incomprehensible; how meaning that lies beyond words can be interpreted in words; how biblical and literary texts might mean differently—these are all sources of reflection and engagement. Recurrent questions across Yang's work condense ultimately into two: the use of language and the pursuit of meaning. These culminate in his promotion of a "Chinese Scriptural Reasoning" and call for a "nonreligious religion." This chapter first considers the question of language before exploring how the creation and explanation of a Chinese form of Scriptural Reasoning is both a natural progression of Yang's work on scriptural texts and a disruptive challenge to received views of Chinese Christianity.

For a scholar whose life quest could be summed up as this search for mean-ing, a number of paradoxes surround Yang's work. Why was a student of medi-eval theology given an appointment in a Chinese literature department? Why would a Communist Party member dedicate his life to supporting the study of Christian theology and the Christian impact in China? How did a quest for hermeneutical resolution end up in the practice of Scriptural Reasoning in China? A glance at Yang's oeuvre shows the range of his publications, which in-clude, among others, *Sin and Atonement: On the Cultural Spirit of Christianity* (罪恶与救赎: 基督教文化精神论, 1995); *The Quest for God: Faith vs. Reason* (追问上帝: 信仰与理性的辩难, 1999); *Theological Hermeneutics: Word of God and Words of Man* (神学诠释学, 2001); and two recent volumes of essays, *At the*

Boundary of Literature and Theology (在文学与神学的边界, 2012) and *China, Christianity and the Question of Culture* (in English, 2014).

Appropriately enough, given that Yang is a comparativist, his work is threaded through with its own intertextuality. *At the Boundary of Literature and Theology*, for example, shares six essays with the English collection *China, Christianity and the Question of Culture* and includes three essays from an earlier volume,[4] while the English-language collection republishes five further essays from Yang's earlier English-language collation *Christianity in China: The Work of Yang Huilin*. An interlocking and overlapping of themes, and threads of argument that build up across several essays, direct us to see Yang's work as an integrated whole. It might be packaged differently according to audience, with prefaces and section headings framing different narratives of content (so, for example, the recent Chinese-language essay collection coheres around the problem of meaning, whereas the English edition, with its foreword by David Lyle Jeffrey reevaluating the missionary legacy, circles around the binary China-Christianity), but the same key questions recur. Like a painter who returns to a canvas, Yang comes back to previous works and adds a new touch, a new layer. His essay on the book of Job, for example, reworked for *At the Boundary of Literature and Theology*,[5] gains two new opening paragraphs that set the essay in a new frame of wisdom literature and discussion on theodicy, bringing attention to the Chinese term (the justice/righteousness of God) and drawing the essay into an ongoing discussion in Yang's work of the meaning of "righteousness." The reworking of material is in part a function of a busy academic and administrative life and an ever-present demand for new material but also recalls one of the central themes of the current book: the fluidity of Chinese textual form. Yang, working between texts, translations, and commentaries, is at home in a world of multiple editions, commentaries, and textual variants, with little interest in final authorial text or urtext, a stance that has implications for biblical reading.

SINO-CHRISTIAN THEOLOGY AND ITS QUEST FOR MEANING

In his recent writings, Yang Huilin has drawn together the themes of texts and comparative literature to new theological resonances. The co-editor of a volume on Sino-Christian theology in 2006, he has promoted this new field through his institutional leadership.[6] The Sino-Christian theology movement, a broad coalition of academics working on topics related to Christianity, may be seen as a form of contextual theology for the global, post-Marxist setting of Chinese academia, providing, as its proponents hold, a critique of methodological assumptions in the humanities from the vantage point of theological studies.[7] This context is the backdrop to Yang's work, but that framework addresses the motivations of individuals involved only at the level of their desire to do social good and overlooks any personal element that may be discerned in the work of Yang and other academics studying Christianity. As in the 1930s and 1940s, a strong impetus to serve and better the nation acts as an underlying motivator for many in Sino-Christian theology, and as in the Republican era, a commitment to "truth" provides both an academic and a personal stimulus to research in the face of an uncertain social environment. In Republican times, as explored in Chapters 2 to 5, angst at the turmoil that prompted such a drive for "truth" was directed outward to imperialist aggressors. For the current generation of leaders in Chinese society and the church, whose adolescence was shaped by the Cultural Revolution, an equally, if not more chaotic environment, the iconoclasm had no external target, and the confusion and soul-searching has had to be turned inward, to China's own cultural frustrations.

The Cultural Revolution is an underexplored background factor to Sino-Christian theology and may be posited as causal in the choice of field of various scholars in the generation that includes Liu Xiaofeng, He Guanghu, and Yang Huilin.[8] Many Chinese academics now in their late fifties or early sixties spent their teenage years or early adulthood as "sent-down youth" (*zhiqing* 知青) in the countryside, making restitution for an educated upbringing or the "intellectual" background of their parents. This generation attended university or seminary once education was again accessible in the late 1970s and early 1980s, some in their twenties or even thirties by then, and pursued careers just as Zhao Ziyang's "primary stage of Socialism" embraced a shift in the CCP's role from creating a classless society to promoting economic development, paving the way for Deng Xiaoping's full-blown Socialist market economy.[9] Their experiences of family life, language, Communism, and religion have been markedly different from those of their children, especially the generation who grew up after 1989. From uniform clothing, assigned housing, and political study sessions to private property, second homes, and sending children to study abroad: the generational differences for this cohort have been as marked as for those who lived through 1911 or 1949. The multiple directions that Chinese theological thinking has taken in recent years cautions against a simplistic correlation of social background with theological output, but the parameters of thought set during the nation's drive toward Socialist, atheist utopia have shaped the questions and expressions of faith of this generation in ways that are still emerging.

The influence of a period now "thoroughly negated" still lingers, and not just in the revival of Red tourism and nostalgia-making in China.[10] It is well-documented that the parody of religiosity of the Cultural Revolution—in pictorial representation, with ubiquitous posters of Mao crowned with a halo of light; in slogans glorifying Mao the Savior of the people; and in the requirement to constant self-confession and self-abasement—alienated many of those now in their fifties or sixties from religious practice. A residual distaste for organized worship, combined with unease at the low level of priests' education, has been cited as the reason for the so-called cultural Christians' avoidance of church and liturgy.[11] Yang Huilin himself writes of the associations of confession, reading the Bible, and church rites with reporting one's thoughts, studying the works of Mao, and "seeking instructions in the morning and reporting in the evening" and suggests that the resultant distancing from Christianity "may be especially strong among middle-aged intellectuals, who retain the deepest memories of the Cultural Revolution."[12] In the intellectual realms, the experience of profound immersion in a single, rigidly enforced ideological system, during which time the praxis of that ideology all but destroyed both base and superstructure, followed by a period when the destruction could not be openly discussed or acknowledged has inevitably left traces in what individuals have chosen to study, and how. Practical constraints have also informed the questions of this generation: those engaging with academic theology within the university system came to the field not through the study of theology or biblical studies, but from cognate disciplines such as philosophy, sociology, and history and often without a working knowledge of biblical languages.[13] Even today, research funding and conferences are much more readily available for sociological or cultural studies of religion than topics associated with the Bible or confessional modes of thought.

The shadow of the Cultural Revolution may be discerned in a lifelong dissection of language and texts in Yang Huilin's work. The late 1960s and early 1970s was a time of vibrant, saturated language, when language was used to legitimize violence, to denigrate and dehumanize, when words and their meaning were dissociated and reconstituted weekly in new political slogans and formulas; it was a time when the failure to grasp a certain shade or layer of meaning might have lifelong consequences.[14] In one essay examining ethical responses to Auschwitz and the Cultural Revolution, Yang explored fanaticism, collective unconsciousness, and the frailty of human values and structures; this essay was notable for its unwillingness to exculpate anyone in the Chinese context, intellectuals included.[15] Elsewhere in his writings the explanation of interpretation is an end in itself. The theological and philosophical analyses of language had close parallels in literary responses to the chaos of the Cultural Revolution and their "language revolt," of which Yang as a literature professor would be keenly aware, from the obfuscation of the *Menglong* school of "Misty Poetry" of the late 1970s to the "root-searching" fiction of the 1980s and especially the more antirealist, avant-garde fiction of the mid-1980s, with its clear break from Maoist language and ideological codes.[16]

The search for, if not fixity, then a theoretical means of codifying how meaning functions, has a broad, outwardly social application. It is this application of theological frameworks and methodologies to the humanities more generally that has been at the center of the Sino-Christian theology movement and a reason why Yang can argue, semiseriously in the epigraph to this chapter, that academic theology has done more for China than seminaries. But such a steadfast quest for meaning is inherently multilayered, and in Yang's work on language, hermeneutics, and the meaning of religious texts, we see the social, the intellectual, and the spiritual all in operation in the search for understanding. To analyze meaning in non-Marxist literary and theological systems was an astute and subtle form of constructive political protest (and one that might be contrasted with the state-inclining theological program of TSPM theologians, for example). From Hannah Arendt to Vaclav Havel, some of the most trenchant studies of revolutionary language in totalitarian societies have come from those with inside experience. Yang Huilin's language is always subtle, removed from any potentially direct political criticism—from which it derives its force within China's intellectual-political system—and mostly directed forward to the theoretical structures of meaning-making, not back to recent history. A notable aspect to Yang's reflection through different fields of Christian inquiry and attempts to theorize Christian thought within the Chinese academy is its positive engagement: the constant imperative to dialogue and to understanding.

LANGUAGE, INTERPRETATION, AND THE LOSS OF CERTAINTY

The quest to understand what understanding means—and so how we read texts, communicate with each other, and speak of God—entrains questions of language, culture, and philosophy. Yang opens the preface to *At the Boundary of Literature and Theology* with a question that Jacques Derrida's life has bequeathed: was his career spent "in dispelling meaning, or in searching for meaning"?[17] Searching for, defining, and questioning meaning is, Yang claims, a central thread in the humanities in the West—the trajectory of which has seen the certainty and objectivity of meaning placed ever more in doubt. While suspicion of the certainty of meaning began with the ancients, the accumulation of questions has proved more acute in the present; indeed, argues Yang, the contemporary "crisis of faith" is actually a crisis of meaning: this loss of certainty and objectivity. The move allows Yang to entwine religious and philosophical questions and to suggest that the problems Christianity must now deal with are no longer just matters of faith, but primarily ones of meaning.[18] In a series of essays on Slavoj Žižek, Martin Heidegger, and Derrida and on the value of theology in the humanities and in literary theory, Yang explores theological methodology as a way to approach and determine meaning. He teases out the hairbreadth of semantic space where theology and literature illuminate each other and where a series of "inter-ness" or "in-between-nesses" in event and language allow for an escape from the impasse of uncertainty and show how the Christian legacy can profit the humanities today as it "affirms the absolute in its fragility, reconstructs the subject in its vulnerability, and aids us in our pursuit of the Real beyond its deadlock."[19]

For Yang, the question of language is the root of this quest for understanding. If the ineffable is the premise of all speaking, the fundamental question for theologians and scholars remains: how can the divine Word be lodged in human words? The relation of the paradox of language to meaning fascinates Yang. Before discussing Barth's aphorism that ministers must speak of God, but as humans cannot, he writes, "The basic issues in hermeneutics emerge from the finitude of human beings and language, and this finitude can be fully opened only in the interpretation of a religious text."[20] Yang points out in an essay on the Chinese Union Bible translation of 1919 that this question constitutes pretty much the whole history of Christian thought. Exploration of language takes various forms in Yang's essays and includes such questions as historic language use, how to theorize dialogue, and the church as a community of discourse. In a study of language choice in missionary-founded universities in China, Yang reflects on how language "not only transmits ideas but at the same time itself stands for ideas and has its own values," and how, in the educational setting of early twentieth-century China, it reflected proponents' understandings of the relationship between faith and culture.[21] Yang contrasts St. John's University, Shanghai, with Shandong Christian University (later Cheloo University). Students protested and went on strike in both: against instruction in English at St. John's and in favor of instruction in English at Shandong. Some missionaries feared the secularization that English would bring, while others saw it as the medium for higher learning; events overtook both when English ceded to Chinese nationally as the language of progress and revolution.

The power dynamics in systems of discourse are as relevant to contemporary interreligious dialogue as to tertiary education in Republican China, and in another essay on Buddhist-Christian dialogue, Yang considers how different understandings of dialogue are determined by different systems of discourse. Taking Raimon Panikkar's five different attitudes to religious dialogue as a base, Yang establishes how human existence is itself a form of dialogic relationship and that recognition of the other is necessary to one's own being; he then argues that "dialogue" is not ultimately among or between religions but "necessarily oriented 'within the religion,'"[22] facilitating an understanding of the limitations of the self at the same time as it activates the self. An examination of two different types of dialogue between Christianity and Buddhism and two between Buddhism and Christianity, as espoused by Paul Knitter and David Tracy, and Sheng Yen and Masao Abe, respectively, shows how very different religious assumptions and interpretations of the terms used for dialogue and for describing such elements as the self, existence, and the purpose of relationship shape the interaction—and just how difficult it is for each partner in dialogue "to grasp the other side's spirituality from within, without imposing its own ontological and axiological categories," as Masao Abe puts it.[23] Yang's rather bleak conclusion that noble objectives and values are often themselves the source of conflict, and his questioning of whether bigotries can ever be set aside in dialogue around a genuine round table, does not bode well for an embrace of Scriptural Reasoning but shows how a decade of probing and theorizing the nature of religious communication prepared the ground for the attempt.

One of the most important threads of discussion on language in Yang examines the issue of "Chinese-language Christianity's cultural identity."[24] As Yang writes, although Christianity plays an important role in religious belief in China, the question of its legitimacy has "never been truly resolved."[25] Yang describes a three-stage historic assimilation of Christianity in China, first via Buddhist terms and language concepts during the period of the Church of the East (the "Nestorian" church) in China, second via Confucian concepts and terminology in Ming and Qing China, and third in the period after 1919 via everyday experience and the language of quotidian modern life.

Language, contextualization, and interpretation are inextricably linked. Yang explores in various essays the dangers of too much contextualization in any period, or extreme or selective inculturation: the early use of Buddhist terminology for concepts like "Christ" or "kingdom" to the point where Christianity failed to gain an independent status and Christian scriptures were included in Buddhist corpuses; the "ethicization" of Christianity in late imperial China where the focus on morality enabled Christianity to gain ground and adherents but ultimately limited it to the sphere of morals and raised the question of why anyone should bother to convert; and the structural assimilation of Christianity in contemporary China that has impaired its ability to critique society and to operate beyond popular modes of faith or received ideological systems.[26] For Yang, the answer lies in Chinese Christianity setting its own theological framework, making its own judgments about the integrity of the tradition and what is paradigmatic about the tradition (in Francis Schüssler Fiorenza's terms) — and quite possibly in finding outside resources for that task, along the lines of Dietrich Bonhoeffer's "nonreligious" discussion of God, for an era characterized by the absence of God.[27]

The importance of the role of translation in the cultural identity of Chinese Christianity is clear. The tension between rendering a language intelligible in another and maintaining a sense of the difference inherent in the source language is, for Yang as for the Victorian missionaries, not just a matter of translation theory but one of theological meaning.[28] In the same manner in which some translation theorists have imploded the notion of transparency, or the "invisibility" of the translator, and have called for a "hermeneutic of resistance" that allows the foreign to remain different — arguing that the attempt to find functional equivalence in the target language masks domestication processes involved[29] — the Sino-Christian theologian Liu Xiaofeng has also opposed theological indigenization, arguing that China should not tame and naturalize Christianity but defend it as foreign, as foolishness.[30] For Yang Huilin, the questions that centuries of translators mulled and argued over — how to render scripture literally into Chinese, the limits of paraphrase in creating a text acceptable to Chinese, whether to adopt the language codes for the divine from Buddhist, Daoist, or Confucian scriptures — were spectacularly reordered with the 1919 Chinese Union version edition of the Bible. If the missionaries' translations through the end of the nineteenth century had done much to "achieve the absolute disparity between 'human words' and 'divine Word'"[31] — and they themselves were aware of this, still hoping for the advent of a Chinese translator of the Bible able to write in good modern Chinese — the ground shifted with the adoption of the modern Chinese language (*baihua* 白话). The codes of modern Chinese allowed writers to distance their thought, should they wish, from Confucian language and connotations: as Yang writes, the "rift" in the existing language carrier that modern Chinese brought "gave unprecedented hermeneutical room to a heterogeneous culture" and allowed for a Bible translation that "distanced itself in a fundamental manner from the semiotic shell of the original culture."[32] The accommodation, or indigenization, was no longer to existing textual and interpretative frameworks, and the use of everyday, oral language allowed the Bible to speak directly to people's lived experiences.[33]

The Union Bible, which is still the most widespread Bible text available in China today, is clearly "foreign" in context (a significant proportion of the text, especially of the Hebrew scriptures, is underlined, to denote proper names to Chinese readers), but Yang's insight here suggests that the revolutionary new language register introduced in the 1910s allowed the Bible for the first time *not* to be transposed into a Chinese cultural context. As Yang notes, underlining the strength of the link between translation and theology, new language systems permit and encourage new ways of thinking; current Chinese theology is an outgrowth of the Union translation. The stripping away of the associations of classical language terms with China's own cultural meanings ushered in new possibilities for a theology working within modern lived life, and not just in tandem with traditional culture. Theological hermeneutics, concludes Yang, is not meant to eliminate the distance between human words and the divine Word but to establish a relation between self and other through "absolute heterogeneity." Yang gives credit for this insight to the work of the Union translators as they sought to create a new language for the Bible.

SCRIPTURAL REASONING WITH CHINESE CHARACTERISTICS

For more than a decade, Yang Huilin has been laboring to bring comparative literature and religious studies, along with sinology, into closer dialogue and interaction. The nexus of texts as scripture and literature, together with religious modes of reading those texts, brought Yang to Scriptural Reasoning and to the development of a Chinese form of the practice. "Scriptural Reasoning" developed in the United States and United Kingdom as a movement to bring together followers of Judaism, Islam, and Christianity in academic and non-academic contexts to discuss and share interpretations of sacred scriptures.[34] "Hospitality" is a keynote in this practice of co-reading, which expanded out of Jewish Textual Reasoning in the 1990s: participants speak from within their own faith perspective on the given text for each session and practice a "deep listening" toward others; there is no center of authority and no aspiration toward consensus. Friendship and dialogue form the foundations for the scripture reading sessions, which have tended to strengthen individuals' faiths and serve as a locus for their developing identity, as ideas and resistances from outside traditions are generative within their own.[35] The aim of the movement has been one of "improving the quality of disagreement," which as Ben Quash notes may be harder for Muslims and Christians than for Jews, who are more used to arguing over their sacred texts. Scriptural Reasoning is characterized, suggests Quash, by the "interrogative mood," an open-ended hypothesizing beyond the common strictures of one's own interpretive tradition or academic discipline.[36]

It is easy to see why Scriptural Reasoning should appeal in a contemporary Chinese setting. It theorizes reading practices and shared reading, considers the materiality of texts and their signifying relations in interpretation, and is tied to an academic setting; it is both a way of thinking and interpreting and an ethical activity, a social practice.[37] Scriptural Reasoning can mediate between academic and nonacademic interpretations and modes of reading and between disciplines: for example, between "confessional" theology and "neutral" religious studies, or between philologists and classical studies scholars concentrating on the "original" meanings, and theologians or ethicists seeking contemporary or applied meanings. The encouragement to dialogue fits well with the recent Chinese emphasis on harmonious society (*hexie shehui* 和谐社会). The use of scholarship in the service of a broader human flourishing echoes the vision of Chinese intellectuals earlier in the twentieth century and chimes with more recent criticism of the rote learning demanded by the *gaokao* 高考, the university entrance exam. As David Ford notes, "apart from the theological basis and dimension" (a significant caveat!), the features of Scriptural Reasoning relate well to classical Chinese interpretive activities of *jingxue* 经学, or study of the Confucian canon.[38]

The institutional location of theological thought is a question that Yang Huilin and others, including particularly Zhuo Xinping at CASS, have spent time reconsidering over the past few years, as political ideology and directives on religious faith from central authorities have shifted. For Yang, university theology is in essence a theorizing of theology itself. The Chinese model of academic engagement with theology developed during the Deng era has parallels with the one in the United States, where "theology" is mostly relegated to seminary study and "religious studies" is undertaken in universities, but the separation has been more extreme in China, for ideological and structural reasons.[39] The study of religion within universities has only gradually evolved from a narrow ideological model to some acceptance of the role of religion in society and its amenity to philosophical or social science research; a further openness to subdisciplines like church history is still ongoing. In his Cadbury lectures in 2013, which comment on the Chinese case, David Ford argues that the institutional presence of both religious studies and theology makes for the best inquiry. Ford defines the field of theology and religious studies, notably for the Chinese case, as "the pursuit, through a range of academic disciplines, of questions of meaning, truth, practice, goodness and beauty raised by, between and about the religions."[40] Ford's interpretation and lyrical defense of the integrated system in many British universities show one reason why Scriptural Reasoning, with its possibility of cross-over between faith and reason, might appeal in the current Chinese structure, where it can balance the "cut and dried indicatives and imperatives" of academic discourse with more "unsettling interrogatives" and "experimental hypothesizing."[41]

Ever since a Chinese version of Scriptural Reasoning first gained traction a decade or so ago, commentators have queried whether the concept makes any sense in a Chinese context.[42] At the outset, the skeptics do seem to have a strong suit: for Chinese to take part in Scriptural Reasoning via Confucian texts on the same basis as other participants would require the acceptance of jing (经, canonical texts) as scripture and of the practice of reading such texts as a religious act, and would seem to demand a comparable level of identification with the text, its meaning, and its place in believers' spiritual and moral lives as for other religious participants. The case is much easier to make for Chinese Buddhists and Daoists, but it is the Chinese (Confucian) classics that have been the focus of much of the discussion, including Yang Huilin's work. As a practice to be theorized rather than theory to be enacted, Scriptural Reasoning throws up an odd paradox in the Chinese case: in a system that has heavily valorized theory, a chaotic or unpredictable practice whose grounds are resistant to ultimate theorizing has been used as a testing pit for textual and religious meaning.[43]

The early experience of Scriptural Reasoning practice in North America and Europe gives some pointers as to how a Chinese movement may develop and differ. As Peter Ochs and William Stacy Johnson describe, one of the reasons the practice was initiated was to rebut Western media claims that the three scriptures involved followed conflicting paths of devotion; another was so that the modern academy was not the only player involved in defining interreligious study. All three Abrahamic religions have undergone interpretive crises in recent decades in relating to changing society and to other traditions. The "interpretive hospitality" of Scriptural Reasoning provides a space where the more sharply defined boundaries of modern discursive thought, which have brought new ways of defining self and other, can be challenged or recast.[44] Is the motivation for Scriptural Reasoning in China similarly a question of interreligious harmony and of the public image of religion, or a question of the location of religious study, or something else? One question that the Chinese experience raises is what difference a pluralistic religious frame might make to a model of Scriptural Reasoning developed for agnate religions, especially where traditions are not distinct and when dialogue is intrareligious as well as interreligious, as "Confucian Christians" and Christians in Buddhist households live their daily lives in an ongoing mode of interreligious reasoning. Another question arises as to how Scriptural Reasoning might offer a new form of praxis for religious dialogue in China where sharp, and often artificial, delineations of religions have been fostered by official definitions of "five religions" in China and the segregating effects of specified locations for religious services.

Ford identifies four innovations in Chinese Scriptural Reasoning: the addition of three "Eastern" religions, a combining with comparative theology, the role of Confucianism as a player, and the disciplinary setting of comparative literature.[45] The first question above, about religious pluralism, is addressed by one of the four innovations, as developed by You Bin at the Institute for Comparative Scripture and Inter-religious Dialogue at Minzu University: combining Scriptural Reasoning with comparative theology so that participants are competent with, and can speak from, more than one religious tradition. This interior dialogue between religions is taken up in another innovation associated with Yang Huilin: the location of Scriptural Reasoning within comparative literature. Here, the dialogue may happen within the translators and interpreters of the Confucian canon, and this innovation entrains the third, the role of Confucianism as a textual/religious dialogue partner in Chinese Scriptural Reasoning. Several of Yang's essays on Scriptural Reasoning focus on James Legge, the great missionary translator of the Chinese classics and first professor of Chinese at Oxford University. Through studies of Legge's work, Yang sets out to answer the questions of the skeptics: whether *jing* can be regarded as scripture and why literary texts are apposite for Scriptural Reasoning; whether the moral and spiritual formation of Confucianism is akin to that within (other) religions; and how a Chinese intervention may provide answers to important questions of how we interpret texts, and what the interpretation means.

A SCOTTISH MISSIONARY AND INTERTEXTUAL SCRIPTURAL REASONING

If Abrahamic Scriptural Reasoning began with theists and theologians, Chinese Scriptural Reasoning has been developed by textual theorists and comparativists. In one essay on Legge, Yang begins by setting out the Chinese side of the relation between literature and religion, as a basis for a comparative and interactive reading with Western theology and literature. He starts not from a collective co-reading of scripture, but from an exploration of the links between literature and religion, since, as he argues, any Scriptural Reasoning using the Chinese classics will necessarily be interdisciplinary. The reason for this lies in the classics themselves. Knowledge of the *Liu Yi* 六艺, the six classics attributed to Confucius's editorship that became the basis for education and the selection of government officials for more than a millennium in China, was intended to lead to a fully rounded, moral human being, with the essence of the learning focusing on "moral behavior, self-cultivation, and metaphysical thinking, so that the *Dao* (道, wisdom), *jiao* (教, teaching), and *xing* (行, behavior) in one person can simultaneously grow and become integrated, which might be something like *animus et factum*."[46] This single form of training—in the classics—served to nurture both moral formation and literary scholarship, and the integration of scholarship with moral formation is central, Yang implies, to the association of the classics with scriptures. Other links between literature and religion include training in philology and the arts of grammar and logic as precursors to reading sacred texts, in the Chinese case just as in the medieval liberal arts, and the fact that spontaneous composition of poetry (following years of study) was frequently seen as akin to religious enlightenment.[47] Another affinity comes from the methodology of each discipline. Yang reiterates that both literary and religious studies are inherently comparative in nature, based on the principle embodied in a phrase he is fond of quoting from Goethe via the German sinologist Max Müller: "He who knows one knows none." As a new comparative and interdisciplinary process of reading scripture takes shape with the inclusion of Confucian texts, writes Yang, "we may find ourselves being confronted with a boundary-crossing 'liturgy,' in which the presence of Truth might be identified in various ways."[48]

James Legge (1815–1897) emerges as a critical figure in Yang's configuration of a Chinese Scriptural Reasoning. As Norman Giradot's door-stopping study of Legge explores, the Scottish pastor, missionary, teacher, comparativist, "cross-country pilgrim," heretic (?), and translator was at the forefront of the new human sciences of comparative religion and of sinology in the late nineteenth century.[49] For Yang Huilin, Legge provides a model of inter-interpretation and a template for an intercultural Scriptural Reasoning. In Yang's view, Legge's translation and interpretation of the Chinese classics into English and for a non-Chinese audience was itself an act of Scriptural Reasoning. Legge, like Max Müller, sacralized the Confucian texts through reading them as "Sacred Scriptures,"[50] or, in Yang's terms, by regarding Western and Chinese "sacred books" as "mutually inclusive and illustrative."[51]

Legge's way of approaching the classics is perhaps best exemplified by his translation of and commentary on the *Yijing* (易经 Yî King, I-Ching), the most arcane of the classics, whose base text is a series of sixty-four trigrams and whose "peculiarity" of style made it "the most difficult of all the Confucian classics to present in an intelligible version."[52] Legge acknowledged that he had let his translation sit for twenty years until he could give it the attention necessary "to make it reveal its secrets." The key to his grasp of the text's meaning was a moment of inspiration when Legge realized, contra received scholarship, that he had to separate the commentaries from text to understand it and that Confucius could not have been the author of various appendices.[53] The key to his translation was an equally significant breakthrough, a fundamental shift in the concept of rendering Chinese into English. Whereas in his earlier translation of the *Yijing* text in 1854 Legge had endeavored "to be as concise in my English as the original Chinese was," this rendered the version "all but unintelligible" in English. The clue was something Legge had already subconsciously acted on in other translations, "namely, that the written characters of the Chinese are not representations of words, but symbols of ideas, and that the combination of them in composition is not a representation of what the writer would say, but of what he thinks."[54] (This is a linguistic as well as a metaphysical point, since classical Chinese is effectively a written language, not a transcript of speech, although the divergence between the oral and written forms was much greater in Legge's time than in Confucius's time.) A translation for Legge was now a meeting of minds, rather than of languages, which meant that, in terms of the classics, "there is not so much an interpretation of the characters employed by the writer as a participation of his thoughts; — there is the seeing of mind to mind."[55] Legge drew support in this passage for his version of translation theory (and all that it implies in terms of a contextual theology) from the philosopher Mencius, whose rule for interpreting the old Zhou poems was "we must try with our thoughts to meet the scope of a sentence, and then we shall apprehend it."[56]

Elsewhere in Legge's translations and his own commentary we see the principles of his work spelled out, principles on which Yang Huilin draws in his more recent construct of a Chinese Scriptural Reasoning. Legge draws out for readers points that he is interested in, such as the principles of benevolent rule in the minds of early philosophers. On occasion he interpolates his own political commentary, such as when he praises Mencius's exposure of the errors of those who would advocate a classless society ("the conduct of government should be in the hands of a lettered class").[57] Legge is keen to point out to foreign audiences the merits of Chinese philosophy, commenting that Mencius "does not need to hide a diminished head" alongside contemporaries Plato, Aristotle, and Zeno. He is willing to concede Chinese cultural superiority where he perceives it, such as in the matter of government involvement in education ("only within a century has Education assumed in Europe the definiteness and importance with which it appeared to Mencius here in China two thousand years ago"),[58] but he is also forward in his criticism, commenting, for example, that the rule of the ancients "affords but poor footing compared with the Word of God," although "still it is to them the truth."[59] As Yang notes, Legge makes occasional cross-correlations for readers to biblical or familiar texts ("his words are akin to those of Paul")[60] as well as in the moral sphere. In some areas, Legge reveals his blinkers, being wont to judge morality in nineteenth-century Christian terms. He censures Mencius severely, for example, for advising one king that as long as he regulated his love of women, war, and money, such things would not interfere with his governance.[61] Legge defends his subjects, however, from what he feels are erroneous interpretations of Chinese thinking among fellow Europeans or Americans. He discusses at length the case of human nature, and, in an important intervention in debates, nuances the general view that Mencius believes human nature to be good, by comparison with the views of the moral philosopher Bishop (Joseph) Butler. While arguing that Mencius's views were "defective rather than erroneous" and that the Chinese notion that sages could and did achieve perfection is a doctrine that "wants an element which Revelation supplies,"[62] Legge defends Mencius against detractors who had simply not read the texts carefully enough. (For Legge, Mencius's position is that the goodness of human nature is an ideal rather than a contradiction of original sin, in that humans are constituted for the good.)

If the above gives some sense of the mechanics of Legge's mode of reading and inter-interpreting, Yang addresses Legge both at this level of textual interpretation and as a meta-narrative of cultural identity and certainty. For Yang, Legge's translations and the hermeneutics of Scriptural Reasoning both pivot around the Mencian phrase quoted above: "we must try with our thoughts to meet the scope of a sentence, and then we shall apprehend it."[63] Yang Huilin heralds this phrase as a "core principle of scriptural interpretation" for Legge, serving as a "bridge" between two different conceptual systems and providing "rich resources for scriptural reasoning between China and the West." While commending Legge for "interpreting scripture by scripture," that is, by other early classics and their commentaries, Yang argues that throughout, Legge's "Christian stance remains persistent and clear." Yang suggests that his Christian preunderstanding governs not just Legge's introductions and commentary to his translations, but the parameters of translation also. In his essay "The Possibilities and Values of 'Scriptural Reasoning' Between China and the West," Yang takes three example translations of words or phrases and discusses in detail their meaning, interpretation, and theological resonances.[64] The essay forms a practical outworking of what Yang intends by Scriptural Reasoning with the Chinese classics: the possibility of "mutual interpretation with Christian culture."[65]

The terms Yang explores include "perfect virtue" or "benevolence" for *ren* (仁) and "reciprocity" instead of "forgiveness" for *shu* (恕), Tao for *Dao* (道), and the phrases "sheathing the light" (韜光) and "the use of emptiness" (虛用). As Yang notes, Legge will comment on some statements; qualify others; make

indirect connections to other texts, both classical and biblical; and on occasion when he approves of a text, or believes the logic will be self-evident to
his Christian audience, leave the text unadorned, as in *Dao de jing* 63:1.[66] In
some instances, which are critical to Yang's sense of how Scriptural Reasoning
might work in the study of the classics, Yang posits that Legge's understanding
of certain passages comes from recognition of parallels in Christian scripture
(Yang gives the example of Chapter 7 of the *Dao de jing*, "the sage puts his
own person last, and yet it is found in the foremost place," and its resonances
with Mark 10:43–45). We can see from Yang's own play of resonances, links,
and inspirations in the texts how he anticipates a textual Scriptural Reasoning
working. The links may or may not carry weight or ring true for everyone, but
the propositions and suppositions can be seen as part of that "experimental
hypothesizing" that is a hallmark of traditional Scriptural Reasoning. Yang's
explanation of his assumption that Legge makes a link between "an empty pair
of bellows" in *Dao de jing* 5 and the kenotic "emptying" in Philippians 2:7 via
the emptiness of a vessel, for example, seems potentially off kilter because there
is no "vessel" in the Philippians passage; the "emptying" metaphor refers to taking the form of a (bond) servant, and not a metaphoric bodily vessel. However,
the commonality in the images that Yang raises—of the emptiness not being a
state of powerlessness in either case—is helpful and provides a good example
of how such an intertextual reading might provoke a fruitful dialogue on the
understanding of power and authority in both religious traditions.[67]

   In the first example term given above, Yang argues that Legge selectively
translates *ren* according to context, so in *Analects* 12.2 when Confucius replies
to the question "what is perfect virtue?" with the Golden Rule ("what you do
not want done to yourself, do not do to others"), the interpretation of *ren* here
as "perfect virtue" is intended to present a correlative to the Christian Golden
Rule. Likewise, Yang argues that if Legge translates *ren* as "perfect virtue," then
shu as an explanation of the Golden Rule has to be "reciprocity," not the more
common rendering of "forgiveness" because otherwise it would end up a divine
not human prerogative. The logic is a little convoluted here, and while it is easy
to agree with Yang that Legge did not see any fundamental difference between
the (positive) Christian version of the Golden Rule and the (negative) Confucian one, to conclude that what Legge focused on was "to make Confucius'
teaching correlative to Jesus Christ's law" and that his attention to shades of
meaning evinces an "attempt to bridge the gap between Chinese and Western
Cultures" may overstate the case.[68] (One could equally well argue that Legge's
exact deployment of terms was an interpretation, not a bridging, of the gap
and that his attention to shades of meaning precisely directs the gaze toward

the differences between terms. "Perfect virtue," for example, does not appear as a phrase in the King James Version and does not readily connote the highest Christian command to love; the phrase itself would seem to point to a Chinese concept, and Legge's choice of the term over "benevolence" here arguably reflects the degree of excellence implied in the question.)[69]

Legge's decision to transliterate not translate Tao/Dao is interesting. He had a minor role in the translation of the Delegates' version of the Bible in the late 1840s and early 1850s; although split over the "principles of translation" and need for closeness to the source text, the translators did advocate retaining certain target language terms, such as the ineffable Dao (道 Tao) for the embodied Word or Logos. Yang Huilin describes this move as "incredible," in as much as it was foreign missionaries not native Chinese speakers who made the association. Legge came to be firmly positioned on the side of his London Missionary Society predecessors Walter Medhurst and William Milne, who valued acceptability in Chinese and Chinese idiom over a more literal rendering—a position denounced by many missionaries with strong views on the Bible but lesser language expertise.[70] For Yang, Legge's knowledge and interpretation of the classics and texts like the *Dao de jing* show his deep familiarity with the Chinese heritage and, time and again, prove superior to modern translations. Drawing an inference from this in terms of Scriptural Reasoning, Yang concurs with David Ford that there is no "native speaker" in wisdom-seeking engagements and that diverse voices help with an understanding both of the other and of one's own scriptures and tradition.[71]

Moving from the textual to the conceptual, Yang reminds that interfaith dialogue arose long before modern scholarship, in texts like Müller's *Sacred Books of the East* series. The task for Chinese scholars now, in Yang's opinion, is to diagnose the motives and subjects of Western academic studies and then dismantle their Western discourse so as to be able to recognize their own standpoints. The gain of Scriptural Reasoning is its creation of a real decentering. There are parallels between sinology and theology, suggests Yang: both need, and both are unable, to talk about their subject (God/China).[72] The questioning of the subject position, however, and the decentering of all discussants, and of "-centric" logic itself, rejects the notion that any occupies a central position. Yang weaves between Barth's "let God be God" and Derrida's "tout autre est tout autre" in a discussion whose frame is the history of readings of "China" and "the West." Scriptural Reasoning here becomes a model not just for dialogue between theology and religious studies, or an interreligious discourse, but a model for intercultural dialogue, a means of going beyond the Western projection of China. The methodological gain of Scriptural Reasoning in getting rid of the "discourse logic of the 'constitutive subject' and the 'projected others'"[73] becomes for Yang a way of obviating the history of orientalism—a theoretically informed response to, and continuing engagement with, Christianity, while implicitly acknowledging the history of the one-sided, imperialist exchange. (It is worth pausing to note that this hospitable move was facilitated by the original reaching out to and into the Chinese classics by Legge, a missionary to China, and the implications of a mission of listening as well as preaching.)

As the translator, according to Mencius, has to comprehend the scope of an entire passage and not allow a single term or sentence to do violence to the whole, so the hermeneutical circle, the subject of Yang's essay "Scriptural Reasoning and the Hermeneutical Circle," has been since Aristotle a matter of relating the parts to the whole. Part of the appeal of Scriptural Reasoning to Yang is undoubtedly its potential for theorizing literature and subjectivity. Yang returns to Peter Ochs's insight that Scriptural Reasoning aims neither to produce certain answers to a question nor to reach any final conclusions and so introduces "something otherwise unachievable within the hermeneutical and epistemological frameworks of the modern university."[74] Yang considers Ochs's framework of a hierarchy of meanings, where an initial indeterminacy of meaning cedes to an interpretive meaning within a particular reading group, whose determinate claims are valid only for that group and in that space; where any determinate "meaning" that presents is always that of the "plain sense" interpretation of scripture for a single interpreter. But if indeterminacy is a source of strength in Scriptural Reasoning, and a determinate reading can come only from a specific time and place—a given gathering of people involved in co-reading scripture, where the determinative reading relates to the performance—how is this still "determinacy," asks Yang, and where does it leave universality?

Yang's own preference is to focus on the theoretical logic of achieving determinacy, rather than to attempt to point to any specific determinate meaning. For Yang, the "impossibility" of Christian theology provides a way to resolve the paradox, through an acceptance of the "impossible possibility" of Paul Tillich's "Theological Circle," which no one can ever escape because all interpretation, inductive or deductive, starts out from a priori assumptions, where every theologian is always ever in faith and doubt, inside and outside the theological circle. Linking this line of thought back to language and the meeting of minds, Yang points to medieval exegesis as an attempt to "escape from language through words"[75] and to theological logic as possessing a unique ability to "present its 'possibility' through 'impossibility,' to define 'determinacy' through 'indeterminacy,'" and to hold in tension a similar perfection in different instantiations.[76] The need to define not determinacy but "the definition of the 'determined' hermeneutical logic" brings Yang back to his starting point: a discussion of the foundation of theology as the end of theology. The awareness of human finitude that pushes theologians always to the meaning of understanding itself gives the discipline, for Yang, an interpretative advantage in the humanities, and one from which other subjects in the academy could learn.

The awareness of the finitude of human beings and language brings the discussion across several essays back to the unifying question of language. If, as the work of Legge and other translators suggests, there are some concepts—like the range of meanings for the Chinese term "heaven," for example—that cannot be directly translated, this implies that there are thoughts that can be fully grasped only in a given language, and that the grasp of God is therefore also culturally limited. For Yang, one of the radical strengths of Christianity is the disconnect between its language base and its written expression, between Jesus's Aramaic and the Greek New Testament, that "natural chasm" between scripture and the Word, which has forced Christian thinkers throughout the ages to acknowledge the nature of God as wholly other.[77] This remains the effective starting point, and end point, of theoretical discussion about, and between, readers of *jing*.

CONCLUSIONS

Yang Huilin has written of the value of Christianity outside of religious confession lying in the methodology of its search for the truth.[78] As this chapter has explored, Yang pursues this methodology wherever he finds it—among theologians, philosophers, and poststructuralists; in literary criticism, linguistics, and translation theory—to broach questions of how we can know and speak; how we can know and speak of God in different cultures and transmit that knowledge through writing in different languages; and what this exploration means for other forms of inquiry into the truth. Yang's development of "nonreligious religion" and of the theoretical basis for a Chinese Scriptural Reasoning can be seen as modes of mediation, between Christian and non-Christian cultures, between the gospel and Chinese culture, between an atheist or Marxist academic worldview and a theistic methodology. For Yang, Christianity has to make sense in Chinese, has to make its meaning make sense, and has to be useful to meaning-making in China.

The writings of academics studying Christianity or engaging with academic theology in China intersect with the church at a tangent. They help the Christian church through their historical research into what the church has been, in the theoretical articulation of what the church and its theology are, and in reasoned insight into what the church might become. These academic writings are also an important means of disseminating a better understanding internationally of the scope of the Chinese church. Yang Huilin's engagement with Scriptural Reasoning presents a rich example of cross-over between historical textual study and theoretical grappling with a contemporary religious practice in a Chinese cultural setting that has potential for church development.

Questions remain as to whether the Chinese innovations in Scriptural Reasoning, (especially the theoretical positionings of Yang Huilin) stretch the parameters of the project beyond its elastic point. They also offer further commentary on the relationship between church and academic practices. The commonality that Yang establishes between literary and religious texts in the term *jing* allows him to bring a literary classic to the table on a par with religious classics and to establish a form of textual reasoning between the two. But is this comparative literature dialogue anything more than just an academized version of the personal religious engagement of Scriptural Reasoning? What sense is there in which Chinese participants are bringing texts that are personally formative? Is what is being gained, or brought to others, being brought solely at the level of methodological insight, or with the anticipation of spiritual gain? If Chinese Scriptural Reasoning is essentially an attempt to put the meaning-making of *jingxue* (Chinese textual study of the classics) alongside scriptures, a variant of Zhuo Xinping's "self-realization through Chinese cultural identity,"[79] is this just another secularizing, Confucian-Christian move in the manner of 1930s scholars? Is the aim to take Chinese participants deeper into their own scriptures, to live as better Confucians, or is text study itself the moralizing force, a vehicle for introspection and self-reflection, in the manner of ancient Chinese text study—in which case it is essentially an a-religious practice and an example of the "overinculturation" that Yang dismisses in Ming Christianity? How exactly does what Yang describes differ from translation studies, in terms of methodology and outcome?

The intrareading of James Legge that Yang proposes diverges from the original (Abrahamic) version of Scriptural Reasoning in some fundamental ways. The face-to-face encounter and engagement with the other here becomes an individual, not communal affair, an encounter with a text, not a living human who can argue back and shape a new narrative. The danger in facing an unfamiliar text alone is that we allow it to mean what we want it to mean,[80] a tension played out in Yang's study of Legge's recourse to the Bible to interpret the *jing*. While Yang discusses this possibility obliquely in his essay "Inculturation or Contextualization"—describing the extreme or selective inculturation of 1930s ethical responses to Christianity, which were toned down to the point of no-difference with Confucianism, and the tendency to find oneself reproduced in the new—the potential loss to a text-only version of Scriptural Reasoning is underexplored.

Legge's own writings, introductions, and commentaries on his work show that he followed the same path of textual and philological work as the Chinese scholars and ancients whose texts he was translating. Again: does this make the Chinese Scriptural Reasoning that Yang is proposing just a modern version of traditional Chinese textual and philological study? And does what Legge understood himself to be doing in his translations matter to the debate? The question ties in with the decentering that Yang places at the center of the hermeneutical gain of Scriptural Reasoning. But is the method really, then, a decentering? or is it more a finding of that which resembles one's own in the other? Yang speaks of the scriptures and the classics as "inter-illustrating and inter-interpreting" each other, and of Louis Althusser and Alain Badiou, whose subject and thought, respectively, always required decentering; but the question of whether we can have a truly dialogic relationship with a text is surprisingly undertheorized. The question has a practical answer, however: Chinese Scriptural Reasoning, when modeled on the Abrahamic version of roundtable discussion of scriptural texts, clearly works in practice. In his reflections on the experience of "Six-Text" Scriptural Reasoning in China, David Ford describes the same experience of argument, understanding, and laughter as in Scriptural Reasoning sessions elsewhere in the world.[81]

One of the things that Chinese thinking can bring to Scriptural Reasoning is a fluidity of interpretation. In Yang's estimation, the lack of fixity of interpretation is seemingly more of a problem for (Western) sacred texts: that there is "no permanent interpretation of the *Shi jing* has little impact for Chinese intellectuals, but for sacred texts and their exegetical tradition, such a situation is intolerable and a paradox that must be solved."[82] Citing Legge's ability to change over time in his opinions on Confucianism as he read and understood more, Yang argues for a "fluid dogmatics" and for the dynamic process of the word "religion" itself. The fluidity of texts, of human identity, and of religion itself are all linked. Yang associates the "fluid variety of possibilities" of religion with the "coming into being" of the self through interpretation, the experience that Legge and other translators of the classics underwent of interpreting the self. Scriptural Reasoning, concludes Yang, in line with Abrahamic reasoners, "reconstitutes the self-understanding of each tradition."[83] But it also sheds light on how Chinese theology reflects traditional Chinese textual practice in its patterns of thinking. Yang Huilin's writings share with many Sino-Christian and Chinese church theologians a propensity to what may seem to be random textual connections. In one sequence, for example, where Yang is considering Legge's use of "reciprocity" as a translation of *shu* (恕), he moves from first president of the European Council Herman Van Rompuy's (twenty-first century) notion of "strategic partnership" to John 14:23 and back to Legge and Zhu Xi's (twelfth-century) commentary on the *Analects*. The model here is a textual web of association around a keyword—not a linear thought line developing all of the possibilities of that thought, but a text line, thinking through all the associations of that term in texts. Those who profess surprise that China has not developed a systematic theology tradition of its own need to consider anew China's own textual histories and patterns, and the theological writings that have developed out of these. Yang's work on religious language and meaning offers both comment on, and worked example of, such a practice.

Visible and Voluble: Protestant House-Church Writings in the Twenty-First Century

The Three-Self is a state monopoly set-up, with exactly the same
characteristics as state-owned industries; you could call it the
"state industry" of the religious sphere. Just as state-owned industries have no means of responding to challenges of the market
economy, the Three-Self has no means of responding to people's
spiritual needs in a timely and accurate way in this new era.
—Yu Jie and Wang Yi[1]

In the epigraph above, Beijing house-church leader and former TSPM pastor Rev. Jin Mingri suggests a comparative reason for the strength of the Protestant new urban house-church ministries. Arguing that the TSPM has lost its
"life force," Jin concludes that the decline of the Protestant patriotic church
"is inevitable," yet his objections to the Three-Self Movement are pragmatic
and spiritual as much as ideological, and in this he represents a conciliatory
wing of the house church. That Jin could articulate such a pessimistic vision
for the body that is the sole recognized Protestant authority in China is little
short of astonishing and shows the new ideological assurance of many in the
"unregistered" or "house" churches in China. The growth of unregistered
churches, which now surpass state churches in number by some margin, is one
of the remarkable stories of modern China. This brief final chapter expands
on the discussion in Chapter 8 by presenting an initial survey of the writings of
three Christians—Lü Xiaomin, Wang Yi, and Yu Jie—who are committed to
the house churches out of theological allegiance or who, like Jin, see the state
church as irrelevant to the future of Chinese Christianity.

One striking facet of the new urban house-church movement is the interconnectedness of its leaders: with each other, with overseas Chinese and overseas Chinese churches, and with the wider society. The pastor and former lawyer Wang Yi is equally at home discussing the philosophy and legality of the death penalty with French intellectual Robert Badinter as he is defining the nature of Christianity as it emerged in Antioch. The writings of these engaged, elite urban pastors are in continuous dialogue with official church theologies and with academic Christian writings and presage a greater cross-over in shared theological discourse than during much of the twentieth century. In Wang's writings we might detect a dialogue both with the likes of academic Liu Xiaofeng in discussions of the need to be part of the church to be "Christian," and with separatist-leaning Christians within the house-church movement in his formula "the local church is a city within a city."[2]

This chapter begins, however, in the countryside, the nucleus of growth for the house churches during the 1980s. Lü Xiaomin comes from rural Henan, where she was an itinerant evangelist for many years. Lü's Christian heritage includes Pentecostalism and the Little Flock/Shouter teachings brought back into China in the 1980s by followers of Li Changshou,[3] and her faith and theological thought is expressed in the medium of the hymn. Lü's work from the 1990s and 2000s is representative of a type of enduring acceptance of state persecution, a "suffering servant" model of Christian living. Her hymns are hugely popular across China, and her life is the subject of documentaries, garnering her a strong following. The promotion of her life and her music (by U.S.-based Chinese American backers) are interlinked; this theology places a high premium on personal holiness and testimony. The new urban house-church ministries can also call on a number of superstars, or public figures with a strong media presence, and the chapter then considers the work of Wang Yi, the pioneer urban house-church minister from Sichuan, and Yu Jie, who was prominent in activist and Christian circles in Beijing before leaving China for the United States in 2012. Wang and Yu are urban, savvy rights activists; their work and experience leading churches and speaking nationally and internationally represent a new stage in the evolution of the Chinese Protestant church.

THE CANAAN HYMNS: LÜ XIAOMIN

The story of the prolific hymn writer Lü Xiaomin is well-known in evangelical and house-church circles: born in 1970 to a peasant family, Lü dropped out of junior high school because of ill health, became a Christian at age nineteen, and started writing hymns a year later, producing more than seven hundred during the next decade, with well over a thousand circulating in the early twenty-first century. Since she does not read or write Western musical notation, the hymns are transcribed by others; they are sung throughout China, crossing over between house-church and TSPM congregations. Recordings and hymn scores in Chinese notation are available online, and the documentary *The Canaan Hymns*,[4] orchestral remixes, and various video clips and versions have made Lü and the lyrics famous beyond China.

The power of the hymns comes both from their congregational use across China and from the life story of their author. Lü spent her formative years as a Christian, during the early 1990s, as an itinerant evangelist in the rural church and experienced, alongside other members of her church, at least two periods of imprisonment for speaking or publishing outside of official channels. A quiet introvert at the time she began to use her own songs in worship and teaching, Lü evinces through her hymns the struggles of the unregistered church—its hopes and mission calling. The documentary of her life and work, *The Canaan Hymns*, tells the story not just of an unassuming, humble dedication and a life of self-sacrifice and fervor for evangelism, but also of the Chinese Christians who regard her work as "God's gift to China," a means of grace and of guidance for the church, an inspiration in times of difficulty. These are genuinely inculturated hymns, with a folk lilt, Chinese harmonics, and an imagery that blends rural China with biblical themes.[5] The tunes draw on a great repertoire of Chinese folksongs and work in different settings: accompanied by a folk music troupe and fast clapper rhythms or as solos in Chinese operatic style. The hymns are mostly short, and often simple—a few lines of doxology or lament. Few have verses or refrains; many are rhymed, some are not; illiterate congregations can soon sing unaccompanied and worship through the words. A Taiwanese edition of Lü's hymns with composition notes documents how the songs often develop rapidly from a Bible verse that comes to Lü as she is praying.[6] Many of the hymns are spontaneous and circumstantial: a prayer in response to a local need or an outpouring of thanks in a particular situation.

Thematically, the hymns, especially the earlier ones, concentrate on overcoming difficulties, on responding to dark circumstances with faith and courage. One from 1997 speaks of a spiritual escape to heaven while the "hard earth" remains the road underfoot while the next takes up the theme:

A faithful person never loses heart,
and does not retreat when he meets with trouble;
he does not fear how high the mountains or how dark the night,
he knows the one in whom he believes
Come with me, come with me to praise the Lord of the whole earth.[7]

Lü's annotation to the hymn describing the hard earth underfoot notes that it was written at a time when her co-workers in the church were under a lot of pressure from authorities. Another song from the same period affirms, "In the dark nights, I can already see dawn;/In the dark nights, I can already see the morning star."[8] Acknowledgments of suffering come with exhortations to remain steadfast and encouragement for worshippers. A further 1997 song, "The Path of Suffering," affirms that all alike suffer the hardships of the road and have tasted the same bitterness, but "Jesus says you must be loyal, and complete the road that is yours to travel."[9] Nature metaphors abound: high mountains and winding roads may be as physical as metaphysical; snow and high winds are frequent obstacles. The recurrent mentions of inclement weather show that the rural journeys of evangelists even in the 1990s were not without hazards. Some songs bring to mind the "work team" songs laborers used to keep pace:

> Wind and rain refine our bones,
> Rain soaks our clothes; snow piles up on our bodies.
> Do not complain of the burden of work, or suffering;
> We are Christians, we serve the Lord with our whole lives.
> The world is watching, angels are also recording.
> We are Christians, we never fear hardship.[10]

The songs narrate the spiritual and physical journeys of the itinerant evangelists—their fears, failures, pain, and faith. This is a diary in song, a record of a spiritual life of prayer expressed in musical snatches.

Rural sights and everyday figures of speech root Lü's hymns in the countryside: "The times need the Gospel/the threshing floor needs workers," she sings in the song "Sheep Need a Shepherd."[11] The harvest, like the hills, is both real and spiritual, as expressed in the verse "Facing the threshing ground I need your help even more/Lord I need your help."[12] There is a Christological and pneumatological focus running through the praise songs and entreaties, as one might expect, but the biblical references that provide the frame for many of the poem-hymns are often taken from the Hebrew scriptures, especially the Psalms: "I have no way to refuse your love:/If I fly to the ends of the earth, you are there/If I descend to Sheol, you are there"; and elsewhere: "His gates are called praise and his walls are called salvation/blessed are those who trust in the Lord."[13]

One of the strongest threads running through the collection, and which marks it off as notably Chinese (and indeed, as much in line with both government and popular nationalistic sentiment as any TSPM offering), is the yearning for China as a nation. The lyrics to the hymn "China Belongs to the Lord" exemplify the staunch love for country that many Chinese Christians profess:

"If I only had one drop of blood, one drop of sweat left / I would shed it for China / . . . If I only had one breath left, one ounce of strength left / I would dedicate it to China."[14] Some hymns call for a fire of revival to sweep through China;[15] others call on the church to make China God's home. In both cases the revival of China as a nation and of China as a Christian nation are intertwined. There is a human part to play in the revival, as God works together with people in the task.[16] The need to love one's neighbor is paramount, to the point of martyrdom:

> If we don't love our compatriots,
> it is a reproach to the heroic spirits of our ancestors,
> a reproach to the many heroes;
> . . . O Lord, you alone know how much we long for the revival of the
> Church in China—
> even if our lives on earth are cut short by you.[17]

A tension is expressed across the hymns between the desire for China to come to know God and know that the country is loved by God and the call to "shake off the yoke of the homeland" or pray for unity in "turbulent times." This tension reflects the difference between a spiritual vision of China and the earthly political reality in a theology that sees itself in an interim age and looks firmly toward the second coming. More shocking to non-Chinese, another "hymn" is a Christianized parody of a song from the Red China period and draws on the rousing tunes of the 1960s:

> China! China! The Chinese people must arise,
> Silent for so many years, lethargic for so many years,
> Today you must revive like a fierce lion.
> China! China! The Chinese people must arise.
> We bless you with one heart, in unison we acclaim you
> The Lord of ten thousand armies loves you eternally,
> China! China! The Chinese people must arise.[18]

The easy transfer of sentiment between God and country seems out of kilter with the absolute stand against the government of the older generation of house-church leaders like Allen Yuan or Samuel Lamb yet expresses the deep desire of Christians to belong, and an ideological separation of China as people-and-nation from China as nation-under-Communism.

Two features of the theology imbued in the hymn collection are worth noting. The first is the strong eschatological tenor, consonant with much rural nonofficial Protestant theology of the era. This is seen in such hymns as "On That Day the Stars Will Fall," which describes a day of the earth shaking and the skies turning dark and an "angry lamb" returning; it ends with the question, "Who can stand? Only the one wearing white"; or the hymn "Fear Not the Path of Suffering," which advises that "there won't be many more tomorrows/until the world suffers great catastrophe."[19] A second feature is the strong missional emphasis. The first task remains to broadcast the gospel throughout China,[20] but as another hymn proclaims, "the gospel has no national boundaries," so "we will continue, laughing joyfully, until the whole of humanity turns to God."[21] Mission and national revival are closely linked, as they were in the vision of Christians early in the twentieth century: as evangelists spread the seeds of love, "we will eventually be victors/and side by side restore China."[22] A sense of election to this mission is evident in Lü Xiaomin's hymns, and her views chime with a widespread sense in house-church communities of a call to mission westward, through Central Asia back toward Jerusalem.[23] This call to mission is amply clear in the hymn "The Great Commission":

> The gospel doesn't distinguish between nationalities, it must surely be
>   transmitted to all nations,
> We are a blessed generation, the envoys of Heaven,
> The camel bells of the Gobi desert, the bleat of sheep in mountain valleys,
> The Holy Spirit constantly moves us, urges us forward,
> To go throughout the whole world and spread the gospel for all people
>   to hear.
> This is the great mission to all nations, the great mission to all nations.[24]

Lü Xiaomin's theology, including the sense of the great commission, is rooted in the praxis of worship and prayer. If the composition of the hymns derives from moments of prayerful worship, the hymns themselves frequently speak of prayer. One of her best-known songs is "Five a.m. in China," which evokes the prayer meetings that Chinese Christians wake early for and describes the revival, peace, and harvest that prayer brings. In commenting on the song, Lü reportedly quipped that "because I wrote that song, I'll use it to discipline myself for the rest of my life"—an apt reflection on the formative nature of praxis and surely a pointer toward the way worship has shaped theology and revelatory experience for this sector of the Chinese church in a fashion not dissimilar to the "intense 'micro-climate'" of the Jesus devotion of early Christian circles.[25]

WRITER, PREACHER, PASTOR, BLOGGER: WANG YI

The works of Wang Yi (b. 1973) showcase the breadth of writings among prominent intellectual figures associated with the house churches. Wang, still in his early forties and a pastor since 2011, had published articles on constitutional law as well as volumes of *suibi* notes and of poetry before he became a Christian in 2005. With well over ten thousand followers on *weibo* 微博, the Chinese micro-blog site akin to Twitter, he was heralded in 2004 as one of the fifty leading public intellectuals of influence in China (by *Nanfang Renwu Zhoukan*) and in 2013 as one of the twenty-five most influential Chinese to watch (by the *Financial Times*).

Carsten Vala and Huang Jianbo have analyzed the postings of Wang on religion and politics as part of a study of high-profile *weibo* users.[26] Their findings show how the micro-blog site has provided an opportunity for Christians to engage in intellectual dialogue with each other and beyond church boundaries about issues of religion and politics—and how *weibo* can paradoxically be a medium for deepening and complexifying discussions of doctrine. One of the most interesting discussion threads, in a series of posts from April 2013, explores how Wang Yi distinguishes between patriotism and nationalism. Wang is, of course, keen to emphasize that house-church members can be just as "patriotic" as TSPM members but makes a clear distinction between patriotism and nationalism. As Vala and Huang show, Wang grounds patriotism in biblical motifs—the "seeking the peace of the city" of Jeremiah 29—or conjugal love (where patriotism equates to loving one's spouse, but nationalism to loving one's mistress).[27] Patriotism, Wang argues, values the local community, whereas nationalism leads to universalism and disables a loving response to the wider group. The TSPM, Wang argues, is bound to the Nationalist agenda of the CCP—and so to the totalitarianism that twentieth-century nationalism led to.

The span of Wang Yi's writings tells us much about current restrictions and laxity in Christian publishing. Beyond his church sermons and public debates via micro-blog, Wang has also served as a film review columnist in a mainstream weekly, but he has found it easier since becoming a Christian to publish book-length works outside of the mainland. His first book after coming to faith, *On Constitutionalism: Turning Points in Views and Systems* (宪政主义：观念与制度的转换), was an attempt to revisit questions such as "why do we have laws?" through a scriptural perspective; the second, *Kissing God* (与神亲嘴), was a self-published volume of essays discussing Christian faith that was aimed at fellow liberal intellectuals, for whom he felt a particular burden.[28] Since then, Wang has co-edited with Yu Jie two volumes of biographical interviews published with a Taiwanese press and, in a separate series with the same press, co-written a volume with Liu Tongsu on urban house churches; he has also published a collection of his own writings, a sequel to *Kissing God* with the English subtitle *Revolution in the Depth of the Soul* (灵魂深处闹自由).[29]

   The title of this collection of essays, speeches, and reprinted reviews is taken
from a film review Wang published on the Hollywood blockbuster the *Wolverine*. Like the *suibi* entries of Xu Zongze discussed in Chapter 4, Wang's writings
are accessible to (educated) Christians and non-Christians alike, and also like
Xu, Wang's didactic intent is clear yet not obtrusive. In a review of Bonhoeffer's biography, for example, he makes common cause between intellectuals
and activists of conscience everywhere, while explaining further Bonhoeffer's
beliefs and his views on church-state relations.[30] Eclectic in his references, flitting within a single page from Jane Eyre to Zhuangzi to rock and roll lyrics,[31]
Wang moves effortlessly between popular culture and philosophy. In his piece
on the *Wolverine*, for example, he discusses the Gnostic element of arcane saving knowledge running through commercial films, quoting writers from Milton to Novalis, and considers the theme of mutants and what it means to be
human in a perfected world via Shelley, Byron, and Hobbes. Shelley's "free,
uncircumscribed" human, "the King/Over himself," is met with Zhou Enlai's
"We must ourselves liberate ourselves, we must teach ourselves, we must be our
own masters," as Wang notes that tales of mutants are always metaphors for human nature and the state. The state is Hobbes's Leviathan, a "living God" who
chooses to release mutants, while the false promise of freedom that Byron's Lucifer gives to Cain reveals the mutant in each of us and provides, Wang suggests,
the most apt footnote to *Wolverine*. Wang starts from the premise that no film
is rubbish—the rubbish is always us[32]—and concludes his review with a more
elevated plea: "Freedom is not found on the street, or in the narrative poems of
the Romanticists. The freedom of a republic lies in the depths of each person's
soul; it's just that there is too much rubbish in our minds."[33]
   In his reviews Wang uses Hollywood films to introduce questions of a broad
religious and ethical nature to readers and to analyze structures of belief and
knowledge in the films. Questions such as the nature of religious freedom and
its relation to Anglo-American property rights, or the combination of Puritanism and Gnosticism in so many U.S. box-office hits, are discussed across several
reviews, including one on *Avatar* under the strapline "The Householder of the
Soul." (His wife, Wang notes, questioned whether readers really wanted to hear
about religion in every single film review—but he thought they seemed content
to do so.) Others of Wang's essays frequently turn to the nature of life, death, or
responsibility, whether he is musing on scattering a father-in-law's ashes or the
Sichuan earthquakes of 2009. Some articles are transcripts of speeches (such as
"Why Do I Believe in Christianity?"); others are more academic in nature and
fully footnoted (e.g., "Romans 13 and the Separation of Church and Government"). Still others are more evidently political, such as the hard-hitting speech

Wang gave at the seventy-first PEN International Congress in 2005, when he represented the imprisoned Liu Xiaobo, head of the independent Chinese Writers Association (and later Nobel laureate), and lamented the lack of freedom for writers in the years since 1989;[34] or the text of the prayer Wang wrote for a May 2006 prayer meeting with President George W. Bush at the White House.[35]

The trope of writing is a point to which Wang, like other Chinese Christian intellectuals throughout the centuries, frequently returns, and one that integrates the personal and the public in his work. He is sharply self-critical of his former self as a writer and public intellectual, as he considers the arrogance to which workers for justice or human rights are prone. There is also a bleaker side to Wang's musings, as he circles back to the oldest Chinese figure of all—that of writing as a means of perpetuating the self, as an alternative to progeny.[36] Wang admits to an earlier unwillingness to have children, born out of disaffection, a hopelessness, the lack of a role model for fatherhood, and the sense of the limits of his own capacity to love. It was, he notes, a "strange person" who wanted to produce a book but not a child. Tying writing to a gendered division between multiplying and governing, Wang suggests that writing is as difficult and as precious as giving birth. He discerns a falsity in his own position, especially after conversion: how could he be an intellectual, an upstanding citizen, an advocate of democracy, and yet be unwilling to have a child—since that would signal that the future of the nation had no purchase on him? How could you claim to love your neighbor if you were unwilling to love a child?, he asks.[37] A spirit-led change of mind (and a willingness to procreate, resulting in a son) led also to a new understanding of the significance of writing, as Wang saw his individual life as a writer and his corporate ideals now linked in Jesus. Christian hopes tie in with old Chinese intellectual visions of the power of writing: "through writing," Wang writes, "God uses these humble vessels, and entrusts to us the mission of renewing culture through our faith, and pastoring the earth with the gospel."[38]

The stakes for Christian writing are high. Wang describes his profound hopes for the cause of Chinese Christian literature and the need for moving laments, great confessions, pious hymns, and descriptions of a biblical worldview. Wang wants his writing to be an agent of cultural transformation in China, "to pierce the Chinese people's spiritual world and the depths of their moral values, to tear open the hidden idols and cut through dead-end roads in the journey of the soul."[39] But if writing is a supreme act of creativity which gives the sense that "when we write, we feel like God," then it is also one of the main forms of idolatry for a Christian intellectual, as Wang explores in "Am I Writing for Christ?"[40] Constant vigilance and discernment of motive are needed. Wang identifies four themes in his own writing that chime with Chinese intellectual concerns: "from Su Wu to Moses," the theme of exiles and the meaning of wilderness; "from 'easy wandering' to 'salvation'" (echoing Liu Xiaofeng) or from Buddhism or pantheism to Christianity and monotheism, the theme of freedom; "from Prometheus to the Cross," from pessimism and heroism to a new understanding of redemption, the theme of salvation; "from death to resurrection," the theme of life.[41] The first two of these take up the Chinese classical tradition and interreligious dialogue, respectively, and show the textual and thematic breadth of Wang's theological engagement; all four clearly show movement around a hinge to a new Christian life. The sea change that Wang underwent on conversion (and perhaps, too, the fervor of the newly converted) is evident in his appraisal of the nature of writing as divided into two categories: that which witnesses to Christ and that which does not stem from faith in Christ. In Wang's opinion, all writings since Christ's Incarnation that do not acknowledge Christ are false witnesses and can only be idolatrous.[42] With this, he steps beyond cultural heritage and apart from his more liberal peers.

THE LIFE OF A HOUSE CHURCH:
BIOGRAPHIES OF CHRISTIAN LEADERS

There is a programmatic and ambitious nature to the publishing endeavor of dissident and prolific author Yu Jie.[43] His three volumes of biographies of prominent Chinese Christians, two of which are co-edited with Wang Yi, form the series "Christ and Life" (基督與生命), a three-part, multivolume set whose other major divisions are "Christ and the World" and "Christ and China." The project as a whole intends to envision, and play its part in realizing, a transformation from "humanity as the root" to "God as the root" within Chinese culture.[44] China's success and very future, the authors argue, are linked to what sort of faith and values the country chooses, as they set out very different futures for "China's rise" in a materialist scenario and within a theistic future. Pointing to the role of Christianity in the transformation of South Africa, South Korea, and Eastern Europe, the authors suggest that religious freedom is a necessary precondition to social change, which will follow a set order: "First there is Christian faith, and then comes the reconstruction of society, which then develops into social transformation."[45] The biographical interviews collected in this series represent the cornerstone to any such project of transformation, since "if there is no individual coming to faith, no changed life, no experience of salvation and being reborn, then a change of direction and redemption for the state and the people remain just hoped-for but unattainable mirages."[46] The biographies are couched, in other words, not so much as theological reflection on the shape of a life or of biographical narrative as a source of theological self-understanding for certain groups in society,[47] but in terms of the nation. The social activism and interest in moral regeneration of these Protestant intellectual leaders, and the parallels with the ideas of progressive reformers of the early twentieth century, have not escaped notice.[48]

The Chinese Christian pastors, public intellectuals, and artists Yu and Wang interviewed were selected, according to the authors, for being committed to an open and public ministry, rooted in the church while facing out toward society, and for possessing such quality of action that their lives would change public understandings of Christianity.[49] In the first volume of the series, they are also notably all men.[50] Although later volumes attempt to provide a better balance of mainland voices (and of gender), five of those interviewed in this first volume are based not in China, but in North America. There is a variety of experience but also common threads in the life stories. Many are alumni of Peking University (e.g., Jin Mingri, Liu Tongsu, Zhang Boli, and Yu Jie himself) or other key universities such as Fudan or Renmin; some had privileged Red backgrounds as children of high cadres or army personnel; and some like Yuan Zhiming were themselves CCP members. Many are connected through the events of Tiananmen Square. The lives of the mainland interviewees in the volume collectively tell a story of disaffection and rediscovery, whether ditching a doctorate in Marxist philosophy, like Yuan Zhiming, or moving away from the Three-Self church, like Jin, or from an identity as a Cultural Christian, like Liu. Their stories present powerful testimonies of faith and renunciation, commitment and blessing, but also provide an authoritative, and at times pathos-filled, insight into the development of the house-church movement and the questions facing it in the 1990s and 2000s.

The interviews are structured so as both to narrate individual biographies and to open up a space for discussion on house-church issues such as the legal ramifications of registration or the challenge of whether to create new denominations in China. The interviews with pastors Jin Mingri and Liu Tongsu articulate especially clearly some of the biographical commonalities and particularities among this circle of highly educated and high-achieving leaders. The despair of students following the events of 1989, which provided a catalyst for many to seek meaning in the church, and the sense that "the old world had been completely destroyed" and of being "rejected, cast off, cheated" by the society that provided for students' every need, is voiced by Jin Mingri.[51] Jin, a Chinese of Korean ethnicity (as are several Beijing house-church leaders) is unusual in the extreme poverty of his farming background—four of seven siblings died as children—in his going to church as a student in the late 1980s before it was popular to do so, and in training as a Three-Self pastor before starting the Beijing Zion Church in 2007. The first graduate of a key university since the Cultural Revolution to attend Yanjing Seminary, Jin shares with other evangelical or charismatic Christians a two-stage conversion narrative and a strong desire to "live for the truth" and spread the gospel. Incisive in his account of the reasons for house-church growth and development, Jin is clear about some of the challenges a house church faces in the building of an identity and collective consciousness, in its unity within and relation with the universal church, and in discerning God's will in its future direction. Like others, Jin believes that with the Western church "waning," and the global demise of U.S. or U.K. church leadership, the Chinese church, "like the early morning sun," needs to develop a vision for the whole world.[52]

Jin's experience with registration regulations provides an amusing and salutary account, given the legislation covered in Chapter 8. Jin is among those promoting the normalization of the house churches and in favor of regular contact with local officials. On setting up Zion Church, he explains how he sent a report to Chaoyang governmental offices—not an application to register, but a "self-introduction." He gave a detailed account of his résumé and theological training and of plans for the new church—and heard nothing in return. A year later, in the run-up to the Beijing Olympics in 2008, the church was involved in organizing a citywide workshop for pastors and suddenly came under pressure, with the landlord being leaned on to break the building lease. Jin responded by pointing out that the church had been clear about the building use at the outset, that there were no grounds for revoking the contract, and that if the landlord were to break the contract, he should state that he was doing so under pressure from the authorities and bear any financial losses of the church, which would also publicize the case in the media. This resulted in direct contact from the local government authorities and a robust discussion on what the church would do to keep its doors open during the Olympics.[53] Jin's own view on registration stems from an appreciation that the church belongs to God but is at the same time a group within society and so should develop links with those charged with maintaining social order. Jin's position on legality adds a new angle: from a legal point of view, he argues, since only the TSPM and China Christian Council are legal persons, churches under the control of the TSPM are in no different position from that of the house churches. Moreover, he argues, the church should not have a privileged position in society: a few house churches gaining legal status will not change the overall situation, and the church must suffer and struggle alongside others for its rights and work to enlarge the growing sphere of citizen society.[54] Such a bold and unapologetic, yet conciliatory, approach is plying open a space for house churches to exist but also driving forward the need for a solution to the impasse created by the regulatory requirements for registration through patriotic bodies.

A second interviewee, Liu Tongsu, exemplifies the international nature of the contemporary house church, as he writes and thinks about the Chinese church yet leads a congregation in San Francisco. Liu's congregations have from the outset been composed of mainland immigrants, and he has remained involved in supporting and training house-church leaders and researching the church in China; he is well-known for his books and numerous articles on house churches and church-state relations.[55] Liu is one of the growing generation who converted while studying abroad. In Liu's case he was researching European and American legal philosophy at Yale University in the early 1990s and switched programs to the Divinity School, joining his wife in training for ordination. His honest account of his faith journey spotlights some of the difficulties for Chinese intellectuals in coming to faith, including the stumbling block of the church itself, which Liu found to be characterized by low-level preaching and apathetic congregants, "practically like the CCP back home."[56]

Liu constructs his conversion narrative as a tale of moving away from a cerebral, "Cultural Christian" faith based on rational grasp toward a notion of faith as life in Christ.[57] The gain of seminary for Liu was not in the intellectual pursuits it offered, but in the rare individuals who modeled a Christlike life and allowed him to see that Jesus was not found just in the abstract thinking of the likes of Paul Tillich but in renewed life—prompting the comment from interviewer Wang Yi that "when Cultural Christians come into contact with the church, they die. When real believers come into contact with the church, they live."[58] Liu's ministry, as he describes it, began with a testing time, as he came to terms with the realization that his own abilities, organizational skills, and social prestige were not going to be the basis of church growth and that spiritual maturity was reached only via the way of the Cross.[59] The narrative draws less on Chinese biographical models of moral exemplars and more on an evangelical confession after the model of the desert fathers and mothers, who recounted their own faults to bring others to clarity and repentance.[60] Liu's accounts of posting church notices in New Haven, Connecticut, and of tiny startup congregations in New York, meanwhile, show something of the humble reality, hard work, and discouraging setbacks that have driven Chinese church growth.

The second half of the interview with Liu concentrates on the nature of the house church and offers some important theoretical insights as to its present and future status. Central tenets for Liu include the unconditional independence of the church, the continuation of its character of devotion and self-sacrifice across any rural/urban divide, and the need for the church to adapt to changing social conditions by worshipping openly and taking a full part in public life. House churches, argues Liu, are a specifically Chinese phenomenon, a manifestation of the church under an authoritarian government; the term cannot be applied to U.S. Chinese or others meeting for worship in homes. Given that the essence of the church is its common (or "public") life of faith, the retreat of the churches to the private sphere of the household was a means to safeguard a public faith in a private manner, and was time-limited in nature. Now that society is taking steps toward public life, the church can, and must, argues Liu, discard its private or family nature and take its place in public life. As Wang and Liu clarify, a church that is able legally to maintain a public faith but does not is not a "house church" even if it meets in a home; conversely, a house church may meet in an office or a barn as long as it retains its independence from government ideological control.[61] Meeting in houses is merely the external form of the church: its substance lies its independent, spiritual, and public (or communal) nature.

For Liu, two essential components have allowed house churches to hold onto an independent faith: their devotion, or piety, and their spirit of sacrifice. The Red martyrdom of the early PRC has ceded to a "white martyrdom" in the urban church: self-sacrifice is rarely now a question of bloodshed or the loss of livelihood but an equally challenging one of maintaining purity in the face of the contemporary temptations of money, pleasure, and possessions.[62] This sort of purity is not about separation from the world, suggests Liu, arguing (with a hint of revisionism) that an antagonism to society was never an aim of the house church but a means to preserve faith.[63] Given that independence of faith is a central theological tenet for Liu, it is unsurprising that this forms the focus of his critique of the TSPM, which, he argues, was never a truly independent social body but an extension of the state, along with other "mass groups." Lack of independence meant that the Three-Self Movement by nature could not be "the house of the eternal God," but a function of an excessive and utilitarian government, a state-owned industry, an "official organ and monopoly of an ideologized government."[64] The house church naturally held the same antagonistic attitude toward the state church as it did toward the government.

If there is a paradox in house-church leaders wanting to be open toward the government yet remain independent, a hardening tone emerges regarding the TSPM. In an earlier article Liu had accepted that the early postliberation generation of Protestant church leaders had believed that the church might work together with Communist governments, and that in the high Communist years leaders like Ding Guangxun genuinely believed they had chosen the "lesser evil" of cooperation. For Liu, the problem came in the Reform era and the church's choice to cling to the benefits of its attachment to power.[65] Liu is bold in his condemnation: during the transition period, he claims, while the TSPM still enjoys a monopoly, it will do all it can to protect its interests and delay competition, to the point of resisting the de-ideologization of society and others' freedom.[66] Unlike the house churches, suggests Liu, the TSPM has no base in the new social life of civic society and has not contributed to its progress. The TSPM will, he claims, disappear when civil society is fully formed and the state is de-ideologized. (This chimes with then-leader Ding Guangxun's own thinking, who also assumed that the TSPM was a time-limited organ, "scaffolding" until the church was built up.)[67] The house churches, meanwhile, need to see that the current battle is no longer a spiritual one over faith but a struggle with the government over civil society and the place of the church in that future society.[68] The role of the church in political struggle and democracy advocacy elsewhere in East Asia (Hong Kong, Taiwan, Korea) adds immediacy to Liu's vision for the urban house churches in China, but it is concerning that the views of Liu and allies do not seem to allow for any future for the (former) registered church in the broader church economy.

CONCLUSION

It would be foolhardy to take a crystal ball, or yarrow stalks, to attempt to look into what the future holds for the Chinese church. While the vibrancy of thought and of artistic creativity within the house churches has been amply demonstrated in the writings considered here, putting to rest any notion of a protest theology or a narrow anti-TSPM platform, the broader political situation and the ongoing lack of reconciliation between house churches and the TSPM tempers any blithe optimism—and this is only to consider divisions within the Protestant church. Meanwhile, broader political developments do not bode well: Xi Jinping's measures against "the promotion of Western values in education" in early 2015; greater Internet censorship; a contraction of civil society; images of the bulldozing of Chinese churches and cathedrals, such as that destroyed in Wenzhou in April 2014; and the recent campaign to remove crosses from church buildings—all are disconcerting to China-watchers at the time of writing. The existence of draft government documents normalizing the existence of the house churches gives grounds for optimism—despite the gainsayers arguing that this is just a further mechanism of control—but when these will be ratified and become law is as yet unclear.

Two things seem more sure: the first is the greater public role and visibility of house-church leaders and representatives, in social media and publications, if not in traditionally authorized venues. The legal challenges mounted by some high-profile house churches over the curtailment of their activities or property leases is one aspect of this. Another is the increasingly self-confident nature of theological pronouncements, exemplified by a recent web document from Wang Yi's church in Chengdu, provocatively titled "Reaffirming Our Stance on the House Churches—95 Theses."[69] The document covers a range of church issues including the sinicization of Christianity and relations between church and state, with its most confrontational clauses being those opposing the TSPM and its actions. While the degree of interdependence between the state, unregistered churches, and registered churches is growing, and there can be no illusion of a church entirely separate from the state or society as in the time of the Jesus Family communes of the 1920s and 1930s, theological differences between different sectors of church are also becoming more visible once again. Worshippers may be choosing their churches for pragmatic reasons, or moving between registered and unregistered congregations, but divisive articulations of faith by church leaders may yet stem this trend.

A second aspect that is also clear from this chapter considering just Protestant writings is the continuation of the strong imperative of individuals to publish, to reach an audience through the written word, and to create networks of readers in new media. The interests and theologies of the Chinese church remain as diverse in form and format as they were during the Ming dynasty, and, despite the voluminous recent translation and availability of Western theological classics, a healthy disinclination persists to mimic anything that even remotely resembles a tome of Western systematic theology.

AFTERWORD

Standing in a Sunday service at a Roman Catholic church in central China recently, an impressive and lively church with discreet electronic boards on the pillars displaying the liturgy in real time, I was struck with renewed force by the difficulty of worshipping with a sense of inauthenticity. This was a rare occurrence; there is usually no occasion to doubt a priest's or minister's faith as expressed in the sermon or worship. That morning, however, a disturbing unease at the perception of an inauthentic leader—perhaps not even in the sense of unbelieving, but for presenting a homily that did not ring true and came across as a government circular or directive—was a bleak reminder of the choices that Chinese congregations and theologians have faced for decades.

The relation of church to state, and the locus and nature of authority, has been one of the central issues of modern Chinese theology, inspiring a spectrum of writings and responses from extreme separatism to the programmatic adaptation of theology to Socialism. The relation between church and government has interacted in complex and surprising ways with a second prominent aspect of twentieth-century Chinese Christian thought: nationalism. While nationalism has mostly been a positive, pro-China yearning bound up with the good of the people and supported by biblical exploration of the history of Israel, it has also entrained an antiforeign element, which has had positive aspects (the drive toward a self-sustaining church, postcolonial emancipation) as well as more invidious strands (the matrix of foreign/national/authority being an especially convoluted doctrinal and practical problem for Roman Catholics). Add in the close relationship for many people between the well-being of the nation and salvation itself—and their direct connection in certain Protestant writings combining a universal soteriology with a Confucian connection between right rule and national well-being—and it starts to become clear why separating out the elements of Chinese theology into discrete interests of (Western) systematic or biblical theologies, or even categorizing them by church type or belonging, might prove challenging.

A colleague once asked, in a slightly exasperated tone, following a protracted discussion of Chinese theology: "but is it systematic"? For some, there is a paradox at the heart of this volume: that Chinese theology is not "theology" at all. For the most part it does not address the core historic concerns of Euro-American theologies in a systematic form, and where it does, in writings on Christology or the Incarnation, for example, its methods or interests may be unorthodox. The rejection of systematic forms and norms is not a rejection of theology, however, but a comment on that theology—an assertion that the "universal" theologies of the Western canon may be seen as culture- and time-bound forms relating to their own textual and philosophical traditions. The tendency still perpetuated in seminaries and universities across different continents to label historical Euro-American writings "theology" and all else "contextual theology," to be taught in a separate section of the curriculum, is no longer tenable. It is not only pedagogically patronizing—the pivot around certain forms of logical reasoning is not axiomatic to theological thought itself—it also fails to recognize the shifts in geographic and intellectual centering of the world church. As this volume has shown, China has its own long history of theological writings. These might not fit readily into a systematic corpus, but why should they? Chinese thought has historically been organized and categorized along various principles, and these have formed the bone structure for Chinese theology.

The Chinese theology explored in this volume comprises elements of biblical theology, constructive theology, contextual theology, and liberation theology. Much Chinese theology shares common ground with other liberation theologies, in mediating between Christianity and the wider cultural situation and in its questioning of established church structures. Chinese theology also conforms to a degree to characterizations of "Asian theologies" as engaging in dialogue with their socioeconomic contexts, cultural contexts, and religiously plural contexts. If theology moves continually between the two poles of eternal truth and the "temporal situation in which eternal truths must be received" (in Tillich's much-quoted terms), Chinese theologies have consistently situated themselves toward the applicable end of inquiry, at the junction between truth and society, rather than reaching between human understanding and God. Lai Pan-chiu has characterized Chinese theology in terms of the inculturation and contextualization of the foreign into China, and there is much to support this approach too (when seen as a bilateral process): the urgent need for a "relevant" religion and the use of Christianity to shape society dominated thinking in the Republican and Nationalist eras just as it has done in the recent Sino-Christian movement.[1]

This volume has taken an alternative approach, highlighting the text as a defining aspect of Chinese theology and the textual context as an important base in reading any Chinese theology. The text has operated in at least three ways: most fundamentally, in an interest in language, translation, and transmission. From Matteo Ricci in the sixteenth century to Yang Huilin in the twenty-first, the process of linguistic and textual inculturation—of how to name God in Chinese, at the most basic level, and why that choice matters, because of the textual resonances in the Chinese tradition of whichever term chosen, and of how to create texts in which that God can be received by readers—has preoccupied some of the best minds in Chinese Christianity. Others have written on the language aspect of this process of accommodation, or entextualization, while this volume has drawn more attention to the textual elements. (These are closely linked: so, for example, the choice of "Tianzhu" or Lord of Heaven for "God" by Roman Catholics opens up a pantheon of references to "heaven" in the Chinese classics as potentially relating to the Christian God, while the Protestant choice of "Shangdi" offers a separate set of religious resonances from the canon.) A second realm of the text has been writers' use of classical Chinese texts, or their dialogue with canonical tradition, seen not just in late imperial writings like those of Li Jiubiao or Wang Zheng, but also throughout the modern era, in the work of a Wu Leichuan or Zhao Zichen. These resonances extend beyond allusions, references, and the networks of associations they inspire, to the whole context of the text, including the reading methods and understanding of the function of the text in the life of the believer and in society and education—functions that are derived from Chinese canonical traditions and imperial examination systems.

A third area of textuality explored in the volume has been the use of specific Chinese writing genres in which Christian texts are composed. The examples of Xu Zongze (in his *biji* notes and jottings) and Zhao Zichen (with his biography, or *zhuan*, of Jesus) come most obviously to mind here, where the associations brought to life by a particular genre or textual form create new readings of scripture, new insight into theological truths. Given the centrality of the textual tradition to Chinese education, history, and sense of national identity, it is not surprising that Chinese theology has drawn on its own hermeneutical traditions in its reading of the Bible. These may overlap with other traditions of exegesis—in reader-based approaches or an emphasis on the historical nature of canonization processes—or be more distinctive, such as the continuous, communal interpretation as texts circulate or the lack of distinction between text, paratext, and commentary. The volume has drawn on sinological perspectives and methodologies and suggested that these might form an important component in approaching Chinese theology, alongside the insights of earlier theological traditions, since textual, historical, and literary studies are all needed to make sense of the texts and contexts of Chinese theology.

The theology surveyed here has deliberately engaged with China's cultural heritage(s) and indigenous philosophical and religious traditions and insights as a central element in its own construction, whether directly or indirectly through the connotations of the literary form in which it is written. The volume has concentrated precisely on those texts that actively reflect not just on God, but on God as explored through a range of Chinese social, philosophical, or literary frames of perception. The selection of texts was made in an attempt to explore this vein of theology and its history, but such an approach has inevitably left unexplored, and undertheorized, alternative channels of Chinese theology, including more influential ones in numeric or ecclesial terms. The self-referential "Chinese theology" studied here sits alongside a range of other Chinese theologies in play. It may be contrasted not just with other Christianities or theologies in mainland China, but also with traditions in other Chinese-language spheres, such as the Homeland or Chhut-thau-thin (出頭天) theologies of Taiwan or the writings of diasporic Chinese communities in Southeast Asia or North America.

There is a natural connection between beliefs regarding the relation of the church to the world and the relation between Christianity and Chinese culture, and so these texts that engage with broader (non-Christian) traditions of Chinese thought or ritual have, in the postimperial period at least, tended to come from elite, liberal-leaning writers in the historic denominations. My hope is that a concentration on this strand of Chinese thinking will not just offer a methodology for studying its texts, but open up new conversations and comparisons with other Chinese theologies. The singular noun of the book's title is not an attempt to appropriate the term "Chinese Theology" for this particular style or emphasis—although the term is particularly apposite here—but is merely a preference for the more succinct abstract noun. This too is Chinese theology: these texts and literary works whose themes and interests and rootedness in the quotidian sometimes show little resemblance to the key questions of other theological traditions.

The volume has taken a broad, perhaps presumptuously broad, definition of "theology," incorporating a range of writings on God, the church, and Christian perspectives on human nature or society—and has done so on the basis of the

Chinese writings themselves. If, as one British theologian suggests, the task of a systematic theologian is "doing constructive, rigorous and imaginative thinking for the contemporary church and world,"[2] this is precisely what the theologians discussed here were doing (with the possible exception of Yang Huilin, whose horizon is much more "world" than "church"): rigorously testing out what it meant to be a Christian in Chinese society and to conceptualize Christ and Christian truths from within Chinese traditions, expressing these through writing. The scale of the task, and the almost insurmountable challenges of language and conceptual barriers, can be seen in the early experiences of speaking of and writing of Christ in Chinese, but the "rigorous and imaginative thinking" remains just as demanding in the present.

This process of interpreting Christianity into, and through, Chinese languages and cultures has been going on continuously for four hundred years. Text, as discussed here, is an aspect of theology, but also a mode of theology itself—theology as text understanding. The theologies of Chinese Christians—working out of their own textual traditions of composition, circulation, and the social function of the text, in conjunction with acquired patterns of reading the Bible—have shown in various ways how a relationship with God is mediated through texts and predicated on a particular world of textual meaning. One aspect of the indigeneity of Chinese theology in the incarnations described here is thus its textuality. This has proved a dynamic, collaborative process, often very aware of its human-centered nature, and catholic in the scope of its networks and references.

Foregrounding the textual element to Chinese theology provides a complementary approach to other readings of Chinese Christian texts. Reading textually enhances thematic approaches, by showing how, and in what forms, theological topics have been addressed. The key theme of God and the church can be traced in this volume through the writings of Wu Leichuan and Ni Tuosheng on the Kingdom of God in the 1930s and in their recensions of earlier arguments between Johannes Weiss, Albert Schweitzer, and others; in the debates among Roman Catholic leaders and between Wang Mingdao and Ding Guangxun on cooperation with the government-imposed church structures in the 1950s; and in the writings of contemporary urban house-church leaders like Liu Tongsu on God and Caesar. Thessalonicans or Corinthians? The Chinese church has embodied the very tensions that caused Paul to exhort and lament during the first decades of the Christian church's existence between too great an accommodation to local custom and too great a tendency to holy separation. The depths of pain experienced, and vitriol of the arguments on the nature of the church on earth, show how close to the heart of belief in God this issue has been for so many in the Chinese church. The political nature of religion in the twentieth and twenty-first centuries in China has foregrounded this as *the* critical issue of Chinese theology; but Chinese Christian writings, as this volume has explored, have also always shown a strong social focus. The great divide within the churches on the question of church and state can be seen to parallel the division between Chinese theologians who do and do not engage proactively with their non-Christian cultural heritage(s) in the writing of their theology, since both are grounded in questions of textual (biblical) authority.

A textual reading may inform other approaches, but it also creates its own focus of interest. The centrality of dialogue in the construction of a written Chinese theology is one trait, for example, that a textual reading highlights (and which links Christian theology to other Chinese religious texts). If all three of the late Ming texts explored in Chapter 1 were essentially transcripts of dialogue, dialogue also recurs in the interviews of Wang Yi and Yu Jie with contemporary church leaders and is present in a removed form in the debates between Ding Guangxun and Wang Mingdao. The dialogue of Wang and Yu's interviews draws also on another literary form — the biography — in inviting participants to reflect on their own spiritual and church journeys; and on the tradition of the moral exemplar as the source of biographical writing, a tradition explored (and subverted) more fully in Zhao Zichen's *Life of Jesus*. Zhao's imaginative reconstruction of Jesus's life, with its many allusions to Chinese literary texts and tropes, may not have represented his mature theological thought but provides a resonant resource for intertextual reading as a source of theology, and a helpful comparator for the related images of Jesus in Wu Leichuan and Ding Guangxun.

One of the most enjoyable aspects of writing this volume has been the reading, precisely because Chinese theology — as defined here — has not followed the style of the scholastics or the prolixity of a Barth but emerged in a range of Chinese literary forms beyond the standard essay. The *biji* jottings of the Jesuit Xu Zongze in the 1930s share not just a formal similarity with the blog postings and film reviews of independent Protestant church pastor Wang Yi in the 2010s, but a similar approach, range of references, and subject matter and a dual purpose of personal reflection and of community building, bringing Christian thinking into contemporary media debate. One aim of the volume has been to illuminate such connections and show that these commonalities in literary genre and their associated patterns of meaning-making are integral to the question of what Chinese theology is, and how it should be read.

Intersecting debates on "inculturation" or "indigenization" have been addressed here only tangentially, in part because a textual indigenization has not been a central focus of inculturation studies, which have usually been concerned more with ritual or liturgical and language-translation issues, and in part because the particularity of the Chinese literary field may not lead to particularly productive theorizing on inculturation globally. This study has focused on sinicization as a long-term process of adaptation and imaginative creation, as distinct from any programmatic attempts to make the church "more Chinese" in, say, the early twentieth century. (There is also the complicating factor that an "indigenized" Chinese church, as studied by Lian Xi and others, often refers to denominations or sects that are essentially Christianized popular religions— which highlights the problematic elitism of separating highbrow philosophical assimilation from local ritual praxis in addressing the question.) The complex relation of Chinese Christianity to the foreign, and its centrality to developing theologies, has been raised throughout the volume, including in discussions of those periods of anti-Christian and anti-imperialist fervor when Christianity needed most acutely to define itself as Chinese to outsiders. Also highlighted has been the vacillation within individual thinkers on this issue, exemplified by Ding Guangxun's shift from skepticism over whether the Chinese church was ready to cut ties to its progenitors to an adamant espousal of the need for independence.

One question to ponder further in discussing the nature of "Chinese theology" is where the drivers for creating a distinct Chinese theology have come from in each period: whether the preoccupation was more politically or theologically motivated, intended to contribute to a universal theology or to respond to directives to demarcate an exclusive and ideologically sound Chineseness. As in the project of Theological Reconstruction, it may not be possible to separate political and theological motivations quite so easily. As the volume has discussed, a term like "nationalism" needs reading carefully, with much more benign connotations of internal well-being and flourishing in earlier eras obscured by later expressions of a popular or jingoistic nationalism. Nationalist sentiments notably cut across church boundaries, as examples from Lü Xiaomin's hymns and elements within the academic Sino-Christian theology movement show. If the cause of China has been central to a spectrum of recent Chinese theologies, the notion that China could, if it wished, create a theology that eschewed its common Christian heritage or be formed without foreign influence has been debunked throughout the volume by the emphasis on the foreign links and interactions of the writers considered. From Ming times to the present—when a significant number of mainland citizens are studying theology abroad in seminaries and universities—Chinese theology has always been in conversation with theologies and philosophies taught elsewhere in the world, whether the Counter-Reformation curriculum, John Nelson Darby's dispensationalism, or a resurgent Neo-Calvinism. The great project of Chinese theology has been to take these, select from, argue with, deconstruct, and then reanimate as a tertium quid via Chinese literary and textual forms.

A learned colleague once commented on this project, asking how it was possible to speak of scholastic Catholic theology in the same breath as Protestant Social Gospel writings—or find any meaningful Chineseness in both. As the volume has begun to suggest, the answer is methodological as well as metaphysical and lies in the fact that both exist in broader textual networks and understandings of writing that shape the theology that emerges. The textual aspect has often been overlooked in studies of Chinese theology, but, as the volume has explored, written forms and the social meanings of different literary genres need factoring into the discussion. Just as the social, religious, and philosophical backgrounds that comprise "China" imbue its theology, so broader reading histories and patterns of literary and textual construction inform the theological writings produced. One of the two major traditional theories of writing held, after all, that *wen yi zai dao* 文以載道 (literature conveys the Way): we cannot understand the Christian Dao, or Way, without also grasping *wen*, or how it is conveyed in Chinese.

NOTES

1. Song, *Tell Us Our Names*, 4.
2. The argument, as will be seen, bears a resemblance to Hong Kong theologian Archie C. C. Lee's "cross textual reading strategies," but here there is no "cross" text from an Asian canon; the readings are not comparative but within Chinese textual networks. Very few volumes consider the nexus between textuality and Chinese Christian writing, but a notable exception is the pioneering book edited by Lee, *Wenben shijian yu shenfen bianshi* 文本实践与身份辨识.
3. Vermander, "From Ethnography to Theology," 8.
4. There is still a significant divide in the field between scholars working with classical Chinese sources, predominantly on Roman Catholic thought, and those working with modern sources, where the majority of the output relates to the Protestant church. The excellent work done by scholars and philologists on late imperial church thought and doctrine is rarely utilized by those working in the modern era, and the two sets of writings are effectively treated as pertaining to two separate churches (the Chinese government and public perception see Roman Catholicism and Protestantism as distinct religions). Combining the two in one narrative provides a stronger methodological perspective.
5. Cf. e.g. McIntosh, *Divine Teaching*, 28.
6. There were some interesting Chinese theological developments in the nineteenth century in, for instance, the writing of Liang Fa, a London Missionary Society evangelist working alongside Robert Morrison, and particularly in the theology and biblical commentaries of the scholar-priest He Jinshan, but these are exceptions rather than the rule. On He Jinshan, see e.g. Pfister, "Transmitter But Not a Creator."
7. See e.g. Harrison, *Missionary's Curse*, or Menegon, *Ancestors, Virgins and Friars*.
8. See e.g. Lian Xi, *Redeemed by Fire*, or Fällman, *Salvation and Modernity*, respectively.
9. Quash, *Found Christianity*, 34. Both, as Quash writes, lacked an "intrinsic openness to the *found*."

10. Cf. Williams, *On Christian Theology*, 141–42, and discussion in Quash, *Found Christianity*, 26–30.
11. Tsao and Ames, eds., *Xu Bing*, xiii.
12. Ames, "Reading Xu Bing's *A Book from the Sky*," in Tsao and Ames, *Xu Bing*, 35, 36.
13. Tsao and Ames, *Xu Bing*, xv.
14. See Chapter 2 below.
15. See Meyer-Fong, *What Remains*, 98, 2. As the author notes, the multiple allegiances and agendas of the Qing resistance were reduced in contemporary records to "a morality play of absolute identities and loyalties."
16. Medhurst, *China*, 441.
17. This is usually attributed to the pioneering work of Paul Cohen, Nicolas Standaert, and others.
18. See e.g. Malek, "Shaping Reciprocity," 424–50.
19. Max Müller held the new chair in Comparative Philology at Oxford from 1868, and James Legge the first chair in Chinese Language and Literature from 1876.
20. Newman, "Sublime Is Now."

CHAPTER 1. FROM MISSIONARY WRITINGS TO CHINESE CHRISTIAN TEXTS

1. Wang Zheng, *Renhui yue* 仁會約, 554.
2. See Handlin, *Action in Late Ming Thought*, 108; on benevolent societies see Handlin's more recent *Art of Doing Good*.
3. Wang Zheng, *Renhui yue*, 549. Erik Zürcher sees in Wang's work an extreme example of "Confucian monotheism," where Christianity is reduced to belief in the Lord of Heaven alone, but this position underplays the teachings of Jesus as the basis of *Renhui yue*; it may also be ambitious to look for a strong Christology in the statutes of a humanitarian society. See Zürcher, "Jesuit Accommodation," 50; and Zürcher, "Christian Social Action in Late Ming Times," 274–76.
4. Wang Zheng, *Renhui yue*, 535. Cf. Deut 30:11, 14.
5. The "Regulations" note that God loves all and the society welcomes all in membership, making no distinction between civil and military, rich and poor, even lowly merchants and those in technical professions (just not Buddhist and Daoist priests, see p. 541; and women, although the latter may contribute financially).
6. For detail on Wang's collaboration with Jesuits in Beijing, see e.g. Ren Dayuan's essays in Malek, ed., *Western Learning and Christianity in China*, Vol. 1, 339–58 and 359–68.
7. Wang Zheng, *Renhui yue*, 523, 550, 557.
8. As Zürcher notes, Wang had the Jesuits Giacomo Rho's and Giulio Aleni's texts on charity before him as he wrote; see "Christian Social Action," 270–71.
9. See Wang Zheng, *Chongyi tang riji suibi* 崇一堂日記隨筆. For discussion of the text and sources of the biographies, see Dudink, "Religious Works."
10. For a helpful discussion of Jesuit formation in the late sixteenth century and its relevance to China, see Criveller, *Preaching Christ in Late Ming China*, Part One. For

a counterplea for more attention to non-Jesuit, nonelite Christian preaching in seventeenth-century China, see Menegon, *Ancestors, Virgins and Friars*. As it discusses theological texts, this chapter naturally focuses on the minority of elite, literate converts.

11. The friars (Dominicans and Franciscans) in China might win the argument over ritual "accommodation" or praxis and over terminology (using transliterations over translations for terms like "Deus" or "sacrament"), but written texts have to engage with Chinese textual practices.

12. When, after long debate among missionary orders in China and with Rome, Pope Clement XI condemned in 1705 ancestral rites and Confucian temple rituals and forbade Christian participation, or further discussion, reinforced by Papal Bull in 1715. Emperor Kangxi responded by banning Catholic missions.

13. The process could be termed "entextualization," if a label were necessary.

14. Cf. Young, *East-West Synthesis*, 12.

15. Scholarly and popular biographies of Ricci abound, e.g. Spence, *Memory Palace of Matteo Ricci*; a recent readable version is Hsia's *Jesuit in the Forbidden City*.

16. On the contemporary Jesuit Ratio Studiorum, see e.g. Criveller, *Preaching Christ in Late Ming China*, 4–6.

17. See e.g. Peterson, "Learning from Heaven," 789.

18. Saussy, "Matteo Ricci the Daoist," 176–78.

19. For examples in this paragraph, see Criveller, *Preaching Christ in Late Ming China*, 7–8, 17–19, 21–28.

20. See Criveller, *Preaching Christ in Late Ming China*, 26. Fellow Jesuit Giulio Aleni prevaricates on the question, advising merely that before the transmission of the scriptural canon, the Lord of Heaven will surely have compassion on those who make every effort to practice goodness; see Zürcher, *Kouduo richao*, 377.

21. On the question of Ruggieri's language capacities, whether his recall to Europe was a positive move, and the destruction of the woodblocks of Ruggieri's text, see e.g. Meynard, *Le Sens Réel*, xiii, xxviii.

22. Luo Mingjian 羅名堅 (M. Ruggieri), *Tianzhu shilu* 天主實錄. On the existence of a prior manuscript of conversation notes for catechistical conversations, a possible working draft of the *Tianshi shilu*, see Criveller, "Matteo Ricci's Ascent," 48. As Meynard notes, Ricci claimed joint authorship of the Ruggieri catechism, but since he had been in China for only two years, he cannot have input much; see Meynard, *Le Sens Réel*, xii. For simplicity, the text is referred to here as Ruggieri's.

23. Confucianism, Daoism, and Buddhism were all designated by the term "teaching" at this point.

24. *Tianzhu shilu*, 4.

25. *Tianzhu shilu*, 18. We see things without form, such as God, or spiritual things, with *li* (reason, principle) rather than with the eye, adds Ruggieri.

26. Cf. *Tianzhu shilu*, 77–78. The implication of a super-league of Christians was undoubtedly confusing, given the underlying question of who can get to heaven.

27. *Tianzhu shilu*, 22, 23.

28. *Lunyu* (論語 "The Analects") were the "recollections of conversations" between Confucius and his disciples or Confucius and rulers of the feudal states he visited;

see De Bary and Bloom, *Sources of Chinese Tradition*, 42. For a helpful exploration of the centrality of discussion and conversation to scholarly learning and revival of academies in the Ming, see Standaert, *Yang Tingyun*, 9–10. As Gernet notes, *China and the Christian Impact*, 17, Ricci opened a "preaching house," that is, a 書院, or academy, early on in his ministry, grasping that in China one preached "more fruit-fully through conversations than sermons."

29. *Tianzhu shilu*, 70.

30. Cf. "天主化為男子" or "自化為男子," "西竺國," and "仙媽利呀天主聖母娘娘."

31. *Tianzhu shilu*, 82–83.

32. For one of the best introductions to the text and background, see Introduction to Meynard, *Le Sens Réel*; see also Ricci, *True Meaning*, 3–53; and discussion in Hsia, *Jesuit in the Forbidden City*, 224–44. Fuller analysis is given in Zhang Xiaolin 张晓林, *Tianzhu shiyi yu zhongguo xuetong* 天主实意与中国学统—文化互动与诠释; and Sun Shangyang, 孫尚揚, *Mingmo Tianzhujiao* 明末天主教.

33. Ricci, *Tianzhu shiyi*, 5. Ricci rather labors the point with an analogy of a robber, but the illustration does imply that he hopes those who can "speak the tones properly" will come along afterwards and take up the cause.

34. Cf. Huang, ed., *Male Friendship in Ming China*. For English translation of 交友論 (originally 友論), see Ricci, trans. Billings, *On Friendship*. Billings shows the "stag-gering popularity" of the essay and how Chinese readers copied, excerpted, reprinted, and anthologized it (pp. 2–4). Importantly for our discussion, Billings notes that the combination of patristic sources and Chinese innovations means that "the essay can be read either as a European text translated into Chinese or as a Chinese text com-posed by a European" (p. 19), with reading patterns as translation or creative work splitting along cultural lines.

35. Cf. Chinese text and French translation in Meynard, *Le Sens Réel*, 256–57.

36. See Criveller, "Matteo Ricci's Ascent."

37. Criveller, "Matteo Ricci's Ascent," 53–54.

38. Despite Ricci's relative caution on the matter; cf. Zürcher, "Jesuit Accommodation," 50–52.

39. Ricci, *True Meaning*, 51.

40. Ricci, *Tianzhu shiyi*, 4. This idea is picked up in later seventeenth-century Christian writings, such as the opening to Li Jiugong's *Shensi* 慎思.

41. Ricci, *Tianzhu shiyi*, 5. Lancashire and Hu Kuo-chen suggest (Ricci, *True Meaning*, 62) that Ricci's source for the slenderest knowledge of higher things being greater than certain knowledge of the lower is Aquinas (*Summa Theologica* I, q.1.5.1) follow-ing Aristotle; the concept also echoes the "pearl of greatest price" of Matt 13.

42. Meynard, *Le Sens Réel*, xxxvi.

43. This last chapter, which moves toward doctrinal questions, explores the notion of chastity and the purpose of "setting aside" some believers who may travel freely and expound the teachings of the Lord of Heaven and, finally, describes the surpass-ing, supernatural nature of Christ, whose deeds and teachings were recorded by four saints.

44. Ricci's use of translated terms over transliterations, a key strategy in texts aimed at nonbelievers, went against agreed mission strategy and was contested, and over-turned, by later Roman Catholic missionaries.

45. Sun Shangyang, *Mingmo Tianzhujiao*, 94. As Sun notes, Ricci was selective too in his presentation of Western theology.

46. Ricci, *Tianzhu shiyi*, 8.

47. Ricci, *Tianzhu shiyi*, 11.

48. Ricci, *Tianzhu shiyi*, 12–14.

49. Ricci, *Tianzhu shiyi*, 15–16. Western allusions such as to Augustine are not usually cited: Ricci cannot appeal to textual authority through them, merely to the strength of what is said; the two textual worlds are treated differently. One might have thought, as others have noted, that the apophatic, or via negativa, would have endeared Ricci to Daoist philosophy of and language of the Ultimate, but there are few overtly posi-tive references to Daoism in Ricci. For an alternative view of how Ricci introduced himself as a paradoxical and exceptional foreigner via Daoist tropes, see Saussy, "Mat-teo Ricci the Daoist."

50. See e.g. Ricci, *True Meaning*, 47–48; Meynard, *Le Sens Réel*, xxv. Examples might include Ricci's grasp of *kong* 空, or emptiness in Buddhism; his interpretation of *li* 理, principle, as accident; or his insistence on the necessity of a motivating force to do good, against prevailing views on goodness as the fulfillment of innate human nature.

51. See Zhang Xiaolin, *Tianzhu shiyi yu Zhongguo xuetong*, 68.

52. See Meynard, *Le Sens Réel*, xxvi, xxix. Meynard's reconstruction of which sections of text relate to which historical debates and interlocutors shows the "real" nature of the conversations and improvements to the text over time, with a five-year gap between draft and additions in some cases.

53. In an extraordinary article with a deceptively simple basis, Erik Zürcher details par-allels in terminology in the reception of and accommodation to Confucianism in earlier Chinese Judaism and Islam. See Zürcher, "Jesuit Accommodation." Zürcher argues that not only was such accommodation inevitable, but that it enabled the teachings of the Lord of Heaven to be seen as "a marginal religion" in the Chinese context, not a missionary construct (p. 32).

54. The *Catechismus christianae fidei*, written with Luís Froís and Ōtomo Sōrin. See Meynard, *Le Sens Réel*, xviii. Meynard provides tables of the content overlap with Ruggieri's and Valignano's catechisms, see pp. xvi–xvii, xx–xxi.

55. While the Japanese catechism separated the philosophical arguments from the his-torical and dogmatic, another Chinese-language work, Juan Cobo's introduction to the faith of 1593 written for the Chinese community in Manila, had already presented a purely rational explanation of the faith. Cf. Meynard, xxxiii; and Menegon's discus-sion in *Ancestors, Virgins and Friars*, 50–58.

56. Menegon, *Ancestors, Virgins and Friars*, 22.

57. Including not just the intuitive and individualistic Wang Yangming school, but off-shoots like the populist "wild Chan" school of Wang Gen and iconoclasts like Li

Zhi. On Ming syncretism, see e.g. Berling, *Syncretic Religion of Lin Chao-en*; on the synthesis of Pure Land and Chan, see e.g. Yu, *Renewal of Buddhism in China*.

58. For a helpful chapter outlining the background to the Ming scholarly debates in *Tianzhu shiyi*, see Zhang Xiaolin, *Tianzhu shiyi yu Zhongguo xuetong* 44–68.

59. Reordered arguments include, for example, placing the judgment of the dead in Chapter 6 as a component of ethics or reworking creation as a two-stage argument.

60. See Sun Shangyang, *Mingmo Tianzhujiao*, Chapters 2 and 3, respectively.

61. Meynard, *Le Sens Réel*, lxii.

62. For a biography of Aleni and brief notes on Rudomina, see Zürcher, *Kouduo richao*, 54–75; see also the excellent volume of essays on Aleni, Lippiello, and Malek, eds., *Scholar from the West*; also Gang Song, "Learning from the Other," which discusses the "hybrid Christian-Confucian identity" emerging out of dialogue and negotiation between Jesuits and converts. The text used here is *Kouduo richao* 口鐸日抄 in Standaert and Dudink, eds., *Chinese Christian Texts, Vol. 7*, hereafter ASJ (Archives of Society of Jesus) *Kouduo richao*.

63. The former are listed as *da* 答, "answer to x," the latter as *lun* 論, "general discourse on y." A comparison between the "Western Confucian" or "Western Saint" Aleni and Confucius in the text is implicit in the form.

64. For discussion of this earlier text of Aleni's conversations, the 三山論學記 "Records of Discussions in Sanshan on the Teachings" (which are much more theological and philosophical than those of the *Kouduo richao*), see Luk, "Serious Matter of Life and Death." Menegon describes these as the "high point of missionary propagation within literati circles in the provincial capital," *Ancestors, Virgins and Friars*, 29 (and emphasizes the fact that they are among the last missionary writings before Chinese-authored texts take precedence) and locates them in Aleni's shift from gospel propagation via scientific texts to a more direct religious propaganda. As Zürcher noted, however (*Kouduo richao*, 9), the anti-foreign atmosphere in Fuzhou during the 1620s precluded more direct evangelism.

65. ASJ *Kouduo richao*, 187, 205; translation from Zürcher, *Kouduo richao*, 330. Yan led a small Christian community in Zhangzhou and was a subeditor of Books I and II of the *Kouduo* (see Zürcher, *Kouduo richao*, 94).

66. The entries are presented in the *biannian* 編年 mode, or chronology. In commenting on the original *biannian* chronology, the *Zuozhuan* commentary and its poetics of narrative, Sheldon Hsiao-peng Lu notes that "objectivity in recording, accuracy in details, and an aesthetics of realistic narration are the ideals of Chinese historiography," a description that fits the *Kouduo richao* well. Lu, *From Historicity to Fictionality*, 55.

67. ASJ *Kouduo richao*, 345; cf. Zürcher, *Kouduo richao*, 449.

68. *Kouduo richao*, 43.

69. See Zürcher, *Kouduo richao*, 263.

70. ASJ *Kouduo richao*, 47.

71. ASJ *Kouduo richao*, 67.

72. One of the most fascinating aspects of the *Kouduo richao* is the re-creation in words of Western art texts with their florid allegories (e.g., the human soul as an infant bathed

in blood) using Chinese vocabulary and experience; see e.g. the detail Li Jiubiao gives of eighteen depictions of the human heart he is shown by Rudomina (from Anton Wierix's 1585 Cor Iesu amanti sacrum series). On the pictures' use as catechetical tools and aids in the spiritual journey, see Menegon, "Jesuit Emblematica." A second set of images on "Time and Opportunity" shown to Li (ASJ *Kouduo richao*, 110–16) shows more clearly how the shading is lost as the pictures are de-allegorized and concretized and the lessons are drawn out by Li.

73. "On the Meaning of the Sacrifice [of the Mass]," see ASJ *Kouduo*, 228–29. As Zürcher notes (p. 365), the text Aleni refers his disciple to has few details on the topic!

74. These include both symbolic and material texts. The disciples and Aleni acknowledge that the Chinese language, with a great number of characters but limited ways to pronounce them, means that texts cannot always be understood aurally and need reading to be comprehended; see ASJ *Kouduo richao*, 81. The moral that Aleni takes from this, echoing Confucius, is that one should read more and speak less; cf. Zürcher, *Kouduo richao*, 243.

75. See Lewis, *Writing and Authority*. In their earliest form as ox scapula and turtle plastrons, Chinese texts had a religious function tied to the state, as the records of—or idealized record of—divinations.

76. See Zürcher, "Jesuit Accommodation."

77. Cf. ASJ *Kouduo richao*, 21. This is also a perfect parallel to Neo-Confucian tropes of lost transmission.

78. On this tradition of records of conversations (the "stenographic efforts of their disciples") in later dynasties, see e.g. Gardner, "Modes of Thinking." The tradition took place in Neo-Confucian and Chan settings; Christian parallels are again part of the indigenization process.

79. See Lewis, *Writing and Authority*, 58. The role of Confucius as editor, expurgator, and abridger—but not author—of canonical texts is such a banal construct that its effect shaping the value of editorial practices can be taken as given. On Confucius as editor, see e.g. Henderson, *Scripture, Canon and Commentary*, 26–30.

80. ASJ *Kouduo richao*, 19; translation from Zürcher, *Kouduo richao*, 186.

81. ASJ *Kouduo richao*, 16; translation from Zürcher, *Kouduo richao*, 185.

82. ASJ *Kouduo richao*, 271–72. When Aleni's discussant is unable to reproduce anything of a text he claims to have read, Aleni explains how texts on Heavenly Studies are food for the soul and need savoring slowly lest the stomach be damaged (a metaphor that Xu Zongze repeats three hundred years later; see Chapter 4 below).

83. ASJ *Kouduo richao*, 38.

84. ASJ *Kouduo richao*, 40.

85. ASJ *Kouduo richao*, 55

86. ASJ *Kouduo richao*, 55. Cf. Zürcher, *Kouduo richao*, 217. Again, this is a common trope.

87. ASJ *Kouduo richao*, 43–45. Zhang was a son of the preface writer Zhang Geng.

88. ASJ *Kouduo richao*, 142

89. ASJ *Kouduo richao*, 106.

90. See Zürcher, *Kouduo richao*, 258–59. As Zürcher points out, the fact that Wang refers to the *Kouduo richao* in early 1637 shows that the first four volumes (*juan*) were already circulating as far away as Shaanxi.

91. ASJ *Kouduo richao*, 582. In the same entry, Aleni points to a preface to his own *Sanshan lunxue ji*, in which Duan Xi compares the merit of writing and printing Christian texts to the luminous sun and the reflected light of the moon, respectively; see Zürcher *Kouduo richao*, 610–11, n. 42. Aleni elsewhere suggests that the merit of Duan and his brothers in printing Vagnone's books is "a minor matter" compared with their cheerful strength in rebuilding a destroyed church; see ASJ *Kouduo richao*, 583.

92. ASJ *Kouduo richao*, 56.

93. ASJ *Kouduo richao*, 59.

94. ASJ *Kouduo richao*, 62.

95. ASJ *Kouduo richao*, 91.

96. ASJ *Kouduo richao*, 58. Zürcher notes (*Kouduo richao*, 221) that the discussion is "sinicized" by the editor at this point and "obscured" by Neo-Confucian terminology for human nature. The discussion echoes debates within the *xinxue* School of the Mind over innate goodness.

97. ASJ *Kouduo richao*, 72–74. Rudomina's point here is that most Confucian scholars are not practicing what is written in their texts and that even souls returning from hell would not persuade them to do otherwise, but the stress on practice holds.

98. ASJ *Kouduo richao*, 266. Moreover, as Aleni notes, following the parable of the talents, the more merit we gain, the more debt we incur and the greater the opportunity for bankruptcy.

99. See Brokaw, *Ledgers of Merit and Demerit*; also Yu, *Renewal of Buddhism in China*.

100. *Elajiya*, 額辣濟亞, is given in transliteration, but it is clear that even Christians need a translation for the term, since an interlineal comment notes, "which translated says the Lord of Heaven's favor." See ASJ *Kouduo richao*, 240.

101. "不賞其所為而賞其所為," p. 241.

102. As Zürcher shows, the teaching of the three stages of revelation allowed for the possibility that Chinese sages were in heaven but also allowed later Chinese writers to question the need for Atonement or conversion at all if "natural revelation" could lead to salvation and Confucians could reach perfection before God. See Zürcher, "Jesuit Accommodation."

103. ASJ *Kouduo richao*, 64.

104. Zürcher, *Kouduo richao*, 231.

105. An excellent example is Nicolas Standaert's study of the thought of Yang Tingyun, Neo-Confucian ex-Buddhist and key apologetics writer for Christianity, showing how Yang's writings were attuned to answering Neo-Confucian questions, but also in dialogue with Jesuit and Buddhist texts, and evolved over time. See Standaert, *Yang Tingyun*, 205. For an example of Yang amplifying and explaining Christian thinking via Chinese texts, see Standaert's discussion of Yang's preface to *Qi Ke* and discussion of Christian love, pp. 119–22.

106. See Gernet's account of Xu Dashou's questions in Gernet, *China and the Christian Impact*, 148–49.

107. See Gernet, *China and the Christian Impact*, 168, 235, 154, 99, for these examples.

108. See e.g. Gernet, *China and the Christian Impact*, 9–10, and discussion on Longobardo's text of 1622–1623, "Traité sur quelques points de la religion des Chinois," refuting the idea that the ancient Chinese had known God/angels/the rational soul.

109. Cf. Gernet, *China and the Christian Impact*, 45, 57.

110. Cf. Menegon, "Yang Guangxian's Opposition to J. A. Schall," 314.

111. Standaert, *Yang Tingyun*, 162.

112. Gernet, *China and the Christian Impact*, 129.

113. See e.g. Peterson, "Learning from Heaven," esp. 112–18.

114. When writers suggest that many were "converts in no more than appearance" or presume that for conversion to be real, there had to be an absolute, once and for all, metanoia, the theological preconceptions in these assertions need challenging. The belief that a sinicized Christianity is somehow not really Christianity is evident in claims such as the Chinese language "deforms" the Christian message, a stance that ignores the history of Christian mission, as well as recent scholarship showing translatability as the bedrock of Christianity. See Gernet, *China and the Christian Impact*, 49; cf. Sanneh, *Translating the Message*.

115. Cf. Gernet, *China and the Christian Impact*, 7, 11–12. Counter-Christian writings evince the same pattern of collaboration, personal networks, multistage compilation, and borrowings as the Chinese Christian ones.

116. Zürcher, *Kouduo richao*, 7.

117. It was not just Ricci who interpreted the classics to the Chinese; Franciscans such as Antonio de Caballero also composed texts glossing quotations from the Four Books. See Gernet, *China and the Christian Impact*, 27–28.

118. Peterson, "Learning from Heaven," 801. As Peterson noted, writing "entailed using Chinese vocabulary to express non-Chinese concepts, and losing important distinctions in the translation"; in studying the Confucian texts Ricci and confreres "were indoctrinating themselves" at the same time, a fact Ricci acknowledged in noting that the doctrines of the literati were instilled with study of the canon.

119. See e.g. Mungello, *Forgotten Christians of Hangzhou*, 5. Mungello's fascinating study of Hangzhou Christian Zhang Xingyao's writings suggests that Zhang was "flowing against the cultural tide of the day" in the late seventeenth century by blending Confucianism and Christianity.

120. Menegon, *Ancestors, Virgins and Friars*, 6–7. Menegon names Standaert, Zürcher, and Dudink as examples. In fact, this bold introductory argument is a little specious as the remainder of the study shows how Jesuit texts circulated throughout Fujian and were used by friars too.

CHAPTER 2. THE CHRISTIAN IMPRINT

1. Suh Hu (Hu Shi), "Christianity and the Chinese People," 6.

2. Cf. Schwarcz, *Chinese Enlightenment*, 4.

3. On the May Fourth Movement, see e.g. Schwarcz, *Chinese Enlightenment*, Chapters 1–3; Mitter, *Bitter Revolution*.

4. There are many excellent studies of Republican history and literature. The centrality of print to mission work in Qing (as opposed to Republican) China has long been established; see e.g. Wilson Barnett and Fairbank, eds., *Christianity in China*, 6; McDermott, *Social History of the Book in China*; Ho, *Jidujiao zai Hua chuban shiye* 基督教在华出版事业.

5. O'Neill, "Report on Church in Manchuria."

6. Marx, "Progress and Problems," 92.

7. For details of the import of the plenary and of the extensive preparations for it, see Wang, *Le Premier Concile Plénier Chinois*, 244–52. For an overview of developments, see Carbonneau, "Catholic Church in China," 516–25.

8. Fisher, "Report on Church in South China."

9. A highly readable account of the independent sector as the new center of indigenizing Christianity in China is Lian Xi, "Search for Chinese Christianity."

10. The term "historic churches" is used here to separate new independent Chinese churches and twentieth-century mission plants from Roman Catholic and mainstream Protestant churches. "Mission churches" is avoided as this implies a perpetual outsider status or absence of Chinese leadership within the churches.

11. Carbonneau, "Catholic Church in China," 516.

12. For example, the ratio grew from 3:1 to 6:1 between 1913 and 1922. Communicants also increased from 207,000 in 1913 to 366,000 by 1920; see Marx, "Progress and Problems," 91.

13. See e.g. Lomanov, "Russian Orthodox Church," 553–63. The split in the Orthodox church (with the new Russian Orthodox Church Abroad) and influx of Russian refugees after 1917 changed the character and focus of the church operation in China, complicating the narrative of sinicization in the 1920s and 1930s.

14. Koo, "What Does the National Christian Convention Mean to Me?," 80.

15. See Zui, "Present Tendencies," 160.

16. Cf. Willard L. Beard, untitled report, *CCYB* 12 (1924): 112.

17. The arrival of dozens of newer, more fundamentalist groups had threatened "the old missionary consensus," as did modernist theologies. By 1920, when the Bible Union of China was formed as a federation of conservative groups, it was evident that the NCC would not be able to mediate for all. The Presbyterian conservatives were soon the first to defect, setting up their own (popular) seminary. See Bays, *New History*, 105.

18. Wiest, *Maryknoll in China*, 205.

19. Latourette, *History of Christian Missions in China*, 724.

20. See Clarke, *Virgin Mary and Catholic Identities*, 118–25.

21. Chinese priests composed 41 percent of the total in 1923; Chinese sisters composed 72 percent of the total female religious in 1926; Latourette, *History of Christian Missions in China*, 725. Despite steady growth in Chinese vocations and in seminary facilities, there was in effect a diminution in Chinese leadership during the late nineteenth century as the number of foreign priests grew more rapidly. While Chinese priests grew from 90 in 1845 to 471 in 1900, foreign priests increased from 80 to 904 during the same period; see Jean-Paul Wiest, in Tiedemann, ed., *Handbook of Christianity*, 239.

22. The arrival of Apostolic Delegate Celso Costantini in 1922 sped up change but not without opposition; see e.g. Tiedemann, ed., "Chinese Clergy."

23. Latourette, *History of Christian Missions in China*, 727.

24. See e.g. Yard, "Recent Changes in Mission Organization," and Chandler, "Status of Self-Support."

25. Chao, "Strengths and Weaknesses," 208.

26. Lobestine ("What Practical Steps?"), the co-chair of the NCC, for example, wrote of the "handicap" and "disability" of a divided denominational approach, noting that there were sixty-seven separate missions in China in 1907.

27. See Yamamoto, *History of Protestantism*, 40. Others have parsed the church scene slightly differently; cf. three categories of Protestant church in Xiaojing Wang, "Church Unity Movement."

28. Those who joined the Church of Christ were almost all Calvinist, see Yamamoto, *History of Protestantism*, 78. Xiaojing Wang, "Church Unity Movement," 8–10, highlights the theological basis for new understandings of church unity among young leaders.

29. There were also foreign-run independent churches, such as the congregations fostered by J. Campbell Gibson in the 1890s. Much excellent recent work exists on the independent churches and their growing number and importance. See e.g. Lian Xi, *Redeemed by Fire*; Xiaojing Wang, "Church Unity Movement"; Inouye, "Miraculous Mundane"; Tao Feiya, "Christian Utopia in China."

30. Lian Xi, "Search for Chinese Christianity," 857.

31. See e.g. Bays, *New History*, 130. The True Jesus Church baptized in the name of Jesus, not the Trinity.

32. See Wang, "Church Unity Movement," 8; Lian Xi, *Redeemed by Fire*, 132.

33. See van de Ven, *Breaking with the Past*, 176; for examples of historians' reevaluations, see p. 6.

34. Van de Ven, *Breaking with the Past*, 176.

35. Jing Tsu, *Failure, Nationalism and Literature*.

36. Cf. Tiedemann, ed., *Handbook of Christianity*, xii, xiv.

37. Cf. Stauffer, ed., *Christian Occupation of China*. This publication was one of the flash-points for anti-Christian demonstrations in 1923. Although the report was produced by a committee with equal Chinese representation and followed other similarly titled publications (such as Thomas Cochrane's 1913 *Survey of the Missionary Occupation of China*) that had drawn no ire, the title provoked significant unrest at a time of heightened sensitivity.

38. Van de Ven, *Breaking with the Past*, 50. Like many late Qing missionary-scholars, Hart was educated in the Chinese classics.

39. See e.g. van de Ven, *Breaking with the Past*, 65, 155–58. It was civil servants like Hart who pursued judgments in the British courts during the 1860s setting the limits of foreign merchants' extraterritorial rights in China; Hart also instituted a Customs College in 1907 to draw recruits for the Customs Service from China.

40. Van de Ven, *Breaking with the Past*, 134, 169. In fact, China had regained tariff autonomy by the late 1920s and ceased foreign recruitment for the Customs Service, two

key demands of protesters, but perceptions (and protests) persisted. The post–World War I generation of foreign leaders within the Customs Service was different again, typified by Inspector General Francis Aglen, who displayed, in van de Ven's words, a "racist disdain for Chinese and a belief in Western superiority" (p. 170).

41. Cf. Fairbank, ed., *Cambridge History of China*, Vol. 12, 132. Foreign leaseholds included areas of Shandong (German leaseholds ceded to Japan) and of Liaodong under Russian rule, Manchuria under the Japanese, and Hong Kong and the New Territories under British rule. World War I much reduced the spheres of influence.

42. Jean-Paul Wiest, in Tiedemann, ed., *Handbook of Christianity*, 239.

43. This was not a new trend. Exceptional Chinese priests tipped as candidates for the episcopacy as early as 1735 never progressed; see Criveller on the moves to block progress against Rome's will, "Chinese Priests," 147–82.

44. See e.g. Tiedemann, ed., *Handbook of Christianity*, 296–302.

45. Bays, *New History*, 59.

46. There was a genuine problem, in that Chinese could not legally set up and run their own churches, unlike foreigners protected under treaty rights. Only when the legal categories of person were collapsed into the one of "citizen" in 1912 could individual Chinese found churches.

47. By Tao Feiya, Daniel Bays and Ellen Widmer, Ryan Dunch, Jessie Lutz, and others.

48. They were, of course, a small minority among Chinese Christians. Missionaries were actually the most geographically dispersed group of foreigners; see Fairbank, ed., *Cambridge History of China*, Vol. 12, 28, 149, 165.

49. On Christian colleges, see Widmer and Bays, eds., *China's Christian Colleges*; Lutz, *China and the Christian Colleges*; and Hayhoe, *China's Universities*. Thirteen represents the number of colleges through the 1920s and 1930s; various amalgamations took the number down from a high point of twenty-one.

50. For a helpful survey of studies on education, see Cong, *Teacher's Schools*, 8–14.

51. For details on dates of founding and stories of amalgamations, intradenominational disputes, and conversions to university status, see e.g. Yamamoto, *History of Protestantism*, 42–43.

52. Feuerwerker, "Foreign Presence in China," 174. Around 170,000 pupils were in missionary schools in 1915 (Bays, *New History*, 94).

53. On extracurricular activities, from study societies to arts and sports groups, service projects and campus newspapers, see Shi and Wang, *Jidijiao jiaoyu yu Zhongguo zhishi fenzi*, 197.

54. On upward mobility see e.g. Bays, "Chinese 'Public Sphere'?"

55. See Widmer and Bays, eds., *China's Christian Colleges*, which explores the cultural hybridity that the college campuses fostered in their re-creation of American undergraduate life. See also Yang Huilin's study of Chinese education at Chefoo and English education at St. John's Shanghai, and student dissatisfaction in both. See Yang, *China, Christianity, and the Question of Culture*, 3–8.

56. See Bays, *New History*. The term is useful shorthand but comes more from the perspective of the Christian colleges' experience than wider society; the contention of

the present volume is that these individuals were in the main trying to eschew such hyphenation by integrating their Western experience into the Chinese whole and emphasizing their Chinese Christian identity.

57. For biographical essays in English on Zeng, Wu, and Liu, see Hamrin and Bieler, eds., *Salt and Light*. Ng, *Chinese Christianity*, devotes individual chapters to the thought of various of these figures. On the career of Chen Chonggui, see Bays, "Foreign Missions." On Zhao Zichen's role as an educator, see e.g. articles by Xu Yihua or Han Zongyun in Wang Xiaochao, ed., *Zhao Zichen xiansheng jinian wenji*.

58. The campaigning voice of church figures on "women's issues" in church and society was significant in conscious-raising, such as the prominent Christian voice in campaigns against foot binding; missionaries also influenced the political thought of the reformers and revolutionaries on female emancipation, cf. Zarrow, *After Empire*, 278, 284; Dunch, "Christianizing Confucian Didacticism."

59. See Ryan Dunch's careful examination of the topic in "Christianizing Confucian Didacticism."

60. Kwok, *Chinese Women and Christianity*, 17, suggests that Christian schools educated more girls than government ones; Dunch, "Christianizing Confucian Didacticism," 69, gives figures of 60,000 to 70,000 in Roman Catholic and Protestant schools in 1912–1913 out of a total of 140,000 in school, with Christian colleges educating more than a third of women in higher education through the 1920s. As Kwok notes (p. 85), female Chinese church workers received lower salaries than male counterparts and had less status in the wider church, but they were leaders in their own church communities.

61. See e.g. Dunch, "'Mothers to Our Country'"; Mittler, *Newspaper for China?*.

62. Some churches, such as the Methodist Episcopal (North circuit) did ordain female ministers, but they were a minority.

63. See e.g. Lian Xi, "Search for Chinese Christianity"; Inouye, "Miraculous Mundane."

64. For a biography of Wang, see Barwick, "Promoting a Protestant Vision."

65. Lian Xi, *Redeemed by Fire*, 132.

66. Cheng, "Women and the Church," 240.

67. The continuity of the social role of the intellectual would prove one of the strongest links between Republican and post-Deng Christianities. As Goldman wrote of those involved in liberal challenges in the 1960s and 1970s: "Even those whose purpose was also to enhance their political position regarded themselves as the conscience of society. Although they held diverse views and spoke many voices, their intellectual work had a similar purpose: to point out society's imperfections in order to rectify them" (*China's Intellectuals*, 1).

68. Legge, *Chinese Classics, Vol. II, Mencius*, 55.

69. The exception is Ding Guangxun. Zhao Zichen became an Anglican priest later in life. On the role of intellectuals (and Christians) in Republican China, see Shi and Wang, *Jidijiao jiaoyu yu Zhongguo zhishi fenzi*. In their examination of the difference between Chinese and "Western" notions of the intellectual, Shi and Wang reiterate the social aspect.

70. See Tiedemann, "Indigenous Agency," 210–13, and Teidemann, ed., *Handbook of Christianity*, 224–33. The pattern of leadership that Tiedemann outlines is closer to that of rural Protestant Christianity than either side might have imagined.

71. See e.g. Zürcher, "Jesuit Mission in Fujian."

72. See e.g. Bays, *New History*, 24, 80–81.

73. Bays, *New History*, 73. Ma left the Jesuits in 1876, protesting the discrimination of French superiors against Chinese novices and priests, and pursued an official career under the Qing; he returned to religious seclusion later in life. See Li Tiangang, "Christianity and Cultural Conflict in the Life of Ma Xiangbo," and for an excellent short biography, Jean-Paul Wiest in Hamrin and Bieler, eds., *Salt and Light*.

74. The bivocational ministry of aid-worker missionaries appealed to Chinese leaders; famine relief was also an astute mission activity, see Bohr, *Famine in China and the Missionary*.

75. Cheng Jingyi, "Some Problems."

76. On Chiang Kai-shek, his Methodism, and the Christian leader China had for a quarter of a century, see Taylor, *The Generalissimo*.

77. Cheng Jingyi, "Some Problems."

78. On Anti-Christian movements, see Cohen, *China and Christianity*; Yang Tianhong; on religious and scholarly challenges to Jesus's divine nature, etc., see e.g. Chen Jianmin, "Modern Chinese Attitudes Towards the Bible."

79. The images and texts of late Qing Anti-Christian movements have been widely reproduced in scholarly volumes on these movements, such as Cohen, *China and Christianity*.

80. The rebellion also handed Rome the opportunity to suppress the strong lay leadership that had evolved in the absence of foreign priests and bring the church back under tighter control. See Tiedemann, "Indigenous Agency," 217. On gentry reaction to Taiping values, see Bays, *New History*, 55.

81. For this and other examples in this paragraph, see Lam, *Chinese Theology in Construction*, 11–14.

82. "科學萬能 科學救國."

83. Fairbank, ed., *Cambridge History of China*, Vol. 12, 303, 319.

84. On Kang Youwei's plan for a state-sanctioned "Confucian Church," proposed separation of church and state, and use of Christianity as a structural model for religious organization, see Kuo, "'Christian Civilization.'" On the difficulties for Nationalists in achieving the separation of state and religion, see Nedostup, *Superstitious Regimes*, Chapter 8. Where the early reformists had tried to argue that Confucianism would be a means to national salvation, later the argument shifted to the assertion that all civilized governments had a state religion so China should too, a move satirized in fiction and news media; see Zarrow, *After Empire*, 290.

85. Nedostup, *Superstitious Regimes*, 68. The move to "nationalist secularism" was, Nedostup argues, a two-stage process: the completion of transfer of sovereignty from the emperor to the people and subsequent separation of religion from public life (p. 4).

86. See Nedostup, *Superstitious Regimes*, Chapter 3.

87. As Nedostup explores, the critique of religion became not heterodoxy vs. orthodoxy, but *mixin* 迷信, superstition, vs. (scientific) religion; the idea that religion could be divested of superstitious elements was key to cultural reform (*Superstitious Regimes*, 8). Elsewhere, Nedostup lists the background factors in the Qing and Republic to this anti-superstitious rhetoric as the political philosophy of figures like Liang Qichao or Zhang Binglin, social reform literature, anti-superstition debates within religions, and the influence of new theologies of world religion (p. 13).

88. See e.g. Lam, *Chinese Theology in Construction*, 3.

89. See Zhang, *Origins of the Modern Chinese Press*.

90. Readers reportedly included the emperor as well as reform-minded scholars. See Zhang, *Origins of the Modern Chinese Press*, 3, 50–52. Kang Youwei and Liang Qichao recycled the *Wanguo gongbao* name—as well as some articles—for their first periodical.

91. It has also since opened them up to charges of cultural imperialism, cf. Zhang, *Origins of the Modern Chinese Press*, 11.

92. In her important study of indigenization, Yamamoto separates the process into two spheres: the growth into "Asian" organizations and the autonomous interpretation of Christianity, complicating the account of apologetics as a response to nationalism; see Yamamoto, *History of Protestantism*.

93. On vernacular and classical Bible translation, see Zetsche, *Bible in China*; Lai, *Negotiating Religious Gaps*. On textual indigenization, see e.g. Starr, "Reading Christian Scriptures"; on indigenized language, see e.g. Ma Hongli, "*Guanhua heheben.*"

94. See Lomanov, "Russian Orthodox Church," 205–6.

95. Wang established the journal in 1927 (i.e., before his church), reportedly after he could not get articles accepted to the Nanjing *Lingguang bao*. Like others, he later collated articles into monographs.

96. See van de Ven, *From Friend to Comrade*, where he argues that the CCP began as a series of study societies, bound up with scholarly journals, and emerged as a mass Marxist-Leninist party only in 1927. On literary societies and the sociology of literary production, see Denton and Hockx, eds., *Literary Societies of Republican China*.

97. See "Report of the Christian Literature Council," 412.

98. The report generously acknowledged the work of its missionary predecessors in building up a Christian literature in Chinese, including the Christian Literature Society of China (廣學會), the tract societies, and the Bible societies.

99. "Report of the Christian Literature Council," 192.

100. "Report of the Christian Literature Council," 419.

101. As late as 1923 a unified language for China was still just an aspiration. It is clear across journals of the period that there was no uniform written Chinese at the time. Some of the articles and editorials in *Zhen guang* and the *Sheng kung hui pao*, for example, were in a relatively unmodified literary (classical) Chinese; others were in a simplified *baihua*, or modern Chinese ("Mandarin").

102. National Christian Council, "Report on Christian Literature," 21.

103. Chao, "Indigenous Church," 177–86; quotation from p. 178.

104. Chao, "Indigenous Church," 185.

105. For the data of Gu Ziren (T. Z. Koo), see Ho, *Jidujiao zai Hua chuban shiye*, 219; cf. Crouch, *Christianity in China*.

106. Ho, *Jidujiao zai Hua chuban shiye*, 219; Zhang, *Origins of the Modern Chinese Press*, 73. Even though many missions started outsourcing their publishing, there were still fifty-three mission publishing houses in 1917, rising to sixty-nine by 1933. See Ho, *Jidujiao zai Hua chuban shiye*, 70.

107. See Lam, *Chinese Theology in Construction*, 18.

108. See *The Life: A Journal of Christian Thought and Practice*, 3. Boger notes, "Protestant Pragmatism in China," that *Shengming* produced occasional English editions in the hope that it might publicize its thought among English-speaking missionaries and complement the *Chinese Recorder*.

109. Lew, ed., *The Life*, 6.

110. Lew, ed., *The Life*, 7.

111. The merger in 1926 was with *Shengming yuekan* (The Life), the publication of the Life Fellowship (*Shengming she*) apologetics society. The editorial staff of *Truth and Life* reads like a Who's Who of Chinese intellectual Christianity, including Zhao Zichen, Wu Leichuan, Xu Baoqian, Liu Tingfang, and Wu Yaozong. Like non-Christian publications, many of the magazines struggled financially. See Ho, *Jidujiao zai Hua chuban shiye*, 158.

112. Schwarcz, *Chinese Enlightenment*, 2, notes that the pursuit of truth for May Fourth intellectuals was notably less abstract than for predecessors of the European Enlightenment, with reflections on "what is truth" conveying "an urgent, almost inchoate desire for emancipation from the ethic of self-submission."

113. Chao, Editorial.

114. Jin Bingdao, "Wo duiyu zhenli de jianjie he xinyang."

115. Cheng Zhiyi, "The Idea of Faith in the Fourth Gospel."

116. Xia Yibing, "Moral Evidence of Christianity," 143.

117. Wang Wenxiang, "Yige xiaomi feijidujiao yundong de fangfa."

118. *Juewu* 24 (supplement to *Minguo Ribao*), 19 Aug. 1924, 2.

119. Ms. A, "Yi ge jiaohui xuexiaosheng xie gei youren de xin."

120. Huang Renyi, "Geming qingnian di zhongyao gongzuo." Huang writes: "You who pray in church every day—do you know who the Jesus you worship actually is? I guess you will all reply in unison 'the Son of God who came down from Heaven.' Ha ha, that's funny—you really are stupid!"

121. Chao, "Open Letter." While confessing his Socialist sympathies, Zhao sets out why he was convinced that Communism was "utterly opposed to Chinese culture and ethics" and created a "tyranny" of class distinctions where none had existed in China.

122. Chao and Lew, "Relation of the Chinese Church to the Church Universal."

123. Barker, Editorial on Lambeth 1930. Barker's Chinese-language editorial was additionally published in English.

124. Chao, "Strengths and Weaknesses," 208.

125. Chao, Editorial.

CHAPTER 3. ZHAO ZICHEN AND A CREATIVE THEOLOGY

1. Zhao Zichen, *Yesu zhuan* 耶穌傳; page numbers here are given to the more widely available five-volume anthology, *Zhao Zichen wenji* 赵紫宸文集, Vol. 1. A shorter version of this chapter was published as "Surveying Galilee from a Chinese Observation Tower."

2. Chao, "Church-Consciousness of the Chinese People," 224.

3. Chao, "Jesus and the Reality of God," 343.

4. Much research has focused on his role as an educator, see e.g. articles by Xu Yihua or Han Zongyun in Wang, ed., *Zhao Zichen xiansheng jinian wenji* 赵紫宸先生纪念文集, and by Tang Xiaofeng in Tang and Xiong, eds., *Yeying zhi zhi* 夜鹰之志. Zhao remained convinced that Christian education was a good thing but argued that religious classes should be an elective component of the curriculum. See Chao, "Future of Religious Education in Christian Schools," 258, 263.

5. Zhao was dean of the School of Religion at Yanjing from 1928 to 1952, when he was removed from the post. His life had its share of pain: two brothers whom he supported through university died of illness in their twenties, he was imprisoned six months by the Japanese, and his thought was publicly criticized during the 1950s. His prison memoir is worthy of greater attention: see Zhao Zichen, *Jianyu ji* 監獄記.

6. Chao, "Indigenous Church," 180.

7. He lists those of Giovanni Papini, W. B. Hill, and James Moffatt as examples available in Chinese.

8. For discussion of other fictional depictions of Jesus from the 1920s to 1940s, see Zhange Ni, "Rewriting Jesus in Republican China."

9. Zhao Zichen, *Yesu zhuan*, Preface, p. 2.

10. The suspicion with which Western-educated believers have been regarded is reflected even in recent writings on Zhao that stress his secularized, contextualized vision. See the preface and his children's foreword to his collected works, "My Father Zhao Zichen," in *Zhao Zichen wenji*, Vol. 1, 4.

11. On transformations in Zhao's theology during the 1930s and 1940s see e.g. Ying, "Xunsuo jidujiao yu Zhongguo wenhua de guanxi"; Chow, *Theosis*, 79–80. Glüer, *Christliche Theologie in China*, proposed three phases in Zhao's thinking and writing: before 1927, approaches to chaos, indigenization, and Confucian-Christian synthesis; "Theological Reorientation," 1927–1948; and post-1948, "Theology in the New China." Ying Fuk-tsang, whose study highlights the relationship between Zhao's evolving theology and his changing view of the relationship between culture and religion, broadly agrees (pre-1930s liberal phase; 1930s and 1940s neo-orthodox; 1950s, related to New China); Ying, "Xunsuo jidujiao yu Zhongguo wenhua de guanxi," 66. Hoi Ming Hui (Xu Kaiming) divides Zhao's Christology into four periods: 1915–1922 focused on character; 1922–1927 on moral character; 1927–1937, on religion and ethics; and 1937–1949 on revelation and incarnation. See Xu Kaiming, "Lun Zhao Zichen xiansheng" 论赵紫宸先生, 112–14.

12. Zhao Zichen, *Sheng Baoluo zhuan* 聖保羅傳, Introduction, 1.

13. Zhao Zichen, *Sheng Baoluo zhuan*, 13. This passage is quoted by several commentators.

14. It is clear also that Zhao did not reject his earlier writings: he writes proudly a decade later of the fact that the *Life of Jesus* was a best-seller and used in at least one university course as an exemplar of new literature.

15. In German, Glüer, *Christliche Theologie in China*; in English, Hui, "Study of T. C. Chao's Christology"; in Chinese, Ying, *Xunsuo Jidujiao de dute xing*; Lam, *Qu gao he gua* 曲高和寡; Tang, *Zhao Zichen shenxue sixiang yanjiu* 赵紫宸神学思想研究.

16. See Kwan, *Post-colonial Resistance and Asian Theology*.

17. See Wan, "Emerging Hermeneutics of the Chinese Church." For a longer study which argues that Zhao's theology is constructed around ethical redemption and individual moral behavior, see Tang, *Zhao Zichen shenxue*.

18. Cf. several articles in the Tang and Xiong collection *Yeying zhi zhi*.

19. See Lin, *Ethical Reorientation for Christianity in China*.

20. An exception is Zhange Ni, "Rewriting Jesus in Republican China," within the context of the role of Christianity in nation-building and the "mutual appropriation" between Christianity and the emerging national literature.

21. Zhao Zichen, *Zhao Zichen wenji*, Vol. 1, 466. Translations are my own unless specified. Page numbers are given to the more readily accessible version of *Yesu zhuan* in Zhao's collected writings.

22. *Zhao Zichen wenji*, Vol. 1, 466.

23. See Moloughney, "From Biographical History to Historical Biography"; Twitchett, "Problems of Chinese Biography."

24. Wright, "Values, Roles and Personalities."

25. Wilkinson, *Chinese History*, 120.

26. Twitchett, "Problems of Chinese Biography," 28–29.

27. Wright's list includes "submissiveness to authority," "love of traditional learning," choice of the "middle course," and "esteem for force of example." Valorized characteristics more descriptive of Jesus include a preference for nonviolence and a noncompetitiveness. See Wright, "Values, Roles and Personalities," 9.

28. The *biezhuan* 别传 or *waizhuan* 外传, see Twitchett, "Problems of Chinese Biography," 25.

29. See Twitchett, "Problems of Chinese Biography," 38; Moloughney, "From Biographical History to Historical Biography," 16–18. Liang termed these 傳編 or 專傳, later termed 傳記. Adaptations included, e.g., the practice of quoting extensively from the subject's writings or the detail of chronological biographies.

30. Cf. Moloughney, "From Biographical History to Historical Biography," 23–24.

31. Moloughney, "From Biographical History to Historical Biography," 16.

32. There was some precedent in classical literature for this type of layered biography: see Shen Fu's autobiographical *Six Records of a Floating Life* (浮生六記), a well-known, exceptional text. Zhao's own chapter headings point to Chapter 5 as describing Jesus and clashes with the world, Chapter 6 as Jesus selecting and teaching disciples, and Chapter 8 as Jesus's teachings.

33. *Zhao Zichen wenji*, Vol. 1, 465.
34. *Zhao Zichen wenji*, Vol. 1, 479.
35. The incorporation of anecdotes showing the qualities of a child prodigy was a standard trope in biographies, although the normative virtue was the submission of the young to the old; cf. Wright. "Values, Roles and Personalities," 9.
36. *Zhao Zichen wenji*, Vol. 1, 501.
37. *Zhao Zichen wenji*, Vol. 1, 466.
38. *Zhao Zichen wenji*, Vol. 1, 486.
39. *Zhao Zichen wenji*, Vol. 1, 503.
40. *Zhao Zichen wenji*, Vol. 1, 497.
41. *Zhao Zichen wenji*, Vol. 1, 546. The text reads, "一個十八歲的女孩子，打扮得像紅綻的春梅一樣，出來跳舞侑酒。她又跳又唱，跳得像點波的輕燕，悄蝶的飛鶯，唱得像泣露的芙渠，吟風的綠竹。"
42. The dangers of contextualization are exposed in the temptations, however, when Jesus is tempted to use Greek and Roman culture to spread justice and fulfill Israel's mission to bring all to worship God. "So, how to go about it?" the implied narrator asks. "Accommodation! Only through accommodation!" The voice cedes to another: if you worship me, I will give you all this. "Get behind me, Satan!" cries Jesus, dismissing the cause of compromise and demonstrating how cultural accommodation can be a temptation in itself. *Zhao Zichen wenji*, Vol. 1, 498.
43. *Zhao Zichen wenji*, Vol. 1, 490. Trans. Legge, *Great Learning*, 5.1.2, p. 271.
44. *Zhao Zichen wenji*, Vol. 1, 492.
45. Chao, "Jesus and the Reality of God," 343–51.
46. Chao, "Jesus and the Reality of God," 345.
47. The quatrain reads roughly: The thousand league chain sinks to the bottom of the river / an array of flags emerges at Shitou / how many times in human life do circumstances rise and fall? / but mountains still, as of old, nestle the valley pass and the river course."
48. *Zhao Zichen wenji*, Vol. 1, 509.
49. *Zhao Zichen wenji*, Vol. 1, 458.
50. *Zhao Zichen wenji*, Vol. 1, 464.
51. *Zhao Zichen wenji*, Vol. 1, 574.
52. *Zhao Zichen wenji*, Vol. 1, 579.
53. Trans. in de Bary and Bloom, eds., *Sources of Chinese Tradition*, 683. For a discussion of the passage and its effects on Ming Christians, see Standaert, *Yang Tingyun*, 119–20. Zhang Zai lived in turbulent times and had himself considered military options in his youth, but in later life he regretted seeking material needs and not attaining righteousness. Zhao may have had these resonances in mind.
54. *Zhao Zichen wenji*, Vol. 1, 580.
55. One of Zhao Zichen's most powerful poems, "Bethany," written in 1922 and published in his collection of religious poetry *Da yu* 打漁 (Out into the Deep), presents a very tender reading of Jesus's relationship with Mary (and Martha's annoyance).
56. *Zhao Zichen wenji*, Vol. 1, 492.

57. *Zhao Zichen wenji*, Vol. 1, 544.
58. *Zhao Zichen wenji*, Vol. 1, 494.
59. *Zhao Zichen wenji*, Vol. 1, 527.
60. *Zhao Zichen wenji*, Vol. 1, 556.
61. *Zhao Zichen wenji*, Vol. 1, 508.
62. *Zhao Zichen wenji*, Vol. 1, 527–28.
63. *Zhao Zichen wenji*, Vol. 1, 487.
64. *Zhao Zichen wenji*, Vol. 1, 469.
65. *Zhao Zichen wenji*, Vol. 1, 496. On Zhao's mature-period Christology and how he comes to envision atonement, see e.g. Lin, "Tongyi de jiufa," 80–82.
66. *Zhao Zichen wenji*, Vol. 1, 475.
67. The paradox of John the Baptist, for Zhao, is that the least person in the kingdom is greater than this pure, selfless prophet, who has not understood that love has succeeded God's anger and punishment (*Zhao Zichen wenji*, Vol. 1, 530).
68. *Zhao Zichen wenji*, Vol. 1, 493.
69. *Zhao Zichen wenji*, Vol. 1, 493.
70. Zhao is no friend to the CCP at this point in his life and argues strongly in 1936 with Wu Leichuan over the gulf between Christianity and Communism, but the rhetoric of the masses and the valorization of the underclasses in Zhao has clear Marxist overtones. See Zhao's review of Wu's *Christianity and Chinese Culture* and discussion in Wan, "Emerging Hermeneutics of the Chinese Church," 353–55. In "An Open Letter," 9–12 (see Chao), Zhao confesses his Socialist sympathies and acknowledges that he could have become a Communist had it been merely a matter of common ownership of the means of production, but he outlines the problems he saw in Communism: its outdated philosophical base, methods of terror and violence, suppression of the individual, and denial of the autonomy of intellectuals.
71. *Zhao Zichen wenji*, Vol. 1, 535.
72. *Zhao Zichen wenji*, Vol. 1, 521.
73. *Zhao Zichen wenji*, Vol. 1, 557. The notion of the 新人, or new person, runs through early twentieth-century thought, from Yan Fu or Liang Qichao on literature creating the new person and new society, through to Mao's talks at Yan'an on literature and art creating the new (Socialist) person; Zhao both affirms and challenges these with his Christian version.
74. *Zhao Zichen wenji*, Vol. 1, 565.
75. *Zhao Zichen wenji*, Vol. 1, 567.
76. *Zhao Zichen wenji*, Vol. 1, 546.
77. *Zhao Zichen wenji*, Vol. 1, 510.
78. *Zhao Zichen wenji*, Vol. 1, 512.
79. *Zhao Zichen wenji*, Vol. 1, 513.
80. *Zhao Zichen wenji*, Vol. 1, 513.
81. *Zhao Zichen wenji*, Vol. 1, 516.
82. *Zhao Zichen wenji*, Vol. 1, 516.
83. The same term is the name of an anti-Christian magazine discussed in Chapter 2.

84. *Zhao Zichen wenji, Vol. 1,* 553, 555.

85. Chao, "Indigenous Church," 180–82.

86. *Zhao Zichen wenji, Vol. 1,* 478.

87. Our resonance with the landscape in Western Europe is just not as strong: visits to North Yorkshire bring to life the bleak scenes of the likes of the Brontë sisters, and Dublin trades on James Joyce tourism, but these are not the same as the specific site-related memories and layering of the Chinese geotextual landscape.

88. Wang Liqun (*Shanshui youji yanjiu* 山水游记研究) argues that travel literature must always comprise three elements: a record of whereabouts, a description of scenery, and an expression of reaction or feelings. Cf. Hargett, *On the Road in Twelfth Century China.* The introduction to Strassberg, *Inscribed Landscapes,* gives a good sense of the differences in mode and purpose of European and Chinese travel writing.

89. *Zhao Zichen wenji, Vol. 1,* 482.

90. The landscape is, as in English in the term "country," inseparable from its political extent. Just as Jerusalem became England in the minds of generations of schoolchildren who were brought up on William Blake's hymn ("And did those feet . . ."), *jiangshan* 江山 ("rivers and mountains") is metonymy for the state itself.

91. *Zhao Zichen wenji, Vol. 1,* 485.

92. *Zhao Zichen wenji, Vol. 1,* 485–86.

93. *Zhao Zichen wenji, Vol. 1,* 517.

94. *Zhao Zichen wenji, Vol. 1,* 523.

95. Xunzi, Youzuo (宥坐) chapter, also quoted in Xu Zhongyu, *Zhongnan youji xuan* 中南游记选, Introduction, 3.

96. Quotation from *Lunyu,* Yongye 雍也 section, also quoted in Wang Liqun, *Shanshui youji yanjiu,* 36. Zhao himself quotes this passage in an essay on Christianity and Confucianism, arguing that there is "a slight suggestion of an appreciation of nature as that in which man could find a reality which is both permanent and transient, both transcendent and immanent, both changeless and all-changing"; *Collected English Writings,* 249.

97. Renan, *Life of Jesus,* Preface, vii.

98. Zhao notably viewed the movement as "a sign of the need for a deeper manifestation of religion"; Chao, "Present-Day Religious Thought and Life in China," 198.

99. Chao, "Christianity and Confucianism," 588.

100. Zhange Ni, "Rewriting Jesus in Republican China," 241.

101. Zhange Ni also notes the "ambiguous attitude of the New Culture toward traditional culture" ("Rewriting Jesus in Republican China," 234) or this paradox of wanting to turn away from "the ancient culture" while drawing on it for a sense of Chineseness. It is the same tension that Moloughney discusses in Liang Qichao's call for a revolution in historiography while using hagiographies to foment patriotism ("From Biographical History to Historical Biography," 16).

102. See Ying Fuk-tsang, *Xunsuo Jidujiao de dute xing.*

103. See Ying's discussion of Zhao's 1935 essay "Zhongguo minzu yu jidujiao" 中國民族與基督教, *Xunsuo Jidujiao de dute xing,* 70.

CHAPTER 4. THE PUBLIC AND PERSONAL FACES OF THE CHURCH

1. Xu, "Tianzhujiao zenyang jiejue shehui wenti" 天主教怎樣解決社會問題 (How Catholicism Resolves Social Questions), 514.

2. Xu, *Sui si sui bi* 隨思隨筆, 76 (#95).

3. Xujiahui is rendered Zi Ka Wai in its older Romanization. There were other contenders for leading Catholic magazines, including the *Shengxin bao* 聖心報 of the Apostleship of Prayer (1887–1949) and especially the Tianjin-based *Yishi bao* 益世報 (1915–1949). The *Huibao* (1908–1911) formed out of the first Catholic journal, the *Yiwen lu* 益聞錄 (1879–1911), also from Xujiahui; once this ceased publication, the *Shengjiao zazhi* emerged (1912–1938).

4. Xu, "Shehui jingjixue gailun" 社會經濟學概論, 31.

5. Including an edited tome celebrating the three hundredth anniversary of his illustrious forebear Xu Guangqi.

6. The phrase means something like "straight from one's thoughts to the brush." The title echoes Yuan Mei's famous volume *Sui yuan sui bi* 隨園隨筆 (Random Jottings from the Garden of Contentment). The first edition of Xu's book includes an imprimatur showing that the bishop of Shanghai had bestowed approval.

7. Xu edited the church journal from 1923 until it was shut down during the war in 1938; many of his books began life as long essays in it. See Lei, *Lun Jidujiao zhi da yu xiao* 论基督教之大与小, 213. Lei (Leopold Leeb) lists an inventory of Xu's works.

8. For a précis of research on Xu Zongze to date, see Li Lili, "Tianzhujiao shehui xundao" 天主教社會訓導, 15–17.

9. In calling for greater indigenization and higher-level training for priests. See Xu Wenhua, "Xu Zongze de shengping zhushu" 徐宗泽的生平著述, 3. Other understudied intellectuals who were born in late imperial China include e.g. Li Wenyu 李問漁, Pan Gusheng 潘谷聲, and Zhu Zhiyao 朱志堯. Xu Wenhua conjectures that Xu Zongze's work is not better known because his writings took a fairly straight Vatican line or because writers have found little detail on his life or personal reflections, a stance that seems to exclude the *biji*.

10. See Xu Wenhua "Xu Zongze de shengping zhushu," 4–5.

11. Accounts of the fields of Xu's doctorates and their number (two? three?) do not tally. Fang Hao lists doctorates in "philosophy and the sciences"; Fang, *Zhongguo Tianzhujiao shi renwu zhuan* 中国天主教史人物传, 677.

12. See Bailey, "Cultural Connections in a New Global Space."

13. These were all published under the aegis of *Shengjiao zazhi* and printed at the Shanghai Tushanwan church press. The volumes listed are, respectively, 勞動問題 (1924), 天主教與婦女問題 (1925), 共產主義駁論 (1926), 社會問題 (1928), 天主造物論 四末論 (1930), 聖寵論 (1930), and 天主降生救贖論 (1932).

14. These were part of a set of six volumes intended as an overview of theology for secondary school students, with one volume per school year, again printed by the Tushanwan press.

15. Xu's work, Li argues, draws deeply on traditional Catholic teaching in formulating his constructive social critique, at the same time as making "adjustments" to faith

teachings in the light of local circumstances. Preeminently a "dialogue between faith and contextualization," the accommodations that Xu was making were no longer to official Confucian thought, as with his Jesuit predecessors, but to modern Western thinking and new scholarship. See Li Lili, "Tianzhujiao shehui xundao," 2. Li examines three different aspects of Xu's writings: Catholic teachings on women in the light of the "churchization" of traditional Chinese views on women, the sinicization of education in China in the light of the Anti-Christian Movement, and labor issues in the light of human dignity and justice. As she states, Xu "tries to blend Roman Catholic doctrine with developing social science theories, to correct clashes in thought between the new theories and Roman Catholic doctrine" (p. 7).

16. Xu Wenhua, "Xu Zongze de shengping zhushu," 12–13, provides a table listing all article themes before and after 1924. Xu also notes that Xu Zongze wrote 17 percent of the articles himself during his tenure.

17. "Laodong qiyue" 勞動契約, and "Tianzhu jiao zenyang jiejue shehui wenti" 天主教 怎樣解決社會問題.

18. Leo XIII, "Rerum Novarum."

19. Xu, "Xu Zongze de shengping zhushu," 15.

20. Pius IX, "Quadragesimo Anno," §15.

21. Xu, "Tianzhu jiao zenyang jiejue shehui wenti," 516.

22. Xu, "Tianzhu jiao zenyang jiejue shehui wenti," 519.

23. Xu, "Zheyang zuo xianqi liangmu" 這樣做賢妻良母, 167–71.

24. Xu quotes the *Daxue* (Great Learning) of Confucius to shore up the point.

25. Xu, *Sheng chong lun*, 3.

26. In a moment of wry candor, Xu comments on his habitual writers' block and how others in his position can alleviate the symptoms by good tobacco or good Longjing tea, but since he doesn't smoke and has only cheap tea leaves, he cannot write. Still, he contends, each job has its own troubles—better to be at peace with one's lot. And as the reader notes, this very thought has provided him with the entry that eluded him.

27. Fu, "Flourishing of *Biji* or Pen-Notes Texts," 107.

28. Owen, *Readings in Chinese Literary Thought*, 272. Liu Xie is here commenting on the distinction, rather than affirming it; as Owen suggests, the grounds for distinctions of the basis of literary style, prose/poetic voice, or whether a text was "written" or the transcription of the oral words of sages were "confused."

29. See Dudbridge, *Books, Tales and Vernacular Culture*, 10. The writer was Huan Tan.

30. See e.g. *Sui si sui bi* #54.

31. *Sui si sui bi*, 46 (#52).

32. Mitter, "Writing War."

33. Mitter, "Writing War," 197.

34. Mitter's Xu shares other pertinent traits with Xu Zongze: a lack of inclination to draw any lessons from, or larger framework around, the disparate entries—that task is left to the reader—and an alternative subjectivity as arch-rationalist and taxonomist in the author's other writings. In an interesting note on Song dynasty *biji*, Fu Daiwie in "The Flourishing of *Biji*" asserts that while authors jotted down discontinuous

notes and reflections, they later assigned them categories according to subject—
except *biji* from chaotic periods, like dynastic transitions, which had no clear order
or taxonomy.

35. Liu, "Poetics of Miscellaneousness," 6.

36. Liu, "Poetics of Miscellaneousness," Abstract.

37. As Leeb points out, the volume includes Dark Ages and medieval philosophy, including Arab thought, at a time when most thinkers in China were looking only to
modern Western thought; Lei Libo, *Lun Jidujiao zhi da yu xiao*, 214.

38. *Sui si sui bi*, 27 (#31).

39. *Sui si sui bi*, 31–32 (#37). Xu notes that when asked about their content, he has a set
response: they discuss "matters east, west, north, and south"; all compass points and
all manner of thing are covered, otherwise "we would hit a brick wall, with 'No Thor-
oughfare' ahead!"

40. Extract numbers throughout refer to the volume *Sui si sui bi* and not to the original
entry numbers in the magazine volumes of *Shengjiao zazhi*. There is a slight discrep-
ancy because Xu cut some of the entries when he collated the volume.

41. *Sui si sui bi*, 16 (#17).

42. *Sui si sui bi*, 87 (#115). On the fascinating history of the Zi-ka-wei Observatory, its
personnel, and its innovative typhoon warning systems, see www.hko.gov.hk/blog/en/
archives/00000047.htm.

43. *Sui si sui bi*, 12–13 (#13).

44. Elsewhere, Xu points out the gains to individuals from amassing texts, including
monetary ones. A note that Xu received from a Suzhou bureau enquiring about past
sets of newspapers provided the impetus for Xu to enlighten his readers as to the material value of the magazine, as well as other newspaper sets they may have. Totting
up the prices of historical sets of newspapers, with a premium for whole runs, Xu
shows the value of buying (and keeping) *Shengjiao zazhi*.

45. *Sui si sui bi*, 28 (#34).

46. *Sui si sui bi*, 4–5 (#5).

47. "Their persons being cultivated, their families were regulated. Their families being
regulated, their States were rightly governed. Their states being rightly governed, the
whole empire was made tranquil and happy"; Legge, *Great Learning*, 266.

48. *Sui si sui bi*, 77 (#97).

49. He writes, for example, "We Chinese have a particular characteristic, that we know
how to praise European and American civilization, but we look down on our own
past civilization"—a clear failing; *Sui si sui bi*, 32 (#39).

50. *Sui si sui bi*, 35–36 (#42). Xu returns to the "movement for the construction of a
Chinese literature" in later musings, noting that its appearance had created a lot of
interest in the press, mainly as correspondents picked up on the use of the word *wenhua*, culture, and debated what it meant. For Xu, who was aware of parallel debates
in Europe over *kultur* and high culture, "Culture is the action of the intelligence,
since only those who have intelligence are cultured; culture is a product of human
talent, which, when it is manifest externally, becomes culture. . . . Thoughts which
accumulate in a person's mind are expressed as action, and when these are built up

over a long time culture is produced" (*Sui si sui bi*, 62). For Xu, all systems of cultural artifacts, customs, and habits are "action," and culture is definitely material as well as spiritual.

51. *Sui si sui bi*, 38 (#45).

52. *Sui si sui bi*, 61 (#74). Xu reports conversations with a colleague ("Old 97") on philosophy, where the latter was advocating that Chinese scholars should all learn some Western philosophy, particularly logic, to force them to greater clarity in their thinking: "If you do not read any Logic, you cannot make your thought clear, and end up speaking backward and forward on even a very simple matter, and you cannot ascertain exactly what's meant; the reason is due to not starting out from definitions–an error of a hair's breadth leads you miles astray!"

53. *Sui si sui bi*, 98–99 (#134).

54. Elsewhere, Xu acknowledges the difficulty of the editorial writer's task and the tension between wanting the reader's approval and writing a spirited editorial—a tension compounded during an era when a small error could result in a fine and a serious error in the imprisonment of the lead writer; see p. 66 (#80).

55. Xu is not oblivious to the weaknesses of the old pedagogy. In an entry entitled "Education ought to develop all faculties of the student" (#107) he considers how the old curriculum and its rote learning led to an overdevelopment of the memory at the cost of other faculties. Education should foster the whole person and allow the development of heaven-given capacities, which include perception, and the spiritual, as well as the faculty of memory—which if overdeveloped can consume too much strength and etiolate other faculties in the developing brains of the young.

56. *Sui si sui bi*, 50 (#57).

57. *Sui si sui bi*, 47 (#53).

58. *Sui si sui bi*, 94 (#128).

59. *Sui si sui bi*, 96 (#130).

60. *Sui si sui bi*, 36–37 (#43).

61. *Sui si sui bi*, 49–50 (#56).

62. See e.g. *Sui si sui bi*, 51 (#58).

63. *Sui si sui bi*, 52 (#61).

64. *Sui si sui bi*, 83 (#108).

65. *Sui si sui bi*, 74 (#93).

66. *Sui si sui bi*, 55–56 (#64).

67. *Sui si sui bi*, 56 (#64).

68. *Sui si sui bi*, 92–93 (#125). Xu uses the unusual compound 偽假 here; the first character is used for "puppet" (government), a subtle reference to avoiding the appearance or the sham of compliance/collaboration with the Japanese.

69. *Sui si sui bi*, 82 (#106).

70. Sometimes the sheer practicality of Xu's advice is amusing (or paternalistic). For example, if you want to live a long time, he notes, you should avoid overeating, "since the stomach is like a stove, and when a stove is full of coal, it doesn't draw well and it is difficult to heat up." When the stomach gets over full and can't digest properly, over time this damaged stomach leads to illness and debilitation (p. 78, #98).

71. *Sui si sui bi*, 93 (#127).
72. *Sui si sui bi*, 54 (#62).
73. *Sui si sui bi*, 79–80 (#102).
74. *Sui si sui bi*, 80 (#102).
75. *Sui si sui bi*, 61 (#73).
76. Perhaps "examenometer" is a better term, given that Xu was a Jesuit.
77. *Sui si sui bi*, 92 (#123).
78. The text of Chiang's speech "Essentials of the New Life Movement" is given in de Bary and Lufrano, eds., *Sources of Chinese Tradition*, 341–44.
79. *Sui si sui bi*, 78 (#99).
80. "The state has four cardinal virtues. If one is eliminated, the state will totter. If two, it will be in danger. If three, it will be overthrown. If all four are eliminated, it will be totally destroyed. . . . What are these four cardinal virtues? The first is propriety, the second is righteousness, the third is integrity, and the fourth is a sense of shame. Propriety consists in not overstepping the bounds of proper restraint. Righteousness consists in not pushing oneself forward at the expense of others. Integrity consists in not concealing one's faults. Having a sense of shame consists in not following those who go awry. Therefore if no one oversteps the bounds of proper restraint, the position of the sovereign will be safe. If no one pushes himself forward, the people will be free of artfulness and deceit. If no one follows those who go awry, evil practices will not arise." Translation from Rickett, *Guanzi*, 54.
81. De Bary and Lufrano, eds., *Sources of Chinese Tradition*, 341.
82. See e.g. Ferlanti, "New Life Movement in Jiangxi Province." As Ferlanti notes, moral revival and self-strengthening formed part of Nationalist and Communist discourse. Debates between Chiang Kai-shek and Wang Jingwei on suasion/coercion and morality/the law have been echoed in English-language scholarship on the movement, which has gradually moved from a fascist to a state-building narrative.
83. 禮義廉恥; translated by Rickett as "cardinal virtues," see *Guanzi*, 51, and by Ulrich Theobold as "social guidelines," see www.chinaknowledge.de/Literature/Diverse/guanzi.html.
84. An alternative choice of virtues would have been the better known list of Mencius, listed in Gongsun Chou Part I, where "benevolence" and "wisdom" appear instead of modesty and a sense of shame.
85. Peter Lee, "Images of Society in the Early Chosun Literary Miscellany," Abstract.
86. Li Lili, "Tianzhujiao shehui xundao," 6
87. Li Lili, "Tianzhujiao shehui xundao," 8.
88. Similar arguments have been made for Chinese philosophy, which was earlier seen as not-philosophy because of its nonlinear, unsystematic form.

CHAPTER 5. WU LEICHUAN, *CHRISTIANITY AND CHINESE CULTURE*, AND THE KINGDOM OF HEAVEN

1. Wu, *Jidujiao yu Zhongguo wenhua*, 5.
2. Eddy, *Religion and Social Justice*, 206.

3. See e.g. Chu, *Wu Leichuan*; Liang Hui, "Interpreting the Lord's Prayer."

4. A helpful survey by Li Wei can be found in Zhao Shilin and Duan Qi, eds., *Jidujiao zai Zhongguo* 基督教在中国, Vol. 1, 160–294, which draws on material in the author's monograph *Wu Leichuan* 吴雷川; see also Chan, *Liji liren* 立己立人.

5. Nedostup, *Superstitious Regimes*, 1.

6. Nee, *Normal Christian Life*, 79; on faith in the party/state, see Nedostup, *Superstitious Regimes*, 4.

7. See West, "Christianity and Nationalism," esp. 236–37, 241–43. As West charts, these shift from achieving national salvation through education, moral example, or talented individuals to achieving it via armed struggle and revolution.

8. West, "Christianity and Nationalism," 243.

9. The minister of education was Cai Yuanpei, who became president of Peking (then National Peking) University in 1917 and later founded the Academica Sinica in 1928. Cai supported Peking students in their anti-imperialist (and anti-Christian) protests.

10. Details of Wu's biography can be found in English in Chu, *Wu Leichuan*, 5–15.

11. For details on the situation, and judgment on the relative merits of Stuart and Wu, see Chu, *Wu Leichuan*, 10–15; West, *Yenching University and Sino-Western Relations, 1916–1952*, 108.

12. Wu, *Jidujiao yu Zhongguo wenhua*, 37–38.

13. Nee, *Normal Christian Life*, 79. Ni's thinking in the late 1930s was compiled and published in English "without reference to Nee," as editor Angus Kinnear notes, following a European tour.

14. Nee, *Normal Christian Life*, 79. This was because, for Ni, the old, once put through the Cross, was wiped out; all creation from the old world, under Satan's "absolute dominion," must die. Ni's emphasis on the transformation of the person and Wu's on society inflates their differences, since they are often not addressing the same question when discussing "the kingdom."

15. Nee, *Glorious Church*, 65–71, quotation from p. 14. For Ni, Christ's redemption deals with the problem of Satan's authority, but "the responsibility of executing the sentence is upon the church" (p. 71), a work that can be done only through weakness, and allowing God to work, rather than human strength. *The Glorious Church* gathers talks from 1939 to 1942.

16. There are in reality, however, only six types of actions, since the seventh appears as a footnote, a concession to readers: Jesus's healings and exorcisms.

17. Wu, *Jidujiao yu Zhongguo wenhua*, 20.

18. See *jianguo* 建国 versus (建) 天国 and translation of *guo* as both "kingdom" and "state." On the broad factors influencing the anti-superstitious rhetoric of the late Qing and Republican eras, and on the 1927–1937 campaign, see Nedostup, *Superstitious Regimes*, 13–15.

19. Wu, *Jidujiao yu Zhongguo wenhua*, 21.

20. Nationalist rhetoric proposed a two-stage transfer of sovereignty to the people followed by a separation of religion from public life; see Nedostup, *Superstitious Regimes*, 4. Zhang Zhenzhi's volume *Revolution and Religion* called for a clear separation of political authority from "numinous power"; see discussion in Nedostup.

21. Wu, *Jidujiao yu Zhongguo wenhua*, 21.
22. Wu, *Jidujiao yu Zhongguo wenhua*, 21.
23. Wu, *Jidujiao yu Zhongguo wenhua*, 23.
24. This passage again echoes Charles Gore (see below), who notes that Jesus devoted more and more attention to training the disciples—as witnesses and rulers of the New Jerusalem—after seeing that the majority of Israel would not listen to the message; and that as Jesus organized the new community, he gave the sacramental rites of baptism and the breaking of bread to them. Gore, *Christ and Society*, 40–41.
25. Wu, *Jidujiao yu Zhongguo wenhua*, 23.
26. Wu, *Jidujiao yu Zhongguo wenhua*, 8.
27. Wu, *Jidujiao yu Zhongguo wenhua*, 24.
28. In this section on the typology of Jesus's actions, Wu adumbrates his logic through selected quotations from the classics. "If the will be set on virtue, there will be no practice of wickedness," *Li ren*, 4.4 苟志于仁矣，无恶; therefore, the healing power lies in the effect of the will of the heart/mind. The orientation of one's heart, or will, is central to Wu, giving strength and enabling right action. If a person were able to apply strength to virtue for just one day, "I have not seen a case in which his strength would be insufficient," as the *Analects* continues.
29. Lk 11:8–13.
30. *Analects*, Shu Er.
31. *Analects*, Shu Er. Translation from Legge, *Chinese Classics, Vol. I*, 204, modified.
32. *Mencius*, Gaozi Part I, Translation from Legge, *Chinese Classics, Vol. II*, 414.
33. "The Master said: If a man be without the virtues [*ren* 仁] proper to humanity, what has he to do with the rites or propriety? If a man be without the virtues [*ren* 仁] proper to humanity, what has he to do with music?" (*Analects*, Ba Yi, trans. Legge, *Chinese Classics, Vol. 1*, 155).
34. "夫仁，　天之尊爵也。" *Mencius*, Gongsun chou.
35. "而棄其天爵，　則惑者深者也，　終必亡而已矣。" *Mencius*, Gaozi. Translation from Legge, *Chinese Classics, Vol. II, Mencius*, 322.
36. Wu, *Jidujiao yu Zhongguo wenhua*, 33–34.
37. Since both the Holy Spirit and *ren* are innate to humans, here we have to follow Confucius's understanding that "through mortifying the body one achieves *ren* virtue" (the phrase has become a proverb meaning to die a martyr, or die for a cause); Jesus's words "unless I go the Holy Spirit will not come" may not to taken literally.
38. Wu, *Jidujiao yu Zhongguo wenhua*, 35
39. Wu, *Jidujiao yu Zhongguo wenhua*, 37.
40. For example, Jesus giving the keys of the kingdom to Peter as a speaking of the Holy Spirit, or *ren*.
41. Wu, *Jidujiao yu Zhongguo wenhua*, 24.
42. Wu, *Jidujiao yu Zhongguo wenhua*, 25.
43. There is nothing particularly novel in Wu's interpretation of what the temptations might really mean, but the demythologizing of all figurative language leads him to the rather prosaic conclusion that undertakings need careful consideration at the outset, "like planning a game of chess before the first move" (*Jidujiao yu Zhong-*

guo wenhua, 26). Wu comments (pp. 25–26) that there were three false suppositions playing on Jesus's mind as he took some time out to plan his extraordinary work: the temptation of nonnatural means, of giving material aid to the people; a playing on the inherited psychology of the people and use of "miracles"; and political compromise, throwing his lot in with the leaders to gain power, i.e., worshipping the devil.

44. Wu cites Matt 13; *Jidujiao yu Zhongguo wenhua*, 40.

45. Wu, *Jidujiao yu Zhongguo wenhua*, 40.

46. Wu, *Jidujiao yu Zhongguo wenhua*, 23.

47. Cf. Wu, *Jidujiao yu Zhongguo wenhua*, 34.

48. These were translated into Chinese by Yu Ensi 俞恩嗣 and published by the Anglican Church in China in 1931.

49. Translated into Chinese and published by the Youth Association, in its Books and Newspapers Translation Journal in 1930.

50. Eddy, *Religion and Social Justice*, 9

51. Gore, *Christ and Society*, 154.

52. Gore, *Christ and Society*, 15–16. Gore writes of the "bewilderment" of trying to reconcile an apocalyptic Christianity and its insistence on world renunciation with the reality of the permanent, organized social life of the present, and sets out in his lectures to outline historical attempts to create the Kingdom of God on earth in different ages through to the present. One of his conclusions is that previous centuries give "no model" for the present but that the "passion for co-operation with God" is "the deepest and most enduring motive which can stir us to action and sustain us within it" (p. 29). It is, we can surmise, this passion that sustains Wu in the face of skepticism, self-doubt, and delay in achieving any of the goals of national salvation.

53. Rauschenbusch, *Theology for the Social Gospel*, 137.

54. Rauschenbusch, *Theology for the Social Gospel*, 139–42.

55. Matt 7:21. Wu's emphasis on the kingdom as a society to be established on earth has divided critics, probably along preexisting theological lines. Yamamoto Sumiko, for example, writes that Wu's understanding of the kingdom as an issue facing contemporary society rather than the mind, and his conclusion that "Thy kingdom come" meant reforming the social order, "is a diversion to say the least"; Yamamoto, *History of Protestantism*, 269.

56. Wu, *Jidujiao yu Zhongguo wenhua*, 55.

57. Examples in this paragraph are taken from Wu, *Jidujiao yu Zhongguo wenhua*, 41.

58. Wu, *Jidujiao yu Zhongguo wenhua*, 42.

59. Wu draws here and in other writings on Karl Kautsky, the Czech/Austrian/German Marxist (and atheist) theoretician who discusses these issues in *Foundations of Christianity* (1925), translated into Chinese in 1932 by Tang Zhi 汤治 and Ye Qifang 叶启芳. Wu quotes Kautsky at length in Chapter 5, pp. 57–58, including his comments on the shift in Christianity from a communal organization to one that "pillages all classes."

60. Gore, *Property*, xv, xi. Gore is quoting "Bartlett of Mansfield College" in the first part. Gore also wrote of the strong sense of brotherhood in community, and in founding an Anglican monastery at Mirfield had sought to put into practice his ideals of social reform in a new type of community.

61. Wu, *Jidujiao yu Zhongguo wenhua*, 43. Wu is assuming public ownership of property and work for "the common good" or "the state" here.

62. Wu, *Jidujiao yu Zhongguo wenhua*, 43.

63. Matt 10:8; Wu, *Jidujiao yu Zhongguo wenhua*, 45.

64. Wu, *Jidujiao yu Zhongguo wenhua*, 45.

65. Wu, *Jidujiao yu Zhongguo wenhua*, 46.

66. The debates that Wu engages with, and his Marxian readings of the parables, prefigure remarkably closely the Liberation Theology debates of the 1980s, including those between Pope John Paul II and the South American theologians Gustavo Guttiérez, Leonardo Boff, Oscar Romero, and others. The Congregation for the Doctrine of the Faith argued in the 1980s that seeing salvation in terms of social justice deprived Christianity of its power to transform daily life and that the church should not be inspired in its work for the poor by a political vision of a perfect world (Wu's "ideal kingdom" of Jesus) or some Marxist utopia; true liberation begins with individual redemption from "the radical slavery of sin." Cf. Congregation for the Doctrine of the Faith, "Instruction on Certain Aspects of the 'Theology of Liberation.'"

67. Congregation for the Doctrine of the Faith, "Instruction on Certain Aspects of the 'Theology of Liberation.'"

68. Wu, *Jidujiao yu Zhongguo wenhua*, 61.

69. Wu, *Jidujiao yu Zhongguo wenhua*, 55.

70. Wu, *Jidujiao yu Zhongguo wenhua*, 47.

71. Wu, *Jidujiao yu Zhongguo wenhua*, 55.

72. Legge's translation, amended, *Chinese Classics, Vol. III*, 283. The original reads, "The sincere, intelligent, and perspicacious among men becomes the great sovereign." The remainder of the quotation reads "and the great sovereign is the parent of the people."

73. Wu, *Jidujiao yu Zhongguo wenhua*, 48.

74. Wu, *Jidujiao yu Zhongguo wenhua*, 47.

75. The reference here is to Lk 9:34–48.

76. Mencius, *Jin Xin II*, quoted by Wu, *Jidujiao yu Zhongguo wenhua*, 49. Legge translates as "If the ruler of a State love benevolence, he will have no enemy in the kingdom"; *Chinese Classics*, Vol. II, 479.

77. Wu, *Jidujiao yu Zhongguo wenhua*, 50.

78. Wu, *Jidujiao yu Zhongguo wenhua*, 51.

79. Wu, *Jidujiao yu Zhongguo wenhua*, 53.

80. Wu, *Jidujiao yu Zhongguo wenhua*, 54.

81. Li Wei, *Wu Leichuan de jidujiao chujinghua sixiang yanjiu*, 12. Cf. also Chao and Lew, "Relation of the Chinese Church to the Church Universal," 350–51.

82. Cf. Li Wei, *Wu Leichuan*, 10–17. Wing-Hung Lam makes a similar point.

83. Li Wei is drawing on Stephen Bevan's definitions of the terms; for a contrary view on the definition of "inculturation," see e.g. Arbuckle, *Culture, Inculturation and Theologians*. Li also quotes Wing-Hung Lam's schematization of five Chinese models of inculturation, from Wu Leichuan's "Christian faith within traditional Chinese culture" through the "cultural blending" of Wang Zhixin and Zhao Zichen's "Chris-

tianity completing Chinese culture" to Wang Mingdao's separation of culture and religion, or the final category of Christianity judging Chinese culture. The scheme is helpful, but characterizing Wu Leichuan as operating entirely within a traditional cultural mode underplays the novelty of much of his thought as well as the scope of his sense of culture.

84. Wu, *Jidujiao yu Zhongguo wenhua*, 58–59. On different periodizations and models of culture, see e.g. Tanner, *Theories of Culture*, Chapters 1 and 2.

85. Wu, *Jidujiao yu Zhongguo wenhua*, 62.

86. Wu, *Jidujiao yu Zhongguo wenhua*, 144.

87. Chu Sin-jan (*Wu Leichuan*, 101) argues that Wu's advocacy for a "totalitarian regime" is misguided and that his economic thought lacks data and is "amateurish"; the latter may be true, but it is not clear that Wu is advocating anything more than unified, or joined-up, centralized government to tackle flood and drought control as well as rural education, etc.

88. As Chu Sin-jan explains (*Wu Leichuan*, 106), Wu's "shift to socialist and revolutionary means" on land reform followed years of thought on this topic; his earlier ideas had included sending experts out to rural provinces and setting up university courses in rural reconstruction. The take-up for experts or students to go out and enact reforms was low.

89. Wu, *Jidujiao yu Zhongguo wenhua*, 162. Wu is here talking about the New Culture Movement, the brain child of Chiang Kai-shek, which was predicated on encouraging a return to the traditional moral values of the countryside, i.e., "propriety, justice, integrity, and a sense of shame;" see discussion in Chapter 4 above.

90. Wu, *Jidujiao yu Zhongguo wenhua*, 14.

91. Wu, *Jidujiao yu Zhongguo wenhua*, 15.

92. Wu, *Jidujiao yu Zhongguo wenhua*, 5.

93. Zhao Zichen was skeptical of Wu's notion that Jesus understood his mission as building a new country for the contemporary Jews; see Zhao Zichen, "Yesu wei Jidu."

94. Wu, *Jidujiao yu Zhongguo wenhua*, 18.

95. Wu, *Jidujiao yu Zhongguo wenhua*, 17.

96. "择善而固执之" and "得一善则拳拳服膺而弗失之." The quotations are from the *Zhong yong* (Doctrine of the Mean), Chapters 8 and 20, trans. Legge, *Chinese Classics, Vol. I*, 389, 413. The first quotation in full is "[He who attains to sincerity is] he who chooses what is good and firmly holds it fast."

97. Wu, *Jidujiao yu Zhongguo wenhua*, 18.

98. Wu, *Jidujiao yu Zhongguo wenhua*, 19.

99. Wu, *Jidujiao yu Zhongguo wenhua*, 19.

100. Wu, *Jidujiao yu Zhongguo wenhua*, 19–20.

101. On the rather slick double act of John and Jesus, Yamamoto (*History of Protestantism*, 268) comments: "this idea of Christ and John as co-conspirators in grabbing political power from the Romans is a remarkably secular biblical interpretation."

102. Tillich, *Systematic Theology*, 357.

103. And quite possibly his Confucian heritage, too. Cf. Liang Hui ("How Do Modern Chinese Christian Intellectuals Read the Bible?"), who argues that Wu's emphasis on

religion as continuously evolving, from a primitive belief in prayer and magic to more noble ideas and empathy, was a way of mitigating the science-religion conflict.

104. Wu, *Jidujiao yu Zhongguo wenhua*, Preface, 6.
105. Wu, *Jidujiao yu Zhongguo wenhua*, Preface, 6.
106. Chen Duxiu, "Christianity and the Chinese People."
107. Liang Hui, "How Do Modern Chinese Christian Intellectuals Read the Bible?"

CHAPTER 6. THE CHURCH AND THE PEOPLE'S REPUBLIC OF CHINA

1. Zhang, *Wo de putishu*, 4–5. Zhang was labeled a rightist in the 1957 Anti-Rightist campaign and spent many years in labor reform camps.
2. Jin, *Memoirs of Jin Luxian*, 212.
3. This paragraph draws on Starr, "Chinese Church."
4. Divisions among Protestants can be seen, for example, in a document from the Word of Life church, a large house-church network, whose formulation of the principles of theological education in the 1980s included an article requiring members to "clearly discern that the TSPM does not represent the true church" but exists as an "adulterous political organism" serving atheism. See Xin, *Inside China's House Church Network*, 89.
5. E.g. Donald McInnis or Jonathan Chao, cf. Lian Xi, Review of Mariani, *Church Militant*.
6. A move accentuated by theorization of the means by which the Chinese church developed its autonomy as "breakaway" from Western "control." See Chapter 2 above and brief discussion of Duan Qi's writing in Starr and Dunch, "Introduction," in Zhuo Xinping, ed., *Christianity*, xxiv.
7. Coulet, *Actes de Béda Chang*, 10. Jesuit sources indicate that Coulet was the pseudonym of Claude Larre, S.J.; Zhang took the name Boda after seminary; Béda was his baptismal name and Zhengming his *zi*, courtesy name.
8. Pius XII, "Ad Sinarum Gentem," §22.
9. Mariani, *Church Militant*, 42.
10. Jin, *Memoirs of Jin Luxian*, 40.
11. Nathan, *Chinese Democracy*, 153.
12. A series of articles in newspapers like the *South China Morning Post* began to appear in summer 2013 of individuals apologizing for their part in Red Guard torment of teachers and others.
13. Mitter, *China's War with Japan*, 5, 14.
14. Coulet, *Actes de Béda Chang*, 7; cf. Mariani, *Church Militant*, 38. Zhang's death was understood immediately: one of the many requiem Masses held in the days after his death was celebrated in red vestments, the liturgical color for martyrs. *Liberation Daily*, meanwhile, hailed him an "imperialist running dog and counter-revolutionary" who entertained Japanese and sent students to America for "slavery education" (Mariani, 88). Zhang's relationship to martyrdom is interesting; in his ordination memorial in 1940 he had written of Ignatius of Antioch, saying "he died a martyr; we cannot hope for such grace" (Coulet, 4). After the suicide of a pupil at his college, Zhang spoke of

the only way of overcoming such inclinations: by forcing ourselves to incarnate our ideal in the realities of concrete life—a tenet that led him to prison.

15. Merwin and Jones, *Documents of the Three-Self Movement*, 15.

16. Yale Divinity School Pamphlet Collection, HR 124. It was not out of any conscious sense of imperialist superiority, one assumes, that an American Thanksgiving Day service held at the same church chose William Merrill's hymn "Not Alone for Mighty Empire" to follow the anthem. "Not alone for mighty empire / stretching far o'er land and sea / not alone for bounteous harvests / lift we up our hearts to thee . . . Not for battleships and fortress / not for conquests of the sword / but for conquests of the spirit / give we thanks, O Lord." "An American Association of Peking Thanksgiving Day Service" at Peking Union Church, 29 Nov. 1934; Yale Divinity Pamphlet Collection, HR 124.

17. Jin, *Memoirs of Jin Luxian*, 57–58.

18. Merwin and Jones, *Documents of the Three-Self Movement*, 66. The article was translated from the Shanghai *Liberation Daily*, 31 Mar. 1951. Djang writes of Jinling (Ginling) College in her disavowal that "not only had English been the medium of instruction, but we had even thought it a mark of distinction to use English in writing letters, in casual conversation, and in holding meetings."

19. "Regulations Governing All Organizations Subsidised with Foreign Funds," 29 Dec. 1950, drafted by Zhou Enlai. See MacInnis, *Religious Policy and Practice*, 25. Details in this paragraph are taken from MacInnis, 25–30.

20. MacInnis, *Religious Policy and Practice*, 29.

21. In line with other political action to create larger economic and industrial conglomerates, the amalgamation of small churches was presented as a "movement to eliminate confusion and waste." See MacInnis, *Religious Policy and Practice*, 180–81.

22. New China News Agency. Dispatch. The statistics presented show that the government knew that, for example, only 17 percent of Protestant preachers were foreign, propaganda on "foreign influence" notwithstanding.

23. "Allegedly," as Bays notes, *New History*, 162. *Tian Feng* documented new signatories over several months of editions, but it is impossible at this distance to assess duplicate names, forgeries, etc., as were documented for the pro-government Catholic manifestos.

24. Merwin and Jones, *Documents of the Three-Self Movement*, 19–20.

25. NCC report on the 1951–1952 Three-Anti Campaign, June 1952, published in *Xie Jin*; trans. in Merwin, *Documents of the Three-Self Movement*, 70–71. The Three-Self name was subsequently changed from the Three-Self Reform Movement to the Three-Self Patriotic Movement (TSPM) to ease doubts that religious "reform" was required.

26. MacInnis, *Religious Policy and Practice*, 147.

27. Merwin and Jones, *Documents of the Three-Self Movement*, 17.

28. As Harrison writes (*Missionary's Curse*, 120), "Money extracted from the local economy by the foreign powers, not foreign donations, funded the diocese in the early twentieth century."

29. Harrison, *Missionary's Curse*, 131.

30. Harrison, *Missionary's Curse*, 128.

31. Harrison, *Missionary's Curse*, 133.

32. Harrison, *Missionary's Curse*, 148.

33. Jin, *Memoirs of Jin Luxian*, 215.

34. Author interviews, Sichuan, 1991, 1993; see also Yang Huilin, "Contemporary Significance of Theological Ethics," 52, and discussion in Chapter 9 below.

35. "The Communists and the Intellectuals," *CMB* IV.V (May 1952), 391. Confession translated from *Renmin Ribao*, 6 Nov. 1951.

36. "Communists and the Intellectuals," 394. Confession translated from *Renmin Ribao*, 10 Nov. 1951.

37. Harrison, *Missionary's Curse*, 165.

38. Bays, *New History*, 165.

39. Editorial, "Yunniang sheng zhong de Zhongguo jiaohui gaizao" (Reforms brewing in the Chinese church), *Tian Feng* 176 (20 Aug. 1949), 1.

40. Wu Yaozong, "Renmin minzhu zhuanzheng xia de jidujiao" 人民民主專政下的基督教, 3.

41. "A Pastoral Letter to Fellow Christians of the Chung Hua Sheng Kung Hui," 5 July 1950, Yale Divinity Pamphlet Collection, HR 114.

42. Throop, *General Statistics of the Chung Kuo Sheng Kung Hui*, 1915 and 1933. The Anglican church was on relatively safe ground on its self-governing statistics, which gave its voice some authority; whereas in the 1910s there were still twice as many foreign priests as Chinese ones, by 1933 the ratio of Chinese to foreign employees was already 10:1 for men and 3:1 for women, with 235 Chinese priests to 85 foreign ones. The trend only accentuated during the civil war and into the PRC.

43. Wu Yaozong, "Quanguo jidujiao kang Mei" 全國基督教抗美, 313.

44. See Bays, *New History*, 162–63.

45. "Guanyu libaitang nei xuangua lingxiu xiang de wenti" 關於禮拜堂內懸掛領袖像的問題, 318.

46. Wan Fulin, "Jidutu! Kuaikuai juanxian wuqi, dabai diren!" 基督徒快快捐獻武器, 打敗敵人, 1.

47. Mo Guang, "Jidutu yao juanxian wuqi" 基督徒要捐獻武器, 2–4.

48. See Whitehead, ed., *No Longer Strangers*, 7.

49. Cf. Whitehead, ed., *No Longer Strangers*, 7–9.

50. Wu Yaozong, "Gongchandang jiaoyu le wo" 共產黨教育了我, 6–7.

51. "Chinese National Christian Conference Successfully Concludes," *Tian Feng* 425–27 (3 Sept. 1954), 406.

52. As Daniel Bays notes (*New History*, 162–65), all three of the major independent Chinese churches that could legitimately claim to be fulfilling the three-self clauses had lost their leaders to imprisonment by the mid-1950s: Ni Tuosheng to the Five-Anti campaign against business owners and Jing Dianying and Paul Wei to the anti-imperialist and anti- counterrevolutionary denunciation campaigns of 1951–1952, a situation that suited those aiming for "only one competitor on the Protestant playing field." But by the time of the Anti-Rightist campaign of 1957, even figures like Chen Chonggui, part of the new establishment, were being purged.

53. Letters of "Uncle Nystrom" (1 Feb. 1954) and William Kelly, quoted in Jones, "Our Continuing Witness."
54. Mariani, *Church Militant*, 20–21.
55. Madsen, *China's Catholics*, 34.
56. Mariani, *Church Militant*, 56.
57. Mariani, *Church Militant*, 20.
58. Madsen, *China's Catholics*, 22, 62.
59. Mariani, *Church Militant*, 23, 25.
60. CMB Vol. II (III), Sept. 1950, No. 8, 707.
61. CMB Vol. II (III), Oct. 1950, No. 9, 796. Riberi was placed under house arrest in June 1951 and expelled from the country in September. Since he had been accredited to the Guomindang and the Vatican did not recognize the PRC, he had operated without any official diplomatic status for some time.
62. E. Dépret, "La Propagande," CMB Vol. III (IV), Aug.–Sept. 1951, No. 7.
63. Luo Zhufeng, *Religion Under Socialism in China*, 61.
64. See Mariani, *Church Militant*, 60–62, for detail of the takeover and opposition.
65. Mariani, *Church Militant*, 61.
66. The Vatican kept China as a mission territory under the Propaganda Fide and did not transfer control to a Chinese council of bishops until 1946. Cf. Madsen, *China's Catholics*, 33.
67. Jin, *Memoirs of Jin Luxian*, 181, 190.
68. Mariani, *Church Militant*, 64–65.
69. As Mariani (*Church Militant*) notes, the set-up, theology, and documentation of the legion lent itself to misinterpretation; the 1928 handbook spoke of it as "a legion for service in the warfare which is perpetually waged by the Church against the world and its evil powers" (p. 48).
70. Jin, *Memoirs of Jin Luxian*, 180.
71. "To the Venerable Brethren and Beloved Sons the Archbishops, Bishops and Other Local Ordinaries of China and to the Clergy and People in Peace and Communion with the Apostolic See," CMB Vol. IV (V), Mar. 1952, 164. An alternative translation is found in Wurth, ed., *Papal Documents*, 33–37.
72. Mariani, *Church Militant*, 45. This has pretty much been axiomatic throughout mission history but has all too rarely been dwelt on in mission history accounts.
73. The Roman Catholic Church system was also, as Madsen discusses, a hierarchy that had parallels to the imperial Chinese cosmic hierarchy; and the ritual hierarchy was entwined in the political structures of Western imperialism, to the point where "Catholics belonged to a different world" than other Chinese, with a different ritual and political hierarchy. Madsen, *China's Catholics*, 31.
74. "Church Hierarchy in Communist China," CMB Vol. IV (V), May 1952, No. 5, 500.
75. CMB Vol. IV (V), May 1952, No. 5, 411.
76. Cf. Mariani, *Church Militant*, 86.
77. "Honors to Priest Martyr Called 'Imperialist Plot,'" CMB Vol. IV (V), June–July 1952, No. 6, 506.

78. Mariani, *Church Militant,* 96.
79. Jin, *Memoirs of Jin Luxian,* 205.
80. Jin, *Memoirs of Jin Luxian,* 191. Cf. Mariani, *Church Militant,* 157.
81. As Madsen, Harrison, and others have documented, "weak" or infrequent church-goers in communities might display the most courageous or strong responses to threats. See e.g. Harrison, *Missionary's Curse,* 166.
82. Whitehead, ed., *No Longer Strangers,* 99.
83. Whitehead, ed., *No Longer Strangers,* 100.
84. Madsen, *China's Catholics,* 36.
85. Harrison, *Missionary's Curse,* 164.
86. For some of the best studies on the need for and language of reconciliation, see Tang and Wiest, eds., *Catholic Church in Modern China.*
87. Fraser, "Western Political Theatre."

CHAPTER 7. DING GUANGXUN

1. Ting, "Why Must We Still Be Preachers?" 23.
2. Wang, "Obey God or Men?" 28.
3. Ding retained a strong preference for the Wade-Giles Romanization of his name (K. H. Ting); however, since Ding is now a historical figure and pinyin is the standard Romanization in China, his name is given here in the current standard form, which also aids pronunciation.
4. A task that has been admirably executed by Philip Wickeri, in *Reconstructing Christianity in China.*
5. See e.g. "Bishop's Funeral Reflection of His Life," *South China Morning Post,* 29 Nov. 2012; also Verna Yu, "Two Settings at Bishop Ding Guangxun's Funeral Reflect His Life," at www.scmp.com/news/china/article/1093337/two-settings-bishop-ding-guangxuns-funeral-reflect-his-life. The Xinhua news report of the funeral (whose headline pointed to the fact that Ding was cremated) lists those sending condolences in the official press report, a list that reads as a Who's Who of Chinese leadership, including Hu Jintao, Wen Jiabao, and Xi Jinping.
6. This contention cannot have been helped by the official acclamations that Ding was "a good friend of the CPC."
7. Ting, "Y. T. Wu—Our Forerunner," in Ting, *Chinese Contribution,* 47. This eulogy to Wu Yaozong was published in 1981.
8. On national patterns, see e.g. Yuan, Kuiper, and Shu, "Language and Revolution"; Lu Xing, *Rhetoric of the Chinese Cultural Revolution.*
9. See Wickeri, *Reconstructing Christianity in China,* 32–33, 47–51.
10. Ting, "Youth and Religion," 7.
11. Ting, "Dilemma of the Sincere Student," in Ting, *Chinese Contribution,* 5.
12. Ting, "Reading the Bible at Christmas," in Ting, *Chinese Contribution,* 1.
13. Ting, "Reading the Bible at Christmas," 2, 3.
14. Ting, "Does God Call Us?" in Ting, *Chinese Contribution,* 8.

15. Ting, "Does God Call Us?" 9, 10.

16. Ting, "Two Reflections on Evangelism: Why Force My Religion on Others?," 16, 17.

17. For example, Christians' one concern, writes Ding, is "that people should worship no false gods but realize their true being and calling by knowing and glorifying the One True God, the Lord and Father of Jesus Christ"; "Two Reflections on Evangelism: Why Force My Religion on Others?," 17. On Anglican influences on Ding's theology, see e.g. Wickeri, *Reconstructing Christianity in China*, 49–50.

18. Ting, "Two Reflections on Evangelism: Why Force My Religion on Others?," 16.

19. Ting, "Two Reflections on Evangelism: How Can They Claim Christianity Is Better?"

20. Ting, "Two Reflections on Evangelism: How Can They Claim Christianity Is Better?," 17, 20.

21. Ting, "Realizing the Gospel," in Whitehead, ed., *No Longer Strangers*, 40.

22. Ting, "Realizing the Gospel," 41.

23. Ting, "Realizing the Gospel," 41.

24. "怎样读圣经"; English edition: Ting, *How to Study the Bible*.

25. This latter is "听取微小的声音," the "tiny" or "micro" could refer too slight, or menial voices, as well as barely audible ones.

26. Ting, *How to Study the Bible*, 5, 15, 29.

27. Ting, *How to Study the Bible*, 29.

28. Ting, *How to Study the Bible*, 30.

29. See for example the *dufa* 读法, or "how to read" commentaries and essays discussed in Rolston, ed., *How to Read the Chinese Novel*.

30. Ting, *How to Study the Bible*, 16, 20, 25; quotation from p. 27.

31. Ting, "How Can They Claim Christianity Is Better?"

32. "The Nature of Witness" (1953), an amalgam of a three-part article carried in *Tian Feng*, repr. in Whitehead, ed., *No Longer Strangers*, 89.

33. Ting, "American Interventions," 112.

34. Ting, "Civil War in China," 114.

35. Ting, "How Can They Claim Christianity Is Better?"

36. Ting, "Christianity in Tension" (1948), in Whitehead, ed., *No Longer Strangers*, 38.

37. On the Denunciation Movement as a "government inspired initiative of TSPM activists," see Wickeri, *Reconstructing Christianity in China*, 393, n. 15.

38. See Wickeri, *Reconstructing Christianity in China*, 98–103.

39. Ting, "Between God and Humankind."

40. See "The Simplicity of the Gospel," in Whitehead, ed., *No Longer Strangers*, 28–29.

41. Ting, "The Nature of Witness," in Whitehead, ed., *No Longer Strangers*, 89.

42. Ting, "Why Must We Still Be Preachers?" 25.

43. Paton, *Christian Missions and the Judgement of God*, 78–80. As Paton reflected, in line with Ding's thinking, "it became evident to some of us, and to many more of our Chinese friends, that our mandate had been withdrawn; that the time for missions as we had known them had passed; that the end of the missionary era was the will of God" (p. 82). In Ding's foreword to the 1996 edition, he comments that Paton had

overstated aspects, but this was not an "anti-missionary" work; rather, it was a book of "prophetic vision," which initiated "a reevaluation of the whole cause."

44. Tony Lambert, Introduction to Li Xinyuan, *Construction—Or Destruction?*, 15. Lambert does accept that Ding's rhetoric has been toned down since.

45. Li Xinyuan, *Construction—Or Destruction?*, 29.

46. Ting, "The Nature of Witness," in Whitehead, ed., *No Longer Strangers*, 90.

47. Ting, "Lamb of God."

48. Ting, "The Nature of Witness," in Whitehead, ed., *No Longer Strangers*, 91.

49. Ting, "The Nature of Witness," in Whitehead, ed., *No Longer Strangers*, 91; Ting, "Lamb of God."

50. See e.g. Ting, *How to Study the Bible*, 32–35.

51. For one of the many polarized expressions of opinion on Ding, see e.g. Thomas Wang, Foreword, in Li Xinyuan, *Construction—or Destruction?*, 7, where Wang claims that Ding's "central theme is the replacement of the doctrine of justification by faith with a new doctrine of justification by love (i.e., salvation by good works)," a move whose "potential damage to Christianity in China cannot be overstated."

52. See e.g. Ting, "Unity Against Nuclear Threats" (1955), in Whitehead, ed., *No Longer Strangers*, 117.

53. Ting, "Unity Against Nuclear Threats," 117.

54. Ting, "Why Must We Still Be Preachers?" 16.

55. The task of relating Christianity to a religiously plural society and to a majority poor population has of course been seen as central to the development of an Asian Christian theology over the past several decades; see e.g. the well-known work of Aloysius Pieris in Sri Lanka or the proceedings of the Asian Bishops' conferences, e.g. Office of Theological Concerns, "Doing Theology in Asia Today."

56. Ting, "Why Must We Still Be Preachers?" 19–20.

57. Ting, "Why Must We Still Be Preachers?" 22.

58. Bickel, "Wise as Serpents and Harmless as Doves."

59. Ting, "Church in China Today," 119–24.

60. See e.g. the disgust of Carl McIntire in his "The National Council of Churches: An Appraisal" (1957), as discussed above.

61. Ting, "Church in China Today."

62. Ting, "Church in China Today," 120.

63. Ting, "Church in China Today," 120.

64. Ting, "On Christian Theism."

65. See Janice and Philip Wickeri's editorial note in Ting, *Chinese Contribution*, 27.

66. Wickeri, *Reconstructing Chinese Christianity*, 143; see also Wickeri's discussion of the full text, pp. 142–49. It is also worth recalling that religion as opiate was, for Marx, a good thing: the opiate of the working class, who had no access to actual opiates.

67. On the reinterpretation of history in the binary materialism and idealism, see e.g. Defoort and Zinda, "Ren Jiyu."

68. Ting, "On Christian Theism," 28–29. In a similar move, his later discussion of the existence of God uses pagans like Marcus Aurelius to demonstrate God via natural law.

69. Ting, "On Christian Theism," 29.
70. Circumstances, as Ding wrote, "in which we are being prepared by God; as we ourselves are re-evangelized, and the church is cleansed and built up." See Ting, "Church in China Today," 122.
71. Ting, "Church in China Today," 122, 123.
72. As he writes: "If we have love, people will not mind coming to a western style building to listen to what the church has to say to them. But without love, no amount of Chinese 'native forms' can really be of much help in preaching the gospel"; Ting, "Church in China Today," 121.
73. Mo Yan, who is a vice chair of the Chinese Writers' Association, was one of those who boycotted a panel of fellow Chinese writers at the 2009 Frankfurt Book Fair. For comment on the Mo Yan prize, see e.g. the pithy article by Chinese literature scholar Perry Link "Does This Writer Deserve the Prize?" where Link compares the different routes Mo Yan and Zheng Yi took, given government strictures. Link's article ends: "It would be wrong for spectators like you and me, who enjoy the comfort of distance, to demand that Mo Yan risk all and be another Liu Xiaobo. But it would be even more wrong to mistake the clear difference between the two."
74. Cf. Cusset, *French Theory*, 144.
75. ChinaAid Association, "ChinaAid Releases 2012 Annual Report on 'Chinese Government Persecution of Christians & Churches in Mainland China,'" www.chinaaid. org/2013/02/chinaaid-releases-2012-annual-report-on.html.
76. Wang, "Missing Voice," 41.
77. Ting, *How to Read the Bible*, 2.
78. Wang, "Nitty-gritty Faithfulness," 19.
79. Wang, "Obey God or Men?" 24.
80. Jiang Peifen, "An Appeal to Mr. Wang Mingdao," 57.
81. Ting, "Cosmic Christ," 14.
82. See Ting, "Why Must We Still Be Preachers?" 14–26.
83. Ting, "Unity Against Nuclear Threats," in Whitehead, ed., *No Longer Strangers*, 117.
84. Ting, "A Response to Wang Mingdao" (1955), trans. as "Truth and Slander," in Whitehead, ed., *No Longer Strangers*, 141.
85. Ting, "A Response to Wang Mingdao," 142, 143.
86. Wickeri, *Reconstructing Christianity in China*, 121.
87. Wickeri, *Reconstructing Christianity in China*, 122.
88. Whitehead, ed., *No Longer Strangers*, 17.
89. A helpful comment on this is found in Robert Whyte's discussion of Ding's Anglicanism: its incarnational character and history of learning how to relate to the state and maintain a distance from the state; its tendency to be both catholic and reformed, as well as to value civil society; see Whyte, "With Regard to Anglicanism." It is also seen later in Ding's call for a greater distance between church and government in the China of the late 1980s, since the TSPM was never meant to direct the church but only to guarantee self-governance. Ding is clear that reordering relationships within the church alone would not work and that both internal relations *and* those with the

government needed addressing simultaneously. See Wang Weifan, "Church Leader of Vision."

90. Ting, "Love and Optimism," 62–63. Although many of those imprisoned for their faith may well have held views to this effect, parading them in this way, even as self-defense, does little to advance the cause of reconciliation.
91. Ting, "Cosmic Christ," 110.
92. Barth, "Current Discussion," 80.
93. Barth, "Letter to a Pastor," 47, 48.
94. Barth, "Letter to a Pastor," 54, 55.
95. Barth, "Letter to a Pastor," 56, 57, 58.
96. Barth, "Letter to a Pastor," 60, 63, 68.
97. Barth, "Christian Community and the Civil Community," 269.
98. Barth, "Christian Community and the Civil Community," 272.
99. Barth, *Church Dogmatics* IV/2, 616.
100. Cf. Whitehead, *No Longer Strangers*, 14.
101. Ting, "My View of God," 38–39.
102. Ting, "My View of God," 68.
103. Nor was Ding's a passive presence at gatherings of such bodies: when an American missionary was invited to talk about the Chinese situation at the septennial World Council of Churches conference in Illinois in 1954, for example, the first and only one to be held in the United States, and a conference that spent much time discussing the Cold War, Ding let the council members know precisely how and why this was unacceptable to the Chinese church.

CHAPTER 8. STATE REGULATION, CHURCH GROWTH, AND TEXTUAL PROFUSION

1. Estimates for current numbers of Chinese Christians vary greatly, from the ca. 25 million of government statistics to scholars' estimates of ca. 60 million to 115 million, with most assuming that around two-thirds of the total worship is in unregistered churches (see e.g. Pew Research Center, "Global Christianity"; Johnson and Ross, *Atlas of Global Christianity*, 140; Stark, Johnson, and Mencken, "Counting China's Christians."
2. These exist alongside a much smaller Russian Orthodox community and numerous, often short-lived, para-Christian groups that have been subject to the harshest suppression as "heretical sects," discussed further below.
3. Others have categorized life differently: Zhuo Xinping's threefold division of Chinese theology is discussed below, with its attendant dangers of losing sight of unofficial publications or of artificially slicing confessional theology off from "neutral" academic theology. These categories here are evidently not theological ones but are related to the production of theology.
4. See e.g. several essays in Ashiwa and Wank, eds., *Making Religion, Making the State*, which move away from the binary of state control and religious response; or essays in Lim, ed., *Christianity in Contemporary China*. There are also interesting studies of

religious mapping of urban spaces as reflecting the interaction between state strategies and individual or community tactics; see Vermander, "From Ethnography to Theology."

5. A good example of writing on how church figures have shaped policy is Philip Wickeri's study of Ding Guangxun, which does examine in detail Ding's contribution to legislation though his role on national committees; see Wickeri, *Reconstructing Christianity in China*, Chapters 8–10.

6. The designation "extralegal" (法外) rather than illegal (非法) began to be used in the late 2000s and represents a positive move toward acknowledging the continued existence of mainstream house churches and their in-between status. Yang Fenggang ("Red, Black and Gray Markets of Religion in China") describes red (official, permitted), black (prohibited), and grey (in-between) markets in the Chinese "oligopoly" of religion.

7. See e.g. Potter, "Belief in Control."

8. Cf. voices in the documentary *The Cross in China*, dir. Yuan Zhiming. Some official churches had opened earlier; the first Catholic one to do so, for example, opened in 1972.

9. For detail, see e.g. Wickeri, *Reconstructing Christianity in China*, Chapters 7 and 8.

10. "The Basic Viewpoint and Policy on the Religious Question During Our Country's Sociality Period," issued Mar. 1982. For English text see MacInnis, *Religion in China Today*, 10–26.

11. See discussion in e.g. Hunter and Chan, *Protestantism in Contemporary China*; MacInnis, *Religion in China Today*; Wickeri, *Reconstructing Christianity in China*.

12. Trans. Janice Wickeri, in MacInnis, *Religion in China Today*, 10. It took until 2002 for Jiang Zemin to admit that even after Communism was realized, religion may yet continue; see Ying, "New Wine."

13. MacInnis, *Religion in China Today*, 25

14. MacInnis, *Religion in China Today*, 23

15. Ying Fuk-tsang, Wickeri, and others have discussed the importance of the definition of "normal" and the fine line between protecting religious freedom and regulating religion according to the law where "public interest" trumps that freedom; see e.g. Ying, "New Wine," 348.

16. See discussion in Wickeri, *Reconstructing Christianity in China*, 210–13. Church leaders with political power like Ding Guangxun attempted to ensure that gatherings in homes remained acceptable.

17. MacInnis, *Religion in China Today*, 18.

18. On sects, see e.g. Lian Xi, *Redeemed by Fire*, 215–30. Government fear of religious sects is as deep-rooted as their role throughout Chinese history in challenging the state, from Buddhist sectarian groups to the Taiping in the late Qing. Vigilance remains high: even in 2014 churches display posters encouraging all to "severely attack heresies."

19. The "Campaign to Eliminate Spiritual Pollution 清除精神污染" ran for the last three months of 1983. For a short history of the campaign and its enduring aspects, see Barmé, "Spiritual Pollution Thirty Years On."

20. English text available in Leung, *Sino-Vatican Relations*, 376–78. The twenty-five underground bishops approved by the Pope and some two hundred priests ordained by these are described in the circular as "a political force defying the government and an element that can seriously affect public security" (p. 377).

21. See e.g. Reardon, "Chinese Catholic Church," 235.

22. E.g. in works like the recklessly cathartic and much-discussed TV series *Heshang* (河殇 River Elegy, 1988).

23. See e.g. Chai, *Heart for Freedom*, or Yuan Zhiming's China Soul for Christ organization and website, www.chinasoul.org. Chai Ling was a prominent student leader at Tiananmen Square; Yuan a script writer for River Elegy. Both are examples of the many who converted while abroad.

24. Former constitutional scholar Wang Yi sees two phases of this "administrative regularization" process (形式合理化), from 1991 to 1994 and from 2004 to 2007, when new sets of regulatory documents appeared. See Wang Yi, *Linghun shenchu nao ziyou*, 311.

25. "Some Problems Concerning Further Improving Work on Religions"; English translation in Human Rights Watch/Asia, *Freedom of Religion in China*.

26. It can be quite shocking to read of the stark rejection of believers by believers during this period. The depths of divisions are evident, for example, in a document from the Word of Life house-church network (see Xin, *Inside China's House Church Network*, 89; and discussion above). Among Roman Catholics, the strengthening of the Bishops' Conference vis-à-vis the CCPA, and measures that allowed for the recognition of the Pope as the spiritual leader of the church in the 1990s, began to reduce the grounds for division between the open and underground churches. At that stage documents were still circulating underground that claimed it was a mortal sin to receive sacraments from CCPA priests. Rapprochement is proceeding unevenly; the younger generation does not share a personal animosity and has not experienced the same level of suffering, but a sense perdures of reverence for the suffering grandees of the underground/house churches adamantly opposed to reconciliation with a "Communist" church. Cf. Jeroom Heyndrickx, "The Need for Reconciliation," in Tang and Wiest, eds., *Catholic Church in Modern China*, 202–3.

27. Order of the State Council of the People's Republic of China No. 144, "Regulations on the Management of the Religious Activities of Foreigners Within China's Borders," and No. 145, "Management of Places for Religious Activities Ordinance Order of the State Council of the People's Republic of China."

28. See Potter, "Belief in Control"; cf. Leung, *Sino-Vatican Relations*, 172; Madsen, *China's Catholics*. Potter argues that with the shift in political aims, the grounds for legitimacy have also shifted, so in a market system the provision of material well-being is now the litmus test of government efficacy.

29. A case in point being the widely reported demolition of the brand new church in Sanjiang, Wenzhou, in Apr. 2014.

30. "关于加强宗教工作的决定" (Decision on Strengthening Work on Religion), issued by the State Council, 20 Jan. 2002.

31. An excellent summary of the regulations is found in Ying, "New Wine," 350–51; quotation from p. 347. On dating: the document was signed by Wen Jiabao in Nov. 2004 and came into effect in Mar. 2005.

32. See e.g. Tong, "New Religious Policy in China," 859–87. Carol Hamrin saw "some improvement" in comprehensiveness and transparency but deemed the regulations "cautious and conservative" overall, noting, as others have, the problem with ill-defined terms, such as "normal" religious activity; meanwhile, Daniel Bays and representatives of Human Rights in China and Human Rights Watch saw no paradigm shift evident; see Congressional-Executive Commission on China, "China's New Regulation on Religious Affairs."

33. See Tong, "New Religious Policy in China," 862–64.

34. Wang Yi, *Linghun shenchu nao ziyou*, 312.

35. Yu Jie and Wang Yi, *Yi sheng yi shi de yangwang*, 64.

36. See e.g. Wang Yi, *Linghun shenchu nao ziyou*, 314–15; Ying, "New Wine," 354–55. These three examples are taken from Ying.

37. See Ying, "New Wine." Regulation may suit the state, as Ying suggests, since administrative regulations, determined by the State Council, may be more closely aligned with ideological aims than laws established by an independent judiciary; but this leaves religion an anomaly in society and its "foreign links" strangely vilified in an era of pervasive foreign presences and investment.

38. This and the next two examples are detailed in Wang Yi, *Linghun shenchu nao ziyou*, 312–13.

39. For a clear and detailed discussion of this see Lian Xi, "'Cultural Christians.'"

40. See Lian Xi, "'Cultural Christians,'" 74–75; Wielander, *Christian Values in Communist China*, Chapter 5.

41. See discussion of the work of de Smith and Triska in Leung, *Sino-Vatican Relations*, 142.

42. See e.g. McLeister, "A Three-Self Protestant Church." "Preacher Zhang's" canny use of his (rescinded) Three-Self license as well as his use of extensive local *guanxi* to smooth relations over irregular building use or leafleting exemplify this.

43. See e.g. Zimmerman-Liu and Wright, "Making Sense of China's State-Society Relations," esp. 221–22. The authors discuss four key variables: location; personal connections and ties, especially to local governmental officials; degree of pressure on the local authorities themselves, including any quota requirements (repression rises at the New Year, during political campaigns, etc.); and the behavior of group members, with more public or aggressive action or worship more heavily repressed.

44. Yang Fenggang, *Religion in China*, 159.

45. For details on early reconciliation negotiations and on the Vatican directive of Sept. 1988 on dealing with China, which sets out the curia's position on issues such as papal supremacy and relations between CCPA and non-CCPA Catholics, see Leung, *Sino-Vatican Relations*, 275–87 and 321–26.

46. For details see e.g. Reardon, "Chinese Catholic Church."

47. Benedict XVI, "Letter." In this the Pope rescinded the outright rejection of the CCPA, among other concessions and clarifications. Reiterating that an autonomous Chinese Catholic Church was "incompatible" with Catholic doctrine, the Pope's letter nevertheless acknowledged the pastoral difficulties the split had caused and confirmed, for example, that sacraments received from illegitimately ordained bishops or priests were valid. In ceasing further "underground" ordinations, Pope Benedict made great demands on Catholics who had remained loyal to Rome, asking that they now support moves toward unity with CCPA hierarchies.

48. See Wickeri, *Reconstructing Christianity in China*, 247.

49. See Zhuo, ed., *Christianity*. For a fuller discussion of Zhuo's classification and characterization of Chinese theology, and some countersuggestions, see Starr and Dunch, "Introduction," to Zhuo, ed., *Christianity*, xix–xxxi. For Zhuo, true theology is philosophical theology, the search for ultimate truth, while devotional theology is exclusive and isolationist, intent on promoting its own dogmatic claims. The issues at stake in the understanding of what "theology" is and its institutional location will continue to shape the development of Chinese research and thinking.

50. Both examples taken from *Tianzhujiao* 天主教, 2014 (04).

51. See Editorial, *Tripod*, Vol. 23, No. 130 (Autumn 2003). As Gianni Criveller commented ("Three Documents"), "'democratic running' means simply the total control of the Church by the Party and political authorities." In this edition of *Tripod*, Criveller and others consider the documents passed in 2003 by the Standing Committee of the CCPA and the Chinese Catholic Bishops College: "The System for the Joint Conference of Chairpersons of the Chinese Catholic Patriotic Association and of the Bishops Conference of the Catholic Church in China"; "Work Regulations for the Chinese Catholic Patriotic Association"; and "A Management System for Catholic Dioceses in China." In his commentary Anthony Lam enumerates the differences between Roman Catholic canon law and the "management system" regulations passed in China.

52. See Jiang Jianyong's speech given in July 2013 and published 20 Aug. 2013 as "蒋坚永副局长在中国天主教民主办教'三项制度'颁布十周年座谈会上的讲话," available at www.chinacatholic.cn/html1/report/1405/2729–1.htm. The "三项制度" (Three Documents and Systems) refers to documents passed in 2003 (note 51). In official terms, the model has been developed under China's own auspices without external pressure, it joins the patriotic organizations with the masses of believers, it promotes unity, and it is good for evangelization.

53. Current book recommendations at the Guangqi Press include e.g. Zhan Delong's 詹德隆 (Basic Moral Theology), Zhang Chunshen's 张春申 (Eschatology in Christian Faith), and Shi Lihua's 施礼华 (Warmly Love the Church).

54. Respectively, the 天主教资料研究汇编 and 天主教研究论辑, the latter published by the Religion and Culture Press (宗教文化出版社), a SARA imprint.

55. Some churches, such as Haidian in Beijing, publish printed volumes of all Sunday sermons, enabling an overview of topics. At Haidian preachers concentrate on

biblical exegesis and moral exhortation and rarely address policy directly. Academic theology may have little to do with Sunday preaching elsewhere in the world too, of course, but expectations are higher for "theology with Chinese characteristics."

56. Ding Guangxun, Preface, *Chinese Theological Review*, 1985. English-language readers are extremely well-served by the work of Janice Wickeri and others in translating and editing Chinese Protestant articles in the *Chinese Theological Review*.

57. Representative writings are found in Chen Zemin, *Qiusuo yu jianzheng* 求索与见证.

58. Zhuo, ed., *Christianity*, xx.

59. See Towery, *Christianity in Today's China*, 83.

60. On Shen's "theology of life," see Chen Qirui, "Christ the Everlasting Lord"; on Wang Weifan, see Yuan Yijuan, *Shengsheng shenxue* 生生神学. Several English-language collections of Ding's writings from the 1980s and 1990s are available, including *God Is Love: Collected Writings of Bishop K. H. Ting*; *No Longer Strangers: Selected Writings of K. H. Ting*, ed. Raymond Whitehead; and *A Chinese Contribution to Ecumenical Theology*, ed. Janice and Philip Wickeri.

61. See Wickeri, *Reconstructing Christianity in China*, 248–51.

62. See Wang Weifan, *Zhongguo shenxue* 中国神学, and discussion in Hai Jinhua, "Inherit and Renew."

63. See e.g. *Chinese Theological Review* 20 (2007), an issue in which all of the articles are by female scholars and theologians; several of them consider questions relating to women's experience in the Chinese church.

64. E.g. Xu Xiaohong, "Obstacles in the Path of Theological Reconstruction."

65. Cf. Cao Shengjie, "Mission in the Chinese Church."

66. Gao Ying, "God's Promise and Eschatological Hope." This is not to undermine the genuine danger that some cultic preaching represents in China.

67. Ting, Foreword to *Theological Writings from Nanjing Seminary*.

68. See Xu Rulei, "Brief History."

69. Han Wenzao, "Guanyu jiaqiang shenxue sixiang" 关于加强神学思想.

70. Chen Yongtao, "Interpreting Christian Faith in Our Own Time and Context."

71. Cao Shengjie, "Mission in the Chinese Church," 4.

72. The term is used both in this narrow sense and in a broader sense of all Chinese-language work in Christian studies from the Ming onward. For a discussion of the term *Hanyu shenxue* and its implications, see Starr, "Sino-Christian Theology."

73. See Lai Pan-chiu, "Typology and Prospect of Sino-Christian Theology."

74. Cf. Yang and Yeung, *Sino-Christian Studies in China*, xvi; see also discussion in Starr, "Sino-Christian Theology."

75. As research shows, the younger generation of scholars researching Christianity is more likely to identify as Christian; see Gao Xin, "Preliminary Survey." Greater crossover between church-attending Christians and academic scholars means that the relationship between Sino-Christian theology and church theology is also evolving.

76. Such as the series *Shijie yu zongjiao* (世界与宗教 The World and Religion), still one of the largest and most influential series, whose texts include the writings of Paul Tillich, Rudolf Bultmann, and Rudolf Otto.

77. Liu Xiaofeng, *Zhengjiu yu xiaoyao* 拯救与逍遥; see also discussion in Fällman, *Salvation and Modernity*; He Guanghu, "Hanyu shenxue de genju yu yiyi" 汉语神学的根据与意义 and "Hanyu shenxue de fangfa yu jinlu" 汉语神学的方法与进路.

78. See Lai and Lam, *Sino-Christian Theology*. Chinese volumes include the three-set Li and Yang, eds., *Xiandai xing* 现代性.

79. Yeung, ed., *Hanyu shenxue chuyi* 漢語神學芻議. The Institute for Sino-Christian Studies has been a strong supporter of, and conduit for, the movement since the 1990s, funding translation series of Christian classics, summer schools, and programs for mainland students. It also published the first collection of articles on "Sino-Christian Scriptural Hermeneutics" in 2010, which included articles on scriptural interpretation, cross-textual hermeneutics (between classical Chinese and biblical texts), and literary studies of the Bible; see Jason Lam, ed., *Hanyu jidujiao jingxue chuyi* 漢語基督教經學芻議. The different naming of "Chinese theology" or "sino-theology" in English and Chinese in the titles points to long arguments over the terms involved.

80. Jin Mingri 金明日 suggests five prime reasons for the later urban growth: urbanization itself, the relaxation of *hukou* (residence permit requirements) in the mid-2000s, post-1989 loss of hope in system reform among intellectuals, the failure of the Three-Self Movement, and globalization and the concentration of foreign missionary staff in urban areas. See Yu Jie and Wang Yi, *Yi sheng yi shi de yangwang*, 59.

81. See e.g. Aikman, *Jesus in Beijing*; Lambert, *China's Christian Millions*, etc.

82. See Wielander, *Christian Values in Communist China*. There are entire virtual communities of Christians, whether as web-based church congregations or communities centered round a particular publication.

83. Some, such as Liu Tongsu, would strongly oppose any such labeling or distinction, arguing that the urban church merely reflects mainstream cultural life. For Liu, the urban house churches are a confluence of two traditions: the piety and self-sacrifice of the Chinese house churches, and theology and management structures that are taken from the worldwide mainstream evangelical church. See Yu and Wang, *Yi sheng yi shi de yangwang*, 232. A very readable overview of distinctions between TSPM churches, non-TSPM churches, and quasi-TSPM churches and between three models of urban house churches, namely the "Beijing," "Wenzhou," and "Pearl River Delta" models, is found in Hai Jinhua, "Inherit and Renew," esp. pp. 17–22.

84. Yu and Wang, *Yi sheng yi shi de yangwang*, 58.

85. Yalin Xin's study of one of the largest house-church networks, the Word of Life group, documents one such movement and shows how it developed from a single itinerant leader linking together reemerging congregations in the early 1980s, to a network of more than three thousand churches by the late 1980s, to an organization implementing new hierarchies, pastoral regions, and a multistage program of theological education in the 1990s. A subsequent trend was the uniting of several of the major new house-church networks, including the Word of Life, the Fangcheng Fellowship, and the China Gospel Fellowship; Xin, *Inside China's House Church Network*.

86. Lian Xi, *Redeemed by Fire*, 222.

87. Gao Shining, "Impact of Contemporary Chinese Folk Religions on Christianity," 178.

88. See Bays, *New History*, 193; on Eastern Lightning with its female Christ, Ms. Deng, or the reincarnated Jesus of the Established King sect, Wu Yangming, see Lian Xi, *Redeemed by Fire*, 215–30.

89. Wielander, *Christian Values in Communist China*, 119. Wielander's study examines also the link between Christianity and prominent human rights activists and lawyers in China.

90. Wielander, *Christian Values in Communist China*, 120, 119.

91. Wiest, "Understanding the Roman Catholic Church in China."

92. Gao Shining, "Cong shizheng yanjiu kan jidujiao" 从实证研究看基督教. With only 57 of 827 church "meeting points" in Beijing registered, proximity to home is one of the single strongest factors determining place of worship.

CHAPTER 9. YANG HUILIN

1. Yang Huilin, "Impact of Christianity," 6 (text edited).

2. "Denominations" in the "postdenominational" church in China here refers to Roman Catholicism and Protestantism, widely (and officially) regarded as two separate religions. Academics like Yang Huilin belong to neither church, and their work may draw on Catholic/Orthodox/Protestant thinking. See also Starr, "Chinese Church."

3. See Yang Fenggang, *Religion in China*, 64. Yang regards religious research as an increasingly important force, alongside believers and the authorities, in the outworking of religious practice.

4. See Yang, *Jidujiao de dise yu wenhua yanshen* 基督教的底色与文化延伸.

5. Yang, "对《约伯记》的再读解," in *Zai wenxue yu shenxue de bianjie*, 3–9. See discussion on righteousness (义), pp. 4–5.

6. Yang heads the Centre for Christian Studies and organizes the World Sinology Conference at Renmin University and is a committee chair for the Institute of Comparative Scripture and Interreligious Dialogue at Minzu University.

7. See Starr, "Sino-Christian Theology," 402.

8. While the connection is understood, it is rarely commented on. Yang Huilin is unusual in making not infrequent references to the CR throughout his writings, especially his English-language essays. It might seem foolhardy to overplay the events of forty years ago as determinative for contemporary Chinese theology, but that argument would scarcely be made against writers in the aftermath of other state-sponsored mass atrocities, including the Shoah, against which Yang evaluates responses to the Cultural Revolution in his essay "The Contemporary Significance of Theological Ethics."

9. See e.g. Zhang, *Ideology and Economic Reform*, 159–65.

10. "Thoroughly negated" from Yang, "Contemporary Significance of Theological Ethics," 52.

11. See e.g. Bays, *New History*, 203.

12. Yang, *China, Christianity, and the Question of Culture*, 41–42. Yang writes of the similarities Christian fellowship can display with CR-era traditions in the context of a Christian convergence with contemporary ideology.

13. Cf. Lam Tsz-Shun, *Duoyuan xing Hanyu shenxue quanshi* 多元性漢語神學詮釋, 29–30.

14. Among studies on the language of the Cultural Revolution, see e.g. Lu Xing, *Rhetoric of the Chinese Cultural Revolution*.

15. Yang, "Contemporary Significance of Theological Ethics," 59–61. Yang's critique extended to the diabolicization of later literary narratives—pointing to the many English-language accounts of CR life with their tendency to idealize the protagonist as a "clear-headed, rational dissenter" uncontaminated by the "monsters" perpetrating the crimes.

16. See e.g. Feuerwerker, *Ideology, Power, Text*, 200. This link does not seem to have drawn the research attention it deserves.

17. Yang, *Zai wenxue yu shenxue de bianjie*, 1.

18. Yang, *China, Christianity, and the Question of Culture*, 138.

19. Yang, *China, Christianity, and the Question of Culture*, 135. Yang's "religion without religion," or "nonreligious religion" or "perverse" theology, follows a trajectory of thinkers from Bonhoeffer to Žižek to Milbank and Pickstock and on to Derrida, each with their contributions to the theory.

20. Yang, *China, Christianity, and the Question of Culture*, 191.

21. Yang, *China, Christianity, and the Question of Culture*, 6.

22. Yang, *China, Christianity, and the Question of Culture*, 12.

23. Quoted in Yang, *China, Christianity, and the Question of Culture*, 21.

24. Yang, *China, Christianity, and the Question of Culture*, 52,

25. Yang, *China, Christianity, and the Question of Culture*, 42.

26. See Yang, *China, Christianity, and the Question of Culture*, 37–41, 48–52, 55–60.

27. See Yang, *China, Christianity, and the Question of Culture*, 43–44, 56–57. For a helpful discussion of Yang's views on sinicized Christianity and the "distortion of integration," see Leeb, "Yang Huilin," 57–63. Yang discusses the notion further in an editorial, "Being Absent in Place."

28. Yang is one of the few who defend the language of the extant *Jingjiao* (景教 "Nestorian") scriptures, including the section titled "On One God," suggesting that the rendering of the biblical texts into Chinese in the Tang was not as poor as many have claimed, especially if read in terms of Chinese grammar and textual construction (where new parallelisms are introduced, as well as omissions to cut repetition). Yang is clearly sympathetic to the cause of translation that is sensitive to the target language, especially given that the Church of the East texts were translated indirectly, from an oral rendition through a Chinese writer.

29. See e.g. Venuti, *Translator's Invisibility*. One of Venuti's arguments is that the "domesticizing" betrays an Anglo-American privileging of the author.

30. See Chin, "Paradigm Shift."

31. Yang, *China, Christianity, and the Question of Culture*, 208. As Yang suggests, missionaries accepted the new language carrier of modern Chinese (*baihua*) much ear-

lier than Chinese scholars. Others, such as the Qing literature scholar Yuan Jin, have contended that they may have done much toward creating that new language. Yang touches on the debate only briefly, leaving hanging the question of who was right: Zhou Zuoren (the missionaries did create the early Europeanized *baihua*) or Hu Shi (the Bible contributed nothing to the preparation for the new language); see p. 210.

32. Yang, *China, Christianity, and the Question of Culture,* 209.

33. Yang, *China, Christianity, and the Question of Culture,* 210.

34. Yang gives a brief history of the movement and its institutional settings in *Zai wenxue yu shenxue de bianjie,* 203–4. This essay also appears in English in *China, Christianity, and the Question of Culture,* 163–84.

35. See e.g. Ticciati, "Scriptural Reasoning."

36. Quash, "Deep Calls to Deep."

37. See Ford, "Flamenco, Tai-Chi and Six-Text Scriptural Reasoning," and Quash, "Deep Calls to Deep." On the practice of reading itself, see Fodor, "Scriptural Reasoning as a Desert Practice."

38. Ford, "Flamenco, Tai-Chi and Six-Text Scriptural Reasoning."

39. Since Chinese seminaries operate outside the national university system, their degrees have not been recognized by the state, which means, inter alia, that students cannot transfer to universities for further study. The resultant low level of theological study—seminaries admit students straight from high school, or even junior high, and few have been able until very recently to travel abroad for further study—has hampered both theological research and the status of Christianity vis-à-vis other religions in secular academic estimation. Rare attempts to mitigate this include a master's in religion program at Renmin University that does admit seminary graduates.

40. Ford, "Deep Reasonings."

41. Ford, "Deep Reasonings." The passage reads: "We recognize the neat, closed, conclusive packages of meaning and truth that are offered by some versions of religion and by some academic accounts of it, the decisive indicatives or imperatives of a confident or defensive faith, and the neat analyses, descriptions or explanations of academic mastery. We also recognize the counterpoint of open questioning, of tentative, experimental hypothesizing or speculation, and of the desire always to make room for the *semper maior,* the 'ever greater' of ultimate transcendence. How are these unsettling interrogatives, adventurous subjunctives and longing, self-transcending optatives to be balanced with cut and dried indicatives and imperatives? A fine line indeed . . ."

42. E.g. talks by Geng Youzhuang at International Comparative Literature Association (ICLA) Paris 2013, and King's College London, 2012.

43. On the question of grounding, see Adams, "Making Deep Reasonings Public," 41–59.

44. See Ochs and Johnson, eds., *Crisis, Call and Leadership,* Introduction.

45. See Ford, "Flamenco, Tai Chi, and Six-Text Scriptural Reasoning." The four are the addition of three "Eastern religions," the combination with comparative theology (Francis Clooney is an advisor at Minzu), the role of Confucianism, and the disciplinary setting of comparative literature.

46. Yang, *China, Christianity, and the Question of Culture*, 153.
47. In the Zen/Chan tradition. See Yang, *China, Christianity, and the Question of Culture*, 154.
48. Yang, *China, Christianity, and the Question of Culture*, 155.
49. Giradot, *Victorian Translation of China*.
50. See Müller's edited series, *Sacred Books of the East* (1879–1910).
51. Yang, *China, Christianity, and the Question of Culture*, 165. The Chinese reads "mutually explanatory," a term referring particularly to oral explanation or commentary; cf. Yang, *Zai wenxue yu shenxue de bianjie*, 205.
52. Legge, *Sacred Books, Yî King*, xiv.
53. It was, Legge notes, "a relief not to be obliged to receive them as his"; *Sacred Books, Yî King*, xxxi.
54. Legge, *Sacred Books, Yî King*, xv.
55. Legge, *Sacred Books, Yî King*, xv. Legge wrote, "When the symbolic characters have brought his mind en rapport with that of his author, he is free to render the ideas in his own or any other speech in the best manner than he can attain to."
56. *Mencius* 5A: 4(2), as quoted in Yang, *China, Christianity and the Question of Culture*, 166.
57. Legge, *Chinese Classics, Vol. II, Mencius*, 52.
58. Legge, *Chinese Classics, Vol. II, Mencius*, 52.
59. Legge, *Chinese Classics, Vol. II, Mencius*, 55.
60. Legge, *Chinese Classics, Vol. II, Mencius*, 50.
61. Legge, *Chinese Classics, Vol. II, Mencius*, 69.
62. Legge, *Chinese Classics, Vol. II, Mencius*, 70.
63. The English translation of Yang's essay retranslates Legge ("they must try with their thoughts to meet the intention or the scope of the author with a sympathetic understanding, and then we shall apprehend it"), adding an element that seems to comment on Legge's own approach and answer the question Yang follows up with: whose (sympathetic) understanding is to meet the "intention" of the ancients? See Yang, *China, Christianity, and the Question of Culture*, 166.
64. Yang, "中西 '经文辨读' 的可能性及其价值," in *Zai wenxue yu shenxue de bianjie* 203–22; English version in Yang, *China, Christianity, and the Question of Culture*, 165–80.
65. Yang, *Zai wenxue yu shenxue de bianjie*, 215.
66. See Yang, *China, Christianity, and the Question of Culture*, 172. The text that Legge tacitly commends reads, "(It is the way of the Tao) to act without (thinking of) acting; to conduct affairs without (feeling the) trouble of them; to taste without discerning any flavor, to consider what is small as great, and a few as many; and to recompense injury with kindness."
67. Yang, *Zai wenxue yu shenxue de bianjie*, 217. It is not entirely accurate to suggest, as Yang does, that the negative stream in the Western tradition was "broken off" for a time or is just found in the linguistic concerns of continental philosophers; it has remained alive and well in the writings on apophaticism of theologians like Denys Turner and in studies of the contrast between theological apophaticism and the mod-

ern versions of Derrida or Anthony Kenny. (On the latter, see e.g. McDonough, "Grounding Speech and Silence"). Yang has developed ideas on kenosis in various articles, suggesting that if God's kenosis is a relinquishment of divine attributes, human kenosis should be a "relinquishment of self-insistence" (*pozhi* 破执) or letting go of our own subjective role, which he argues parallels a "being absent in place." See e.g. Yang, Editorial, *Jidujiao wenhua xuekan* (What Do We Mean by "the Poor"?).

68. Yang, *China, Christianity, and the Question of Culture*, 168.

69. "Virtue" is an uncommon word in the King James Version, used in the sense of "virtue gone out of him" as in Mark 5:30 and Luke 8:46 as well as in the more common sense of a positive character attribute, as in 2 Pet 1:5 or Phil 4:8. It is true that biblical instances of "perfect" do allow for a human attainment of perfection, as in e.g. "Be ye therefore perfect, even as your Father which is in heaven is perfect" (Matt 5:48, King James Version).

70. On debates among those involved in the Delegates' version, see Hanan, "Bible as Chinese Literature." During the 1830s Walter Medhurst was involved in a series of debates on translation with detractors like Samuel Kidd, who held, for example, that "the object of a translation is not that the Scriptures should appear to be a book originally written in Chinese, but to enable Hebrew writers to describe their own manners, customs and habits," and that "I always find great difficulty in dissuading the Chinese from the attempt to identify divine doctrines with their own dogma; and in proportion as we adopt their names for spiritual objects, we increase this difficulty"; quoted in Hanan, 212.

71. Yang, "James Legge: Between Literature and Religion," in Yang, *China, Christianity, and the Question of Culture*, 158. Yang is quoting from Ford's *Christian Wisdom: Desiring God and Learning in Love* (Cambridge: Cambridge University Press, 2007), Chapter 8.

72. Yang, *Zai wenxue yu shenxue de bianjie*, 221.

73. Yang, "Scriptural Reasoning and the Hermeneutical Circle," in Yang, *China, Christianity, and the Question of Culture*, 185.

74. Ochs, "Introduction to Scriptural Reasoning," quoted in Yang, *China, Christianity, and the Question of Culture*, 186.

75. See Yang, *China, Christianity, and the Question of Culture*, 189.

76. Yang, *China, Christianity, and the Question of Culture*, 190. Yang quotes David Ford on the latter point.

77. This is a central insight for other modern cross-cultural theologians too; cf. e.g. the writings of Lamin Sanneh.

78. Yang, "The Value of Theology in Humanities: Possible Approaches to Sino-Christian Theology," in Lai and Lam, eds., *Sino-Christian Theology*, 102–3.

79. See Ford, "Flamenco, Tai-Chi and Six-Text Scriptural Reasoning."

80. Ben Quash ("Deep Calls to Deep") warns of the dangers of both inductive and deductive modes of scripture reading done in isolation, when scripture can lose its "own internal 'logic' and power to resist and reconfigure the reader's expectations and understanding."

81. Ford, "Flamenco, Tai-Chi and Six-Text Scriptural Reasoning."

82. Yang, *China, Christianity, and the Question of Culture*, 192. The statement is complicated by the immediate assertion that "sacred scriptures" in Western scholarship refers to Chinese classics as well as to religious texts, and here Yang suggests that the distinction is not related to religion, but meaning itself is "endowed with some kind of sacredness."

83. Yang, *China, Christianity, and the Question of Culture*, 194, 197.

CHAPTER 10. VISIBLE AND VOLUBLE

1. Yu and Wang, *Yi sheng yi shi de yangwang*, 61.

2. Wang Yi, *Linghun shenchu nao ziyou*, 170–84 and 270–86; quotation from p. 272. As the discussion of the nature of the church hints, not all house-church adherents agree with, or support, the version of faith that the likes of Wang Yi or Jin Mingri promote; this is again a stream within a stream of theology.

3. See Lian Xi, *Redeemed by Fire*, 216–20.

4. One of the four parts of the film *The Cross–Jesus in China* (2003) is the episode *The Canaan Hymns*.

5. For a fuller study of Lü's hymns, see Sun, "Songs of Canaan." Sun's article considers the "theological-liturgical inculturation" of the hymns in terms of their imagery and theology under the six categories of nature allegories, relationship with the divine, worship as allegiance, suffering, unity, and loyalty.

6. Lü Xiaomin, *Jia'nan shixuan* 迦南诗选.

7. Lü Xiaomin, *Jia'nan shixuan*, Vol. 1, #3, "翱翔的地方是天空;" #4, "一個有信心的人."

8. Lü Xiaomin, *Jia'nan shixuan*, Vol. 1, #8, "在黑夜."

9. Lü Xiaomin, *Jia'nan shixuan*, Vol. 1, #2, "都有走路的艰难."

10. Lü Xiaomin, *Jia'nan shixuan*, Vol. 1, #24 "因著耶稣爱的缘故."

11. Lü Xiaomin, *Jia'nan shixuan*, Vol. 1, #22, "你要知道，羊需要牧人."

12. Lü Xiaomin, *Jia'nan shixuan*, Vol. 1, #22, #9, "你要知道羊需要牧人," "每一天我都需要你的帮助."

13. Lü Xiaomin, *Jia'nan shixuan*, Vol. 1, #20, #14 "除祂以外别无拯救," "关上窗."

14. Canaan Hymn selection No. 551, "中国属于上帝."

15. "Flames of a reviving fire must burn throughout China," in "复兴的火," Lü Xiaomin, *Jia'nan shixuan*, Vol. 1, #16.

16. "Although we are base, the creator God works with us," in "这是奇妙的事," Lü Xiaomin, *Jia'nan shixuan*, Vol. 1, #19.

17. Lü Xiaomin, *Jia'nan shixuan*, Vol. 1, #18 "因为我们先听见." Other hymns in this particular selection with a focus on China include nos. 26, 28, 45, 48, 82, and 90.

18. Canaan Hymn selection No. 184, "中国人要起来."

19. Lü Xiaomin, *Jia'nan shixuan*, Vol. 1, #19, #13. It was widely perceived that TSPM churches were banned from preaching on Revelation, and this was a reason for the nonregistration of many pastors. The latest "Church Order of Protestant Churches in China," agreed to by the joint Seventh Standing Committee of the Three-Self Movement and Fifth Standing Committee of the China Christian Council (2008), is clear in its belief in the historic creeds and that "He will come again to judge the world."

20. See e.g. Lü Xiaomin, *Jia'nan shixuan*, Vol. 1, #41

21. Lü Xiaomin, *Jia'nan shixuan*, Vol. 1, #42 "我们欢笑着继续."

22. Lü Xiaomin, *Jia'nan shixuan*, Vol. 1, #10 "我们终于成为赢家."

23. See e.g. Hattaway, Brother Yun, Xu, and Wang, *Back to Jerusalem*.

24. Lü Xiaomin, *Jia'nan shixuan*, Vol. 1, #6, "万国的大使命."

25. Cf. Hurtado, "Early Devotion to Jesus." Quotation from ChinaSource Team, "Xiao Min on Preparing for the Lord's Return," at ChinaSource, www.chinasource.org/resource-library/chinese-church-voices/xiao-min-on-preparing-for-the-lords-return.

26. Vala and Huang, "Three High-Profile Protestant Microbloggers in Contemporary China."

27. As Vala and Huang translate one posting: "Patriotism is a war of self-defense, nationalism is a war of aggression. For the patriots, the country is my wife, but to nationalists, the country is a sleeping beauty that hasn't woken up. For the former, opposing corrupt officials is capturing traitors. For the latter, patriotism is mistresses. Healthy patriotism and faith are consistent with each other, but nationalism is a substitute for religion. 2013–04-22." See Vala and Huang, "Three High-Profile Protestant Microbloggers in Contemporary China."

28. Wang Yi, *Linghun shenchu nao ziyou*, 19. Wang had self-published an earlier volume, "Aesthetics Alarm the Centre" (美德惊动了中央), of which eight hundred copies were sequestered during mailing.

29. With Liu Tongsu, 观看中国城市家庭教会, and with Yu Jie, 一生一世的仰望 and 我有翅膀如鸽子, the latter two with Taipei-based Christian Arts Press, 基文社.

30. "You Opened the Mouths of the Dumb: A Spoke in the Wheel: A Life of Bonhoeffer," Wang Yi, *Linghun shenchu nao ziyou*, 34–36. Renate Wind's biography of Bonhoeffer was translated and published in simplified Chinese (from the 1992 English translation of John Bowden?) in 2006.

31. See Wang Yi, *Linghun shenchu nao ziyou*, 73.

32. Wang Yi, *Linghun shenchu nao ziyou*, 210.

33. Wang Yi, *Linghun shenchu nao ziyou*, 213. Wang is fairly loose in his paraphrase of Lucifer from Byron's *Cain: A Mystery*.

34. "We Are Not Writers, We Are Hostages," in Wang Yi, *Linghun shenchu nao ziyou*, 216–22.

35. "Prayer Text Prepared for White House Meeting," in Wang Yi, *Linghun shenchu nao ziyou*, 338. The prayer includes the following invocations: "In your great power, we beseech you not to let Chinese leaders' hearts harden further . . . we ask that you would prepare a way forward for those in China pursuing free democracy . . . Hallelujah, your children thank you, and ask that you would be with your child President Bush, and keep his burden on his mind, that he may be continuously established in Christ and would serve his people in his post with the same heart as serving God." It also included prayers that China and the United States might share a mutual respect and live in harmony on earth.

36. The trope derives from the decision of Sima Qian (b. ca. 145 BCE) to choose the punishment of castration over death so that he could finish his monumental history, the *Shiji* 史記.

37. Wang Yi, *Linghun shenchu nao ziyou*, 20.

38. Wang Yi, *Linghun shenchu nao ziyou*, 20. Wang adds that receiving this gift was, for him, "a beautiful and profound spiritual process," but more prosaically, as a book-worm, it was the only one of the three Confucian virtues (merit 立功, speech 立言, and virtue 立德) that he was fit for.

39. Wang Yi, *Linghun shenchu nao ziyou*, 26

40. Wang Yi, *Linghun shenchu nao ziyou*, 17–28.

41. Wang Yi, *Linghun shenchu nao ziyou*, 26–27.

42. Wang Yi, *Linghun shenchu nao ziyou*, 21–22. Wang's condemnation of non-Christian writings sits oddly with his liberal political views. Before Christ, Wang suggests, there were two types of writer: those who received special revelation and wrote the Old Testament, and those who called out in response to general revelation, of whom the greatest were Plato and Laozi. The latter had no revelatory knowledge of salvation, but their probing moved hearts and touched souls. Christ's death and resurrection changed everything: all writing now had to face the Christ event, and the greatest writing became testimony.

43. The author of more than thirty volumes, including the divisive *Wen Jiabao—China's Best Actor*, and a political activist involved in Charter 08 and the PEN movement, Yu, a Christian since the early 2000s, emigrated to the United States in 2012 after suffer-ing incarceration and alleged torture over his activities and support of Liu Xiaobo.

44. I.e. from "以人为本" to "以神为本"; see Yu Jie and Wang Yi, *Yisheng yishi de yang-wang*, 11.

45. Yu and Wang, *Yisheng yishi de yangwang*, 10.

46. Yu and Wang, *Yisheng yishi de yangwang*, 13.

47. Cf. e.g. Ford, *Shape of Living*, or a collection like Phan and Lee, eds., *Journeys at the Margin*.

48. See e.g. Lian Xi, "'Cultural Christians,'" 73.

49. Yu and Wang, *Yisheng yishi de yangwang*, 14.

50. Selection bias among the male authors may be a strong factor here, but on gender dis-parities in ministry and cultural reasons for these, see e.g. Chung, *Chinese Women in Christian Ministry*; on gender separation in modern Protestant nonofficial churches, see e.g. Cao Nanlai, *Constructing China's Jerusalem*. In the TSPM churches, female priests are far from unusual, and young female academics in Christian studies pro-grams are now forging careers; however, female leaders are still rare.

51. Yu and Wang, *Yisheng yishi de yangwang*, 51.

52. Yu and Wang, *Yisheng yishi de yangwang*, 61.

53. Yu and Wang, *Yisheng yishi de yangwang*, 62–63.

54. Yu and Wang, *Yisheng yishi de yangwang*, 63, 64. Jin is highly critical of the situation where Document 19 trumps the constitution regarding religious rights and is insistent on the need for the CCP to clarify its position regarding religious legislation—and for a strong leader to change Deng's legacy.

55. Liu's book-length publications *Shangdi yu kaisa de jiangjie* 上帝与凯撒的疆界 and, co-written with Wang Yi, *Guankan Zhongguo chengshi jiating jiaohui* 观看中国城市家庭教会 are available in print and online; the first discusses the relationship be-

tween God and Caesar. Liu was one of those invited by the Chinese government to attend the State Council workshop on "Christianity and Social Harmony" in 2008.

56. Yu and Wang, *Yisheng yishi de yangwang*, 226.

57. On cultural Christians, see e.g. Fällman, *Salvation and Modernity.*

58. Yu and Wang, *Yisheng yishi de yangwang*, 227.

59. Yu and Wang, *Yisheng yishi de yangwang*, 229.

60. See e.g. Williams, *Silence and Honey Cakes.*

61. Yu and Wang, *Yisheng yishi de yangwang*, 230–31. Current regulation may be attempting to limit the church's public life to the private sphere, but the church needs to assert its public nature to claim a role in public life, Liu reiterates.

62. Yu and Wang, *Yisheng yishi de yangwang*, 238.

63. Yu and Wang, *Yisheng yishi de yangwang*, 236, 244. The power of the Cross lay in its transcendence, not isolation, he writes; true spirituality was not an independence from social existence but "the embodiment of the Lord's rule in all layers of life."

64. Yu and Wang, *Yisheng yishi de yangwang*, 233.

65. See Liu Tongsu, "Zhongguo jiaohui de chushi yu rushi" 中国教会的出事与入世. Liu's website contains (to date) nearly two hundred substantial articles on topics ranging from church and state to constitutional law, church history, and spiritual life. This particular article is discussed in more detail in Wielander, *Christian Values in Communist China*, 123–24.

66. Yu and Wang, *Yisheng yishi de yangwang*, 233–34. Liu uses the metaphor of Qing reformers, or the "protect the Emperor faction," to describe the TSPM.

67. See Wickeri, *Reconstructing Christianity in China*, 306. Not everyone in the TSPM felt this way.

68. Yu and Wang, *Yisheng yishi de yangwang*, 234, 250. Liu's argument on the TSPM's place in the new society may have some merit, given the contribution of the Christian rights activists to social awareness, but he cheapens the point by claiming the TSPM had merely made use of new freedoms to reclaim its buildings and safeguard clergy pensions.

69. Accessed at http://weibo.com/p/1001603881634431670754.

AFTERWORD

1. Lai Pan-chiu, "Chinese Theology."

2. David Ford, discussing Stephen Sykes's encouragement given to younger Anglicans, Cambridge, 14 Feb. 2015, "fulcrum," "Stephen Sykes Memorial Address (Proverbs 1.1–34, John 1.1–18)," www.fulcrum-anglican.org.uk/articles/stephen-sykes-memorial -address-proverbs-1–1-34-john-1–1-18/.

BIBLIOGRAPHY

Adams, Nicholas. "Making Deep Reasonings Public," in David Ford and C. C. Pecknold, eds., *The Promise of Scriptural Reasoning*. Chichester: Wiley-Blackwell, 2006.

Aikman, David. *Jesus in Beijing*. Washington, DC: Regnery, 2003.

Arbuckle, Gerald. *Culture, Inculturation and Theologians*. Collegeville, MN: Liturgical Press, 2010.

Ashiwa, Yoshiko, and David Wank, eds. *Making Religion, Making the State*. Stanford: Stanford University Press, 2009.

Bailey, Paul J. "Cultural Connections in a New Global Space: Li Shizeng and the Chinese Francophile Project in the Early Twentieth Century," in Pei-yin Lin and Wenping Tsai, eds., *Print, Profit and Perception: Ideas, Information, and Knowledge in Chinese Societies 1895–1949*. Leiden: Brill, 2014.

Barker, T. M. (柏基根). Editorial on Lambeth 1930, *Zhenli yu shengming* 真理與生命 [Truth and Life: A Journal of Christian Thought and Practice], Vol. 5.1 (Nov. 1930).

Barmé, Geremie R. "Spiritual Pollution Thirty Years On," Australian Centre on China in the World, *The China Story*, 17 Nov. 2013. Available at www.thechinastory.org/2013/11/spiritual-pollution-thirty-years-on/.

Barth, Karl. "The Christian Community and the Civil Community" (1954), in Clifford Green, ed., *Karl Barth: Theologian of Freedom*. Minneapolis: Fortress, 1991.

———. *Church Dogmatics*. Edinburgh: T & T Clark, 1967–1988.

———. "Letter to a Pastor in the German Democratic Republic," in Karl Barth and Johannes Hamel, *How to Serve God in a Marxist Land* (New York: Association Press, 1959).

Barth, Markus. "Current Discussion on the Political Character of Karl Barth's Theology," in Martin Rumscheidt, ed., *Footnotes to a Theology: The Karl Barth Colloquium of 1972*. Waterloo: Corporation for the Publication of Academic Studies in Religion in Canada, 1974.

Barwick, John. "Promoting a Protestant Vision of the Modern Chinese Woman," in Hamrin and Bieler, eds., *Salt and Light*, Vol. 3.

Bays, Daniel. "Foreign Missions and Indigenous Protestant Leaders in China, 1920–1955," in Brian Stanley, ed., *Missions, Nationalism and the End of Empire*. Grand Rapids, MI: Eerdmans, 2003.

Bays, Daniel H. "A Chinese 'Public Sphere'?: Socioeconomic Mobility and the Formation of Urban Middle Class Protestant Communities in the Early Twentieth Century," in Kenneth Lieberthal, Shuen-fu Lin, and Ernest P. Young, eds., *Constructing China: The Interaction of Culture and Economics*. Ann Arbor: University of Michigan Press, 1997.

——. *A New History of Christianity in China*. Chichester: Wiley-Blackwell, 2012.

Benedict XVI. "Letter of the Holy Father Pope Benedict XVI to the Bishops, Priests, Consecrated Persons and Lay Faithful of the Catholic Church in the People's Republic of China," 2007. Available at w2.vatican.va/content/benedict-xvi/en/letters/2007/documents/hf_ben-xvi_let_20070527_china.html.

Berling, Judith. *The Syncretic Religion of Lin Chao-en*. New York: Columbia University Press, 1980.

Bickel, Simone Frutiger. "Wise as Serpents and Harmless as Doves." *Chinese Theological Review* 10 (1995).

Boger, Gretchen. "Protestant Pragmatism in China 1919–1927," in Leigh E. Schmidt and Sally Promey, eds., *American Religious Liberalism*. Bloomington: Indiana University Press, 2012.

Bohr, P. R. *Famine in China and the Missionary: Timothy Richard as Relief Administrator and Advocate of National Reform, 1876–84*. Cambridge, MA: Harvard University Press, 1972.

Brokaw, Cynthia J. *The Ledgers of Merit and Demerit: Social Change and Moral Order in Late Imperial China*. Princeton, NJ: Princeton University Press, 1991.

Cao Nanlai. *Constructing China's Jerusalem: Christians, Power and Place in Contemporary Wenzhou*. Stanford, CA: Stanford University Press, 2011.

Cao Shengjie. "Mission in the Chinese Church." *Chinese Theological Review* 20 (2007): 1–23.

Carbonneau, Robert E. "The Catholic Church in China, 1900–49," in Tiedemann, ed., *Handbook of Christianity in China*.

——. "'We Have Been Thrown into a Vicariate': Passionists in West Hunan: The Struggle to Bring to Life a Chinese Voice of Faith, 1922–26," in Rachel Lu Yan and Philip Vanhaelemeersch, eds., *Silent Force: Native Converts in the Catholic China Mission*. Leuven: Ferdinant Verbiest Institute, 2009.

Chai Ling. *A Heart for Freedom*. Carol Stream, IL: Tyndale, 2011.

Chan, Frank K. P. (Chen Guangpei 陳廣培). *Liji liren: Wu Leichuan bense shenxue chonggou* 立己立人: 吴雷川本色神学重构. Hong Kong: Chinese Mission Seminary, 2008.

Chandler, Robert E. "The Status of Self-Support," *CCYB* 12 (1924): 139.

Chao, T. C. (see also Zhao Zichen). "Christianity and Confucianism." *International Review of Mission*, Vol. 17 (1927).

——. "The Church-Consciousness of the Chinese People." *Truth and Life*, Vol. 2, No. 1 (Feb. 1927): 32–46; repr. in Chao, *Collected English Writings*, 224.

———. *The Collected English Writings of Tsu Chen Chao*. Beijing: Shang wu, 2009. Vol. 5 of *Zhao Zichen wenji* [趙紫宸 Collected Works of Zhao Zichen].

———. Editorial. *Zhenli yu shengming*, Vol. 5, No. 1 (1 Nov. 1930).

———. "The Future of Religious Education in Christian Schools." *Education Review*, Vol. 20 (1928); repr. in Chao, *Collected English Writings*, 258–68.

———. "The Indigenous Church." *CR* 56 (Aug. 1925); repr. in Chao, *Collected English Writings*, 177–86.

———. "Jesus and the Reality of God." Speech delivered in Edinburgh in 1933, published in *Truth and Life*, Vol. 7, No. 5 (1933): 1–10; repr. in Chao, *Collected English Writings*, 343.

———. "An Open Letter." *Zhenli yu shengming*, Vol. 5, No. 2 (Dec. 1930): 9–12.

———. "Present-Day Religious Thought and Life in China" (1926); repr. in Chao, *Collected English Writings*.

———. "The Strengths and Weaknesses of the Church in China," in *The Chinese Church 1922 National Christian Conference*. Shanghai: Oriental Press, 1922.

Chao, T. C., and T. T. Lew. "The Relation of the Chinese Church to the Church Universal." NCC speeches abridged in *CR* 54 (1923): 350.

Chen Duxiu. "Christianity and the Chinese People." Trans. Y. Y. Tsu, *CR* 51 (July 1920).

Chen Jianmin. "Modern Chinese Attitudes Towards the Bible," in Starr, ed., *Reading Christian Scriptures*.

Chen Qirui 陈企瑞. "Christ the Everlasting Lord—Bishop Shen Yifan's Thinking on Incarnation." *Jinling shenxue zhi* 94 (2013): 137–65; trans. in *Chinese Theological Review* 25 (2013): 31–78.

Chen Yongtao 陈永涛. "Interpreting Christian Faith in Our Own Time and Context." *Jinling shenxue zhi* 2 (2004): 42–56; trans. in *Chinese Theological Review* 19 (2005): 1–18.

Chen Zemin 陈泽民. *Qiusuo yu jianzheng* 求索与见证: 陈泽民文选 [Seeking and Witnessing: Selected Writings of Chen Zemin]. Shanghai: CCC/TSPM, 2007.

Cheng, Ruth. "Women and the Church," in *National Christian Conference: The Chinese Church as revealed in the National Christian Conference held in Shanghai, Tuesday, 2 May, to Thursday, 11 May 1922*. Shanghai: Oriental Press, 1922.

Cheng Jingyi. "Some Problems Confronting the Christian Movement in China as Seen by a Chinese Christian." Shanghai: NCC, 1927.

Cheng Zhiyi (誠質怡 Andrew C. Y. Cheng). "The Idea of Faith in the Fourth Gospel." *Zhenli yu shengming*, Vol. 5.2 (Dec. 1930).

Chin Ken-pa. "The Paradigm Shift: From Chinese Theology to Sino-Christian Theology—A Case Study on Liu Xiaofeng," in Lai and Lam, eds., *Sino-Christian Theology*.

Chow, Alexander. *Theosis, Sino-Christian Theology and the Second Chinese Enlightenment*. New York: Palgrave Macmillan, 2013.

Chung, Mary Keng Mun. *Chinese Women in Christian Ministry*. New York: Peter Lang, 2005.

Chu Sin-jan. *Wu Leichuan, A Confucian-Christian in Republican China*. New York: Peter Lang, 1995.

Clarke, Jeremy. *The Virgin Mary and Catholic Identities in Chinese History*. Hong Kong: Hong Kong University Press, 2013.

Cohen, Paul. *China and Christianity: The Missionary Movement and the Growth of Chinese Antiforeignism, 1860–1870.* Cambridge, MA: Harvard University Press, 1963.

Congregation for the Doctrine of the Faith (Joseph Cardinal Ratzinger). "Instruction on Certain Aspects of the 'Theology of Liberation,'" 1984. Available at www.vatican.va/roman_curia/congregations/cfaith/documents/rc_con_cfaith_doc_19840806_theology -liberation_en.html.

Congressional-Executive Commission on China. Roundtable. "China's New Regulation on Religious Affairs: A Paradigm Shift?" Washington, DC, 25 Mar. 2005. Available at www.cecc.gov/.

Coulet, J. C. *Les actes de Béda Chang.* Paris: Procure de la Mission de Chine à Paris, 1954.

Criveller, Gianni. "The Chinese Priests of the College for the Chinese in Naples and the Promotion of the Indigenous Clergy," in Rachel Lu Yan and Philip Vanhaelemeersch, eds., *Silent Force: Native Converts in the Catholic China Mission.* Leuven: Ferdinant Verbiest Institute, 2009.

———. "Matteo Ricci's Ascent to Beijing," in Gianni Criveller and Cesar Guillen-Nuñez, eds. *Portrait of a Jesuit: Matteo Ricci, 1552–1610.* Macao: Macau Ricci Institute, 2010.

———. *Preaching Christ in Late Ming China: The Jesuits' Presentation of Christ from Matteo Ricci to Giulio Aleni.* Taipei: Ricci Institute, 1997.

———. "Three Documents: A Commentary." *Tripod,* Vol. 23, No. 130 (Autumn 2003).

The Cross in China, dir. Yuan Zhiming. Rohnert Park, CA: China Soul for Christ Foundation, 2003.

Crouch, Archie. *Christianity in China: A Scholar's Guide to Resources.* London: Taylor and Francis, 1989.

Cusset, François. *French Theory: How Foucault, Derrida, Deleuze & Co. Transformed the Intellectual Life of the United States,* trans. Jeff Fort. Minneapolis: University of Minnesota Press, 2008.

De Bary, Wm. Theodore, and Irene Bloom, eds. *Sources of Chinese Tradition,* Vol. I, 2nd ed. New York: Columbia University Press, 1999.

De Bary, Wm. Theodore, and Richard Lufrano, eds. *Sources of Chinese Tradition: From 1600 Through the Twentieth Century,* Vol. 2. New York: Columbia University Press, 2000.

Defoort, Carine, and Yvonne Schulz Zinda. "Ren Jiyu, The Marxist View of Chinese Philosophy and Religion." *Contemporary Chinese Thought,* Vol. 41, No. 4 (Summer 2010): 3–17.

Denton, Kirk A., and Michele Hockx, eds. *Literary Societies of Republican China.* Lanham, MD: Lexington, 2008.

Ding Guangxun. See K. H. Ting.

Dudbridge, Glen. *Books, Tales and Vernacular Culture.* Leiden: Brill, 2005.

Dudink, Adrian. "The Religious Works Composed by Johann Adam Schall von Bell, Especially His Zhuzhi Qunzheng and His Efforts to Convert the Last Ming Emperor," in Malek, ed., *Western Learning and Christianity in China,* Vol. 2, 805–98.

Dunch, Ryan. "Christianizing Confucian Didacticism: Protestant Publications for Women, 1831–1911." *Nan Nü: Men, Women and Gender in China* 11.1 (2009): 65–101.

——. "'Mothers to Our Country': Conversion, Education and Ideology Among Chinese Protestant Women, 1870–1930," in Jessie G. Lutz, ed., *Gender and Christianity in China*. Bethlehem, PA: Lehigh University Press, 2010.

Eddy, Sherwood. *Religion and Social Justice*. New York: George H. Doran, 1927.

Fairbank, John King, ed. *The Cambridge History of China. Vol. 12: Republican China, 1912–1949, Part I*. Cambridge: Cambridge University Press, 1983.

Fällman, Fredrik. *Salvation and Modernity: Intellectuals and Faith in Contemporary China*. Chinese Culture Series 2. Stockholm: Stockholm University Press, 2004.

Fang Hao 方豪. *Zhongguo Tianzhujiao shi renwu zhuan* 中国天主教史人物传. Beijing: Zongjiao Wenhua, 2007.

Ferlanti, Federica. "The New Life Movement in Jiangxi Province, 1934–1938." *Modern Asian Studies* 44.5 (2010): 960–1000.

Feuerwerker, Albert. "The Foreign Presence in China," in Fairbank, ed., *Cambridge History of China. Vol. 12*, 128–207.

Feuerwerker, Yi-tsi Mei. *Ideology, Power, Text*. Stanford, CA: Stanford University Press, 1998.

Fisher, A. J. "Report on Church in South China." *CCYB* 12 (1924): 114.

Fodor, Jim. "Scriptural Reasoning as a Desert Practice: Learning to Read in Unchartered Territory." *Journal of Scriptural Reasoning*, Vol. 9, No. 1 (Dec. 2010).

Ford, David. "Deep Reasonings, No Map: Inter-faith Engagement as a Core Dynamic of Theology and Religious Studies," Edward Cadbury Lectures, University of Birmingham, 2013. Available at www.interfaith.cam.ac.uk/resources/lecturespapersandspeeches/Deepreasoningsnomap.

——. "Flamenco, Tai-Chi and Six-Text Scriptural Reasoning: Report on a Visit to China." Available at www.interfaith.cam.ac.uk/resources/lecturespapersandspeeches/chinavisit.

——. *The Shape of Living*. Grand Rapids, MI: Baker, 1998.

Fraser, Giles. "Western Political Theatre Would Struggle to Make Sense of the Violence in Egypt." *The Guardian*, 16 Aug. 2013.

Fu Daiwie. "The Flourishing of *Biji* or Pen-Notes Texts and Its Relations to History of Knowledge in Song China (960–1279)." *Extreme Orient* 27.1 (2007): 103–30.

Gao Shining. "Cong shizheng yanjiu kan jidujiao yu dangdai Zhongguo shehui," 从实证研究看基督教与当代中国社会. *Zhejiang xuekan*, Vol. 4 (2006); English text in Zhuo Xinping, ed., *Christianity*. Leiden: Brill, 2013.

——. "The Impact of Contemporary Chinese Folk Religions on Christianity," in Mikka Ruokanen and Paulos Huang, eds., *Christianity and Chinese Culture*. Grand Rapids, MI: W. Eerdmans, 2010.

Gao Xin. "Preliminary Survey on the New Generation of Scholars of Christian Studies in Mainland China," in Lai and Lam, eds., *Sino-Christian Theology*.

Gao Ying. "God's Promise and Eschatological Hope." *Chinese Theological Review* 20 (2007): 31–55.

Gardner, Daniel K. "Modes of Thinking and Modes of Discourse in the Sung: Some Thoughts on the Yü-lu ('Recorded Conversations') Texts." *Journal of Asian Studies*, Vol. 50, No. 3 (Aug. 1991): 574–603.

Gernet, Jacques. *China and the Christian Impact: A Conflict of Culture*, trans. Janet Lloyd. Cambridge: Cambridge University Press, 1985.

Giradot, Norman J. *The Victorian Translation of China*. Berkeley: University of California Press, 2002.

Glüer, Winfried. *Christliche Theologie in China: T. C. Chao: 1918–1956*. Gütersloh: Mohn, 1979.

Goldman, Merle. *China's Intellectuals: Advise and Dissent*. Cambridge, MA: Harvard University Press, 1981.

Gore, Charles. *Christ and Society*. Halley Stewart Lectures, 1927. London: George Allen and Unwin, 1928.

——. *Property, Its Duties and Rights, Historically, Philosophically and Religiously Regarded*. London: Macmillan, 1915.

"Guanyu libaitang nei xuangua lingxiu xiang de wenti" 關於禮拜堂內懸掛領袖像 的問題. *Tian Feng* 270 (30 June 1951).

Hai Jinhua. "Inherit and Renew: Ecclesiology in the Indigenous Chinese Church." *Chinese Theological Review* 25 (2013): 1–31.

Hamrin, Carol Lee, and Stacey Bieler, eds. *Salt and Light: Lives of Faith That Shaped Modern China*, Vols. 1–3. Eugene, OR: Wipf and Stock, 2009.

Hanan, Patrick. "The Bible as Chinese Literature: Medhurst, Wang Tao, and the Delegates' Version." *Harvard Journal of Asiatic Studies* 63, No. 1 (2002): 197–239.

Handlin, Joanna F. *Action in Late Ming Thought: The Reorientation of Lü K'un and Other Scholar Officials*. Berkeley: University of California Press, 1983.

Handlin Smith, Joanna. *The Art of Doing Good: Charity in Late Ming China*. Berkeley: University of California Press, 2009.

Han Wenzao 韩文藻. "Guanyu jiaqiang shenxue sixiang jianshe wenti" 关于加强神学 思想建设问题—在济南会议上的闭幕讲话. *Jinling shenxue zhi* 2 (1999); English text "On Strengthening Theological Reconstruction." *Chinese Theological Review* 14 (1999): 28–29.

Hargett, James. *On the Road in Twelfth Century China: The Travel Diaries of Fan Chengda, 1126–1193*. Wiesbaden: Steiner Verlag, 1989.

Harrison, Henrietta. *The Missionary's Curse and Other Tales from a Chinese Catholic Village*. Berkeley: University of California Press, 2013.

Hattaway, Paul, Brother Yun, Peter Xu Yongze, and Enoch Wang. *Back to Jerusalem: Three Chinese House Church Leaders Share Their Vision to Complete the Great Commission*. Downers Grove, IL: InterVarsity, 2003.

Hayhoe, Ruth. *China's Universities 1895–1995*. London: Routledge, 1995.

Hayhoe, Ruth, and Lu, Yongling, eds. *Ma Xiangbo and the Mind of Modern China, 1840–1939*. Armonk, NY: M. E. Sharpe, 1996.

He Guanghu 何光沪. "Hanyu shenxue de genju yu yiyi" 汉语神学的根据与意义. *Regent Journal* 2, 39–47; "Hanyu shenxue de fangfa yu jinlu" 汉语神学的方法与进路. *Regent Journal* 3, 16–24; trans. as "The Basis and Significance of Sino-Christian Theology" and "The Methodology of and Approaches to Sino-Christian Theology," in Yang and Yeung, eds., *Sino-Christian Studies in China*, pp. 120–32 and 106–19, respectively.

Henderson, John B. *Scripture, Canon and Commentary*. Princeton, NJ: Princeton University Press, 1991.

Ho, Herbert Hoi-lap 何凯立. *Jidujiao zai Hua chuban shiye* 基督教在华出版事业, "Protestant Missionary Publications in Modern China 1912–1949," trans. Chen Jianming and Wang Zaixing. Chengdu: Sichuan Daxue, 2004.

Hsia, R. Po-chia. *A Jesuit in the Forbidden City: Matteo Ricci 1542–1610*. Oxford: Oxford University Press, 2010.

Huang, Martin W., ed. *Male Friendship in Ming China*. Leiden: Brill, 2007.

Huang Renyi 黄仁遗. "Geming qingnian di zhongyao gongzuo" 革命青年底重要工作 [The Important Task of Revolutionary Youth]. *Juewu*, 9 Sept. 1924.

Hui, Hoi Ming. "A Study of T. C. Chao's Christology." PhD diss., University of Birmingham, 2008.

Human Rights Watch/Asia. "Some Problems Concerning Further Improving Work on Religions," in *Freedom of Religion in China*. New York: Human Rights Watch, 1992. Available at www.hrw.org/reports/pdfs/c/china/china921.pdf.

Hunter, Alan, and Kim-Kwong Chan. *Protestantism in Contemporary China*. Cambridge: Cambridge University Press, 1999.

Hurtado, L. W. "Early Devotion to Jesus: A Report, Reflections and Implications." *Expository Times* 122/4 (2010): 167–76.

Inouye, Melissa Wei-Tsing. "Miraculous Mundane: The True Jesus Church and Chinese Christianity in the Twentieth Century." PhD diss., Harvard University, 2011.

Jiang Peifen. "An Appeal to Mr. Wang Mingdao." *Chinese Theological Review* 1987: 57–59.

Jin Bingdao 金秉道 (Chin Pin tau). "Wo duiyu zhenli de jianjie he xinyang" 我对于真理的见解和信仰 [My Views on and Faith in Truth]. *Zhen guang*, No. 24, Vol. 5 (15 May 1925).

Jing Tsu. *Failure, Nationalism and Literature: The Making of Modern Chinese Identity, 1895–1937*. Stanford, CA: Stanford University Press, 2005.

Jin Luxian. *The Memoirs of Jin Luxian*, trans. William Hanbury-Tenison. Hong Kong: Hong Kong University Press, 2012.

Johnson, T., and K. Ross. *Atlas of Global Christianity*. Edinburgh: University of Edinburgh Press, 2010.

Jones, Francis P. "Our Continuing Witness." Report of the Peking Union Church reunion in New York, 3 Oct. 1954. Yale Divinity School Pamphlet Collection, HR 124.

Kautsky, Karl. *Foundations of Christianity: A Study in Christian Origins*. London: Allen and Unwin, 1925. Trans. Tang Zhi 汤治 and Ye Qifang 叶启芳 as 基督教的基础. Shenzhou: Guoguang She, 1932.

Koo, T. Z. (Gu Ziren) "What Does the National Christian Convention Mean to Me?" *CR*, Vol. LIII, No. 2 (Feb. 1922): 80–88.

Kuo, Ya-pei. "'Christian Civilization' and the Confucian Church: The Origin of Secular Politics in Modern China." *Past and Present* 218(1) (2013): 235–64.

Kwan, Simon S. M. *Post-colonial Resistance and Asian Theology.* Oxford: Routledge, 2013.

Kwok Pui-lan. *Chinese Women and Christianity, 1860–1927.* Atlanta, GA: Scholars, 1992.

The Life: A Journal of Christian Thought and Practice. Special Conference Federation Number, n.d.

Lai, John Tzs-Pang. *Negotiating Religious Gaps: The Enterprise of Translating Christian Tracts by Protestant Missionaries in Nineteenth-Century China.* Sankt Augustin: Institut Monumenta Serica, 2012.

Lai Pan-chiu. "Chinese Theology," in Ian A. McFarland et al., eds., *The Cambridge Dictionary of Christian Theology.* Cambridge: Cambridge University Press, 2014.

——. "Typology and Prospect of Sino-Christian Theology." *Ching Feng* 6.2 (2005): 211–30.

Lai Pan-chiu and Jason Lam, eds. *Sino-Christian Theology: A Theological Qua Cultural Movement in Contemporary China.* Frankfurt: Peter Lang, 2010.

Lam, Jason Tsz-Shun 林子淳. *Duoyuan xing Hanyu shenxue quanshi* 多元性漢語神學詮釋 [A Polyphonic View on Sino-Christian Theology]. Hong Kong: Institute of Sino-Christian Studies, 2006.

——, ed. *Hanyu jidujiao jingxue chuyi* 漢語基督教經學芻議 [An Initiative Proposal on Sino-Christian Scriptural Hermeneutics]. Hong Kong: Institute of Sino-Christian Studies, 2010.

Lam, Wing-hung 林荣洪 (Lin Ronghong). *Chinese Theology in Construction.* Pasadena, CA: William Carey Library, 1983.

——. *Qu gao he gua: Zhao Zichen de shengping ji shenxue* 曲高和寡: 赵紫宸的生平及神学 [The Life and Thought of Chao Tzu-ch'en]. Hong Kong: China Alliance Press, 1994.

——. "Tongyi de jiufa: Zhao Zichen de Zhongguo bensehua jidulun" [An Identifying Salvation: Zhao Zichen's Indigenous Chinese Christology], in Wang Xiaochao, ed., *Zhao Zichen xiansheng jinian wenji.* Beijing: Zongjiao Wenhua, 2005.

Lambert, Tony. *China's Christian Millions: The Costly Revival.* Littleton, CO: OMF Books, 1999.

Latourette, Kenneth Scott. *History of Christian Missions in China.* New York: Macmillan, 1929.

Lee, Archie C. C. (Li Chichang 李炽昌), ed. *Wenben shijian yu shenfen bianshi* 文本实践与身份辨识: 中国基督徒知识分子的中文著述 1583–1949 [Textual Practice and Identity Making: A Study of Chinese Christian Writings, 1583–1949]. Shanghai: Shanghai Guji, 2005.

Lee, Peter. "Images of Society in the Early Chosun Literary Miscellany." *Sung Kyun Journal of East Asian Studies* 6(2): 137–75.

Leeb, Leopold (see also Lei Libo). "Yang Huilin and His View of Christian Culture." *Inter-religio* 38 (Summer 2000): 57–63.

Legge, James. *The Chinese Classics, Vol. II, Mencius.* London: Trübner, 1861. *Vol. I* and *Vol. III.* Taipei: SMC, 1994.

——. *The Great Learning*, in *The Life and Teachings of Confucius*, Vol. 1. Philadelphia: J. B. Lippincott, 1867.

——. *Sacred Books of the East, Part II: The Yî King*, trans. James Legge, ed. F. Max Müller. Oxford: Clarendon, 1899.

Lei Libo 雷立柏 (see also Leopold Leeb). *Lun Jidujiao zhi da yu xiao: 1900–1950 nian Huaren zhishi fenzi yan zhong de jidujiao* 论基督教之大与小: 1900–1950 年华人知识分子眼中的基督教 [Christianity in the Eyes of Chinese Intellectuals, 1900 to 1950]. Beijing: Shehui Kexue Wenxian, 2000.

Leo XIII. "Rerum Novarum." Available at www.vatican.va/holy_father/leo_xiii/encyclicals/documents/hf_l-xiii_enc_15051891_rerum-novarum_en.html.

Leung, Beatrice. *Sino-Vatican Relations: Problems in Conflicting Authority, 1976–86.* Cambridge: Cambridge University Press, 1992.

Lew, Timothy Ting-fang 劉廷芳(Liu Tingfang), ed. *The Life: A Journal of Christian Thought and Practice* (Special Federation Conference Number). Beijing: n.p. (1922).

Lewis, Mark Edward. *Writing and Authority in Early China*. New York: SUNY Press, 1999.

Liang Hui, Grace, 梁慧. "Interpreting the Lord's Prayer from a Confucian-Christian Perspective," in Starr, ed., *Reading Christian Scriptures.*

——. "How Do Modern Chinese Christian Intellectuals Read the Bible? The Principles and Methodologies of Wu Leichuan and Zhao Zichen for the Interpretation of the Bible" 中国现代基督徒知识分子是如何读圣经的? 以吴雷川与赵紫宸处理《圣经》的原则与方法为例. *International Journal of Sino-Western Studies*, Vol. 4 (2013): 47–57.

Lian Xi. "'Cultural Christians' and the Search for Civil Society in Contemporary China." *Chinese Historical Review* 20.1 (May 2013): 71–88.

——. *Redeemed by Fire: The Rise of Popular Christianity in Modern China.* New Haven, CT: Yale University Press, 2010.

——. Review of Mariani, *Church Militant: Bishop Kung and Catholic Resistance in Communist Shanghai. American Historical Review* 117 (2012): 1563–64.

——. "The Search for Chinese Christianity in the Republican Period (1912–1940)." *Modern Asian Studies* 38 (Oct. 2004): 851–98.

Li Chichang 李炽昌. See Lee, Archie C. C.

Li Lili 李麗麗. "Tianzhujiao shehui xundao zai Zhongguo de bendihua: yi ge dui Xu Zongze sixiang de yanjiu" 天主教社會訓導在中國的本地化: 一個對徐宗澤思想的研究 [Inculturation of Catholic Social Teachings in China: A Study of Xu Zongze's Thought]. PhD diss., Chinese University of Hong Kong, 2010.

Lim, Francis Khek Gee, ed. *Christianity in Contemporary China: Socio-Cultural Perspectives.* London: Routledge, 2013.

Lin, Manhong Melissa. *Ethical Reorientation for Christianity in China.* Ching Feng Series No. 17. Hong Kong: Christian Study Centre on Chinese Religion and Culture, 2010.

Lin Hong-Hsin 林鸿信 [Lin Hongxin]. "Tongyi de jiufa: Zhao Zichen de Zhongguo bensehua jidulun" 同一的救法——赵紫宸的中国本色化基督论 [An Identifying Salvation: Zhao Zichen's Indigenous Chinese Christology], in Wang Xiaochao, ed., *Zhao Zichen xiansheng jinian wenji.* Beijing: Zongjiao Wenhua, 2005.

Link, Perry. "Does This Writer Deserve the Prize?" *New York Review of Books*, 6 Dec. 2012.

Lippiello, Tiziana, and Roman Malek, eds. *Scholar from the West: Giulio Aleni S.J. (1582–1649) and the Dialogue Between Christianity and China*. Brescia: Fondazione civiltà bresciana, 1997.

Li Qiuling 李秋零 and Yang Xinan 样熙楠 (Daniel Yeung), eds. *Xiandai xing, chuantong bianqian yu Hanyu shenxue* 现代性, 传统变迁与汉语神学 [Modernity, Transformation of Tradition and Sino-Christian Theology]. Shanghai: Huadong Shifan Daxue, 2010.

Li Tiangang. "Christianity and Cultural Conflict in the Life of Ma Xiangbo," in Hayhoe and Lu, eds., *Ma Xiangbo and the Mind of Modern China*.

Liu Gang. "The Poetics of Miscellaneousness: The Literary Design of Liu Yiqing's *Qiantang yishi* and the Historiography of the Southern Song." PhD diss., University of Michigan, 2012.

Liu Tongsu. *Shangdi yu kaisa de jiangjie* 上帝与凯撒的疆界 [The Boundary Between God and Caesar: Dedicated to the Chinese House Churches of the New Era]. Posted 30 Nov. 2010. Available at www.liutongsu.net.

——. "Zhongguo jiaohui de chushi yu rushi" 中国教会的出事与入世 [The Emergence and Involvement in Society of the Chinese Church], 2007. Available at www.liutongsu.net/?page_id=41#zj2.

Liu Tongsu 刘同苏 and Wang Yi 王怡. *Guankan Zhongguo chengshi jiating jiaohui* 观看中国城市家庭教会 [Observing China's Urban House Churches]. 2012. Posted 13 Sept. 2010. Available at www.liutongsu.net.

Liu Xiaofeng 刘小枫. *Zhengjiu yu xiaoyao* 拯救与逍遥. Shanghai: Shanghai Renmin, 1988.

Li Wei 李韦. *Wu Leichuan de jidujiao chujinghua sixiang yanjiu* 吴雷川的基督教处境化思想研究 [On Wu Leichuan's Thinking on Christian Contextualization]. Beijing: Zongjiao Wenhua, 2010.

Li Xinyuan. *Construction—Or Destruction?: An Analysis of the Theology of Bishop K. H. Ting*. Streamwood, IL: Christian Life Press, 2003.

Lobestine, E. C. "What Practical Steps Should Be Taken at This Time in the Home Churches to Overcome the Handicap of Our Divided Denominational Mission Abroad?" Yale Divinity School papers, RG 08, Box 119–20.

Lomanov, Alexander. "Russian Orthodox Church," in Tiedemann, ed., *Handbook of Christianity in China*.

Lu, Sheldon Hsiao-peng. *From Historicity to Fictionality: The Chinese Poetics of Narrative*. Stanford, CA: Stanford University Press, 1994.

Luk, Bernard Hong-kay. "A Serious Matter of Life and Death: Learned Conversations at Foochow in 1627," in Charles Ronan and Bonnie Oh, eds., *East Meets West: The Jesuits in China, 1582–1773*. Chicago: Loyola University Press, 1988.

Luo Mingjian 羅名堅 (M. Ruggieri). 新編西竺國天主聖教實錄 [Newly Edited True Records of the Holy Teaching of the Lord of Heaven from Western India], reproduced in Nicolas Standaert and Adrian Dudink, eds., 耶穌會羅馬檔案館明清天主教文獻 [Chinese Christian Texts from the Roman Archives of the Society of Jesus], Vol. 1. Taipei: Taipei Ricci Institute, 2002.

Luo Zhufeng. *Religion Under Socialism in China*, trans. Donald MacInnis and Zheng Xi'an. New York: M. E. Sharpe, 1991.

Lutz, Jessie. *China and the Christian Colleges*. Ithaca, NY: Cornell University Press, 1971.

Lü Xiaomin 吕小敏. Canaan Hymns. Available at www.chinasoul.org.

——. *Jia'nan shixuan* 迦南诗选 [Canaan Hymns]. Taipei: Taipei CMI Publishing, 2001.

Lu Xing. *Rhetoric of the Chinese Cultural Revolution: The Impact on Chinese Thought, Culture and Communication*. Columbia: University of South Carolina Press, 2004.

MacInnis, Donald. *Religion in China Today: Policy and Practice*. Maryknoll, NY: Orbis, 1989.

——. *Religious Policy and Practice in Communist China*. New York: Macmillan, 1972.

Ma Hongli 马红莉. "Guanhua heheben yu wenli heheben de fanyi yuanze bijiao"《官话和合译本》与《文理和合译本》的翻译原则比较 [A Comparison of Translation Principles in the Mandarin Union and Wenli Union Versions of the Bible]. *Journal of Chinese Christian Culture*, No. 28 (2012).

Madsen, Richard. *China's Catholics*. Berkeley: University of California Press, 1998.

Malek, Roman. "Shaping Reciprocity: Some Remarks on Orders and Congregations in the History of Christianity in China." *Verbum SVD* 54.4 (2013): 424–50.

——, ed. *Western Learning and Christianity in China*. 2 vols. Sankt Augustin: Institut Monumenta Serica, 1998.

Mariani, Paul. *Church Militant: Bishop Kung and Catholic Resistance in Communist Shanghai*. Cambridge, MA: Harvard University Press, 2011.

Marx, Edwin. "Progress and Problems of the Christian Movement Since the Revolution (1911)." *CCYB* 12 (1924).

McDermott, Joseph. *The Social History of the Book in China*. Hong Kong: Hong Kong University Press, 2006.

McDonough, Conor. "Grounding Speech and Silence: Cataphaticism and Apophaticism in Denys and Aquinas." *Irish Theological Quarterly* 76.1 (2011): 57–76.

McIntosh, Mark A. *Divine Teaching*. Blackwell: London 2008.

McLeister, Mark. "A Three-Self Protestant Church, the Local State and Religious Policy Implementation in a Coastal Chinese City," in Lim, ed., *Christianity in Contemporary China*.

Medhurst, W. H. *China: Its State and Prospects*. Boston: Crocker and Brewster, 1838.

Menegon, Eugenio. *Ancestors, Virgins and Friars: Christianity as a Local Religion in Late Imperial China*. Cambridge, MA: Harvard University Asia Center, 2009.

——. "Jesuit Emblematica: The Use of European Allegorical Images in Flemish Engravings Described in the Kouduo Richao." *Monumenta Serica* 55 (2007): 389–437.

——. "Yang Guangxian's Opposition to J. A. Schall: Christianity and Western Science in His Work Budeyi," in Malek, ed., *Western Learning and Chinese Christianity*, Vol. 2.

Merwin, Wallace C., and Francis P. Jones. *Documents of the Three-Self Movement*. New York: National Council of the Churches of Christ, 1963.

Meyer-Fong, Tobie. *What Remains: Coming to Terms with Civil War in 19th Century China*. Stanford, CA: Stanford University Press, 2013.

Meynard, Thierry. *Le Sens Réel de "Seigneur du Ciel."* Paris: Belles Lettres, 2013.

Mitter, Rana. *A Bitter Revolution: China's Struggle with the Modern World*. Oxford: Oxford University Press, 2004.

———. *China's War with Japan, 1937–45*. London: Allen Lane, 2013.

———. "Writing War: Autobiography, Modernity and Wartime Narrative in Nationalist China, 1937–1946." *Royal Historical Society* 18 (2008): 187–210.

Mittler, Barbara. *A Newspaper for China? Power, Identity and Change in China's News Media, 1872–1912*. Cambridge, MA: Harvard University Asia Center, 2004.

Mo Guang. "Jidutu yao juanxian wuqi" 基督徒要捐獻武器 [Christians Should Donate Arms]. *Tian Feng* 271 (7 July 1951): 2–4.

Moloughney, Brian. "From Biographical History to Historical Biography: A Transformation in Chinese Historical Writing." *East Asian History*, No. 4 (1992): 1–30.

Ms. A. "Yi ge jiaohui xuexiao xuesheng xie gei youren de xin" 一个教会学校学生写给友人的信 [Letter to Friends from a Church-School Student]. *Juewu*, 2 Sept. 1924.

Müller, F. Max, ed. *Sacred Books of the East, Part II: The Yî King*, trans. James Legge. Oxford: Clarendon, 1899.

Mungello, D. E. *The Forgotten Christians of Hangzhou*. Honolulu: University of Hawai'i Press, 1994.

Nathan, Andrew J. *Chinese Democracy: The Individual and the State in Twentieth Century China*. London: I. B. Tauris, 1986.

National Christian Council. "Report on Christian Literature." *National Christian Council of China 1928–37* (1929).

Nedostup, Rebecca. *Superstitious Regimes: Religion and the Politics of Chinese Modernity*. Cambridge, MA: Harvard University East Asia Center, 2009.

Nee, Watchman (Ni Tuosheng). *The Glorious Church*. Los Angeles: Stream Publishers, 1968.

———. *The Normal Christian Life*. London: Witness and Testimony, 1958.

New China News Agency. Dispatch. 23 Nov. 1950, repr. in *CMB*, Vol. III (IV), Jan. 1951, No. 1, 50.

Newman, Barnett P. "The Sublime Is Now." *Tiger's Eye* (1948): 51–53.

Ng, Peter Tze Ming. *Chinese Christianity*. Leiden: Brill, 2012.

Ni Tuosheng. See Nee, Watchman.

Ochs, Peter. "An Introduction to Scriptural Reasoning: From Practice to Theory," trans. Wang Hai. *Journal of Renmin University of China* 5 (2012).

Ochs, Peter, and William Stacy Johnson, eds. *Crisis, Call and Leadership in the Abrahamic Traditions*. New York: Palgrave Macmillan, 2009.

Office of Theological Concerns. "Doing Theology in Asia Today." Federation of Asian Bishops' Conference Paper No. 96 (2000). Available at www.fabc.org/fabc%20papers/fabc_paper_96.pdf.

O'Neill, F. W. S. "Report on Church in Manchuria," *CCYB* 12 (1924).

Owen, Stephen. *Readings in Chinese Literary Thought*. Cambridge, MA: Harvard University Council on East Asian Studies, 1992.

Paton, David. *Christian Missions and the Judgement of God*. Repr. ed. Grand Rapids, MI: Eerdmans, 1996.

Peterson, Willard. "Learning from Heaven: The Introduction of Christianity and Other Western Ideas into Late Ming China," in *Cambridge History of China*, Vol. 8, Pt. 2. Cambridge: Cambridge University Press, 1998, 789–839.

Pew Research Center. Pew Forum on Religion and Public Life. "Global Christianity—A Report on the Size and Distributions of the World's Christian Population. Appendix C: Methodology for China." 19 Dec. 2011. Available at www.pewforum.org/files/2011/12/ ChristianityAppendixC.pdf.

Pfister, Lauren. "A Transmitter But Not a Creator: Ho Tsun-sheen (1817–71), the First Modern Chinese Protestant Theologian," in Irene Eber, Sze-kar Wan, and Knut Walf, eds., *Bible in Modern China: The Literary and Intellectual Impact*. Sankt Augustin: Nettetal, 1999.

Phan, Peter C., and Jung Young Lee, eds. *Journeys at the Margin: Towards an Autobiographical Theology in Asian American Perspective*. Collegeville, MN: Liturgical Press, 1999.

Pius IX. "Quadragesimo Anno." Available at www.vatican.va/holy_father/pius_xi/encycli cals/documents/hf_p-xi_enc_19310515_quadragesimo-anno_en.html.

Pius XII. "Ad Sinarum Gentem" (Encyclical on the Supranationality of the Church), 1954. Available at www.papalencyclicals.net/Pius12/P12SINAR.HTM.

Potter, Pitman B. "Belief in Control: Regulation of Religion in China." *China Quarterly* 174 (June 2003): 317–37.

Quash, Ben. "Deep Calls to Deep: The Practice of Scriptural Reasoning." Available at http:// www.interfaith.cam.ac.uk/resources/scripturalreasoningresources/deepcallstodeep.

———. *Found Christianity: History, Imagination and the Holy Spirit*. London: Bloomsbury, 2013.

Rauschenbusch, Walter. A *Theology for the Social Gospel*. Nashville, TN: Abingdon, 1945.

Reardon, Lawrence C. "The Chinese Catholic Church: Obstacles to Reconciliation," in Paul Manuel, Lawrence C. Reardon, and W. Clyde, eds., *The Catholic Church and the Nation-State: Comparative Perspectives*. Washington, DC: Georgetown University Press, 2006.

Renan, Ernest. *The Life of Jesus*. London: Trübner, 1863.

Ren Dayuan. "Wang Zheng: A Scientist, Philosopher and Catholic in Ming Dynasty China." In Chinese and English in Malek, ed., *Western Learning and Christianity in China*, Vol. 2, 339–58.

"Report of the Christian Literature Council on Present State and Future Task of Christian Literature in China," in *Chinese Church 1922 National Christian Conference*. Shanghai: Oriental Press, 1922.

Ricci, Matteo. *On Friendship: One Hundred Maxims for a Chinese Prince*, trans. Timothy Billings. New York: Columbia University Press, 2009.

———. (Li Madou 利瑪竇). *Tianzhu shiyi* 天主實意, in Zhu Weizheng 朱維錚, ed. *Li Madou Zhongwen zhu yiji* 利瑪竇中文著譯集. Hong Kong: City University, 2001.

———. *The True Meaning of the Lord of Heaven*, ed. Douglas Lancashire and Peter Hu Kuo-chen. Taipei: Ricci Institute, 1985.

Rickett, W. Allyn. *Guanzi: Political, Philosophical and Economic Essays from Early China.* Rev. ed. Boston: Cheng and Tsui, 2001.

Rolston, David L., ed. *How to Read the Chinese Novel.* Princeton, NJ: Princeton University Press, 1990.

Sanneh, Lamin. *Translating the Message: The Missionary Impact on Culture.* Maryknoll, NY: Orbis, 1989.

Saussy, Haun. "Matteo Ricci the Daoist," in Qian Suoqiao (钱锁桥), ed., *Cross-cultural Studies: China and the World. A Festschrift in Honor of Professor Zhang Longxi.* Leiden: Brill, 2015.

Schwarcz, Vera. *The Chinese Enlightenment: Intellectuals and the Legacy of the May Fourth Movement of 1919.* Berkeley: University of California Press, 1986.

Shen Fu. *Six Records of a Floating Life (Fusheng liuji),* ed. Leonard Pratt. London: Penguin, 1983.

Shi Jinghuan 史静寰 and Wang Li Xin 王立新. *Jidujiao jiaoyu yu Zhongguo zhishi fenzi* 基督教教育与中国知识分子 [Christian Education and Chinese Intellectuals]. Fuzhou: Fujian Jiaoyu, 1998.

Song, C. S. *Tell Us Our Names.* Maryknoll, NY: Orbis, 1984.

Song, Gang. "Learning from the Other: Giulio Aleni, Kouduo richao, and Late Ming Dialogic Hybridization." PhD diss., University of Southern California, 2006.

Spence, Jonathan. *The Memory Palace of Matteo Ricci.* London: Penguin, 1985.

Standaert, Nicolas. *Yang Tingyun, Confucian and Christian in Late Ming China.* Leiden: Brill, 1988.

[Standaert, Nicolas] Zhong Mingdan 鐘鳴旦, and [Adrian Dudink] Du Dingke 杜鼎克, eds. 耶穌會羅馬檔案館天主教文獻 [Chinese Christian Texts from the Roman Archives of the Society of Jesus]. 12 vols. Taipei: Taipei Ricci Institute, 2002.

Stark, Rodney, Byron Johnson, and Carson Mencken. "Counting China's Christians." *First Things,* May 2011. Available at www.firstthings.com/article/2011/05/counting -chinarsquos-christians.

Starr, Chloë. "The Chinese Church: A Post-Denominational Reality?" in Stanley D. Brunn, ed., *The Changing World Religion Map: Sacred Places, Identities, Practices and Politics.* Dordrecht: Springer, 2015, 2045–59.

———. "Reading Christian Scriptures: The Nineteenth Century Context," in Starr, ed., *Reading Christian Scriptures.*

———, ed. *Reading Christian Scriptures in China.* London: T & T Clark, 2008.

———. "Sino-Christian Theology: Treading a Fine Line Between Globalization and Self-Determination," in Thomas Jansen, Thoralf Klein, and Christian Meyer, eds., *Chinese Religions and Globalization.* Leiden: Brill, 2014.

———. "Surveying Galilee from a Chinese Observation Tower: Zhao Zichen's *Life of Jesus* (1935)." *English Language Notes* 50.2 (Fall/Winter 2012): 63–76.

Stauffer, Milton T., ed. *The Christian Occupation of China.* Shanghai: China Continuation Committee, 1922.

Strassberg, Richard E. *Inscribed Landscapes: Travel Writing from Imperial China.* Berkeley: University of California Press, 1994.

Suh Hu (Hu Shi). "Christianity and the Chinese People." *Sheng ming* Special Federation Conference Number, 1922.

Sun, Irene Ai-Ling. "Songs of Canaan: Hymnody of the House-Church Christians in China." *Studia Liturgica* 37.1 (2007): 98–116.

Sun Shangyang 孫尚揚. *Mingmo Tianzhujiao yu Ruxue de jiaoliu he chongtu* 明末天主教與儒學的交流和衝突. Taipei: Wenjin, 1992.

Tang, Edmond, and Jean-Paul Wiest, eds. *The Catholic Church in Modern China*, Part III. Maryknoll, NY: Orbis, 1993.

Tang Xiaofeng. *Zhao Zichen shenxue sixiang yanjiu* 赵紫宸神学思想研究. Beijing: Zongjiao Wenhua, 2006.

Tang Xiaofeng and Xiong Xiaohong, eds. *Yeying zhi zhi: Zhao Zichen yu Zhong-Xi sixiang jiaoliu* 夜鹰之志: 赵紫宸与中西思想交流. Beijing: Zongjiao Wenhua, 2010.

Tanner, Kathryn. *Theories of Culture*. Minneapolis: Augsburg, 1997.

Tao Feiya. "A Christian Utopia in China: A Historical Study of the Jesus Family (1921–1952)." PhD diss., Chinese University of Hong Kong, 2001.

Taylor, Jay. *The Generalissimo: Chiang Kai-Shek and the Struggle for Modern China*. Cambridge, MA: Belknap, 2009.

Throop, Montgomery H. *General Statistics of the Chung Kuo Sheng Kung Hui*, 1915 and 1933. Shanghai: St. John's University. Yale Divinity School Pamphlet Collection, HR 114.

Ticciati, Susannah. "Scriptural Reasoning and the Formation of Identity," in David Ford and C. C. Pecknold, eds., *The Promise of Scriptural Reasoning*. Oxford: Wiley-Blackwell, 2006.

Tiedemann, R. G. "The Chinese Clergy," in Tiedemann, ed., *Handbook of Christianity in China*.

———, ed. *Handbook of Christianity in China, Vol. 2: 1800–Present*. Leiden: Brill, 2010.

———. "Indigenous Agency, Religious Protectorates and Chinese Interests: The Expansion of Christianity in Nineteenth-Century China," in Dana L. Roberts, ed., *Converting Colonialism: Visions and Realities in Mission History, 1706–1914*. Grand Rapids, MI: Eerdmans, 2008.

Tillich, Paul. *Systematic Theology*, Vol. 3. Chicago: University of Chicago Press, 1976.

Ting, K. H. "American Interventions," repr. from *The Anglican Outlook*, Apr. 1947, in Whitehead, ed., *No Longer Strangers*.

———. "Between God and Humankind." *Sheng Kung* 圣工 (Feb. 1955): 6–8.

———. *A Chinese Contribution to Ecumenical Theology: Selected Writings of Bishop K. H. Ting*, ed. Janice and Philip Wickeri. Geneva: WCC Publications, 2002.

———. "The Church in China Today." *Student World* 1957, extracted as "New Initiatives" in Whitehead, ed., *No Longer Strangers*, 119–24.

———. "Civil War in China," repr. of "The Sociological Foundation of the Democratic Movement in China," *Bulletin of the Society of the Catholic Commonwealth*, Jan. 1948, in Whitehead, ed., *No Longer Strangers*.

———. "The Cosmic Christ," in Ting, *God Is Love*.

———. Foreword to *Theological Writings from Nanjing Seminary*, trans. in *Chinese Theological Review* 8 (1993).

———. *God Is Love: Collected Writings of Bishop K. H. Ting*. Colorado Springs: Cook Communications Ministries International, 2004.

———. *How to Study the Bible*. Hong Kong: Tao Fong Shan Ecumenical Centre, 1981.

———. "The Lamb of God." *Chinese Theological Review*, Vol. 10 (1995).

——. "Love and Optimism," in Ting, *God Is Love*.

——. "My View of God" (1993), in Ting, *God Is Love*.

——. "On Christian Theism," in Ting, *Chinese Contribution to Ecumenical Theology*, 27–40.

——. "Two Reflections on Evangelism: How Can They Claim Christianity Is Better?" (1950/51). Repr. in *Chinese Theological Review*, Vol. 10 (1995): 14–19.

——. "Two Reflections on Evangelism: Why Force My Religion on Others?" (1950). Repr. in *Chinese Theological Review*, Vol. 10 (1995): 14–19.

——. "Why Must We Still Be Preachers?" in Ting, *Chinese Contribution to Ecumenical Theology*.

——. "Youth and Religion" (1937). Repr. in *Chinese Theological Review*, Vol. 10 (1996).

Tong, James W. "The New Religious Policy in China." *Asian Survey*, Vol. 50, No. 5 (Sept./Oct. 2010): 859–87.

Towery, Britt. *Christianity in Today's China*. Waco, TX: Tao Foundation Missionary Heritage Edition, 2000.

Tsao, Hsingyuan, and Roger T. Ames, eds. *Xu Bing and Contemporary Chinese Art*. New York: SUNY Press, 2011.

Twitchett, Denis. "Problems of Chinese Biography," in Arthur F. Wright and Denis Twitchett, eds., *Confucian Personalities*. Stanford, CA: Stanford University Press, 1962.

Vala, Carsten T., and Huang Jianbo. "Three High-Profile Protestant Microbloggers in Contemporary China: Expanding Public Discourse or Burrowing into Religious Niches on Weibo (China's Twitter)?" in Stefania Travagnin, ed., *Religion and the Media in China*. Abingdon: Routledge, forthcoming.

Van de Ven, Hans. *Breaking with the Past: The Maritime Customs Service and the Global Origins of Modernity in China*. New York: Columbia University Press, 2014.

——. *From Friend to Comrade: The Founding of the Chinese Communist Party, 1920–27*. Berkeley: University of California Press, 1992.

Venuti, Lawrence. *The Translator's Invisibility*. London: Routledge, 1995.

Vermander, Benoit. "From Ethnography to Theology: Religious Communities in Contemporary Shanghai and Tasks of East Asian Theology." *Korean Journal of Systematic Theology*, Vol. 39 (2014): 7–35.

Wan, Sze-kar. "The Emerging Hermeneutics of the Chinese Church: The Debate Between Wu Leichuan and T. C. Chao and the Chinese Christian Problematik," in Irene Eber, Sze-kar Wan, and Knut Walf, eds., *Bible in Modern China: The Literary and Intellectual Impact*. Sankt Augustin: Institut Monumenta Serica, 1999.

Wan Fulin 萬福林. "Jidutu! Kuaikuai juanxian wuqi, dabai diren!" 基督徒快快捐獻武器, 打敗敵人. *Tian Feng* 271 (7 July 1951).

Wang, Paul Jiyou. *Le Premier Concile Plénier Chinois (1924)*. Paris: Cerf, 2010.

Wang, Xiaojing. "The Church Unity Movement in Early Twentieth-Century China: Cheng Jingyi and the Church of Christ in China." PhD diss., New College, Edinburgh University, 2012.

Wang Liqun 王立群. *Shanshui youji yanjiu* 山水游记研究. Beijing: China Academy of Social Sciences Press, 2008.

Wang Mingdao. "The Missing Voice," in *A Call to the Church*, trans. Theodore Choy. Ft. Washington, PA: Christian Literature Crusade, 1983.

——. "Nitty-gritty Faithfulness," in *A Call to the Church*, trans. Theodore Choy. Ft. Washington, PA: Christian Literature Crusade, 1983.

——. "Obey God or Men?" in *A Call to the Church*, trans. Theodore Choy. Ft. Washington, PA: Christian Literature Crusade, 1983.

Wang Weifan 汪维藩. "A Church Leader of Vision." *Chinese Theological Review* 10 (1995).

——. *Zhongguo shenxue ji qi wenhua yuanyuan* 中国神学及其文化渊源 [Chinese Theology and Its Cultural Sources]. Nanjing: Jinling Xiehe Shenxueyuan, 1997.

Wang Wenxin 王文馨. "Yige xiaomi feijidujiao yundong de fangfa" 一个消弭非基督教运动的方法 [One Method of Removing Opposition to Christianity]. *Zhen guang*, Vol. 24, No. 5 (15 May 1925).

Wang Yi 王怡. *Linghun shenchu nao ziyou* 靈魂深處鬧自由. Taipei: 基文社 Christian Arts Press, 2012.

Wang Xiaochao 王晓朝, ed. *Zhao Zichen xiansheng jinian wenji* 赵紫宸先生纪念文集. Beijing: Zongjiao Wenhua, 2005.

Wang Zheng 王徵. *Chongyi tang riji suibi* 崇一堂日記隨筆. Bodleian Library, Oxford, MS.chin.e.16.

——. *Renhui yue* 仁會約, in Nicolas Standaert, Adrian Dudink, and Nathalie Monnet, eds., 法國國家圖書館明清天主教文獻, *Chinese Christian Texts from the National Library of France*, Vol. 6. Taipei: Ricci Institute, 2009.

West, Philip. "Christianity and Nationalism: The Career of Wu Lei-ch'uan at Yenching University," in John K. Fairbank., ed., *The Missionary Enterprise in China and America*. Cambridge, MA: Harvard University Press, 1974.

——. *Yenching University and Sino-Western Relations, 1916–1952*. Cambridge, MA: Harvard University Press, 1976.

Whitehead, Raymond L., ed. *No Longer Strangers: Selected Writings of K. H. Ting*. Maryknoll, NY: Orbis, 1989.

Whyte, Robert. "With Regard to Anglicanism." *Chinese Theological Review* 10 (1995).

Wickeri, Philip. *Reconstructing Christianity in China: K. H. Ting and the Chinese Church*. Maryknoll, NY: Orbis, 2007.

Widmer, Ellen, and Daniel Bays, eds. *China's Christian Colleges: Cross-Cultural Connections, 1900–1950*. Stanford, CA: Stanford University Press, 2009.

Wielander, Gerda. *Christian Values in Communist China*. London: Routledge, 2013.

Wiest, Jean-Paul. *Maryknoll in China: A History, 1918–1955*. Armonk, NY: M. E. Sharpe, 1988.

——. "Understanding the Roman Catholic Church in China." 2002. Available at http://www.evangelizationstation.com/htm_html/around%20the%20world/China/understanding_the_roman_catholic.htm.

Wilkinson, Endymion. *Chinese History: A Manual*. Cambridge, MA: Harvard University Asia Center, 1998.

Williams, Rowan. *On Christian Theology*. Oxford: Blackwell, 2000.

——. *Silence and Honey Cakes: The Wisdom of the Desert*. Oxford: Lion, 2004.

Wilson Barnett, Suzanne, and J. K. Fairbank, eds. *Christianity in China: Early Protestant Missionary Writings*. Cambridge, MA: Council on East Asian Studies/Harvard University Press, 1985.

Wright, Arthur F. "Values, Roles and Personalities," in Wright and Twitchett, eds., *Confucian Personalities*.

Wright, Arthur F., and Denis Twitchett, eds. *Confucian Personalities*. Stanford, CA: Stanford University Press, 1962.

Wu Leichuan 吴雷川. *Jidujiao yu Zhongguo wenhua* 基督教与中国文化. Repr. ed. Shanghai: Shanghai Guji, 2008.

Wurth, Elmer, ed. *Papal Documents Related to the New China, 1937–1984*. Maryknoll, NY: Orbis, 1985.

Wu Yaozong 吴耀宗. "Gongchandang jiaoyu le wo" 共產黨教育了我. *Tian Feng* 271 (7 July 1951): 6–7.

———. "Quangguo jidujiao kang Mei yuan Chao sanzi gexin yundong jinkuang" 全國基督教抗美援朝三自革新運動近況 [On Recent Developments in the National Christian Campaign to Resist U.S. Aggression and Aid Korea and in the Three Self Reform Movement]. *Tian Feng* 270 (30 June 1951).

———. "Renmin minzhu zhuanzheng xia de jidujiao" 人民民主專政下的基督教 [Christianity Under the People's Democratic Dictatorship]. *Tian Feng* 176 (20 Aug. 1949).

Xiaoping Cong. *Teacher's Schools and the Making of the Modern Chinese Nation State, 1897–1937*. Vancouver: University of British Columbia Press, 2007, 8–14.

Xia Yibing 夏宜冰. "Jidu renpin de daode mingzheng" 基督人品的道德明證 [Moral Evidence of Christianity]. *Dao sheng* 道声, Vol. II, No. V (1932).

Xin Yalin. *Inside China's House Church Network: The Word of Life Movement and Its Renewing Dynamic*. Lexington, KY: Emeth, 2009.

Xu Kaiming 徐开明. "Lun Zhao Zichen xiansheng de mailuohua Jidulun de shenxue yiyi" 论赵紫宸先生的脉络化基督论的神学意义 [On the Theological Significance of Zhao Zichen's Systematized Christology], in Tang Xiaofeng and Xiong Xiaohong, eds., *Ye ying zhi zhi*, 112–14.

Xu Rulei. "A Brief History of Nanjing Union Theological Seminary, 1952–1992," trans. Philip and Janice Wickeri. *Chinese Theological Review* 8 (1993): 9–28.

Xu Wenhua 徐文华. "Xu Zongze de shengping zhushu ji qi sixiang yanjiu" 徐宗泽的生平著述及其思想研究. Master's thesis, Shanghai University, 2005.

Xu Xiaohong. "Obstacles in the Path of Theological Reconstruction." *Jinling shenxue zhi* 4 (2002): 32–34, trans. in *Chinese Theological Review* 17 (2003): 6–12.

Xu Zhongyu 徐中玉. *Zhongnan youji xuan* 中南游记选. Shanghai: Wenyi Chuban She, 1982.

Xu Zongze 徐宗澤. "Laodong qiyue" 勞動契約. *Shengjiao zazhi*, Vol. 10 (1932): 576–81.

———. *Shehui jingjixue gailun* 社會經濟學概論 (1934). Repr. ed. Beijing: Beijing zhong xian tuo fang keji fazhan youxian gongsi, 2007.

———. *Sheng chong lun* 聖寵論. Beijing: Beijing zhong xian tuo fang ke ji fa zhan you xian gong si, 2007.

———. *Sui si sui bi* 随思随笔. Shanghai: Sheng jiao zazui she, 1940.

———. "Tianzhu jiao zenmeyang jiejue shehui wenti" 天主教怎麼樣解決社會問題. *Shengjiao zazhi*, Vol. 9 (1933): 514–19.

———. "Zheyang zuo xianqi liangmu" 這樣做賢妻良母. *Shengjiao zazhi*, Vol. 3 (1935): 167–71.

Yamamoto Sumiko. *History of Protestantism in China: The Indigenization of Christianity.* Tokyo: Tōhō Gakkai, 2000.

Yang Fenggang. "The Red, Black and Gray Markets of Religion in China." *Sociological Quarterly* 47 (2006): 93–122.

———. *Religion in China: Survival and Revival Under Communist Rule.* Oxford: Oxford University Press, 2012.

Yang Huilin 杨慧林. *China, Christianity, and the Question of Culture.* Waco, TX: Baylor University Press, 2014.

———. "Christianity in China: The Work of Yang Huilin." *Contemporary Chinese Thought*, Vol. 36, No. 1 (2004).

———. "The Contemporary Significance of Theological Ethics." *Contemporary Chinese Thought*, Vol. 36, No 1. (2004): 51–67. First published in Chinese in the *Canadian Weizhen xuekan Regent Chinese Journal* 15, No. 1 (1999): 1–12.

———. Editorial, *Jidujiao wenhua xuekan. Journal for the Study of Christian Culture*, Vol. 14, No. 2 (2005): 1–9.

———. "The Impact of Christianity on Chinese Society from Schall von Bell to Our Days." Unpublished paper presented at Symposium for Cultural Exchange and Applied Ethics, University of International Business and Economics, Beijing, May 2011.

———. *Jidujiao de dise yu wenhua yanshen* 基督教的底色与文化延伸 [The Underpainting of Christianity and Cultural Extension]. Harbin: Heilongjiang Renmin, 2002.

———. *Shenxue quanshi* 神学诠释 [Theological Hermeneutics]. Shanghai: Yiwen, 2002.

———. *Zai wenxue yu shenxue de bianjie* 在文学与神学的边界 [At the Boundary of Literature and Theology]. Shanghai: Fudan Daxue, 2012.

———. *Zui'e yu jiushu* 罪恶与救赎: 基督教文化精神论 [Sin and Atonement: On the Cultural Spirit of Christianity]. Harbin: Heilongjiang Renmin, 1995.

———. *Zhuiwen Shangdi* 追问上帝: 信仰与理性的辩难 [The Quest for God: Faith vs. Reason]. Beijing: Beijing Jiaoyu, 1999.

Yang Huilin and Daniel Yeung. *Sino-Christian Studies in China.* Newcastle: Cambridge Scholars, 2006.

Yard, James Maxon. "Recent Changes in Mission Organization." CCYB 12 (1924): 247.

Yeung, Daniel 杨熙楠, ed. *Hanyu shenxue chuyi* 漢語神學芻議 [Preliminary Studies on Chinese Theology]. Hong Kong: Institute of Sino-Christian Studies, 2000.

Ying Fuk-tsang 刑福增. "New Wine in Old Wineskins: An Appraisal of Religious Legislation in China and the Regulations on Religious Affairs of 2005." *Religion, State and Society*, Vol. 34, No. 4 (2006): 347–73.

———, ed. *Xunsuo Jidujiao de dute xing: Zhao Zichen shenxue lunji* 寻索基督教的独特性: 赵紫宸神学论集 [In Search of the Uniqueness of Chinese Theology: Essays on T. C. Chao's Theology]. Hong Kong: Alliance Bible Seminary, 2003

———. "Xunsuo jidujiao yu Zhongguo wenhua de guanxi-ziyou shenxue yi hou de Zhao Zichen," 寻索基督教与中国文化的关系: 自由神学以后的赵紫宸, in Ying Fuk-tsang, ed., *Xunsuo Jidujiao de dute xing.*

Young, John D. *East-West Synthesis: Matteo Ricci and Confucianism.* Hong Kong: Hong Kong University Press, 1980.

Yu, Chün-fang. *The Renewal of Buddhism in China.* New York: Columbia University Press, 1981.

Yuan, Ji Feng, Koenraad Kuiper, and Shu Shaogu. "Language and Revolution: Formulae of the Cultural Revolution." *Language in Society*, Vol. 19, No. 1 (Mar. 1990): 61–79.

Yuan Yijuan 袁益娟. *Shengsheng shenxue: Wang Weifan shenxue sixiang yanjiu* 生生神学: 汪维藩神学思想研究 [Shengsheng Theology: A Study of Wang Weifan's Theological Thought]. Beijing: Jincheng, 2010.

Yu Jie 余杰 and Wang Yi 王怡. *Yisheng yishi de yangwang* 一生一世的仰望 [The Expectation for Whole Life]. Taipei: Jiwen, 2010.

Zarrow, Peter. *After Empire: The Conceptual Transformation of the Chinese State, 1885–1924.* Stanford, CA: Stanford University Press, 2012.

Zetsche, Jost Oliver. *The Bible in China. The History of the Union Version or the Culmination of Protestant Missionary Bible Translation in China.* Sankt Augustin: Nettetal, 1999.

Zhang, Wei-Wei. *Ideology and Economic Reform Under Deng Xiaoping, 1978–1993.* London: Kegan Paul, 1996.

Zhang, Xiantao. *The Origins of the Modern Chinese Press.* Abingdon: Routledge, 2007.

Zhang Xianliang. *Wo de putishu* [My Bodhi Tree], Part I. Repr. ed. Beijing: Zuojia, 1994.

Zhang Xiaolin 张晓林. *Tianzhu shiyi yu Zhongguo xuetong* 天主实意与中国学统—文化互动与诠释. Shanghai: Xuelin, 2005.

Zhange Ni. "Rewriting Jesus in Republican China: Religion, Literature, and Cultural Nationalism." *Journal of Religion* 91.2 (2011): 223–52.

Zhao Shilin 赵士林 and Duan Qi 段琦, eds. *Jidujiao zai zhongguo: chujinghua de zhihui* 基督教在中国处境化的智慧 [Christianity in China: Wisdom on Contextualization]. Beijing: Zongjiao Wenhua, 2009.

Zhao Zichen (see also T. C. Chao). *Da yu* 打渔 [Out into the Deep]. Shanghai: Christian Literature Society, 1930.

———. *Jianyu ji* 監獄記 [My Experience in Prison]. Hong Kong: Chinese Christian Literature Council, 1969.

———. *Sheng Baoluo zhuan* 聖保羅傳. Shanghai: Qingnian Xiehui, 1947.

———. "Yesu wei Jidu: ping Wu Leichuan xiansheng zhi *Jidujiao yu Zhongguo wenhua* 耶穌為基督: 評吳雷川先生之基督教與中國文化." *Zhenli yu Shengming* [Truth and Life] 10.7 (1936).

———. *Yesu zhuan* 耶穌傳, Shanghai: Qingnian Xiehui, 1935.

———. *Zhao Zichen wenji* 赵紫宸文集, Vol. 1. Beijing: Shangwu, 2003.

Zhuo Xinping, ed. *Christianity*, trans. Chen Zhi and Caroline Mason. Leiden: Brill, 2013.

Zhu Weizheng 朱維錚, ed. *Li Madou Zhongwenzhu yiji* 利瑪竇中文著譯集. Hong Kong: City University, 2001.

Zimmerman-Liu, Teresa, and Teresa Wright. "Making Sense of China's State-Society Relations: Unregistered Protestant Churches in the Reform Era," in Francis Khek Gee Lim, ed., *Christianity in Contemporary China: Socio-Cultural Perspectives.* London: Routledge, 2013.

Zui, David Z. T. (Yu Rizhang). "Present Tendencies in the Y.M.C.A." *CCYB* 12 (1924).

Zürcher, Erik. "Christian Social Action in Late Ming Times: Wang Zheng and His 'Humanitarian Society,'" in Jan A. M. de Meyer and Peter M. Engelfriet, eds., *Linked Faiths*. Leiden: Brill, 2000.

——. "Jesuit Accommodation and the Chinese Cultural Imperative," in D. E. Mungello, ed., *The Chinese Rites Controversy: Its History and Meaning*. Sankt Augustin: Institut Monumenta Serica, 1994.

——. "The Jesuit Mission in Fujian in Late Ming Times: Levels of Response," in E. B. Vermeer, ed., *Development and Decline of Fukien Province in the 17th and 18th Centuries*. Leiden: Sinica Leidensia, 1990.

——, ed., trans. *Kouduo richao: Li Jiubiao's Diary of Oral Admonitions: A Late Ming Christian Journal*, Vol. I. Sankt Augustin: Institute Monumenta Serica, 2007.

INDEX

Abe, Masao, 247

aiguo ("love the country"), and discourse of nation and nationalism by the People's Republic of China, 125, 171–72

aiguo aijiao ("love one's country and love the church"): as a feature of Chinese Christian scholarship, 229; and youth patriotism, 171–72

Aleni, Giulio, 28–30

Allen, Young J., 55, 61, 65

almsgiving, 15–16, 27–28

Anglican church: *Chinese Churchman*, 64; Ding Guangxun's Anglicanism, 188–89, 199, 325–26n89; "A Pastoral Letter to Fellow Christians of the Chung Hua Sheng Kung Hui," 169–70; self-governing statistics, 169–70, 320n42; Zhao Zichen's ordination as priest, 74; Zhonghua sheng gong hui, 47

Anti-Christian writings and movements, 285; and 1950s repression, 154–55, 176; and dual nature of Chinese and Christian identity, 42–43; and nationalism, 45–46, 49; and Republican intellectuals, 56–59; as stimulation for Christian apologetics, 59, 65–67, 74, 96, 117, 129–30, 152, 285; and textual networks, 37–38

antimiracle stance: of Anti-Christian movement, 57; of secular skeptics, 67–68; of Wu Leichuan, 65–66, 134, 136–37, 152, 314–15n43; Zhao Zichen's naturalist mode of explanation, 77, 84, 87–88

Badiou, Alain, 9, 261

Bays, Daniel, 50, 52, 55, 235, 239n32, 320n52

Bethel Band, 48

Bevans, Stephen, 112, 316n83

Bible: commentaries by Nanjing Seminary scholars, 228; Delegates' version, 257, 337n70; Ding Guangxun's Bible-reading guide, 190–92; King James Version, 257, 337n69; patriotic exemplars in, 197

biblical quotes: Enoch 1, 89; Exodus 17:8–14, 172; Hebrews 11:34 and 38, 194; John 14:23, 262; Luke, 135, 314n29, 316n75, 337n69; Mark 1:33–39, 134; Mark 5:30, 337n69; Mark 8:11–13, 136–37; Matthew, 315n55, 337n69; 2 Peter, 337n69; Philippians 4:8, 337n69; Romans 13:1, 202–3

365